HISTORICAL

AND

DESCRIPTIVE SKETCHES.

CITY HALL.

HISTORICAL

AND

DESCRIPTIVE SKETCHES

OF

NORFOLK AND VICINITY,

INCLUDING

Portsmouth and the Adjacent Counties,

DURING A PERIOD OF

TWO HUNDRED YEARS.

ALSO,

SKETCHES OF WILLIAMSBURG, HAMPTON, SUFFOLK, SMITHFIELD, AND OTHER PLACES,

WITH

DESCRIPTIONS OF SOME OF THE PRINCIPAL OBJECTS OF INTEREST

IN

EASTERN VIRGINIA.

BY

WILLIAM S. FORREST.

PHILADELPHIA:
LINDSAY AND BLAKISTON.
1853.

C. SHERMAN, PRINTER,

19 St. James Street.

PREFACE.

WHEN the author of the following historical observations determined to compile a DIRECTORY OF THE CITY OF NORFOLK, he contemplated also, as a suitable appendage thereto, the publication of a brief description of its situation and facilities for trade and commerce, its advancement and prospects of future wealth and importance. On further reflection, however, it was deemed advisable to adopt a more extended plan, and attempt even a somewhat elaborate HISTORY of the place; commencing at an early period, and continuing the account down to the present time; embracing a description of the neighbouring towns and villages, the principal objects of attraction in the vicinity, &c., &c.

The work was accordingly commenced, with a determination to accomplish it with as little delay as possible; and it is scarcely necessary to mention, that the undertaking was attended with both labour and trouble, and required much time as well as considerable patience and perseverance.

It is proper to state, that the difficulty in collecting the various materials for the work was greatly augmented, and the time required to prepare them for the press was considerably prolonged, by other duties, which demanded much of the writer's time during its progress. It will be readily imagined that he would have found the task far more pleasant, could he have given it his undivided attention from its commencement to its completion. But he was compelled to pursue a different course, and devote to its prosecution those intervals by day and by night, which could be spared from other pursuits and engagements.

With regard to the execution of the work under these circumstances, he must abide by the decision of those whom it is designed to interest.

To those persons whose kindness tended to facilitate his progress, he avails himself of this occasion to express his thanks. To the editors of the several city papers, for the privilege of examining their files, his obligations are hereby specially and respectfully acknowledged. The writer is also indebted to the obliging disposition, retentive memory, and politeness of several venerable and greatly esteemed ladies and gentlemen of Norfolk and Portsmouth, for the particulars of many interesting events included in the Sketches. And it is but common courtesy to acknowledge his high appreciation of the valuable suggestions, as well as the frequent expressions of kindness and encouragement with regard to the enterprise, from individuals whose character and judgment entitle them to considerations of great respect.

In gathering, culling, and preparing the subject-matter for the press, many facts and incidents—some of a melancholy and unpleasant nature, and others of no special interest—were cast aside, to be lost, perhaps, in the deep ocean of forgetfulness; while those only were retained, which it was thought would prove valuable and entertaining, and therefore worthy of a place in local history. As the book will not be without readers at a distance as well as in Norfolk, Portsmouth, and vicinage, many remarks of general interest will be found upon its pages.

The writer is well assured that he does not mistake the character of his fellow-citizens in other parts of Virginia, in supposing that they feel interested in the history, present condition, and prospects of their seaport, and of this productive, and we may truly say, interesting and attractive section of the Old Dominion, bordering as it does upon the sea, whose blue waves ceaselessly break and dash along its beautiful shores.

The author trusts that an effort to save from oblivion, and place in form and order, those occurrences of the past, in which many of the present day must feel an interest, will meet with the general approbation of the community. He indulges the hope, also, that the remarks upon the moral, political, literary, and social character of the place, may not be unacceptable to the reader. At the conclusion of the volume is a copious alphabetical index, which adds somewhat to its value, as it will be found useful for reference.

In submitting, though not without unfeigned diffidence, the result of his labours to an enlightened and scrutinizing public, the writer is constrained to express the hope, that its tendency may prove beneficial. And, if his attempt to recall to mind the recollection of interesting incidents long past and forgotten; to perpetuate to posterity some pleasing reminiscences of worthy men, whose mortal remains repose quietly in the silent tomb, shall prove successful, he will not feel that his efforts have been entirely in vain. If he shall succeed in "letting a spark fall upon memory's altar, and lighting up her slumbering fires" with the remembrance of the pleasing and novel occurrences of other days; or in placing fairly and plainly before the public eye, an account of the commercial facilities and advantageous local position of the port of Norfolk and Portsmouth; in arousing to action any portion of the native mental or physical energy, that may have hitherto been partially dormant and unexercised; in awakening a more lively interest in those works of internal improvement with which the welfare of Eastern Virginia, and the prospects of this port in particular, are so intimately connected; or in directing attention to any of the various places of interest in the vicinity—the works of nature and of art, the noble rivers and winding streams; the pleasant villas and cultivated lands; the buildings, ancient and modern; the dense old forests, the boundless ocean, and other attractive objects—he will not hereafter be troubled with the unpleasant reflection that the time and pains which he found indispensable to the accomplishment of the work, were bestowed, without effecting, at least in some degree, the results which were intended and anxiously desired.

W. S. F.

NORFOLK, VA., January, 1853.

CONTENTS.

CHAPTER I.

CHAPTER II.

CHAPTER III.

1650—1736.

CHAPTER IV.

1736—1739.

CHAPTER V.

1746—1765.

CHAPTER VI.

1766—1768.

CHAPTER VII.

1775—1776.

CHAPTER VIII.

1776.

CHAPTER IX.

1776—1777.

CHAPTER X.

1779—1785.

CHAPTER XI.

1787—1799.

CHAPTER XII.

1800—1803.

CHAPTER XIII.

1803—1812.

CHAPTER XIV.

1813.

CHAPTER XV.

1813.

CHAPTER XVI.

1813—1814.

CHAPTER XVII.

1814—1815.

CHAPTER XVIII.

1816—1819.

CHAPTER XIX.

1820—1821.

CHAPTER XX.

1821—1824.

CHAPTER XXI.

1824.

CHAPTER XXII.

1824—1827.

CHAPTER XXIX.

1840—1844.

CHAPTER XXX.

1845—1847.

CHAPTER XXXI.

1847.

CHAPTER XXXII.

1848—1849.

CHAPTER XXXIII.

1850.

CHAPTER XXXIV.

1850.

CHAPTER XXXV.

1850.

CHAPTER XXXVI.

1851.

CHAPTER XXXVII.

1852.

CHAPTER XXXVIII.

CHAPTER XXXIX.

CHAPTER XL.

CHAPTER XLI.

CHAPTER XLII.

CHAPTER XLIII.

CHAPTER XLIV.

CHAPTER XLV.

CHAPTER XLVI.

CHAPTER XLVII.

CHAPTER XLVIII.

CHAPTER XLIX.

CHAPTER L.

CHAPTER LI.

CHAPTER LII.

CHAPTER LIII.

CHAPTER LIV.

CHAPTER LV.

CHAPTER LVI.

CHAPTER LVII.

CHAPTER LVIII.

CHAPTER LIX.

CHAPTER LX.

CHAPTER LXI.

CHAPTER LXII.

CHAPTER LXIII.

CHAPTER LXIV.

CHAPTER LXV.

HISTORY OF NORFOLK

AND VICINITY.

CHAPTER I.

Situation—Relative Position—The Harbour—Superior Natural Advantages—Early Events and Prospects—Ancient Coin found—Aborigines—Pioneers of the Country—The Indians—Their former Home and savage Life—Departure and Extermination.

NORFOLK, the principal seaport town of Virginia, is situated in the northern part of Norfolk County, on the north side of the Elizabeth River, at the mouth of its eastern branch, and immediately opposite Portsmouth, and the confluence of the southern branch.*

The present site of the city is a small, level peninsula, or neck of land, of about eight hundred acres, with the wide, blue river on the south and southwest, Smith's Creek on the northwest, and Newton's Creek on the east. This city is near the south-eastern extremity of the State, in latitude 36° 50′ 50″; longitude, west from Greenwich, 76° 18′ 47″, and east from Washington, 0° 42′ 43″ (taken at the Farmers' Bank, corner of Main and Bank Streets). It is situate about two hundred miles from the Blue Ridge, and thirty-five northwest of the point at which the boundary line of Virginia and North Carolina intersects the coast of the Atlantic. Norfolk is distant from Boston (by sea) about 600 miles; from New York (by sea), 300 miles; from

* The first four paragraphs are inserted in the Norfolk Directory, having been taken from the manuscript of this work.

Philadelphia (by sea), 270; from Washington, 190; from Baltimore, 180; New Orleans, 1300; Charleston, 350; Wilmington, N. C., 240; Richmond, 140; from the Mississippi River, 700; Hampton Roads, only 8 miles; and it is almost within hearing of the deep-toned roar of the ocean.

The relative position of the place is exceedingly favourable. For all the various purposes of trade and commerce, both foreign and domestic, the port of Norfolk and Portsmouth stands almost unrivalled.

With regard to the means of navigation, and other indispensable requisites for commercial advancement, Nature performed her part most admirably and generously for this location: surely more could not be reasonably asked of her lavish hand. The harbour, always open, is sufficiently deep and spacious to float and accommodate with ample room and perfect safety the combined navies of the world. It is situate about the middle of the whole vast extent of our Atlantic sea-coast,—the nearest and most convenient location for the depôt and shipment of the incalculable wealth of the interior of Virginia and North Carolina, and, in fact, of a large portion of the great West,—in convenient proximity not only to the ocean, and the bold and beautiful Chesapeake, but also to rivers, deep and wide, that wash and drain some of the most productive portions of the Union,—with a climate almost always pleasant and remarkably salubrious, and which is seldom uncomfortably warm in summer, and rarely too cold in winter. Indeed, when the peculiar and superior natural advantages of Norfolk and of the sister town on the opposite side of the river are considered, it must be admitted that these places should long since have been numbered among the principal cities of the Union, or that the two, united as one, should now be known as the great commercial emporium of the South, if not of the United States.

A somewhat extended account of the present appearance, condition, and progress of the city will be presented in another part of this work;—the evidences of its growth, indications of future importance, &c., as well as some reasons why it does not now rival the great commercial marts of the Union. This will be given after we shall have viewed the picture from a distant point, and glanced at the early events, and changing scenes, and bright prospects, and blasted hopes, of years long past and gone.

It is not essential, and perhaps it will be deemed quite unnecessary, to attempt here to look farther back into the deep, dim vista of receding ages, than to the time of the first settlers of this section of country; yet it may not be entirely inappropriate to allude to a circumstance, which, how trifling soever it may appear to some, will serve at least to elicit a train of thought or some vague association of ideas respecting those beings who appeared upon the stage of life, and then receded from view, long centuries ago, at or near this particular spot on the eastern border of the Western Continent.

While some men were boring for water, on the opposite side of the Elizabeth, as late as September, 1833, a *coin* was drawn up from a depth of nearly thirty feet. It was about the size of an English shilling, of an oval shape, and unlike anything of the kind ever seen here before by the "oldest inhabitant." Although it had remained embedded thus far below the surface of the earth perhaps for many centuries, the figures upon it were still plainly and distinctly marked, representing a warrior or hunter, and other characters, apparently of Roman origin. This may have some slight bearing upon the traditions respecting the visit to this country of the chieftain Madoc and the Northmen, hundreds of years prior to the date of its discovery by Columbus; or it may strengthen the opinion, entertained by some, that the Indians of North America held communication with the natives of the Eastern Continent, long before its discovery in the latter part of the fifteenth century.

But it has been suggested that this strange coin, with many others of the same kind, might have been circulated by unknown aborigines, who ceased to exist before the Indians became the proprietors of the soil, and whose very name has sunk into oblivion, with numberless unchronicled events, in the wide and deep ocean of the past. Quite certain it is, however, that there was a time when the level tracts of land which are now divided into so many smaller portions, and distributed among the numerous freeholders of Norfolk, Portsmouth, and vicinity, were a part of the vast, unexplored wilderness of North America, the fit abode of the roving red man and the bounding deer. But strange beings suddenly appeared upon the native soil of the tawny sons of the forest; the tall old oaks and "melancholy pines" tottered and fell; the Indian and the wild beast were alike hunted and driven away from their old and peaceful haunts, and the pale-faced adventurers from the Old World asserted their claim to the territory. The shrill war-whoop was succeeded by the sentimental love-song of the undaunted pioneer of the dense, dark wilds; the wolf, the panther, the bear, and other hideous tenants of the thickly-wooded lowlands, receded from the approach of the white man, nor mingled long their discordant voices with the strange and oft-repeated sound of the woodman's axe.

That portion of Virginia which lies between the Atlantic shore and the base of the Blue Ridge, was occupied by about forty different tribes of Indians, thirty of which comprised the confederacy of the brave though hostile Powhatan, whose dominion included a large extent of country, and extended eastwardly entirely to the sea-coast, including, of course, the site occupied by the City of Norfolk. The Manakins, the Nottoways, the Tuteloes, the Nansemunds, the Chesapeakes, &c., belonged, it appears, to this confederation; and it is quite probable that members of each of these tribes frequently extended their rambles in search of fish, game, and plunder, to the green banks of our noble river and its tributaries.

No doubt, however, need be entertained, with regard to the identical tribe that inhabited this particular spot,—the site of the City of Norfolk, as well as that of Portsmouth, and the country for several miles around. The *Chesapeakes*, from whom the Bay of Chesapeake derived its name, occupied the region of country from the western branch of our river, and some distance west of the head of that stream, eastwardly to the Atlantic, embracing a large portion, if not the whole of the counties of Norfolk and Princess Anne.

Here were their hunting-grounds. They swiftly paddled their light canoes over the deep and quiet waters of the Elizabeth and its tributaries—upon these very shores they held their war-councils, and "as the sun wheeled on his broad disk behind the western hills," or, "as the moonbeams melted over the verge of the evening cloud," they gazed intently upon nature's beauties as they were spread out around, and admired them in their wildness, untouched, unaltered as they then were by the ever-changing and self-appropriating hand of civilization. Their brilliant council-fires drove back the darkness of the "deep midnight" to the gloomy recesses of the forest, and lighted up the adjacent shores, while the savage war-cry, or the monotonous battle-song, made the welkin ring as they mingled in the merry dance or the frantic midnight revel.

"The plough may, in after times, turn up their stone calumets, and the railroad excavation reveal their mouldering skeletons; but their forms, their characters, their rugged virtues and wild crimes, will exist only in the records of the pale-face, or, more vividly, upon the canvass of the adventurous artist, who, like Stanley, devotes years of toil and danger to snatch from oblivion the likeness of a passing race."

"Alas, for them! their day is o'er;
Their fires are out, from shore to shore;
No more for them their wild deer bounds—
The plough is on their hunting-grounds;
The pale man's axe rings through their woods—
The pale man's sails skim o'er their floods,
Their pleasant springs are dry;
Their children, look, by power oppressed,
Beyond the mountains of the West,
Their children go, to die!"

"Not many generations ago, where you now sit, encircled with all that exalts and embellishes civilized life, the rank thistle nodded in the wind, and the wild fox dug his hole unscared. Here lived and loved another race of beings. Beneath the same sun that rolls over your head, the Indian hunter pursued the panting deer;—gazing on the same moon that smiles for you, the Indian lover wooed his dusky mate. Here, the wigwam blaze beamed on the tender and helpless, and the council-fire glared on the wise and daring. Here they warred; the echoing whoop, the bloody grapple, the defying death-song, all were here; and when the tiger strife was over, here curled the smoke of peace.

"Here, too, they worshipped; and from many a dark bosom went up a fervent prayer to the Great Spirit. He had not written his laws for them on tables of stone, but he had traced them on the tables of their hearts. The poor child of Nature knew not the God of Revelation, but the God of the Universe he acknowledged in everything around. He beheld him in the star that sank in beauty behind his lonely dwelling; in the sacred orb that flamed on him from his mid-day throne; in the flower that snapped in the morning breeze; in the lofty pine that defied a thousand whirlwinds; in the timid warbler that never left its native grove; in the fearless eagle whose untired pinion was wet in clouds; in the worm that crawled at his feet; and in his own matchless form, glowing with a spark of that light to whose mysterious source he bent in humble, though blind adoration.

"And all this is passed away. . . . Across the ocean came a pilgrim bark, bearing the seeds of life and death. The former were sown for you; the latter sprang up in the path of the simple native. Two hundred years have changed the character of a great continent, and blotted for ever from its face a whole peculiar people. Art has usurped the bowers of Nature, and the anointed children of education have been too powerful for the tribes of the ignorant.

* * * * * * *

"Their council-fires have long since gone out on the shore, and their war-cry is fast fading to the untrodden West. Slowly and sadly they climb the distant mountains, and read their doom in the setting sun. They are shrinking before the mighty tide which is pressing them away; they must soon hear the roar of the last wave, which shall settle over them for ever. Ages hence, the inquisitive white man, as he stands by some growing city, will ponder on the structure of their disturbed remains, and wonder to what manner of persons they belonged. They will live only in the songs and chronicles of their exterminators. Let these be faithful to their rude virtues, as men, and pay due tribute to their unhappy fate as a people."

"Routed from every nook of the broad wild-wood,
Where in grand solitude they passed their childhood—
Their hearth-stones smoking yet, their fathers' graves
The silent resting-places of 'old braves,'

Who ruled the country ere the white man came,
To extend alike his glory and his shame—
Left for the stranger's foot to trample on—
Alas! the red man from our land is gone!
The NOBLE INDIAN, whose defying eye
Gleamed brighter as the thunder-storm went by—
Who learned his lessons from the mystic lore
Traced on the leaves or on the sea-beat shore.
His day is past—and in the distant West,
Heart-broken, home-exiled, he seeks a final rest."

CHAPTER II.

Early Anglo-Saxon Inhabitants—John Smith—First Settlers—Wealth and Hospitality—Civilization—Plentiful Productions of the Country—Names of early Inhabitants—Reign of James I.—Manners and Customs of the old English Settlers—General Character—Habits and Amusements—Charles II. —English Nobility—Manners of the People—Fondness for Sport and Pleasure—Intoxicating Drinks—Industry, Morality, Religion, Aristocracy—The Ladies, their Industry, Activity, Healthfulness, and Admirable Character—Descendants.

THE early Anglo-Saxon inhabitants of this, as well as of other sections of Virginia, are said to have been a noble class of men, combining in their character—many of them—the essential elements of uprightness, energy, and perseverance. The daring and indomitable Smith had laid the foundation of the political structure that was to rise in its beauty for the admiration of the world. He paved the way to its greatness for the benefit of future generations. His stern and unflinching devotion to the cause of justice and the best interest of the people, formed an example that was, perhaps, not without its effect upon the character of those who occupied the territory in after years.

Many of the settlers of this region were dignified, high-minded, and intelligent. From the richness of the soil which they cultivated, and the facilities for trading with foreign countries, many of them became wealthy—independently so. Some of them indeed, possessed—to use the forcible language of Dr. Johnson—"the potentiality of growing rich, beyond the dreams of avarice;" and their hospitality and bountifulness were commensurate with their means.

"In process of time, enterprise and industry overcame every difficulty, every terror. The soil, the wild beasts, the fierce natives themselves, yielded to the superior energies of civilized man. Neat mansions rose where rude Indian huts had stood; the fertilizing ploughshare succeeded the murderous tomahawk, and rich cultivated fields smiled where a rank vegetation had spread for ages its wild luxuriancy.

"The genial climate and transparent atmosphere delighted those who had come from the denser air of England. Every object in nature was new and wonderful. The hospitality of the Virginians became proverbial. Labour was valuable, land was cheap. Competence promptly followed industry. There was no need of a scramble; abundance gushed from the earth for all. The morasses were alive with water-fowl, the forests were nimble with game, the woods rustled with coveys of quails and wild turkeys, while they rung with the merry notes of the singing birds."

Some persons have supposed, from the style of architecture introduced, that this portion of the State was settled by the Dutch; this is, however, a mistake; it was peopled, principally, by settlers from England, although there were some from Ireland, Scotland, Germany, &c. The Thorogoods, Hancocks, Woodhouses, Moseleys, Chapmans, Hayneses, Walkes, Whitehursts, Smiths, Boushes, Drewreys, Cornicks, Keelings, Hunters, Newtons, Tatems, Herberts, Kempes, Butts, Tuckers, &c., were among the first established inhabitants of this portion of southeastern Virginia; and their descendants are now, many of them, most estimable and respectable citizens of the city and county of Norfolk, and also of Princess Anne.

In the early part of the seventeenth century, especially during the reign of James I., the pride of birth greatly prevailed in England. "The gentry and nobility distinguished themselves by a stiff dignity and stateliness of behaviour. The expenses of the higher rank consisted in pomp and show, and a numerous retinue, rather than convenience and pleasure;" and it is quite probable that these distinguishing characteristics were, to some extent, observable among the early English settlers of this region of country. It is more probable, however, that they were, for the most part, quite unostentatious. Their houses were mostly plain and not too extravagantly furnished; there was probably much less of mere superfluity than there is at the present day. Quite enough there was, and to spare, for all the purposes of a people early distinguished for their hospitality and proverbial for good living. Some there were, among the leading and most opulent gentlemen of those days, who exhibited an air of reservedness and self-importance, which showed conclusively that they entertained no mean opinion of themselves. Indeed, it is quite probable, that they acknowledged no superior class of beings in any part of the wide earth. There were among those old Virginia settlers, men of fine talent, sound judgment, and well-cultivated minds. But it is probable they were most noted for incorruptible integrity, industry, and a commendable devotion to the best interests of the community in general, and of the immediate neighbours in particular.

There were many, especially at a later period, who were remarkable for their sociality, and fondness for company and entertainments. Some delighted in a game at cards, others in a fox or deer-hunt. And the jovial parson complained not, if indeed he was not sometimes among the foremost in the chase! Charles II., the reigning sovereign fifty or sixty years after the settlement of this immediate section of Virginia, "was a man of easy and lively manners, and his courtiers affected the same character. They were chiefly men of the world;" and the people here were, no doubt, influenced to a considerable extent by the manners and customs of the old English nobility of those days.

Very many possessed a degree of fondness for hilarity and sport not often observed among their present descendants. They were a pleasure-loving, care-despising class; an occasional frolic they would have, and that sometimes upon a pretty large scale. Like some of old, they were fond of "music and dancing." They sung songs and made merry, while the social glass, too, passed freely around the convivial board. But they drank liquors of superior quality; not the adulterated poisons so frequently used at the present period. They would have (those who could afford it) none but the best. Some, alas! were sadly injured from their effects, and suffered severely in health, business, and property, while others were ruined outright; although the succeeding generations have suffered much more, as is readily acknowledged by all. They were industrious and active in attending to the various duties of the farm, the store, or the office, and would have justly spurned some of the customs prevalent at the present time. They did not burn the midnight taper, nor consume the lamp of life in poring over injurious light reading; a custom too much in vogue at the present time.

With regard to the morality and religion of those days, there was, no doubt, more of principle than profession. There were many worthy men, who felt more than they seemed to feel on this subject. There was, doubtless, not enough of true piety; yet there was, certainly, a considerable regard for genuine Christianity. There were few churches and church members—few bigotted professors, but little empty show and ceremony; and yet there were examples of consistent, devoted, heartfelt godliness, whose genial influence has not been lost amid the changes and innovations that have been made with the lapse of years, and which still follow on in the track of time.

Here, as in other parts of the Old Dominion, there was, as before intimated, quite enough of aristocracy. This, however, could very readily be thrown aside by some, on particular occasions, and was very generally dispensed with on election days.

The ladies were then, as they are now, noted for their personal attractions; and many, in the higher walks of life, for great dignity of character, modesty, and politeness of behaviour, as well as for their activity and frugality in the management of their household affairs. These commendable qualities left their impress and beneficial influence upon succeeding generations. But many of the respected females who figured in the earlier period of our history, were very different, in some respects, from the accomplished and esteemed fair ones of the city at this day. They were generally more robust, and capable of enduring much greater fatigue. The roseate tints upon the full cheek of health were more frequently to be seen, nor so soon gave place to the paler hues of debility, disease, and premature death. They walked early around the fields of waving grain, and gathered the variegated wild-flowers that exhaled their fragrance on the air, while yet the crystal dew-drops sparkled on their delicate petals. They mounted the spirited horse and cantered merrily and cheerily away, ere Aurora had bedecked with gold the eastern sky, or the cheerful lark had concluded her matin song; availing themselves of the benefit of exercise and the invigorating vital fluid. Some spun at the wheel or wove at the hand-loom! and cultivated kitchen and flower gardens. They studied the Bible, and other books of sound moral and religious instruction; instilled correct, honourable, virtuous, and patriotic principles into the minds of their children, and presided with dignity and grace at the social entertainment or the convivial evening gathering. Of many it might then have been said, using the words of King Solomon, "She openeth her mouth with wisdom, and in her tongue is the law of kindness. She looketh well to the ways of her household, and eateth not the bread of idleness. Her children arise up and call her blessed; her husband also, and he praiseth her."

"When the difficulty between the mother country and the colonies began, they immediately gave up their *tea*, and by their example and exhortations encouraged the men to resist her encroachments. When the cry 'to arms' rang through the land, with eager haste they prepared their husbands and sons for the contest. They knit hose, made knapsacks, and even moulded balls of their dishes and plates, while the males were drilling. Then when the hour of parting came, mothers blessed their sons, and bade them go forth in the vigour of youth. Wives and maidens blessed their husbands and lovers, and, smiling through tears, urged them to struggle manfully for their country and their God."

The descendants of some of those excellent old families, whose lofty bearing and sterling worth assisted in giving an enviable and enduring fame to the State, are now numbered among the inhabitants of our growing city and vicinity. Many have gone to other parts of our highly-favoured land of freedom, while the mortal remains of numbers more, quietly repose in the deep, unbroken stillness of the tomb.

CHAPTER III.

1650—1736.

Remarks relative to the name of the City, &c.—Colonel Thorogood—Original Limits of Norfolk County—Upper and Lower Norfolk—Divisions and Subdivisions—Parishes, Churches, and Laws—Nansemond and Princess Anne Counties—The Princess of Denmark—Seat of Justice in Princess Anne County—Court-house and Jail of Norfolk County, and the Borough—Early Owners of the Site of Norfolk—Act of Assembly—Cobham—Singular Provisions—The Land Purchased by Trustees—Original Limits of the Town—Old Deed—The Walke Family—Norfolk established a Town—Increasing Commerce and Population—Prospect of Advancement—Statement of Colonel Byrd—The Borough Charter—Samuel Boush and other Officers of the Corporation—Boundaries—City Limits—Tanner's Creek—Town Bridge—Extract from the Virginia Gazette—First Council, Recorder, &c.—The first Mayor—Other Charter-men and their Descendants.

WE next offer some observations, which, it is hoped, will not prove uninteresting to the reader, relative to the origin of the *name* of this City and County, and to the original limits and subsequent divisions and subdivisions of the latter.

NORFOLK—correctly pronounced *Norfoke*—is a Saxon word, compounded of *North* and *folk*, and may, with some propriety, be rendered *North people.* In the early records of the county and of the State, "*Norff.*" represents the name Norfolk, as an abbreviation. It was also written *Norfolke.* By persons residing in the city and vicinity, the sound of the *l* is omitted in the pronunciation; but it is often improperly sounded by persons residing abroad.

This name was given to this section of the State by Colonel Thorogood, one of the earliest settlers, in honour of his native county in England (celebrated for its woollen goods, sheep, turnips, turkeys, fish, &c.), from which he emigrated at an early period, to Elizabeth City County, which he afterwards represented in the General Assembly, and whence he removed across the water and settled on the Bay shore. To the town was afterwards given the old English name of the county.*

Norfolk County originally included, in addition to its present limits, Princess Anne and Nansemond—formerly called *Nandzimum* and *Nansimum;* Captain Smith wrote it *Nandsamund.* This part of the territory of Virginia, shortly after being explored and named by Colonel Thorogood, was designated as Upper and Lower Norfolk. The portion now known as the county of Nansemond, was called *Upper Norfolk* (formerly written thus—Vpper Norff.), and the rest, now included in the two counties of Norfolk and Princess Anne, was called *Lower Norfolk.* It was also laid off in *parishes;* and there was the parish of Saint Brides, of Lynnhaven, &c. In these subdivisions, churches were soon erected and provided with pastors. The inhabitants were then required, under a penalty of the law, to attend church, and the ministers were amenable to heavy fines for failing to be regularly at their post! The limits of the parishes were generally comprised between two water-courses, commencing at two principal points on the main stream, and embracing all the territory between the river branches, to an indefinite distance up into the country.

Prior to 1761, however, Elizabeth River Parish comprised a large region of country on both sides of the river; and consequently causing inconvenience to the inhabitants, they petitioned the General Assembly to have it divided into three distinct parishes. It was accordingly enacted, "that from and after the first day of May, 1761, the parish should be divided

* Norfolk is a populous maritime county in Massachusetts. Norfolk is the name of a township in Connecticut. Norfolk Island is situated in the Pacific Ocean; it is noted for pine trees, high hills, and beautiful birds—and Norfolk Sound is in lon. 135° 36′ W., lat. 57° 3′ N.

Of the Dukes of Norfolk, much is recorded in English history. About the year 1390, the Duke of Norfolk was sentenced to perpetual exile for attempting to fight a duel; and a nobleman of this title, greatly distinguished as a warrior and statesman, flourished during a considerable part of the 16th century. About 1570, he was considered "the most powerful subject in England." He was, however, convicted of being concerned, with Mary, Queen of Scots, in a conspiracy, and was executed. "A jury of twenty-five Peers passed sentence upon him, and the fatal warrant was signed by Queen Elizabeth with much hesitation and reluctance."

into three, to be called Elizabeth River, St. Brides, and Portsmouth Parishes," which was accordingly done, and Elizabeth River Parish comprised the land on the northward and eastward of the river, and of its eastern branch (Lynnhaven Parish, it appears, was afterwards formed from this). The limits of St. Brides Parish were between the eastern and southern branches, extending to a mill on Mill Creek, thence southwardly into the Dismal Swamp, as far as the Carolina line, and Portsmouth Parish comprised the remaining part of the former Elizabeth River Parish, extending up into the country, on the south of the river, and on the west of its southern branch.

The name of Upper Norfolk was changed to Nansemond; and in 1691, at the instance of the inhabitants in the eastern and northeastern part of Lower Norfolk, including Lynnhaven Parish, another subdivision took place, by act of Assembly, and Princess Anne County was formed from Lower Norfolk. This was warmly opposed by the people in the Parishes of St. Brides, &c., principally on account of the consequent increase in the poll-tax.

The name, Princess Anne, was, of course, adopted in honour of Anne, the amiable Princess of Denmark (daughter of James II.), who ascended the throne in 1702, in the 38th year of her age, and whose loyal subjects gave her the title of "the good Queen Anne."

The first court-house in that county was built upon a branch of the "River of Chesapeake,"—now known as Lynnhaven River—at the "Ferry landing," on the farm now owned by Lieutenant Charles McIntosh, U. S. N. The old building was taken down about twelve years ago; it had been used as one of the outhouses of the farm. The seat of justice was removed from that place to New town, on the eastern branch of the Elizabeth, thence it was removed to the land of Mr. Kempe, at the head of that stream, now the village of Kempsville. In the early part of the present century another change was made, and the present central location was adopted, which is ten miles below Kempsville, and twenty from the city.

Until 1752, the Court-house of Norfolk County was located in the borough, and was used by the citizens thereof, as well as by those of the county. At this date, however, an act of Assembly was passed authorizing the building of a court-house for Norfolk Borough. This was, of course, consumed in the conflagration of '76.

In 1662, two hundred acres of the land now occupied by the City of Norfolk was owned by one Lewis Vandermull, who, in the same year, sold it to Nicholas Wise, sen., a shipwright.

1680. On the 8th of June of this year, one hundred and eighty-eight years after the discovery of America, and seventy-three after the first permanent settlement in Virginia (at Jamestown, in 1607), an act of Assembly was passed, directing the purchase of fifty acres of land for the TOWN OF NORFOLK.

This was called an "*Act for cohabitation and encouragement of trade and manufacture.*" It was very desirable to establish towns for the purpose of concentrating trade, and of increasing the price and facilitating the exportation of tobacco, &c. Fifty acres of land were accordingly purchased by feoffees of several counties then formed, including fifty in "Lower Norfolk County, on Nicholas Wise, his land on eastern branch of Elizabeth River, at the entrance of the branch."

The act states "that the price to be paid by each county for each respective ffifty acres of land nominated as aforesaid, shalbe tenn thousand pounds of tobacco and caske, which summe the owner or owners thereof shalbe and are hereby constrained to accept, take, and receive, as full and valueable price for the said land for ever."

This singular and somewhat amusing act further provided that all persons who would build a dwelling and warehouse upon the land so appropriated, should have assigned them half an acre of said land in fee simple, on paying to the county one hundred pounds of tobacco and cask—the buildings to be commenced within three months after the assignment.

Tobacco and other produce were required by the act to be brought to said locations and there stored, sold, shipped, &c. The penalty for failing to comply with this provision of the act was the forfeiture of all goods that were not so disposed of. It was further provided, that "All goods, wares, English servants, negroes, and other slaves and merchandise whatsoever that shalbe imported into this colony from and after the twenty-ninth day of September, which shalbe in the yeare 1681, shalbe landed on shore, bought, and sould at such appointed places aforesaid, and at noe other place whatsoever, under like penalty and forfeiture thereof."

The tobacco sent to the said settlements was free from all executions, attachments, &c. It was further provided that all lawyers, bricklayers, &c., that would "cohabitt, dwell, and exercise their trades within the said appointed place," should be freed from arrest of their persons or seizure of their estates for debts formerly contracted, for five years after the publication of the act. Other persons were free from "publique levyes," during the same term, showing the great and commendable anxiety to establish towns, attract emigration, and increase trade.*

In 1682, August 16, the land was purchased by trustees from Nicholas Wise, a house carpenter of Elizabeth River Parish, in the County of Lower Norfolk. He was a son of the individual of that name above mentioned. The grant was made "for and in consideration of the sum of ten thousand pounds of good merchantable tobacco and caske, to Captain Wm. Robinson and Lieutenant Colonel Anthony Lawson, feoffees in trust for the said county." The grant embraced all the land on the river, from the eastern to the western end of the present Main Street, bounded on the north by Back Creek, which, at that time, flowed from the river eastwardly nearly to Church Street. Granby and Bank Streets cross this creek, and where the City Hall now stands, was then navigable for small craft and lighters. The greater portion of the land south of Main Street has since been added by filling up the river.

The old deed from Wise to the trustees is quite a curiosity as a legal contract, commencing, "*To all Christian people to whom these presents shall come.*" A portion of the conveyance, after naming the price, &c., reads thus: "I hold myself well satisfied, contented, and paid, and for divers other considerations, me therefore moving, having given, granted, bargained, sold, alienated, enfeoffed, and conformed, by these presents, for myself, my heirs,

* Prior to the establishment of other trading-points, considerable trade and shipping were carried on at a landing called Cobham, opposite Jamestown, on James River. More business was done there at one time than at all other places in the State combined.

exor's, and adm'rs, do give, grant, bargain, sell, alienate, enfeoff, and confirm," &c. The location, boundary, &c., are thus defined: "Situate and lying in Elizabeth River Parish, north side of Elizabeth River, bounded with Elizabeth River to south and west, to the north with a creek, and to the east with several stacks, running partly across an old field, and partly through some points of woodland, it being a small nick of cleared ground and woodland," &c.

The deed thus concludes: "In the year of the reign of our sovereign lord, King Charles the Second, over England, Scotland, France, and Ireland, defender of the faith," &c.

This land was part of the tract of 200 acres which Mr. Wise inherited from his father. The remaining tract of 150 acres, afterwards included in the limits of the town, was purchased by Charles Wilder, who sold it to William Porten, Clerk of the County Court, from whom it was purchased by Anthony Walke, some of whose descendants are now highly respectable residents of the City, and of the County of Princess Anne. That part of this tract extending from Bermuda Street to Plume's Cove, including Fenchurch Street and the whole of Briggs' Point, remained in the Walke family for more than a century; and some of the heirs are, at the present time (1853), proprietors of a portion of this old family estate.

1705. At this period a considerable population had been attracted to the place by its favourable situation for trade and commerce, and in October of this year, Norfolk was, by act of Assembly, regularly established a town.

1728. The business of the place had now greatly increased, and a very considerable number added to the population. Its situation presented all the requisite advantages for commerce, navigation, and a profitable investment of capital. A brisk trade was carried on with tho West Indies, whither large quantities of flour, lumber, beef, pork, &c., were exported; in return for which were imported, abundant supplies of sugar, molasses, rum, and fruits. Twenty or thirty brigs and smaller vessels constantly rode at the wharves; the merchants and mechanics all appeared to be actively engaged, and prospering; a number of stores and dwellings were erected, real estate advanced in price, and there was no good reason for doubting that Norfolk would, ere the present day, be a very large and flourishing city, if not the greatest upon the whole coast.

"The two cardinal virtues," wrote Colonel Byrd, at this period, "that make a place thrive—industry and frugality—are seen here in perfection; and so long as they can banish luxury and idleness, the town will remain in a happy and flourishing condition." And so it did, for many years; indeed, the town appears to have continued in a "flourishing condition" (with some intermissions), until the memorable 1st of January, 1776.

1736, September 15th. This is the date of the Royal Charter of NORFOLK BOROUGH, of which the following is an extract:

"Whereas, a healthful and pleasant place, commodious for trade and navigation, by an act of the General Assembly of our Colony and Dominion of Virginia, hath been appointed and laid out for a town, called by the name of Norfolk; which place of late years, especially during the administration of our trusty and well-beloved William Gooch, Esq., our Lieutenant-Governor of our said Colony, hath been very greatly increased in the number of its inhabitants and buildings, in so much that the said town, not being capable of containing all such persons as have resorted thereto, divers of our loving subjects have seated themselves upon the adjoining land, so far as to a place called the Town Bridge. Know ye, that we being willing to encourage all our good and faithful subjects, as well at present residing and inhabiting, as shall or may hereafter reside and inhabit within the said town of Norfolk, and the places thereunto adjoining, so far as the Town Bridge, at the instance and petition of divers of our dutiful and loyal subjects, inhabitants of the said town and places adjacent, of our royal grace, good will, certain knowledge, and mere motion, with the advice of our Council of our said Colony, have constituted and erected, and by these our Letters Patent, do constitute and erect the said town of Norfolk and the said parts thereunto adjoining, so far as said bridge, a borough, by the name of the Borough of Norfolk; and for us, our heirs, and successors, do, by these presents, grant to the inhabitants of the said borough, and of the parts adjacent, that the said borough and the parts adjacent, shall be a borough incorporate, consisting of a mayor, one person learned in the law, styled and bearing the office of recorder of the said borough, eight aldermen, and sixteen other persons to be common-councilmen of the said borough."

The Charter points out the duties of the mayor, aldermen, &c. Samuel Boush, Esq., was appointed to be Mayor; Sir John Randolph (Knight), Recorder; and George Newton, Samuel Boush, the younger, John Hutchings, Robert Tucker, John Taylor, Samuel Smith, the younger, James Ivey, and Alexander Campbell, were appointed Aldermen. Provision was also made in the charter for the election of councilmen and the different officers of the corporation, the holding of the courts, elections, markets, public fairs, &c.

This Charter was granted, and the letters patent witnessed by William Gooch, Lieutenant-Governor and Commander-in-chief of the Colony and Dominion of Virginia, at Williamsburg, "in the tenth year of our reign."

"It will be seen that the northern boundary of the town, when it was incorporated, was defined by a line running from the head of the cove at Town Bridge, in a westerly direction to the river, embracing the whole of the two hundred acre tract of Mr. Wise." "In 1761, the limits were enlarged, by Act of Assembly, so as to take in all the land south of a line running from the head of Newton's Creek to the head of Smith's Creek." "In 1807, a new survey of the northern boundary was ordered by Act of Assembly; and the line between the heads of the two creeks designated by stone landmarks. The jurisdiction of the city now extends over a space of about eight hundred acres."*

* With regard to extending the city limits, the Herald thus remarks (1850): "The purpose of petitioning the Legislature for the extension of the boundaries of the city to include all the land west of a line from the head of Plume's Creek (now the eastern boundary of the city) to Tanner's Creek, however visionary it may seem at a first glance, will, on a closer inspection, be found at least worthy of consideration. Our city limits now embrace a space equivalent, we believe, to a square of one mile and a quarter. The contemplated extension would make it equal to a square of three miles. It would take in all the farms on the south side of Tanner's Creek, down to the old "Quarantine House," and all from that point to Lambert's Point, and thence to Smith's Point, the present western terminus of the city; and it would then be a great deal smaller than one-half of the site of the city of New York. A ditch or canal from Plume's to Tanner's Creek, about a mile, would completely insulate the

As early as the period at which the borough charter was obtained, the town had spread far beyond the limits of the fifty acres first purchased from Wise, and extended from the river "out into the country" to the cove above mentioned. This cove extended from Newton's Creek west to the spot where Church and Charlotte Streets now intersect each other, at which place there was for a long time, a bridge, which gave the name of Town Bridge to that immediate portion of the town, and which it still retains, although there has been no bridge, nor any necessity for one for many years. During the Revolutionary struggle,

city, while it would afford a ready means of transportation for wood and marketing for all the country on the north side of Tanner's Creek to the lower end of the city.

"It is not at all improbable, we think, that if our city were thus extended it would infuse a spirit of energy and enterprise into the people of the new municipality, which they must remain utterly insensible to while their noses are kept to the grindstone by the powers to which they owe allegiance, and they are not permitted to have the full benefit of the taxes they are called upon to pay: they would feel and estimate their independence, and the value of their city connexion; they would bestir themselves to make their farms more valuable, and find out the secret of cultivating more on a few acres, than they have heretofore done on many, and thus enable them to sell as much land as they can conveniently do without. But we would caution them not to be in too great haste to part with their lands, nor to part with any more than they can do without; for in fifty years from now the whole will be compactly built up and become a part of the flourishing city of Norfolk. We cannot live to see it; but there are those of adult age who will."

The following additional remarks on this subject, are from the Herald of a more recent date:

"Our city authorities should be looking about them for more land for a further extension of the city limits; and while they are about it, why not take in the whole extent of the boundaries so clearly indicated by nature? commencing at the head of Newton's (or Plume's) Creek and running across the narrow strip of territory (three-quarters of a mile in width) between the head of that Creek and Tanner's Creek, and following that water-course to its junction with Elizabeth River, and thence to the present limit of our southern water front. It is not generally known that Tanner's Creek, the northern boundary of the city as it then would be, is a bold stream all the way up to the point where it is proposed to intersect it by a canal from the head of Newton's Creek; and that for more than a mile from its mouth it has a sufficient depth of water for ships of large tonnage. There were formerly several ship-yards on Tanner's Creek, where vessels of large draught were constructed. The last of which we have any recollection was the brig George Loyall, built by the late Isaac Talbot, Esq."

an entrenchment was thrown up from this place across the town to Smith's Point. It has been stated by a person now living (1852), that boats of considerable size were frequently to be seen at Town Bridge, at as late a period as 1780. Many years since, Fenchurch Street was extended across this ravine, and Charlotte Street has been continued through from Church to Fenchurch, (and will be lengthened to Chapel), covering what was formerly the centre of the cove; and on each side of which, buildings are now erected.

The following remarks are copied from the Virginia Gazette of November 26, 1736.

"The inhabitants of *Norfolk* Town, in this Colony, having for several Years past, flourished in Trade, by their sending Vessels to Sea, loaded with the Commodities of this Country, which returned with those of other Countries, by which several of the Merchants are become very considerable, and the Number of their inhabitants increasing, they lately petitioned the Governor for a Charter to incorporate them, which was accordingly granted: and an Act of Assembly passed the last Session, to confirm and strengthen the said Charter, by which they are incorporated by the name of the Borough of *Norfolk*, and are to consist of a Mayor, Recorder, and 8 Alderman; who have power to hold a Court of *Hustings*, &c., and to choose 16 Common Council Men; with several Privileges, Immunities, &c., granted by the said Charter; in which the following Gentlemen are nominated, viz., Samuel Boush, Gent., Mayor, Sir John Randolph, Knt., Recorder, &c. The first Mayor dying soon after the Grant of the said Charter, he is succeeded by *G. Newton*, Gent.

"Sir *John Randolph* being so appointed Recorder of the said Borough, made a Visit to them, and was on *Thursday*, the 18th instant, sworn into that Office accordingly: And he being empowered to appoint a Deputy, to act in his absence, did appoint *David Osheall*, General Deputy Recorder of the said Borough, who was accordingly qualified.

"On this Occasion of Sir John's Visit, the Gentlemen of the said Town and Neighbourhood, shew'd him all-imaginable Respect, by displaying the Colours, and firing the Guns of the Vessels lying there, and entertained him at their Houses, in the most elegant Manner, for several days; amply signalizing their great Respect, on this joyful Occasion."

The first Council meeting was held November 18th. This was the only meeting attended by Sir John Randolph. Two days thereafter, he appointed a deputy.

"Mr. Henry Tazewell, of James City, the father of Governor Tazewell, was the next Recorder, and qualified and took his seat on the bench, the 19th August, 1782, and continued as such until his appointment as a Judge of the General Court. He was succeeded by Edmund Randolph, on the 22d February, 1786; but it does not appear that he ever qualified. After this, by the Act of 1787, the Court and Council being separated, the Recorder was always one of our own citizens, and the appointment vesting in the Court, no notice of course appears on the journal of the Council."

Samuel Boush, Esq., the first mayor of the borough of Norfolk, three years after his appointment, presented to the parish the grounds occupied by St. Paul's Church, including the old grave-yard. The initials of his name may be seen in large capitals, in the brickwork of the south end of the church, with the date, 1739. In that sacred old cemetery his remains have reposed in stillness and security for long years that have past and gone, with the multitudes of the sleeping dead around; alas! how unconscious of the varied scenes and misfortunes, the noise, bustle, commotions, alterations, and improvements, that have been going on in the place in which he had the honour of presiding as its first chief magistrate!

"The third name mentioned in the old charter is that of *George Newton*. In 1706, he married Aphie Wilson, and had nine children. His son Thomas married Amy, daughter of John Hutchings, whose name also appears in the charter. They had five children, all of whom died in infancy, except a son, also named *Thomas*, who married Martha Tucker, a daughter of another of the charter men. The last-named Thomas was the father of the late respected and intelligent citizens, Thomas and George Newton."

No man was better known in Norfolk and the District than the Hon. Thomas Newton, one of the brothers just mentioned.

As a citizen, he was kind, polite, and unostentatious; as a politician, ardent and faithful; possessing the advantage of great experience.

"In the early stage of his life he pursued the profession of law, from which, in 1801, he was called by the voice of his fellow-citizens, whose political sentiments he reflected, and whose confidence he possessed, to represent them in Congress.

"Mr. Newton commenced his political career soon after the elevation of Mr. Jefferson to the Presidency, and was regularly returned from the Norfolk District for thirty years. His manners were plain; indeed they could not have been farther removed from arrogance or repulsiveness than they really were. Such was the good feeling which his republican simplicity and long services created in his favour, that no hostile power could easily shake him in the estimation of the majority of his constituents." He died August 5th, 1847, at the advanced age of 79.

George Newton, Esq., the brother of Thomas, was a very wealthy gentleman. He, also, merited and enjoyed the esteem and confidence of his fellow-citizens, having filled important public offices. They had several estimable sisters, who married in highly respectable families. Two of them are now living.

Some of the individuals comprising the present descendants of the family are now members of this community, while others of them have removed elsewhere. Cincinnatus W., one of the sons of Thomas, has represented the city in the Legislature of the State; and Dr. Thos. Newton, son of George, an accomplished physician, is an efficient alderman of the city.

"The next name in the charter, after Newton, is Samuel Boush, Jr. He was the first clerk of the Borough Court, when its powers were enlarged, and in the year 1766 was one of the committee of correspondence appointed by the *Sons of Liberty;* an association formed by many of our most respectable citizens, to concert measures of defence against the operations of the Stamp Act. He, too, was buried in St. Paul's Churchyard.

"The next name is John Hutchings, who also opposed the Stamp Act, and was one of the committee appointed by the Sons of Liberty. His earthly remains also lie in the yard of old St. Paul's, near the south gate. A daughter of his married Dr.

John Ramsay, a native of Scotland, a warm and fearless patriot, and a Son of Liberty." He was an eminent physician, and a gentleman greatly respected for his intelligence and public spirit. His name will appear in another part of this work, in connexion with some further allusions to the Sons of Liberty.

"The next name is that of Robert Tucker, one of the corresponding committee of the 'Sons.' He at one time had *twenty-one children living!* but now no male descendant bears his respected name. He and most of his numerous family were interred in the lot connected with the Exchange Bank.

"John Taylor's name comes next. He was born in 1691 and died in 1744. He was buried in the lot of St. Paul's, and the spot is marked by a massive tablet. His descendants are among the worthiest members of the community.

"Samuel Smith is the next name. From him the creek that bounds the city on the north side and Smith's Point took their name. He was buried on the left hand, as you enter the northern gate of the old churchyard.

"James Ivey appears next. He was the ancestor of the Iveys, who formerly lived in Norfolk County. He died and was buried at his country seat, on Tanner's Creek."

Alexander Campbell is the last name in the charter. We have not been able to gather any further definite information respecting this gentleman, than the fact, that from him Campbell's Wharf took its name.

CHAPTER IV.

1736—1739.

Distinct Classes of Society—Effect of War—Political Agitation—Changes—Slow Movements—Style of Architecture—Flourishing Commerce—Sports—Fairs—Greased Pole—Pig Chase—Sack Races—Empty Hogshead Affair—Hot Mush—Bull-bait—Old St. Paul's—The Grounds Improved—Church Street—Diabolical Plot—The Old Graveyard, and its Silent Occupants.

The inhabitants of the borough of Norfolk, anterior to the Revolutionary War, were divided into three distinct classes; and the lines of demarcation were more plainly designated than at the present time. "The first included the clergy, the medical faculty, lawyers, merchants, and those who lived on their income. The second was composed of mechanics, who were greatly respected in their class; and the '*tag-rag and bob-tail*' constituted the third."

But when the roar of the Revolution was heard, as it were, booming in the distance—when the commotions and soul-trying events of war were realized, society was shaken to its centre; the different classes were, of necessity, less plainly identified; and while it must be acknowledged that there were some who, from the want of firmness or a lack of principle—from motives of self-preservation, or from considerations entirely of a pecuniary nature, gave their efforts and influence against the oppressed, or withdrew entirely from the scene of contention, still, to a great extent, all parties and classes united against the common foe. And after the din of battle had been hushed by the triumph of an unconquered and unconquerable people; when the sad calamities of war were over; after the smoke from the ruins of Virginia's principal town had passed away, and Norfolk began to rise from its ashes, the different grades and classes here were more united in their efforts, and there was a perceptible, though gradual, abandonment of the old aristocratic views.

But an allusion to the Revolutionary scenes and events that took place here, will not be omitted in its appropriate place; and it is proper now to confine the reader's attention to Norfolk as it was, prior to that memorable period—the infancy of a nation, which now stands majestically forth in its own power and glory, for the eager gaze of an admiring, though jealous world. And yet, not without occasional indications of troublesome and tumultuous events. May they prove to be only as the thunder of the distant storm-cloud, or merely the rumbling and gentle vibratory motions of the far-off earthquake; and not a fell and fearful visitation, by which the whole mighty Union, and perhaps the great nations of the earth, shall be convulsed and shaken, while thousands and tens of thousands shall be involved in the common desolation and ruin.*

* These remarks were written when the public mind was greatly agitated on the Slavery question, and prior to the passing of the Compromise measures.

During the lapse of more than a hundred years, numerous changes have, as a matter of course, taken place here as well as elsewhere. Many have, doubtless, been judicious and advantageous, while some have been of doubtful utility. It will not be insisted that Norfolk has, during the last fifty years, kept pace with very many other places in the country. No, indeed; for it is quite too certain that the people here have been wont to jog along in the march of improvement slowly, very; at least, in some respects. Improvements have, however, been made; and very important and beneficial innovations have marked the history of the place from time to time.

The style of building, for instance, in Norfolk and vicinity, as well as elsewhere, has been wonderfully improved. In the early days of the history of this section, the mode of constructing dwellings was quite singular. They were often built with a Dutch roof, a chimney at each end, or in the middle, with very spacious fire-places, furnished generally with figured cast-iron back-pieces. The walls were, in many cases, built of imported bricks, and were very thick. There were two rooms and a passage on the first floor (which was often within two or three feet of the ground), and several small chambers above. Some preferred a very sharp or acute-angled roof, but the prevailing taste gave the preference to the unsightly plan first mentioned. The mantel-pieces were five or six feet high, and the walls on the inside were wainscotted, or covered with a casing of panel-work. The carpentry was much more heavy and clumsy than at the present day. Some of the buildings of the more wealthy portion of the community were large and tolerably commodious; having, sometimes, one very spacious room for company, balls, social parties, &c., in one end; a dining and sleeping-room in the other, and a wide passage through the middle; and the interior work was often of oak, walnut, &c. But the houses were, many of them, of contracted dimensions, badly ventilated, and very uncomfortable, especially in summer; having small, low-ceiled rooms, with a few diminutive windows, scarcely half the size of those in the light, commodious, and airy mansions of our time. The kitchen was frequently placed at a considerable distance from the dwelling, sometimes as much as fifty paces or more, and often exhibited many of the architectural peculiarities of the principal house.

There are many of these old, ante-revolutionary family residences in the counties of Norfolk and Princess Anne. We shall speak especially of one in the immediate vicinity of Kempsville, about ten miles from this city, and belonging to the descendants of Anthony Walke, Esq., one of the early settlers, to whom we have alluded on another page. This Dutch-roof relic of antiquity is probably two hundred years old, resisting still the effects of time. The walls are more than four feet thick, for some distance above the ground. The interior walls and ceiling are heavily wainscotted with black walnut, the passage is exceedingly spacious; and there are other architectural curiosities about it which form a striking contrast to the present style of building.

The old borough is said to have been "a rare place," before the disasters of the Revolution. The harbour was almost filled with vessels, many of which were very large. Commerce was exceedingly flourishing; money was plentiful. There was but little grumbling about "hard times." The sluggish, lazy, intemperate, or the constitutional grumblers, only, complained; and fortunes were made much more rapidly than at present. Indeed, this port almost monopolized the heavy trade of the West Indies. All were busy; a prosperous state of affairs was plainly exhibited on every hand, and no one doubted the future greatness of the place. And yet, it appears that many found time for amusement and pastime.

The sports and diversions of those days, though principally of English and Scotch origin, were ludicrous enough. Sometimes the most laughable scenes were presented. It was customary and lawful to hold *fairs** in the Market Place; and, on such occasions, the middle of the Square was appropriated to such amusements as the young and mirth-loving portion of the crowd chose to engage in. No objection was made to the noise and

* Fairs and markets were first instituted in England, by Egbert, in 829. In early days, markets were held in Norfolk on Tuesdays and Saturdays, and the fairs were held annually on the 3d of October, and the four following days, Sundays excepted.

uproar which accompanied the sport. They laughed and shouted aloud, without hindrance or molestation. Sometimes a pole, well greased and soaped, with a gilt-laced hat on the top, was erected in the middle of the Market Space; and the unavailing efforts to take the tempting prize that was freely offered to the smartest man, was a source of great merriment to the lookers-on. Young men, and, occasionally, some of the *damsels*, too, ran races. Pigs were turned loose amid the crowd, for those who could catch and hold them by their tails, which had been previously well-shaved and greased.

There were, also, "*sack races*." A purse was made up, and two candidates selected, who were separately enclosed, all but the head, in a bag, the mouth of which was drawn closely around the neck. Then, the unavailing attempts to run, the shuffling, tumbling, and, finally, the rolling, of the ambitious contenders for the prize, afforded great enjoyment to the noisy crowd.

Three or four fellows would undertake to run a race through several sugar-hogsheads, with both heads out, and placed end to end. The empty hogsheads commenced rolling to and fro, both to the dispersion and diversion of the excited multitude. Of course, this contrary hogshead affair ended in "noise and confusion," and the company waited impatiently for another source of hilarity; when, lo and behold! a wag would appear with *a pot of hot mush*, for the hungry fellow who would "gobble it up" faster than the rest; and the wry faces, distorted countenances, and tearful eyes, of the hungry eaters gave joy enough to all others present.

Sometimes a *bull-bait* was introduced, for which the sudden disappearance of the women and the "small fry" made ample room.

In 1739,—one hundred and thirteen years ago,—St. Paul's Church was erected, on the west side of "the road leading out of town." Historians have stated that this venerable old edifice was almost the only building that escaped destruction from the conflagration of '76. All the combustible part of this church was consumed: the walls, however, remained as they are now, alike uninjured by the destructive hand of Time, the raging of the devouring element, or the balls from Dunmore's ordnance,—

excepting the mark made by a cannon-shot, near one of the corners, and on the side facing the river,—another fit and lasting monument of British folly and oppression. The effect of this ball, by the way, was somewhat singular. It struck with very considerable force, about three feet below the eaves of the building, and about one foot from the southeastern corner of the eastern end, ranging with the easternmost wall, starting a portion of the masonry from its position, and leaving a perpendicular fissure of about two feet in length, at each end of which, as well as around the principal indentation, pieces of the bricks were displaced by the concussion. If the ball had struck only a few inches farther from the corner, of course it would not have ranged with the eastern wall, and it would, therefore, have gone entirely through. The portion of the masonry removed from its original place, and forming a part of the angle, looks as if a slight pressure would detach it entirely, and cause it to fall to the ground. Thus it has stood during the long interval of seventy-seven years, and so it will remain, it is probable, to be examined by the curious of coming generations.

Formerly, it was thought that; when the ball struck; it had lodged in the wall, and was removed by some mischievous person shortly after the general conflagration, or had been displaced by the heating of the walls when the house was on fire and the interior destroyed. Several years ago, it occurred to Captain Seabury, an esteemed member of the vestry of the church, that it might be buried in the ground below the spot where it took effect. He accordingly set a man to work with a spade, and after a very short search a ball was found, corresponding in size with the concavity, and which is supposed to be the identical shot that struck the church. It weighs twenty pounds and a half, and measures in diameter about five and a half inches; but, as its size has been much diminished by corrosion, it is reasonable to suppose that it was a twenty-four pound shot, and about six inches in diameter.

The venerable gentleman who brought this old revolutionary relic to light, developes the antiquarian propensities in his character by a commendable intention to have it permanently replaced in its appropriate bed in the wall; and he generally executes his plans. *Nous verrons.*

The ground-plan of the building is in the shape of a Roman cross,—which it was intended by the designers to represent,—the four ends, pointing severally to the north, south, east, and west,—the easternmost wall, forming an angle with the enclosure and the western line of the street, presenting to the eye of the beholder an irregular and unsatisfying appearance. The roof is right-angled, and has now the third, or possibly the fourth, covering of shingles. The windows and doors are arched; and there is a large circular window above the entrance in the northern end, and also in the southern. The walls of this time-honoured structure, as well as of the enclosure of the burial-place attached, were built of very durable materials, and in the most substantial manner,—about every alternate brick in the building having the bluish, glazed appearance caused by extra heat in the kiln.

Since this faithful old sentinel of other days and of other years, that have winged their rapid flight away, took its present position, three generations have passed; and, unless it should be taken down to give place to a more modern structure, it will, in all probability, continue for ages yet to come. Like the sturdy old oak of the mountain, that defies the fury of the levelling tornado, and which has escaped the heavy strokes of the woodman's axe, as well as the scathing thunderbolts of the God of Nature, or like the aged pilgrim, who has long survived all the rest of his generation, and who lingers, almost as a stranger, amid the changes and desolation around him, this ancient temple stands among the silent dead,—the mouldering remains of those who formerly assembled to worship within its consecrated walls and make their vows at its altar; and it points gloomily, though significantly, to the men and the events of years that have gone by.

> "On it Time his mark has hung;
> On it hostile balls have rung;
> On it green old moss has clung;
> On it winds their dirge have sung:
> Let us still adorn thy walls,
> Sacred temple, Old St. Paul's!"

A few years subsequent to the Revolution, the interior of St.

Paul's Church was rebuilt, and put in order for public worship. About twenty years ago, it was again repaired and improved; and ten years since, under the direction of the Rev. Mr. Miller, then the resident pastor, and some of the members of his charge, the church was again improved; a neat lecture-room was erected within the enclosure, and the grounds beautified with ornamental shade-trees, flowers, evergreens, gravel-walks, &c. It has more recently undergone thorough repairs; and the interior now presents a very neat and comfortable appearance. A new square belfry has also been erected in the northeastern angle.

The Rev. Mr. Jackson is the present minister of this church. He is a most excellent preacher, a faithful pastor, and an estimable and devoted Christian gentleman, to whom the numerous members of his charge are greatly endeared.*

St. Paul's having been built upon the principal avenue leading out into the country, gave to it the name of Church Street.

Some have insisted that this old ante-revolutionary building should give place to another, more in keeping with the style of the age, and the improvements of the city: this change has been warmly opposed. Situated as it is, in immediate proximity to the business part of the city, it has also been whispered that the grounds connected with the church should be converted into a public square. This plan, how objectionable soever it might be to many, would not be without a precedent in other cities. The authorities very properly prohibited interments in the lot, many years ago.

There are some circumstances connected with the history of this old sanctuary, which would prove interesting to the reader; but having already continued the description farther than was intended, we shall pass them by for the present, not without alluding, however, to a diabolical plot, many years ago, to destroy

* This church, and also Trinity, in Portsmouth, are strictly under the supervision of the bishop, and are governed according to the old canonical laws of the Protestant Episcopal Church of Virginia. For instance, the minister, after being once elected, remains during good behaviour, and he cannot be ejected unless he should be guilty of some gross violation of his clerical vows.

Christ Church is an independent church, and is governed according to its own peculiar constitution; nevertheless, in every other respect, it is regulated by the canons of the Episcopal Church. The minister and officers are elected annually by the pew-holders, on the first Friday in November.

it, and involve the assembled congregation in ruin. The scheme was actually commenced, but fortunately discovered in time to prevent its consummation.

A walk, or even a look within the walls of the grave-yard attached to this old church, is calculated to produce a train of solemn, if not painful reflections—to inspire the heart of the thoughtful man with melancholy feelings,—

> "The tombs
> And monumental caves of death look cold,
> And shoot a chillness to my trembling heart."

The remains of many, very many, of those whom Time mowed down in the borough and vicinity, repose in that old "city of the dead," and there they have long and quietly slumbered, regardless of the anxious throngs that press by. There, in that densely stored repository of death, lie the tiny crumbling remains of the infant of a day, the once agile form of the stripling youth, the "sordid dust" of the strong man of middle age, and of those of threescore years and ten. Here sleep on profoundly,

> "The ancient venerable dead,
> Sages who wrote and warriors who bled."

Concealed beneath the uneven sod are the earthly relics of many whose familiar voices were heard, and whose active forms were seen in the places now occupied by their living, thinking, dying descendants—not to be disturbed, it may be, but by the Archangel's loud trumpet blast.

> "Here friends and foes
> Lie close, unmindful of their former feuds.
> The lawn-robed prelate, and plain presbyter,
> Erewhile that stood aloof, as shy to meet,
> Familiar mingle here, like sister streams
> That some rude, interposing rock had split.
> * * * * *
> Here are the prude severe, and gay coquette,
> The sober widow, and young green virgin,
> Cropped like a rose before 'tis fully blown,
> Or half its worth disclosed. Strange medley here!
> Here garrulous old age winds up his tale;
> And jovial youth, of lightsome vacant heart,
> Whose every day was made of melody,
> Hears not the voice of mirth."

CHAPTER V.

1746—1765.

Celebration of the Defeat of the Pretender—Privileges of the Borough enlarged —Court-house and Prison—Act of Assembly relative to Ferries—Talbot Street —Captain Talbot's Property—Foot-bridge—Grave-yard—Human Bones— Reflections.

1746, July 23d. The inhabitants on this day manifested their loyalty by celebrating the defeat of the Pretender, by his Royal Highness, the Duke of Cumberland, at the battle of Culloden, fought April 6th of this year.

They had an effigy of the Pretender, seated in an armed chair, which was placed in a cart. A procession was then formed in the following order:—Three drummers, a piper, three violinists, six men with rods, sashes, and significant mottoes; a nurse, carrying a warming pan with a child peeping out of it; the Pretender in the cart; six men with drawn cutlasses; and a vast crowd of people of the town and country.

After the procession had marched through the principal streets, the effigy was hung, and liquor was provided in plentiful quantities. Salutes were fired, at night the town was illuminated, the effigy burnt, the ladies were entertained with a ball, "and the evening concluded with innocent mirth and unaffected joy, becoming a people loyal to their king, and zealous for their country's good."

In 1752 the privileges of the Borough were enlarged by Act of Assembly. Provision was also made for the raising of money to build a court house and prison.

Extract of an Act of the Assembly of Virginia, passed in 1757.

"SECTION 1. Whereas it hath been represented to this General Assembly by the inhabitants of the County and Borough of Norfolk, that on the branches of Elizabeth River and Tanner's Creek in the said county, there are five public ferries, over one of which most of the inhabitants are obliged to pass in order to get to church, court, and general muster, and that by expenses of ferriages, *many poor people are prevented from bringing their small wares and commodities to the market of the said Borough.* Be it therefore enacted, &c., that the Justices of the Court of the County of Norfolk for the time being, be, and they are hereby empowered, and required, to appoint, contract, and agree with proper persons to keep the said ferries, and to levy the expense thereof upon the tithable inhabitants of the said county annually at the laying of the county levy.

"SECTION 2.—That every person appointed to keep the said ferries shall constantly keep such boats and hands as the said court shall from time to time order and direct, to be kept at the said ferries respectively, and shall give immediate passage over the said ferries to all the inhabitants of the said county without *any fee or reward.*

"SECTION 3.—That such ferry-keepers shall and may demand and receive from persons not being inhabitants of the said county of Norfolk, the following rates, that is to say, for a man, four pence; for a horse, the same; on every coach, chariot, or wagon and the driver thereof, the same as for six horses; for every cart or four-wheel chaise, and the driver thereof, as for four horses; for every two-wheel chair, or chaise, the same as two horses; for every hogshead of tobacco, the same as one horse," &c.

In 1765, Talbot Street (twenty-six feet wide, and which now extends north from Main, near Market Square, to William's Street, at the City Hall Square), was opened by Captain Talbot, the proprietor of the land, one of the most respectable and opulent citizens, from whom it took its name, and whose heirs are still the owners of a large portion of the property thereon. This street soon became and continued for some time the most fashionable thoroughfare in the town. Captain T. built upon it large and commodious houses; it was the first street paved in the borough; and, being one of the principal avenues to the Market Place (Bank and Granby Streets were not opened for many years after this), a number of the most respectable and fashionable citizens resided on it.* At its northern terminus, there was a foot-bridge, which extended across the cove, to the land between Cove Street and Williamson's Lane, and east of Avon Street. At the corner of Main and Talbot Streets was situated Captian Talbot's store; in the rear of which, and extending back to the marsh, he had a warehouse.

Many years before Talbot Street was opened, a portion of the land over which it extends, and on the east side, near its north end (part of which is now enclosed, and included in the City Hall Square), reaching as far as the site of the City Prison, and formerly that of Avon Theatre, was a *grave-yard;* sufficient evidences of which were exhibited while making the public improvements at that location. Portions of the slowly mouldering remains of the unknown dead, that have lain there for ages undisturbed,—human skulls and other bones of different sizes—have been dug up from their concealment, and exposed to the thoughtful gaze of the inquisitive denizens of the present day. The old enclosure gradually decayed, and piece by piece fell down and disappeared, or was torn off and removed by sacrilegious hands. The vernal tides came up and blasted the green grass and gentle flowers that were wont to adorn those graves. The tombstones sank down beneath the slow, but heavy tread of Time. These too, were removed, and the "monumental caves of death" filled up. The footprints of the careless passenger were seen there. Names, and titles, and deeds, good and bad, are forgotten. At least one old grave-stone should have been spared, to serve as a silent monitor to succeeding generations of the vanity of all earthly things; and under its old inscription should have been deeply engraved, "*sic transit gloria mundi.*" But

"The time draws on
When not a single spot of burial earth,
Whether on land or on the spacious sea,
But must give back its long-committed dust
Inviolate: and faithfully shall these
Make up the full account! not the least atom

* The property on the west side of this street, and extending from Main to Williams Street, remains in the Talbot family; and the enterprising and respected heirs have had it improved in handsome style, by the erection of a long row of beautiful buildings.

Embezzled or mislaid of the whole tale.
Each soul shall have a body ready furnished;
And each shall have his own.
* * * * *
When the dread trump shall sound, the slumbering dust,
Not unattentive to the call, shall wake;
And every joint possess its proper place,
With a new elegance of form, unknown
To its first state."

CHAPTER VI.

1766—1768.

Protest of the People against the Stamp Act—The Sons of Liberty, and their Patriotic Proceedings—Members' Names—Descendants—Imports of Virginia —A Curiosity—The Revolution and its Calamities.

THE people of Norfolk and its vicinity were among the first and the boldest to protest against the Stamp Act, and to assert on the broadest grounds the rights of the Colony. Accordingly, on March 31, 1766, a number of the inhabitants of the town and county of Norfolk assembled at the Court-house, and an association called "THE SONS OF LIBERTY," was duly organized.

The patriotic object of this society was, to oppose, by all suitable means, that detestable Act, and to unite with others in the country, in a dignified and determined effort to prevent the operation of a measure so manifestly unconstitutional and oppressive.

The Rev. Thomas Davis was chosen moderator, and James Holt and Wm. Roscoe Curle, secretaries. The following preamble and resolutions were adopted, and fifty-seven individuals, of pure and unsullied patriotism, in order to show to that and to future generations their faithful devotion to the cause of liberty, signed the manly protest. These proceedings of the Sons of Liberty have been carefully preserved among the archives of Norfolk as a "monument of their patriotic spirit and love to their country." The following is a copy:

"Having taken into Considerations the evident Tendency of that oppressive and unconstitutional Act of Parliament, commonly called the Stamp Act, and being desirous that our sentiments should be known to Posterity; and recollecting that we are a Part of that Colony who first in General Assembly openly expressed their Detestation to the said Act (which is pregnant with Ruin, and productive of the most pernicious Consequences), and unwilling to rivet the Shackles of Slavery and Oppression on ourselves and Millions yet unborn, have unanimously come to the following Resolutions:

"1. *Resolved*, That we acknowledge our Lord and Sovereign, King George the Third, to be our rightful and lawful King, and that we will, at all times, to the utmost of our Power and Ability, support and defend his most sacred Person, Crown, and Dignity; and shall be always ready, when constitutionally called upon, to assist his said Majesty, with our Lives and fortunes; and to defend all his Just Rights and Prerogatives.

"2. *Resolved*, That we will by all lawful Ways and Means which Divine Providence has put into our hands, defend ourselves in the full enjoyment of, and preserve inviolate to Posterity, those inestimable Privileges of all freeborn British Subjects of being taxed only by Representatives of their own Choosing; and of being tryed by none but a Jury of their peers. And that if we quietly submit to the Execution of the said Stamp Act, all our Claims to civil Liberty will be lost, and we and our Posterity become absolute Slaves. For, by that Act, British Subjects in America are deprived of the invaluable Privileges aforementioned.

"3. *Resolved*, That a committee be appointed, who shall in such manner as they shall think most proper, go upon necessary Business and make public the above Resolutions, and that they correspond as they shall see Occasion with the Associated Sons of, and Friends to, Liberty, in the other British Colonies in America.

Ja. Holt,	Henry Tucker,
Thos. Davis,	Maxln. Calvert,

Robt. Tucker,
Jas. Parker,
Robt. Tucker, Jun.,
Jno. Hutchings,
Lewis Hansford,
Jno. Hutchings, Jun.,
Paul Loyall,
Will. Roscoe Curle,
Anthy. Lawson,
Jos. Hutchings,
Thos. Newton, Sen.,
Jno. Phripp, Jun.,
John Ramsay,
John Gilchrist,
Matthew Godfrey,
Matthew Phripp,
Thos. Newton, Jr.,
Saml. Boush,
Richd. Knight,
James Campbell,
John Lawrence,
Joshua Nickolson,
Nicholas Wonycott,
Matthw. Rothery,
Jacob Ellegood,
Cornelius Calvert,
Edward Archer,
Edward Voss,
Fras. Peart,
Samuel Calvert,
Ja. Gibson,
Nicholas Winterton,
Griffin Peart,
Jno. Wilson,
Wm. Skinker,
Thos. Butt,
Wm. Gray,
Hudson Brown,
John Taylor,
Alexander Moseley,
Jno. Taylor, Jr.,
William Calvert,
Willm. Aitcheson,
Edward Hack. Moseley, Jr.,
Wm. Hancock,
Robt. Brett,
Stephen Tankard,
Thos. Willoughby,
James Dunn,
John Cramond,
Alexr. Kincaid,
George Muter,
Chrisr. Calvert."

There were other resolutions, unanimously passed, in which the most spirited and patriotic sentiments were embodied. The Stamp Act, the result of a strange freak of a misguided though powerful nation—that precipitate measure, which, from its gross injustice, proved worse than a failure, but which thereby gave a wonderful and most desirable turn to the affairs of the world—that miserable and mistaken policy of Great Britain, was denounced in terms of merited severity. And the noble-souled Sons of Liberty, in their firm determination to assist in preventing it from going into operation, agreed, if necessary, to "*sacrifice their lives and their fortunes.*"

With regard to the members of this patriotic association, a learned gentleman, formerly of this city, remarks as follows:

"The two immediate descendants of Paul Loyall and Thomas Newton represented the Norfolk District in Congress for thirty-seven consecutive years; the same gentlemen, and another descendant of Thomas Newton, represented the borough of Norfolk in the General Assembly twelve or more years. The name of Calvert is no longer known as a surname; but his blood runs in a numerous and reputable posterity, some of whom are among the most active business men and public-spirited citizens. James Parker was the ancestor of the mayor of the town in 1806, I believe, and with him, I presume, the present family of Parkers, formerly of Isle of Wight, are connected collaterally. If Colonel Josiah Parker of Isle of Wight is the son of James Parker, the fact would appear that three of the descendants of the Sons of Liberty represented your District in Congress for almost the first consecutive half century after the adoption of the Federal Constitution. The surname of Ramsay no longer exists in Norfolk; but the Steeds, among others, are of his race. A former delegate to the Assembly from Norfolk, but who, to the great regret of all, died before taking his seat, was named John Ramsay Steed. The surname of Joseph Hutchings is extinct; but the most efficient Register of your city bears not only the whole name and the blood of his ancestor, but reflects credit upon them.* A descendant of Lawson I have not seen for some years; there are no doubt some of the race now living in Princess Anne. The Boush family is known to all. The Phripps I have never known; I hope, however, the name exists within the four counties, as it was borne by two patriots at a portentous period. Gilchrist and Lawrence are names not now known; some of our elder citizens may be able to trace the stock. I confess it is with pain that I cannot point to a male descendant of Lewis Hansford. The late Dr. Hansford, a practising phy-

* Joseph H. Robertson, Esq., attorney at law, a most ready, forcible, and attractive speaker, and for a number of years the faithful and systematic incumbent of the responsible office mentioned.

sician and an accomplished gentleman, was the last of the name in active life. He died in middle age, about the year 1822, leaving two sons, one of whom, Casey, a promising youth, died before he reached maturity, a midshipman in the navy; the other resides in Philadelphia.

"One of the representatives in the late Convention, Tazewell Taylor,* represents the Taylors and the Tuckers; and, if the late General Taylor be sprung from those of his name in the proceedings, the genealogy of the Sons of Liberty will receive one of its most splendid illustrations. When we regard the number and character of the posterity of the Sons of Liberty, it might well happen, that, if a great crisis in affairs were imminent, and a chairman of a public meeting were called upon to appoint a committee of citizens for the emergency, he would be apt to select some of the descendants of the Sons of Liberty to fill the important trust committed to their fathers.

"Hence it will appear that the posterity of the old inhabitants, in spite of the invitations to go abroad, which federal legislation for fifty years past has held out, still cling to the home of their ancestry. Some have gone abroad, and founded families; but the old patriarch would tell his children of his early and distant home.

"Et dulces moriens reminiscitur Argos."

1768. "A Curiosity.—The following is a copy of a bill recently found among the papers of one of our old citizens. The charges for tailoring eighty years ago contrast strangely with the prices now charged. $2 75 for making a coat and vest! and $1 67 per yard for cloth!—but it did not pay duty then, and was probably equal to what is charged $4 00 for now. But the trimmings,—$4 54! Didn't the tailors in those days

* Tazewell Taylor, Esq., attorney at law, of this city, has long since acquired judicial distinction. His knowledge of the science of law is extensive and thorough. From an early period, he has devoted himself with great assiduity to the study and practice of his profession, which, with the advantage of an active and vigorous mind, and a ready delivery, have combined to render him deservedly successful and popular as an advocate; while his experience in jurisprudence is considered inferior to that of but few in the State.

know how to charge for them? More than one-third the cost of cloth and making!"—*Herald.*

September 3d, 1768.

MR. JOHN BAYNS To YOUNG & SMITH, DR.

	£	s.	d.
To 3 yards Brown Cloth, at 10*s.*, ...	1	10	0
To 3½ yards Shalloon, at 2*s.* 8*d.*, ...	0	9	4
To 3½ yards Lining, at 1*s.* 6*d.*, ...	0	5	3
To 14 yards Binding, at 3*d.*, ...	0	3	6
To Buckram, Silk, and Twist, ...	0	4	0
To Thread, Buttons, and Oznaburgs, . . .	0	5	2
To making Coat and Jacket, ...	0	16	6
	3	13	9

Norfolk Borough, sc.:

The above account of three pounds, thirteen shillings, and nine pence, proved by the oath of John Smith.

GEO. ABYVON.

September 24th, 1770.

1769. Imports of Virginia, principally of the port of Norfolk, £851,000.

We now approach an eventful era in the history of Norfolk and vicinity, as well as that of the entire country,—the trying yet glorious period of the great conflict with the power of Britain;—years that were dark and gloomy indeed, and still not causing despair.

As before intimated, our town was thriving and prosperous enough until the commencement of this important and unequal contest. And how sudden was the change! how soon were a thousand hopes disappointed, and the brightest prospects blasted! —one day presenting the appearance of wealth and prosperity, and inspiring the most confident hopes of future greatness, and, ere the dawn of the next, a heap of smouldering ruins!

CHAPTER VII.

1775—1776.

Lord Dunmore—Preparations for War—The Battle of the Great Bridge—Glorious Victory—Heroism and Generosity of the Virginians—Miss Polly Miller—Officers, &c., who were in the Battle at the Bridge.

1775. LORD DUNMORE, on hearing of the warlike preparations that had been made in this part of the State, directed special attention to Norfolk. He erected batteries, threw up entrenchments, furnished the blacks and tories with arms and ammunition, concentrated a considerable military force here, and ordered the farmers to send in provisions.

"The government of Virginia despatched, with all speed, a detachment of minute-men, under the command of Colonel Woodford, into the county." Dunmore, with but little delay, took a strong position at the Great Bridge, then a thriving village, situated about ten miles from the town, and which took its name from the bridge over the southern branch of the Elizabeth. "This point was upon the direct route of the provincial troops. Here he threw up works on the Norfolk side, and furnished them with a numerous artillery. The entrenchments were surrounded on every part with water and marshes, and were only accessible by a long dike. . . . The Virginians took post over against the English, at cannon-shot distance. Before them they had a long, narrow dike, the extremity of which they also fortified. In this state the two parties remained for several days, without making any movement."

"Lord Dunmore," says the Virginia Gazette, "had erected his fort in such a manner that his cannon commanded the causeway on his own side, and the bridges between him and us, with the marshes around him." The causeway to our camp was also commanded by the enemy's cannon.

"The causeway on our side, in length, was about one hundred and sixty yards, and on the hither extremity our breastwork was thrown up. From the breastwork ran a street, gradually ascending, about the length of four hundred yards, to a church, where our main body was encamped."

It appears that Dunmore had been induced to believe, by stratagem, that there were only about three hundred *shirt-men* (as the Virginians, who wore a kind of hunting-shirt, were often called); and he despatched to the bridge about two hundred regular soldiers and three or four hundred blacks and tories. Meanwhile, the news of these warlike preparations spread in every direction; and a number of patriotic individuals hastened to the battle-ground, carrying such arms and ammunition as they could procure with the least possible delay. From different sections of Norfolk, Princess Anne, and Nansemond Counties, active and heroic young men, middle-aged and old men, even of threescore years and more, shouldered their muskets, rifles, or fowling-pieces, hurried on to the scene of danger, and rallied nobly around the standard of liberty.

"On Saturday, the 9th of December, the enemy crossed the bridge, fired the remaining houses, and attacked our guard in the breastwork. Our men returned the fire, and threw them into some confusion; but they were instantly rallied by Captain Fordyce, and advanced along the causeway with great resolution, keeping up a constant and heavy fire as they approached. Two field-pieces, which had been brought across the bridge and placed on the edge of the island, played briskly at the same time upon us. Lieutenant Travis, who commanded in the breastwork, ordered his men to reserve their fire until the enemy came within fifty yards, and then they gave it to them with terrible execution. The brave Fordyce exerted himself to keep up their spirits, reminded them of their ancient glory, and, waving his hat over his head encouragingly, told them *the day was their own*. Thus pressing forward, he fell, within fifteen steps of the breastwork. His wounds were many; and his death would have been that of a hero, had he met it in a better cause. The progress of the enemy was now at an end. They retreated over the causeway with precipitation, and were dreadfully galled in the rear.

"Hitherto, on our side, only the guard, consisting of twenty-five, and some others,—in the whole, not amounting to more than ninety,—had been engaged. Only the regulars of the 14th regiment, in number one hundred and twenty, had advanced upon the causeway; and about two hundred and thirty negroes and tories had, after crossing the bridge, continued upon the island. The regulars, after retreating along the causeway, were again rallied by Captain Leslie, and the two field-pieces continued playing upon our men. It was at this time that Colonel Woodford was advancing down the street, to the breastwork, with the main body, and against him was now directed the whole fire of the enemy. Never were cannon better served; yet, in the face of them and the musketry, which kept up a continual blaze, our men marched on with the utmost intrepidity. Colonel Stevens, of the Culpeper battalion, was sent round to the left to flank the enemy, which was done with so much spirit and activity that a rout immediately ensued. The enemy fled into their fort, leaving behind them the two field-pieces, which, however, they took care to spike.

"Many were killed and wounded in the flight; but Colonel Woodford very prudently restrained his troops from pursuing the enemy too far. From the beginning of the attack till the repulse at the breastwork might be fourteen or fifteen minutes; till the total defeat, upwards of half an hour. It is said that some of the enemy preferred death to captivity, from fear of being *scalped*, which Lord Dunmore cruelly told them would be their fate, should they be taken alive. Thirty-one, killed and wounded, fell into our hands; and the number borne off was much greater. Through the whole engagement, every officer and soldier behaved with the greatest calmness and courage. The conduct of our sentinels I cannot pass over in silence. Before they quitted their stations, they fired at least three rounds as the enemy were crossing the bridge; and one of them, posted behind some shingles, kept his ground till he had fired *eight* times, and, after he had received the fire of a whole platoon, made his escape across the causeway to our breastwork. The scene was concluded with as much humanity as it was conducted with bravery. The work of death being over, every one's attention was directed to the succour of the unhappy sufferers; and it is an undoubted fact that Captain Leslie was so affected with the attention of our troops to those capable of assistance, that he gave signs from the fort of his thankfulness. What is not paralleled in history, and will scarcely be credible, except to such as acknowledge a Providence over human affairs, —this victory was gained at the expense of no more than *a slight wound in a soldier's hand;* and one circumstance that renders it still more amazing is that the field-pieces raked the whole length of the street, and absolutely threw double headed shot as far as the church, and afterwards, as our troops approached, cannonaded them heavily with grape-shot.

* * * * * *

"Several of our soldiers ran through a hot fire, to lift up and bring in some that were bleeding, and who they feared would die, if not speedily assisted by the surgeon. The prisoners expected to be scalped, and cried out, 'For God sake, do not murder us!' One of them, unable to walk, cried out in this manner to one of our men, and was answered by him, 'Put your arm around my neck, and I will show you what I intend to do.' Then taking him, with his arm over his neck, he walked slowly on, bearing him along with great tenderness to the breastwork. Captain Leslie, seeing two of our soldiers tenderly moving a wounded regular from the bridge, stepped upon the platform of the fort, and bowing with great respect, thanked them for their kindness. These are instances of a noble disposition of soul. Men who can act thus must be invincible."

Truly, indeed, and most justly, may it be said of the conduct of the Virginians on that occasion, that they manifested a "noble disposition of soul;" added unfading honour to our arms, and undying glory to the State and to the Union. And most true it is, also, that men who can act thus cannot be conquered; for, as in other cases during that struggle for freedom, an unseen power and an influence from above, more powerful than all the dread engines of death, were present, to protect and "save to the uttermost" the heroes who fought and conquered in Liberty's holy cause.

There resided at the Great Bridge, in Revolutionary days, an active, energetic, and patriotic female, who was long known as *Miss Polly Miller;* and who, notwithstanding some eccentricities that marked her life, is well entitled to notice, for her kind and diligent attention to our men.

"It would be the very acme of injustice," said one who knew her, "to consign the memory of this heroine to dull forgetfulness, without a scratch of the pen to perpetuate her name, and record her extraordinary merit and good qualities.

* * * * * * *

"Her services in behalf of her country, during the struggle for independence, deserve the highest strains of eulogy; for having naturally a love of freedom, she took a decided stand on the side of her country. The bustle of war having penetrated as far as the Great Bridge, she had often an opportunity of ministering to the wants of her countrymen in arms, and affording them aid and comfort whenever an exigency required. The defeat of the British, who were sent to dislodge the Americans from their post at the Great Bridge, and the fall of their leader, the gallant Captain Fordyce, are circumstances well known. On this occasion our heroine was not inactive; she ordered refreshments for the soldiers after the battle, and took charge of the wounded men, whose wounds she dressed and attended to until they were cured. Indeed, it is asserted that she saved the lives of more than half a dozen. Her generosity and patriotism acquired her great celebrity, so that her house soon became the resort of all who travelled that way." She lived to rejoice at the success of our arms at the celebrated battle of Craney Island, nearly forty years after the victory at the Bridge, and died Feb. 1st, 1814, aged 73.

In addition to the officers named, who were at this battle, were Major John Marshall, Lieutenant Travis, and others, from the counties of Orange, Culpeper, Fauquier, &c. There were also Captain Thomas Nash, some of whose respected descendants now reside in the city, and who was highly spoken of as an unflinching patriot and accomplished gentleman. There were also William Porter and John Brannam (the latter was afterwards at the battle of the Cowpens), John Brooks (who is still living), and others of Portsmouth and vicinity. There were there, also, from the counties of Norfolk and Princess Anne, Jonathan Denby,

Billy Flora (the man that fired eight times from the pile of shingles, and made his escape so wonderfully), the Butts, Millers, Talbots, Etherages, Wattses, Hodgeses, Culpepers, Sykeses, Taylors, Tatems, Owenses, Grimeses, Lukes, Woodhouses, Whitehursts, Drewreys, Foremans, Moores, Wrights, Wilsons, Herberts, Wilkinses, &c.

CHAPTER VIII.

1776.

Sufferings of Captain Nash and other Revolutionary Patriots—Lord Dunmore on Shipboard—Colonel Woodford—Dunmore's Rage, Arrogance, and Threats—Tories and Slaves—Their Miserable Condition—Norfolk Cannonaded—Misstatements Corrected—Cornstalk, the Sharpshooter—The Town Burned by the Citizens and Soldiers—Woodford Fires upon the British Fleet—Awful Conflagration—Patriotism—Battles—A Sad Contrast—Loss and Distress—The Site of Norfolk Abandoned, and the Silence of Gloomy Depopulation Reigns.

Some of the noble souls who fought and acted a brave and independent part in the cause of liberty, during these trying revolutionary days, were subjected to the greatest hardships and privations; their sufferings indeed, in some cases, were intolerable, and justly called forth the severest denunciations from the inhabitants. That fearless patriot and gentlemanly soldier, *Captain Nash*, and six or eight of his fellow-soldiers, were confined for months in the old sugar-house on the Portsmouth side, and compelled to endure the cruelties and oppression which some of the British officers delighted to inflict upon the Americans. Their food was of the coarsest and most common kind, while the place of confinement was exceedingly loathsome and disagreeable. They were removed from the old sugar-house to Cornwallis's prison-ship, at York, and confined in the hold among a number of men of the meanest and most degraded character. Their fare, companions, and all the circumstances attending their confinement were most revolting. When they were liberated from the old floating dungeon, their condition was in the highest degree pitiable and humiliating. When Captain N. made his appearance on deck, the only remaining portion of his shirt was the ruffles at the wrist; and, in addition to being almost suffocated with foul air, and horrified at the fiendish propensities of some of the prisoners, he was tormented with vermin, and half dead from the want of wholesome food and water. Think of these things, ye favoured sons and daughters of freed and republican America! Ponder on them in these bright and prosperous and peaceful days!

At an early period of the Revolution, Dunmore had fled to the British fleet, which was for some time in Norfolk harbour. A few days after the enemy had been so signally routed in the battle of the Great Bridge, the Virginians, commanded by Colonel Woodford, arrived at Norfolk. They ridiculed and vexed the remaining loyalists; fired upon the vessels, from the houses on the wharves, and endeavoured to prevent the British troops from landing for sport and recreation, and for the purpose of foraging in the country. Dunmore raved like a madman. He swore he would hang the boy that brought the news of the defeat at the Bridge! He informed the soldiers that they must cease firing, and the citizens that they must furnish him with provisions, or he would bombard the town; but his arrogant menaces were disregarded. Meanwhile his troops, with the tories and slaves who had sought his protection, were starving for provisions. His lordship at length determined to drive out the patriotic inhabitants with artillery, and, therefore, directed the women and children to leave.

1776, Jan. 1st. Between the hours of three and four o'clock in the afternoon, a heavy cannonade was commenced upon the town. It has been published by historians and others, that the *British*, "under cover of their guns," on this day "burned the town;" and some have also declared, that the place was set on fire by the *tories*. It has been said, likewise, that the enemy commenced the work of wholesale destruction, and the citizens, to prevent them from enjoying *the pleasure of burning their property*, put the torch thereto themselves; while there are many who assert that the place was burned by the inhabitants, to prevent the British from quartering here. These statements of this important affair, it will be seen, are contradictory, if not unreasonable. Dunmore and his troops were without provisions. They were suffering from the want of bread to eat, and fresh air to breathe. His object was to quarter his troops in the town, and feed them upon the substance of the people. How could this be accomplished by burning all the houses and the goods they contained? Besides, a portion of the property was owned by English and Scotch factors or agents, some of whom were tories, who had fled to the fleet for safety. Their influence was, doubtless, exerted against any design to fire the place. The tories remaining in the town did not set fire to their property, because they desired the place to afford shelter and accommodation to the enemy; and, in fact, the most of them had joined Dunmore's troops on board the ships. And, it is by no means probable that the inhabitants could, as a general plan, have acted so strangely as to put the torch to their dwellings and stores, merely to prevent the British from having the pleasure of it. His lordship threatened more than he ever executed, or intended to execute. He may have declared, as has been stated by some, that he would bombard and burn Norfolk; but a careful inquiry, relative to the facts of the affair, does not justify the belief that he did either; nor is it probable that he intended either. That "a heavy cannonade from the frigate Liverpool, two sloops of war, and the ship Dunmore, opened against the town," is not doubted; living witnesses testify to that, and old St. Paul's is a witness that cannot be set aside; bearing substantial, though silent evidence, that balls were thrown, and with very considerable force; but it is very evident they were not bombs.*

The tories, moreover, had too much property here to be willingly sacrificed, and neither they, nor their regal governor, wished it destroyed or injured. But, it may be asked, why then was the town fired during the cannonade? and what ground is there for the statement that the British put the incendiary's torch to the houses? The circumstances attending the occasion were singular; and, it is believed, by no means satisfactory to

* The author is aware that it is doubted that St. Paul's Church was struck on this occasion.

the enemy, who probably supposed that, as soon as the guns opened upon the place, the inhabitants would leave it, and all it contained, to their mercy and for their benefit.

It is quite evident that at, or more probably just before, the commencement of the firing from the ships, a small company was sent on shore to burn some stores on the wharf nearest the fleet, in order to deprive the patriots of a shelter from which to fire upon the ships; for Dunmore had been greatly annoyed by the sharpshooting of our men from both sides of the river, and he was obliged, for fear of getting aground, to keep his crowded ships in the channel of the river. By the way, there was a tall, fierce-looking rifleman, who was exceedingly fond of shooting at the "red-coats" on board the vessels. He aimed with extraordinary precision, and seldom missed his mark. This was his employment and amusement by day, and sometimes by night. He was called *Cornstalk*, the name of an Indian warrior of the Shawanee tribe, also celebrated for being a superior marksman. Cornstalk would take his station on the shore, and remain concealed, until some unfortunate fellow would appear upon the poop deck, or in some position where he could be plainly seen. Then, the sharp sound of the rifle would be quickly succeeded by a scream, or a groan, and then a tumble, and a few convulsive struggles, and, with the victim, all of this life was over. This was, of course, a very vexatious business to Dunmore, and all others concerned with him.

It has been stated, too, that the fire was communicated from the buildings on the wharf to those of the town, by reason of a strong wind that blew. This is not probable, for the prevailing winds in winter are not from a southerly direction, although the flames might have spread from the stores farther than the British expected. But it is true that, as soon as the firing commenced from the guns of the ships, or immediately thereafter, flames "were seen to shoot up in several parts of the town."

Another statement was, that Norfolk was burnt by direction of the Virginia Committee of Safety; this is also doubted. The Safety Committee gravely proposed to desolate the borough of Norfolk, the town of Portsmouth, and the entire counties of Norfolk and Princess Anne, and thus effectually starve the British out. This plan, necessary as it may have seemed, met with considerable opposition on the part of the citizens, the tories especially, and it was abandoned. We have been informed also that Congress had directed the property to be valued and burned, to prevent the enemy from finding shelter and accommodation here; and that the court met, and properly arranged the whole affair. This appears, also, to be without foundation.

The Virginians, commanded by Colonel Woodford, who had come to Norfolk by order of General Howe, were of course spirited, if not enthusiastic, after the famous victory at the Bridge. Woodford determined to fire upon the fleet, formidable as it was; but, from the favourable position occupied by the vessels for raking the streets and lanes—the town being only a few feet above the level of the river—it was necessary for the Virginians to take a position at some distance from the wharf. Therefore, to remove the obstructions to the view, and to the execution of the balls from our cannon, and in order also, to deprive the enemy of quarters and provisions, many of the buildings were fired by the soldiers and patriotic citizens; and the flames spreading in every direction, the destruction was, at once, awful, rapid, and complete.

The following remarks are the most recent we have seen relative to this subject:—

"Lord Dunmore, to shelter his shipping from the deadly aim of the Virginia riflemen, who ensconced themselves behind the houses on the wharves, set fire to and destroyed that part of the town, which enabled their people to land, and possess themselves of comfortable quarters in the upper part. Seeing this, the commander of the Virginia troops resolved to dispossess them, and accordingly set fire to and destroyed the remainder of the town. It is true that the State paid the owners for their property, but with depreciated paper money, which was equivalent to a total loss; and compensation is still due for the calamity which she had brought upon her citizens—if not to those who had long ago gone to their account, it is due to their successors, and could not be more gracefully and appropriately recognised by the State, than by ministering to their prosperity by acts of wholesome legislation."

Many of the inhabitants occupied and owned costly, elegantly-furnished, and commodious residences, with fine gardens, and every convenience that wealth could procure. Among these were Dr. Ramsay, and other devoted old patriots, some of whose names are connected with the proceedings of the Sons of Liberty. The fire was a great, though necessary, calamity; yet it was borne with astonishing fortitude by a large portion of the citizens.

There was a brave and unflinching patriot—an uncompromising enemy to the British, and whose hatred for a tory was rather more inveterate than for any other living animal—who was playing at billiards in a house which stood near "West's Corner" (now opposite the National Hotel), when the firing from Dunmore's ships commenced. He hurried home, quickly put the torch to his own buildings; and, having confined a quantity of hogs in the cellar of one of his houses, to prevent the British from eating them, he cheerfully went to work, with the rest of the citizens after the conflagration, to procure shelter and provisions for himself and family as best he could.

Dunmore and his troops were sadly disappointed, no doubt, at such rebellious and unexpected proceedings. "The old borough was too republican for them," says a fearless patriot, now living. The last building destroyed was situated on the north side of Bermuda, near East Street, on the spot in front of the recent residence of "the oldest inhabitant." It was the property of the Ingram family. There was only one house left within the immediate limits of the borough, and that was a dairy, with a pigeon-house on the top, belonging to a Mr. Bacon, and situated on what was then called Bacon's Lane. This lane extended from Main Street, a few doors east of Market Square, through to the water, now Union Street. Its location was probably where Loyall or Marsden's Lane now is.

During the frightful progress of the flames, the cannon from the shipping and Woodford's battery continued their thundering roar. Hostile parties frequently encountered each other amid the smoking ruins near the shore; and, in every action, the British were driven off with loss, and in the greatest confusion.

There was a daring and intrepid party under Colonel Stevens, who "rushed with the rapidity of lightning to the water-side, struck a large party of the British who had landed there, and compelled them to retire, with slaughter and dismay, to the protection of their wooden walls. In general, during the whole of this afflicting scene, both officers and men evinced a spirit worthy of veterans.

"Such was the melancholy event, which laid prostrate the most flourishing and richest town in the colony. Its happy site, combining all the natural advantages which invite and promote navigation and commerce, had been actively seconded by the industry and enterprise of the inhabitants. Before the existing troubles, an influx of wealth was pouring into its lap. In the two years, from 1773 to 1775, the rents of the houses increased from £8000 to £10,000 a year. Its resident population exceeded six thousand citizens, many of whom possessed affluent fortunes. The whole actual loss on this lamentable occasion has been computed at more than three hundred thousand pounds sterling; and the mass of distress attendant on the event is beyond all calculation.

"After the conflagration, occasional skirmishes took place between the Virginians and the enemy, in which the latter suffered most severely. On the 6th of February, Colonel Robert Howe, who was now commander of the American troops, abandoned Norfolk, or rather the site on which it had stood; for scarcely any vestige of that ill-fated town was to be seen.

"After the removal of the inhabitants, the few remaining edifices (in the suburbs), had been destroyed; and the mournful silence of gloomy depopulation now reigned where the gay, animating bustle of an active, emulous crowd had so lately prevailed."

CHAPTER IX.

1776—1777.

British Fleet and Soldiers—Pastimes and Depredations—Dunmore's Departure—Removal of the Citizens before the Conflagration—Their Spirit and Fortitude—Tories—Coloured Persons—Small-pox—Dreadful Suffering and Mortality—Money Buried—Mr. Goodchild's Trunk of Specie, &c.—First House Erected after the Conflagration—Return of the Inhabitants—Privations of the People—Dunmore.

PREVIOUSLY to the memorable battle of Great Bridge, the enemy had for some time remained without very serious difficulty in the vicinity of Norfolk; indeed, the fleet to which Dunmore fled rode at anchor in the deep and tranquil waters of our harbour. The officers and troops occasionally came on shore for recreation. There was a large vacant lot on the south side of Main Street, extending down to the sandy shore of the river. It comprised the greater part of the lots between Boush and Loyall's Lanes, fronting on Main Street, and on which now stand the Mechanics' Hall and other valuable buildings. Here, as we have been informed by an aged inhabitant, they assembled and held their pastimes. The forces were formidable enough, even excluding the armed vessels, and the inhabitants were well aware that the town was then at the mercy of the British; resistance, therefore, on the part of the citizens, would have been in vain, how much soever they may have disliked the intrusion of the unwelcome foe. On the spot alluded to, the soldiers assembled. Upon a carpet of Nature's own green, their tables were spread, at which they ate, drank, and frolicked, little dreaming of the sad reverses that were soon to happen, especially on the arrival of Woodford, Stevens, and their fearless compatriots. They had remained too long in confident security, plundering the town, and impoverishing the farmers in the neighbourhood, by enticing away their servants and taking off their stock. It was to be endured no longer; Dunmore's time to leave soon came, and, very much against his will, he was deprived of the privilege of coming on shore again. He is said to have embarked for the last time from Norfolk at the site of the south end of Dunmore Street, which for that reason, it is said, bears his name. It crosses Freemason Street near Smith's Point. The depredations of his soldiers could not be longer allowed, and he therefore determined to cannonade the place; and finally carried out his iniquitous object; which, however, had but little injurious effect upon a town depopulated and on fire.

After he had made known his intention to cannonade the town, great efforts were of course made to get the women and children out of the way; it was reported also that the whole town would be burned. Consequently every description of conveyance was in requisition. Horses, carriages, wagons, gigs, carts, drays, boats, &c., were purchased and hired; and a general removal took place; indeed, almost the entire population took their departure from the place now to be freely sacrificed on the altar of Liberty. Numbers were seen wending their way in different directions; many fled to Portsmouth, some to Princess Anne and Norfolk Counties; very many to Suffolk and other parts of Nansemond; and some to North Carolina. Such house furniture as could be removed, as beds, chairs, tables, &c., and also, clothing, provisions, and cooking utensils, were hastily conveyed out of the reach of the enemy. Many a neat and beautiful dwelling, associated with which there were a thousand pleasing recollections—the home of childhood and youth, the scene of many a happy, joyous day, was left to feed the flames, and never to be entered or seen again.

Yet there was but little complaining. Many, very many, preferred this course to the disgrace of yielding any advantage to the impudent and imperious demands of a hostile force, arrayed against the imperishable principles of justice, and the undying love of liberty, that warmed the hearts of the inhabitants, and nerved them for the privations and sufferings of that unhappy crisis. And although as they journeyed on from their homes, made still more dear by dangers now threatening, and while the booming of the great guns in the distance but too plainly announced the sad fate of their once flourishing, active, bustling, native town, they brooded not over their misfortunes. The big tear of grief that rose and gushed forth, was as quickly brushed away. They sung, engaged in amusements, and kept their spirits up. Some of the more lively even joined in an occasional dance at the house of some old patriot, on their retreat from the depredations of a misguided and revengeful foe.

The regal governor had offered protection and other inducements to all tories and *coloured persons* who chose to embark on board the vessels in the harbour, and act with the British against the Virginians. A few disaffected citizens and very many of the slaves of the town and surrounding counties, accordingly, repaired on board the shipping. Some of the farmers lost large numbers of their servants in this way; and great cause had the deluded fugitives to repent of their course; for, instead of realizing the benefits and blessings which Dunmore had promised, they could not even get enough to eat, drink, or wear. And besides, to increase the horrors of their situation, the *small-pox* broke out among them, and the mortality was appalling. Many of the slaves were glad enough to find their way to the shore again; and, failing in their attempts to reach their homes of plenty, or even to find a place of shelter from the inclemency of the weather, after having been attacked with the symptoms of the dreadful scourge, they died on the roadside and in the woods; their loathsome bodies became a prey to the vultures and beasts, and impregnated the ambient air with the hateful pestilential stench.

Many of the citizens, apprehending that the town would be burned, buried their specie, plate, jewelry, and such other valuable articles as could not be readily and safely removed; and it is quite probable many such articles remain in their places of concealment to the present day. Among those who resorted to this plan was *Mr. William Goodchild.* In order to secure a considerable amount in Spanish dollars, he secretly lifted several planks in the lower floor of his house, made a small excavation, and deposited a trunk containing the money. The trunk was covered with earth, and the planks replaced. Two weeks after this, the house contributed its share to the "sea of fire" that deluged and swept away the town. Being compelled to retire to the country, he occasionally returned to the site of the borough, without an opportunity, however, of exhuming the "needful," although he felt keenly the want of a very small sum. He would stand and gaze wishfully at the rubbish that hid the well-remembered spot from view. He succeeded, however, at an early day after the fire, to regain his buried treasure, without the loss of a single particle of the shining dust; and was the first to erect a house within the borough limits, after the conflagration. Mr. Goodchild purchased a large lot on the north side of Main Street, where now stands the City Hotel, and other large buildings, on the west of that establishment. This lot extended for several hundred feet northwardly to a cove (now Cove Street), and cost him only the small sum of £45. His house was erected at the west corner of Main Street and Mitchell's Lane, at which place there is now a lofty brick building. Mr. G.'s tenement was of wood, and of rather small dimensions. He, nevertheless, kept a public house, and acted a prominent part during the Phœnix-like struggles of the borough to rise from its ashes. Prospering in business, he added another tenement in the rear, considerably higher than the one first erected; and continuing to flourish, he put up another, and yet a third, fourth, fifth, &c., the whole row towering upwards, as it extended back from the street, until the regular succession of roofs, one reaching above another, had the appearance of an immense stairway. This gentleman, after a few years of success, built a house in the fields, and retired from business. The building is still standing, on the north side of Moseley, a few rods east of Church Street. It was used for some time as a house of reception for persons attacked with contagious diseases, which gave it the name of the *pest-house.*

The peculiar advantages of position gradually attracted the attention of fortune-hunters, capitalists, and enterprising men to the scene of ruin. A few stores and dwellings were erected, and commercial operations were resumed to a limited extent. Some of the former residents returned with their families, and built small tenements, which they occupied until it was convenient to erect larger and more commodious dwellings, and the smaller ones were then used as kitchens.

The privations of the people, on the occasion of the fire, were great; and the sufferings of the women and children, especially, very severe. The name of Dunmore was, for many years after this calamitous time, and is even to this day, associated with many a daring adventure, many a scene of distress; and calls to recollection circumstances of the most trying nature, on the part of those whom he was instrumental in depriving of their homes and property. Indeed, it was held in contempt by all classes and parties—the rich and the poor, the old and the young, male and female, and even the detested tories themselves, upon whom he had been the cause of bringing so much scorn and contempt, as well as by the true sons of liberty. But he has passed away. Doubtless he saw and felt, if he did not acknowledge, his errors. We shall recall to memory no more of his deeds; all of which will be scrutinized and tried at a high and just tribunal.

CHAPTER X.

1779—1785.

Extraordinary Winter—The Two Schooners from the West Indies—Harbour Closed—Immense Profits—Destitution of the Citizens—Trying Times—Borough Charter Amended—Mild Winter—Norfolk Improving—Rev. Philip Bruce—Very High Tide—Extraordinary Drought—Terrific Thunder and Lightning—Scarcity of Water—Animals and Vegetation Suffering—Alarming Day—Terrific Explosion—Negro Men Killed—Providential Escapes—The Merchant's Clerk, the Countryman, and the Gimlet—Money Raised by Lottery for Building a Church.

THE winter of 1779–80* was one of extraordinary severity. The harbour was frozen entirely across to Portsmouth, admit-

* "The most unseasonable weather I have ever heard of (in Virginia) was a snow nearly a foot deep, in the month of June, 1774. Cherries and other fruits of the season were ripe. The coldest morning ever known in Virginia, since its first settlement by the English, was January 14th, 1780. The mercury sunk into the bulbs of thermometers. The ice upon our rivers was three feet two inches thick. James River was frozen over at Burwell's Bay, so that

ting a free and uninterrupted communication between the two towns, on the ice, for several weeks. The Atlantic Ocean was frozen as far out from the shore as the depth of forty fathoms. Chesapeake Bay was so thickly frozen that teams crossed for some time from shore to shore, as far down as the Capes. The ice was piled up along our coast, at some places, twenty feet high, large quantities of which remained as late as the middle of May. Of course, the harbour could not be entered;—a truly remarkable circumstance for this latitude, and which, as far as we have learned, has not taken place since.

Two small schooners, returning to Norfolk from the West Indies, in the latter part of February, were compelled to land their cargoes several miles south of Cape Henry, which were conveyed to the town in carts, in which return cargoes were also sent down,—a temporary harbour having been made by the melting and removal of the ice in some places between the shore and the icebergs.

There was of course but little foreign trade during the Revolution; but that little, although it was attended with great difficulty and danger, was exceedingly profitable.

"Tobacco that was bought in Petersburg at from three-quarters to one dollar per hundredweight was readily sold at St. Eustatia for twenty dollars; and the returns, which were generally powder, rum, sugar, and coarse cloths, were equally profitable here.

* * * * * * *

"But few there are now amongst us that could be induced to believe how important the safe arrival of those vessels was to the comfort of a considerable community. Tea, coffee, chocolate, and sugar, were rarities; clothes, but of the poorest description, had nearly disappeared; and if the spinning-wheel had not been resorted to with a degree of patience and industry seldom

the heaviest wagons passed it upon the ice. Chesapeake Bay was frozen quite over, and hundreds of persons walked across it, from Annapolis to Kent Island, and other places. On the 9th of March, 1780, Colonel Charles Dabney's regiment of Virginia Infantry marched from Falmouth to Fredericksburg upon the ice in the Rappahannock, which had been formed there the preceding November."—*Richmond Inquirer.*

equalled, the whole population would have been in as pitiable a condition as our first parents were when they discovered the necessity that beset them."

These facts were gathered from the remarks of a venerable and distinguished citizen,* who died in 1851, an octogenarian, and who also said, "It may not be either unprofitable or unpleasant to look a little into the characters that figured in the times and contests that required the virtue, patriotism, and incessant exertions, of those who should not *yet* be so much forgotten."

In 1782, the charter was so amended as to allow the common council to be elected by the votes of the people.

The winter of 1782–3 was exceedingly mild for those days and this latitude.

Up to this time the town had increased but slowly in population and business. But, after the lapse of about seven years succeeding the fire, a fresh impulse was given to commerce; it began to improve rapidly; and Norfolk, though not what it should be, has become what it is within the space of a little more than sixty years. Had the true interests of the place been properly regarded, and its advantages judiciously fostered, instead of the restraints to which it has been subjected, its prosperity and rapid growth in former days would have been but a suitable prelude to the exalted station which it would have occupied before the present time.

1784. Rev. PHILIP BRUCE (who died, we believe, in 1850), a native of North Carolina, one of the most active pioneers of Methodism on the American Continent, was assistant to Bishop Asbury this year. In 1786, '87, '96, '97, and in 1807–8, he was presiding elder on the Norfolk District. He was one of the heroes of the Revolution, and was very zealous in his efforts to "disperse the tories."

1785. This year was noted for the highest tide ever before known in the borough, completely deluging a large portion of its site on the water-side.

* Commodore James Barron.

The summer of this year was remarkable and long remembered for a most distressing and protracted drought. And what is singular, in connexion with this fact, it was equally noted for the frequent occurrence of dark and lowering clouds, attended with most terrific thunder and lightning. The earth was dry and parched to cracking by the scorching rays of the sun in the forenoon, which were almost daily followed, during the month of June particularly, by a dense collection of dark vapours in the air above, but which gave no rain, save only a few scattering drops, that occasionally fell, and were almost as quickly evaporated,—tending only to excite the anxious hopes of the people, to be as surely disappointed.

The springs were almost dried up. The deepest wells only yielded a scanty supply; "water, bright water," was in great demand, and its inestimable value was very generally appreciated.

The beasts of the field drooped and died for want of the cooling draught. The variegated flowers that had given signs of freshness and beauty in the months of spring, withered upon their slender stalks, and faded ere their soft petals had expanded, and their opening charms perfected. Vegetation was sadly retarded in its progress; the most hardy productions of the garden were stunted, and, when offered for sale, commanded very high prices. The young corn changed from the deep hues of green to a sickly yellow; and, except in the lowest lands, it almost withered in the fields. The wheat crop could not mature; the hopes of the husbandman were sadly blasted; and the traveller by land was almost suffocated by the clouds of dust that were driven by the winds and scattered in every direction.

There was one day, during the continuance of this extraordinary weather in the month of June of this year, that was truly alarming, and which witnessed an event in the old borough that was really terrible and destructive in its effects.

A brilliant flash in the distance announced the approach of the threatening, though tantalizing cloud, with its diurnal and frightful display of electric power, and the deafening roar of its attendant peals. Longer and louder grew the roaring and hoarse murmuring of the thunder, and quicker and more appalling still, "the vivid lightning's glare."

During the continuance of the threatening storm, a man from the country called at the counting-room of one of the principal merchants, to purchase pork, a quantity of which was stored, with other articles of merchandise, in a large warehouse situated near the intersection of Church and Lower Union Streets. One of the clerks was despatched with the customer, who wished to examine the quality of the article, but who remarked, after leaving the office, that he could judge of its quality by *tasting the pickle;* whereupon, the clerk hurried back for a gimlet, and the dealer stepped away to attend to other business requiring his attention for a few minutes.

There was stored in the warehouse a great variety of goods, intended principally for the country trade, which was at this time rapidly increasing. Besides the pork and a quantity of bacon, there were numbers of whip and cross-cut saws, and *three hundred kegs of gunpowder!*

The clerk was soon retracing his steps in the direction of the warehouse; meanwhile, the clouds grew darker; the lightning flashed and crashed and hissed, forking, darting, and resembling a number of monstrous flying serpents, shooting their fiery forms through the air, from the surcharged, though rainless clouds; which had covered, as with a great sombre shroud, the whole face of heaven. The thunder muttered and rumbled angrily overhead; flash upon flash, and peal upon peal, came in rapid succession, until there was almost "one continual blaze and deafening roar." And still the merchant's clerk passes on, until he comes within a few yards of the warehouse, on the steps of which he discovers two negro men, carefully counting over some change they had received at market. But up to this moment the countryman had not made his appearance, since the separation a few moments before. The lightning now ceases, perchance for a short space of time, and seemingly withholds itself, to gather additional force, and concentrate its irresistible powers, to burst forth with still greater terror and sublimity than before; and now comes another "wild electric flash"—an overpowering blaze of dazzling light, which is followed by an explosion that almost causes the very earth itself to tremble. Commingling with the stunning peals of thunder, it echoed, reverberated, and roared for many miles around. The inhabitants were startled as by the shock of an earthquake, and felt the most painful apprehensions of impending danger.

The youth, though stunned by the violence of the concussion, soon recovered; and after waiting a few moments for a dense black cloud of smoke, in which he was enveloped, to pass away, he looked for the warehouse; but it was *nowhere to be seen!* The building, and all it contained, had disappeared; and also the coloured men who were upon the steps. This was exceedingly surprising to the affrighted clerk, but not more so than his own escape. It is scarcely necessary to add, that the lightning had struck the building; having been attracted, perhaps, by the ironware that was stored within, and communicated to the gunpowder, which exploded, and the report thereof was almost simultaneous with the thunder that followed the lightning-stroke. Large timbers and fragments were scattered in every direction. Some of the saws were thrown almost to the southeastern extremity of the town, and twisted in various singular and indescribable shapes. One of them, however, was rolled up, as if it had been done with great care, after the manner of a piece of ribbon or tape. The two negro men were blown many rods from the building, "skewered with splinters," and dreadfully mangled. They were removed from the fatal spot and laid beneath a large sycamore tree, which grew on or near the present site of the Presbyterian Church, and nearly opposite St. Paul's, where an inquest was held, and at which place they were seen by an individual now living (1853), who states that they were frightfully disfigured, and presented a sight too shocking to behold.

Very many of the window-panes, especially on the north side of Main Street, and fronting in the direction of the explosion, were shattered; and, as far off as the location of Bank Street, glassware was raised by the concussion several inches from the tables!

The merchant and clerk alluded to were very respectable citizens, and their names could be given. It is not important, however; they have both gone to their account in another state of existence, and their descendants are now numbered among the inhabitants of Norfolk. A gentleman who was then a youth, said that he was crossing over to Portsmouth at the time, and had a full view of the explosion, which he represented as having been very imposing. Bacon, timbers, &c., he stated were thrown very many feet in the air, resembling the rapid upward flight of an immense flock of large birds. A large quantity of the bacon fell on a vessel lying at the wharf near the ill-fated storehouse. A man was standing on the deck at the time, but was not injured.

The narrow escape of the clerk and the customer, to whom he failed on this occasion to effect a sale, was thought to be, as it doubtless was, by the special interposition of an overruling Providence. The former, who returned for the gimlet, had scarcely arrived at the counting-room, before he recollected that it had been left at the warehouse, whence he had forgotten to take it to the counting-room, where it was generally kept. So, it appears that his *forgetfulness*, on two separate occasions, was the means of saving both his own life, as well as that of the man who started with him to examine the quality of the pork. He lived many years after the affair, and several of his descendants are now highly respectable residents of our city. We have no further information respecting the country gentleman, who also figured on this occasion, and who escaped so narrowly with his life, but we will venture the suppositions: that he was not a little discomposed when he learned the place and circumstances of the explosion; that he had a wonderful tale to tell, when he arrived at his quiet abode in the country; and that he often thought of the pork and the pickle, but more especially of the little gimlet.

In October of this year an Act of Assembly was passed, authorizing the raising of a sum of money, not exceeding £700, by way of lottery (!) for rebuilding a church in the parish of Elizabeth River, in the County of Norfolk. Surely public sentiment, in some quarters at least, has undergone a very considerable change with regard to lotteries.

CHAPTER XI.

1787—1799.

Dismal Swamp Canal—Importance of its Trade—Judicious Management—Average of Tolls—Captain James Cornick—Location of the Canal—An Eminent Subscriber to the Stock—Borough Charter Amended—Tardy Legislation—Newspaper—Religious Revival—Cape Henry Light-house—Court-house—Population—Exports—Norfolk Herald—T. G. Broughton, Esq.—Heavy Exports and Tonnage of the Borough—Cold Weather—Extensive Fire.

1787. THIS year the Dismal Swamp Canal was commenced under a joint charter of Virginia and North Carolina. It is truly an important and valuable work, being the medium of an immense amount of business. It is navigated by sloops and schooners, some of which are of considerable size. Norfolk has, for a long time, received a large portion of her support from the canal trade.

"Few, except those engaged in it, are aware of its magnitude and importance. It makes no noise, no show. The little vessels arrive, and deliver their cargoes at the wharves; take in return freights, and depart for the waters of our sister State, without attracting the least notice from 'the public at large.' The newspapers do, indeed, keep a record of the arrivals, but that is only for the information of the parties interested, and the mass of their readers seldom look at it. Still 'the wonder grows' that Norfolk is increasing in improvements and in population, without any visible way of accounting for it."

We publish the following passage relating to the judicious management of the Dismal Swamp Canal, by the present efficient Directory, from the late Report of the Board of Public Works (1851):—

"The annual report of the Dismal Swamp Canal Company (page 181) presents a favourable view of its present condition and finances. In regard to the former, personal inspection, made by the President and other members of the Board, impressed them with a very high opinion of the great value of this work for general public purposes. Notwithstanding the unexpected interruption of the trade for a short period, by the giving way of the lock at Gilmerton, and other serious casualties, the transportation appears to have been greater during the past year, than it *has ever yet been.* The annual average of tolls for the eight preceding years, was $32,906 06; the amount collected in that year was $39,748 23. A dividend of 4½ per cent. was declared out of the nett profits, leaving a balance of available funds of $13,065 73. The Board deems it but an act of justice to say, that instances of a more systematic, judicious, and successful management of works, of a similar character, are rarely to be met with."

Captain James Cornick, a descendant of one of the oldest and most respectable settlers of this part of our State, and formerly a most skilful and successful shipmaster, has, for a number of years, been the efficient president of the Company.

It is stated that this Company, with a view of extending the canal, intend to renew their application to the next Congress for an appropriation of the amount of dividends which accrue to the United States, upon the $200,000 capital stock owned by the Government.

"The route, which has already been surveyed for the improvement, makes the distance from the end of the canal to the Shingle Landing, the point at which they intend to bring the new cut into the river again, three and a half miles. From this point, by the present route, to the South Lock, the distance is seven miles, and that of the most difficult navigation; the river being narrow, deep, and exceedingly crooked; and, during the winter season, when the swamp is full of water, a strong current sets down, which renders it very difficult for vessels to get up;—they frequently occupy one, two, and sometimes four days to get from this point to the canal. If this improvement were made, the distance to the lock could be accomplished in two hours, and, frequently, boats would reach Norfolk in less time than they now consume in working up this miserable piece of navigation to the South Lock, besides saving much labour and trouble to this important branch of our commerce.

"But a greater improvement might still be made, at a comparatively small expense. The distance from the proposed terminus of the new cut to the mouth of the Narrows, is not more than one and a half miles. If an extension were made to this point, no difficulty would be met in reaching the canal, as the river is sufficiently broad and deep to enable vessels to work up even against a head wind; and the trip from Elizabeth City to Norfolk, which now requires often four and five days, could be easily performed in two, and often in one."

By means of this canal, a communication is opened between the sounds and principal rivers of North Carolina and the waters of the Elizabeth, Chesapeake Bay, and the ocean. The north end of the canal empties into Deep Creek, a branch of our river, and the south end into a branch of the Pasquotank. The canal passes for about twenty miles through the Dismal Swamp, from which, of course, it takes its name. It has been pronounced by travellers to be one of the best in the Union. The name of the great *Patrick Henry* appears among the first subscribers to the stock, having been placed upon the books at Williamsburg, in 1791.

December 7. "An Act to amend the charter of the borough of Norfolk," was passed by the General Assembly. It related, principally, to the election of the councilmen by the people, triennially, on June 24th; vesting also in them the election of mayor, and directing a uniform rate of taxes. It appears that the Legislature was as slow in former days, in correcting unconstitutional usages in the *borough*, as it now is in allowing privileges which are not only reasonable, but absolutely necessary to the prosperity of the *city*.

1788. The first newspaper published in the borough, after the Revolution, appeared this year.* It was the "*Norfolk and Portsmouth Chronicle*," issued weekly, by J. & A. McLean, from

* The First Newspaper in Virginia.—Palmer's Register states that the first press in this State was imported by the city of Williamsburg in 1780. The prices of advertising and subscriptions of those times are thus stated in the following extract from the terms of the paper, contained in the first issue:

"All persons may be supplied with this paper at *fifty dollars a year*, and

New York. Its existence was of short duration, on account of the death of one of the editors.

This year an extraordinary revival of religion commenced in this section of the State. Great multitudes inquired the way to be saved, and thousands professed to have experienced a change of heart. "Vast numbers," said a gentleman writing from Portsmouth to an eminent minister in England, "are flocking into the fold of Christ, from every quarter. In many places, as soon as the preacher begins to speak, the power of God appears to be present, which is attended with trembling among the people. * * * * * *Great is the joy, great is the glory.* Surely America will become the mart of nations for piety."

1789, November 13. Act of Assembly passed, authorizing the Governor to convey certain land to the United States, in the County of Princess Anne, at a place commonly called the head-land of Cape Henry, for the purpose of building a light-house.

1790. Court-house built on Main Street, east of Church. The population of the borough had reached this year to within 50 of 3,000 souls.

1791. Value of exports from Virginia, and principally from this port, $3,130,865.

August 13, 1794. On this day, the first number of the *Norfolk Herald* was published, by Mr. Charles Willet. It was printed on a small sheet, about eighteen by twenty-four inches, and was issued on Wednesdays and Saturdays. Price per annum, twenty shillings. The Herald has since changed hands several times, and has been greatly enlarged and improved; having been altered many years ago to a tri-weekly, and since to a *daily* and tri-weekly publication. It requires only a short allusion here; for, under the judicious auspices of Thomas G.

have advertisements (of a moderate length) inserted for *ten dollars the first week, and seven dollars for each week after.*"

It should be recollected, too, that this was a weekly paper, making the cost to subscribers about ninety-six cents a number.

The Norfolk Herald says: "the year is evidently misprinted 1780 instead of 1680. We once possessed a file of the Virginia Gazette printed in Williamsburg in 1744–5; and there was a press in Norfolk in 1775, which Gov. Dunmore unceremoniously caused to be removed on board the Fowey man-of-war, previous to the conflagration of the town."

Broughton, Esq., it has, for a long time, faithfully told its own history to a very large number of patrons and friends in Norfolk and the neighbouring towns, villages, and counties in Virginia and North Carolina, by whom it is justly regarded as a faithful journal of current events, and a valuable medium for the dissemination of useful information. The Norfolk and Portsmouth Herald has long advocated and supported, in an able manner, the principles and doctrines of the Whig party.

Thomas G. Broughton, Sr., Esq., the oldest editor of our city, and who has been for so many years the able and successful conductor of the Herald, is a native of Princess Anne County. There is, perhaps, no person who has more general information than Mr. B., concerning the men who have lived, and the events that have transpired, in Norfolk and its vicinity, during the last forty years.

It is very certain, that for some of our most judicious local improvements, the citizens are mainly indebted to suggestions that first appeared in the columns of his paper. Mr. B. is justly considered an excellent writer. His style is generally pointed, smooth, and perspicuous. His descriptive articles, especially, are "easy, pleasant, and properly adorned." As was said of Roger North, "he is excellent at a narrative."

Mr. Broughton having, several years since, associated with himself one of his sons (Richard, a gentleman of literary taste and talent), the paper is now edited and published by *T. G. Broughton & Son.**

"In the year 1795, a period of twelve years after the war, the exports, consisting chiefly of tobacco, flour, wheat, Indian corn and meal, salt beef, pork, fish, tar, turpentine, flaxseed, iron, lead, timber of every kind, reached the sum of $1,934,827. In 1804, nine years later, the exports for the last two quarters of the year, reached $2,230,855, and in three quarters of the same

* The late Dr. Charles H. Broughton, U. S. N., a young gentleman of superior talents and fine literary attainments, as well as a devoted Christian, was a son of Mr. B. of the Herald. His religious influence had already been felt, and promised to be most salutary and extensive, when he was unexpectedly summoned to his reward. "On the 22d of December, 1843, he breathed his last, calmly reclining on the bosom of God his Saviour." See tract, No. 486, Am. Tract Society.

year, the foreign articles re-exported were $210,679. In 1805, a period of twenty-three years after the peace, the exports in domestic produce were $3,880,347, and in foreign articles $507,907; making the exports of a single year nearly FOUR MILLIONS AND A HALF DOLLARS. The tonnage owned in the borough was about 31,292 tons. These facts stand almost without a parallel in the history of American commerce. When peace was fairly restored, the town began to rise with wonderful rapidity. In 1796, the number of houses was between eight and nine hundred."

The winter of 1798–99 was unusually cold. In '99 there was an extensive and a most distressing fire, which destroyed a large amount of property in the commercial part of the town.

CHAPTER XII.

1800—1803.

Severe Winter—Act of Assembly—Funeral Solemnities of Washington—Oration—Monody—Minute Guns, &c.—Population—Officers of the Corporation—Exports—Population Rapidly Increasing—Norfolk Advancing—Influx of Foreigners—Brisk Business—Shipping—Buildings on Main Street, &c.—Mud and Water—Dust, Frogs, and Musquitoes—Church Street—Ship-yards—Rev. Mr. Bland and Old St. Paul's—Rev. J. Whitehead—Different Christian Denominations, and their Houses of Worship—Cumberland Street Baptist Church—Number of Buildings—Simmons's Directory—Chamber of Commerce—Members' Names—Norfolk Junior Volunteers—The Council—Amendment of the Charter.

1800. THIS year was also remarkable for the severity of the weather, during the winter months.

January 25. Act of Assembly passed, authorizing the Governor to convey to the United States the property called Gosport, for the purpose of establishing a navy yard.

February 22. On this day took place, in the borough, the

funeral solemnities on the occasion of the death of WASHINGTON, the "Father of his country, the first and greatest of the Presidents," and, may we not truly add, the greatest of *men?*

The following account is taken from the Herald of February 25th:—

"On Saturday last, the 22d inst., agreeably to the notification of Major Ford, the different troops stationed at the Forts and Navy Yard, paraded in this borough, in order to form a procession to pay funeral honours to the memory of George Washington. At twelve o'clock, they were joined by the different volunteer corps, in full uniform. In the Main Street, the whole formed in battalion, and received the word of command from the Major. The bier passed them, attended by the principal gentlemen of the town as chief mourners; then followed the Lodges of the Masons in their orders; then the officers of the Navy; the different artificers from the Navy Yard, and the citizens of Norfolk and Portsmouth in general. The troops then reversed their arms and marched, the drums being muffled, and the music playing the dead march, until they arrived at the church wall, when the ranks faced to each other, and resting on their arms reversed; the bier, &c., passed between them into the church, the troops following; but the church not being sufficiently spacious, a great portion of the citizens were prevented from seeing that part of the ceremony.

"After prayers were given by the Rev. James Whitehead, Dr. Read, Mayor of the town, pronounced a handsome oration, well adapted to the occasion, and was followed by Mr. Blanchard, who delivered a beautiful monody, such as, to quote his own words, made

"'All nerves tremble, and all eyes weep.'

"Mr. Hiort then rose, as one of Captain Myers's Company, and addressed the audience as follows:

"[It is unnecessary for us to transcribe the address, which fills more than a column; but its quality may be guessed by the peroration, which was as follows]:

"'When memory traces back the anniversary of this day, and thinks on the ecstasy that for years hath pervaded every citizen;

imagining they could not celebrate with too much joy and festivity the day that gave their Washington birth; and, when we compare it with the mournful procession of the present, the chords of the human heart are ready to burst with agonizing comparison.

"'But the scene is closed!

"'As we have been unanimous to pay tribute to his memory, let us be unanimous in imitating his patriotism; and, may our unanimity be lasting as the sun that rules the day.'

"After Mr. Hiort had finished, a band of music performed a solemn dirge; the bier was carried to a grave, where the troops fired three volleys over it. The procession then moved to the Market Place, the music playing the President's march, where, after having formed in column, they were disbanded. (Queer way of dismissing troops that—*in column!* Doubtless a mistake of the reporter.)

"A greater concourse of people was never before seen in Norfolk. The attention of Major Ford to the accommodation of every description of citizens was alike, and the whole was conducted with great regularity and order."

A gentleman who was present, wrote as follows:

"Saturday last, February 22d (a day kept sacred to the name of our Washington—a day which convened in their several districts the inhabitants through the whole extent of the United States—a day mourned by a collection of near eight millions of sorrowing citizens), the funeral honours of our departed chief were performed here with a solemnity, order, and decorum, that do credit to those who conducted the procession, and to civilized society.

"Nothing could exceed the order, discipline, and precision of the troops under Major Ford, who conducted the mourning duties of the day; the steadiness of their movements, and their *recline*, when the bier passed, was not an unaffecting circumstance in the ceremony. The procession, consisting of the inhabitants, the orders of Masons, and the military, proceeded at half-past twelve, from Main Street to the church, where the service was begun by prayers from the Rev. Mr. Whitehead, and a very handsome oration by Dr. Read, Mayor of the Borough, followed by Mr.

Blanchard, who rehearsed the beautiful poem on General Washington's death* (first published in the Herald of the 2d of January), and concluded by an address from Mr. Hiort, of Captain Myers's Company, and the blessings of the church.

"The day was so remarkably bright that Heaven seemed to smile on our endeavours to do honour to the deceased and to departed merit; the spirit of emulation was abroad; each wished to contribute his mite. The concourse of people was such as we have never witnessed before in the borough. But not a single act of confusion blotted the scene; and the solemn and masterly strains of music, added to the preceding circumstances, seemed to send us to our homes, resolved to imitate in all his imitable virtues, the man for whom we mourned."

The Herald of August 1st, 1850, adds the following:

"At an early hour the old revolutionary drummer, George Fritz (who had lost an eye in his country's service), took the round with his 'spirit-stirring drum,' to remind the volunteers of the parade. A piece of artillery, worked by a detachment of Captain Lugg's Company, was posted at the foot of Market Square, and fired the minute guns, commencing at nine o'clock, and continuing till the procession was dismissed. The volunteers in the procession consisted of the Norfolk Cavalry, Captain John Nivison; the Norfolk Volunteers, Captain Moses Myers; the Light Infantry, Captain Samuel Smith; Norfolk Artillery, Captain P. Lugg; and the Ancient Artillery, Captain W. P. Pollard.

"The whole arrangement and direction of the ceremonies was deputed to Major Ford, of the U. S. Army, who commanded the troops on this station, having his head-quarters at Fort Nelson (where now stands the U. S. Naval Hospital).

"The Major, with the gallantry of the soldier, placed sentries at the doors of the church (old St. Paul's), for the exclusive admission of the ladies, till the arrival of the procession.

"The flags of the shipping were half-masted during the day; and on the front wall of the Exchange Coffee House, then recently opened by Mr. John Rourke (of eccentric memory), there was hung up a large transparency, representing the apotheosis

* A portion of this poem will be found on another page.

of Washington, with this inscription, '*Washington in Glory—The World in Tears.*' It attracted the special observation of large crowds of admiring spectators."

The resident population of the borough, in 1800, according to the census, was 6,926; showing an increase in ten years of 3,976. The officers of the Borough Corporation elected this year (not one of whom now lives), were as follows:—

Mayor.—Seth Foster.

Recorder.—Thos. Newton, Sr.

Aldermen.—Cornelius Calvert, Baylor Hill, Samuel Moseley, John K. Read, William Vaughan, John Cowper, and John Stratton.

Councilmen.—Robert Boush, President; Thomas Newton, Jr., Thomas Blanchard, John Brown, John Nivison, Luke Wheeler, Robert Taylor, Robert B. Taylor, Harrison Allmand, Richard L. Green, John Bramble, James Bennett, George Wilson, James Woodward, James Tucker, John G. Marsden.

Register.—William Sharp.

State's Attorney for the Borough.—James Nimmo.

Clerk of Hustings' Court and Common Council.—William Sharp.

Sergeant.—James Boyce.

Deputy Sergeant.—Jonathan Williamson.

Chamberlain.—Hance Baker.

Overseer of the Poor.—John Calvert.

Physician.—William O'Grady.

Commissioner of Revenue Tax.—Paul Proby.

Commissioner of the Streets.—Edward Widgeon.

Clerk of the Market.—John Warrington.

Wood Measurer.—Robert Demster.

Harbour Master.—Paul Proby.

Inspectors of Lumber.—John Barret, Frederick Hennicke, and Henry Prescott.

Inspector of Flour.—John Dudgeon.

The value of exports this year from Virginia, and of course principally from this port, was $4,430,689.

Norfolk was a busy, bustling place at this period. The population had nearly reached the respectable number of 8,000, including the transient and floating part of the community, with the permanent residents. There were very many foreigners, principally from England and Scotland, and quite a large number from France, Ireland, &c. Scores of vessels were at the wharves, taking in and discharging cargoes, and "the streets and lanes, from Main Street to the river, were thronged with a heterogeneous mass of human beings." The houses were principally of wood; the greater part of which have since disappeared, and given place to substantial brick buildings. There is scarcely a house on Market Square that stood in 1800; only about twenty on the north side of Main Street, and not so many on the south side. None of the streets were paved; and plentiful supplies of mud and water in winter, and of dust, frogs, and mosquitoes in summer, there must have been. Church Street was the only avenue by which the town could be entered by vehicles; and a noisy, brisk thoroughfare it was. There were on this street a large number of stores, and a very considerable retail trade was transacted with the country people. The three brick buildings, now standing on the east side of this street, near the Princess Anne Road, were built this year by "Monsieur Delisle, a Frenchman from the West Indies, who went largely into the brick-making business."

"There were four ship-yards in Norfolk, and two in Portsmouth; all of them just as busy as they could be. There was no higgling about prices; the only question was, 'How soon can the work be done?'"

The Rev. Mr. Bland, an Episcopal minister, was, at this time, "the regularly-installed pastor of St. Paul's Church, though not the choice of the congregation." He was quite an eccentric gentleman, and besought his small assemblage of hearers "to do as he *told* them; not as he *did*."

Many persons congregated at the town-hall to attend the ministrations of the Rev. J. Whitehead, also an Episcopalian clergyman. The Methodists assembled in an old building on Fenchurch Street, below Holt. The Baptists occupied a house opposite their present church on Cumberland Street. The Catholics worshipped in a small wooden chapel on Chapel Street, on the site of the building which, a few years since, was succeeded by their fine house on Holt Street. The Presbyterians were this year organized into a church, and soon after built the house at the corner of Catharine and Charlotte Streets; and, within the next twelve months, the Protestant Episcopalians and the Methodists, also, had commodious and comfortable houses of worship erected; the former on the site of the present Presbyterian Church, on Church Street, and the latter where their building now stands, on Cumberland near Cove Street. The Cumberland Street Baptist Church was erected in 1816. This was a neat, plain, and commodious brick building. It has been enlarged and greatly improved, and now presents a very chaste and handsome front. The interior has recently been put in good order, and is, perhaps, as beautifully finished as any house of worship in the city. Rev. Reuben Jones is the present pastor.

1801. Up to this time, twenty-five years after the great conflagration, one thousand houses had been erected in the borough, averaging forty a year.

A Directory of Norfolk was published this year by Charles H. Simmons, Esq. It was continued for several years, and proved a profitable undertaking; but the town having suffered severely by fires, and the difficulties which attended the commercial affairs of the United States and Great Britain, having resulted unfavourably for the prospects of Norfolk, this and other enterprises were necessarily abandoned.

On the 2d of May, of this year, "Articles of Association and Rules of the Norfolk Chamber of Commerce" were agreed to at the Exchange Coffee House. The officers were a president, vice-president, secretary, and treasurer. The meetings were held on the first Monday in every month.

We copy the following agreement of the Chamber, with the subscribers' names:—

"Articles of Association and Rules of the Norfolk Chamber of Commerce, agreed on at a meeting of the Chamber, held at the Exchange Coffee House, on Tuesday the 2d of May, 1801.

"We, whose names are hereunto subscribed, do hereby agree to associate together, under the title of 'Members of the Chamber of Norfolk,' for the purpose of aiding trade, the adjustment of mercantile differences, and the carrying into effect such rules and regulations as may, from time to time, be established."

Robert Taylor,	Henry Benbridge,
William Pennock,	William Vaughan,
Robert Gibson,	James Mackinder,
Alexander Wilson,	Edward Johnston,
Christopher Fry,	Francis Smith,
James Taylor, Jr.,	Harrison Allmand,
William Plume,	Thomas Willock,
James Young,	Wright Southgate,
Soulage,	James Thorburn,
John Cowper,	John Proudfit,
Luke Wheeler,	Martin Fisk,
Thomas Newton,	James Tucker,
John Granberry,	Thomas Hamilton,
Alexander Maclure,	Warren Ashley,
Louis E. Durant,	James Douglas,
John Brown,	Alexander Cowan,
Francis S. Taylor,	William Raincock,
Phinehas Dana,	William Hartshorne, Jr.,
Nathan Macgill,	Samuel Kerr,
James Herron,	Daniel Stone,
Moses Myers,	William Cuthbert,
Thomas Higinbotham,	Edward Archer,
James Bennett,	Theodoric Armistead.
Robert Dickson,	

In 1802, that excellent and well-disciplined volunteer corps, the Norfolk Junior Volunteers, now commanded by Captain F. F. Ferguson, was founded.

Until this year the Council was elected triennially, when, by act of Assembly, the term of service was reduced from three years to one year—the election, as heretofore, to take place on the 24th of June.

January 27, 1803. Charter of the borough again amended, so as to allow an alteration in the mode of electing councilmen. The town was accordingly divided into eight wards, each electing, within its own bounds, two Common Councilmen.

CHAPTER XIII.

1803—1812.

William Wirt—Letters, &c.—Norfolk Academy Incorporated, Trustees—Annual Exports and Imports—Prosperous Condition of the Borough—Commercial Advantages—Agriculture—Extensive Fire—Heavy Losses—Distress and Deaths—Market-House—River-side—Parade Ground—Taxes, &c.—Expenditures of the Corporation—Large Bill for Gunpowder—The Poet Moore—Shocking Tragedy—Comparative Statement—Norfolk People—Foreign Trade—Merchants—Commerce—Streets and Houses Labelled—Act of Assembly relative to Paving the Streets—The Harbour filled with Vessels—Immense Business—Transient People—Brilliant Prospects—Norfolk Merchants—Pennock and Myers—Norfolk Bar—Chesapeake Affair—Embargo—Ruinous Effects upon Commerce—Embargo Law Repealed—Mechanical Benevolent Society—Places of Amusement—Public Gardens, Parks, and Groves—Back Creek—Street Lamps—Solemn Funeral Procession—Burning of the Theatre at Richmond—Soldier Sentenced to be Shot.

In the winter of 1803-4, William Wirt, Esq., then a distinguished lawyer and writer, and afterwards Attorney-General of the United States, removed to Norfolk, where he remained till July, 1806. "From this date," says Kennedy, "we may compute Wirt's rapid advancement to eminence in his profession. While here, he wrote many valuable and interesting letters, which have been published; and his practice was very extensive and lucrative." He remarks in one of his letters, "In the Borough of Norfolk every drone feels the pressure of business;" and in another, "Norfolk, as you guess, is very expensive. I keep, for instance, a pair of horses here, which cost me eight pounds per month. Wood is four to eight dollars per cord; Indian meal, through the winter, is nine shillings per bushel; this winter it is supposed it will be fifteen. Flour, eleven and twelve dollars per barrel; a leg of mutton three dollars; butter three shillings per pound; eggs two shillings and three pence, and so on. Having set out, however, with a view of making a provision for my family, in the event of my being called away from them, I live as economical as I can, so as to avoid giving my wife any reason for regret at the recollection of her father's house and table."

1804, January 19. Act of Assembly passed, incorporating the Trustees of the Norfolk Academy, and the following gentlemen were appointed: Thomas Newton, Jr., John Nivison, Thomas Blanchard, Theodoric Armistead, Robert Brough, John E. Holt, Littleton W. Tazewell, Philip Barbour, Alexander Jordan, Richard H. Lee, and Arthur Lee.

The annual exports of the borough, for this and several preceding years, and also for 1805, '6, and '7, varied from five to seven millions; and the importations were scarcely commensurate with the demand.

"It must be kept in mind that we then had no internal improvements, in the common acceptation of the term, excepting a partial use of the Dismal Swamp Canal, which, when compared with the present magnificent work of that name, was as a mole-hill to a mountain. A glance at the map will show whence our exports came. Look at the Chesapeake, which has been aptly called our Mediterranean Sea. Its head stream, the Susquehanna, penetrates far into Pennsylvania. To pass over the tributaries from Maryland, which are alone sufficient to sustain a city, let us come to Virginia. There is the Potomac and its tributaries; the Rappahannock and its tributaries; the Piankitank; the York with its associated streams, the Mattaponi and the Pamunkey; the James with its northern and southern tributaries, which are competent to support a large city; and your own Elizabeth and its tributaries. Look at the position of your port, which seems to be designed to receive the produce of these mighty rivers, and to become the mart of their commerce. But numerous as are these channels of trade, your port received its tributes from many other sources. North Carolina crowded the products of her soil and her rich forests of pine and oak, on your wharves. The Delaware brought you the wealth of the States on its banks. Let me ask in passing, whether these sources of trade are exhausted? Do the skies refuse their genial showers to our lands? Do the waters of your streams refuse to run to the sea. No, no; on the contrary, all the sources of your ancient wealth are still open, and increased tenfold. New scenes are also open. Facilities of intercommunication, not dreamed of half a century ago, now exist. A late Richmond paper announces the wonderful intelligence that a heavily laden canal packet may now pass to Buchanan, a settlement that is nestled among the Alleghanies. Railroads, constructed at great cost, are multiplied and multiplying over our own State and the neighbouring States. Nor is this all. The capacity of production is greater now than ever. We have more people, more cultivated land, and more money. There is hardly an acre of timber standing on the low grounds which were of old given up in despair, but which modern skill has made available for all the choicest productions of agriculture. Not a stream is closed against us; not an acre of land but but may be made to yield the full produce of the virgin soil."

This year, also, the commercial part of the town suffered severely by fires. Many of the houses being built of wood, the progress of the flames was very rapid, and they were subdued with great difficulty. The loss in goods of every description was immense, and the distress occasioned was very great. A respectable old gentleman, seeing his goods consuming, committed himself in desperation to the furious flames, in his own store, from the ruins of which his remains were taken,—a charred mass; and another leaped from the wharf, in a fit of excitement, and was drowned.

The market-house was pulled down to save more valuable property. This was situated in the upper part of the Market Space, on a line with Main Street,—the ends being east and west; and the north side being nearly on a line with the south side of Main Street, east from the square. From the market-house there was a gradual descent to the river-side,—a part of which was near the spot now occupied by Barry's extensive China establishment, corner of Union Street, long known as the Steamboat Hotel. West from this location, the shore extended further south; perhaps as far as Water Street. The parade ground was on the declivity in the rear of the market-house.

Total amount of taxes, and other funds, received by the Corporation this year,	$17,263 72
Moneys paid, as per the Chamberlain's Account,	8,653 72
Balance due the Corporation, January 1st, 1806,	$8,610 00

Of the above amount, for expenditures, the sum of $246 was paid for *powder* to blow up houses.

This year, Thomas Moore, Esq., the poet, who was on a visit to the United States, came to Norfolk, and while here, composed a song, which he called "The Lake of the Dismal Swamp." This affecting poetic effusion will be found in another part of this work, in connexion with a description of that silent and secluded collection of water. Moore was born in Ireland, and educated at Trinity College, Dublin. "His prejudices did not allow him to form a favourable opinion of this country." Some of his poems are justly censured for their licentious character, while others are much admired for their surpassing beauty, pathos, and religious sentiment. He returned to his native land in 1806, and soon after published, "The Two-Penny Post-Bag;" "The Fudge Family in Paris;" "The Loves of the Angels;" and "Lalla Rookh;" an Oriental romance, "which unites the purest and softest tenderness, with the loftiest dignity, and in every page glows with all the fervour of poetry."

1806. This year, a shocking tragedy occurred in a building on the north side of Little Water Street, two doors east of Commerce. "Two gamblers, brothers, of the name of Davis, rented the third story for the purpose of keeping a pharo table. One night an Italian, whose name we believe was Colmini (*Coalminer*, as he was commonly called), visited this establishment, and meeting with an extraordinary run of luck, finally broke the bank. The Davises and another of their fraternity charged him with cheating; he protested his innocence, but it was to no purpose. They attempted to seize him, but he broke from them and fled down the narrow dark stairway, all three in close pursuit. On the second landing he stepped aside, unperceived, and as each passed him on the right, in the dark, he gave him a fatal stab with a stiletto in the left side, and a push down the next flight. The two Davises were mortally wounded and died within twenty-four hours; their companion lingered several weeks and died also. The Italian escaped."

For the following statement, prepared from Simmons's Directory for this year, we are indebted to the kindness of an intelligent citizen.

Corporation.—Mayor, recorder, aldermen, and officers of the court in 1806, fifteen; survivors in 1852, none. Common Council, nineteen; survivor, John Southgate. Constables and watchmen, thirteen; survivors, none. Overseers of the poor, inspectors, measurers, fire wardens, and others, fifty-eight; survivors, none.

Institutions.—Trustees and teachers of the Norfolk Academy, fourteen; survivor, L. W. Tazewell, trustee. Directors and visitors of the Female Orphan Asylum, sixteen; survivors, Mrs. Taylor, Mrs. Chandler, and Mrs. Woodward. President and directors of the Dismal Swamp Canal Company, seven; survivor, F. Whittle. President and directors of the Norfolk Drawbridge Company, six; survivor, C. Fry. Officers and members of the Marine Society, sixty-two; survivors, none. Officers and members of the Chamber of Commerce, thirty-five; survivors, John Southgate and George M'Intosh. President, directors, and secretary of the Marine Insurance Company, eighteen; survivors, John Southgate, and F. Whittle. President, directors, and officers of the United States Bank, twenty-one; survivor, A. Maclure. Virginia Bank, twenty; survivor, John Southgate.

Masonic Lodges.—Royal Arch, fourteen; No. 1, eighteen; No. 51, ten; no survivors.

Militia.—54th Regiment, colonel and staff, majors, and adjutants, eight; survivors, none. Effective rank and file, eight hundred and thirty-five; survivors, unknown. First battalion, twenty-two; survivor, William Maxwell. Second battalion, eighteen; no survivor.

Lawyers and notaries, ten; survivor, L. W. Tazewell. Custom House officers, twenty-one; no survivors. Marine Hospital, three; survivors, none. Post-office, four; survivors, none. Navy Agency, three; survivors, none. Of course, but few remain, after the lapse of nearly half a century. Death could not spare, till the present time, many of those who had come to mature age at the period here alluded to.

Mr. Simmons says of Norfolk, in 1806: "At present, notwithstanding the great fires of 1799 and 1804, which consumed the most extensive commercial part of the town, there are about twelve hundred houses—the suburbs have nearly two hundred dwellings. The number of inhabitants may be computed at nearly ten thousand, and they are characterized by travellers as generally polite, obliging, and hospitable.

"It carries on a brisk trade to Europe, the West Indies, and the States, in tobacco, provisions, naval stores, and lumber, which, in the last two quarters of this year, amounted to $1,852,883. In 1805, the amount in domestic produce was $3,880,317, and in foreign articles to $507,907.

"The number of vessels from foreign ports entered at Norfolk in 1800, were three hundred and fifty-six; in 1801, three hundred and sixty-nine; in 1802, four hundred and fifty-three; in 1804, four hundred and eighty-four; in 1805, three hundred and sixty-eight; in 1806, three hundred and thirteen."

About this time the streets were labelled and the houses numbered.

January 3d, 1807. An Act of Assembly was passed empowering the court of Norfolk Borough to cause the streets to be paved, on certain conditions.

"Your harbour," says an observant visiter, alluding to this period, "capacious as it is, was filled with ships from foreign ports. The coasting trade, which distributed your imports, employed hundreds of vessels, whose streamers, mingling on a gala day with the flags of the foreign ships, presented a cheering spectacle. A gentleman, recently deceased, who had come out of the war in the South with a shattered constitution, and who sought to recover his health by a sea trip to the North, informed me that it was difficult even in 1787 to cross in a ferry boat from Norfolk to Portsmouth, on account of the great number of vessels in the harbour. Your warehouses were full of foreign and domestic products. Besides your stated population, there was always a body of transient people, respectable in point of numbers, and demanding house-room and board. The houses extended from the western end of Main and Broad Water to their eastern extremity. Church Street was lined with tenements from Main Street to the borough limits. The people lived freely, and indulged in those expenses which contribute to fill the treasury of a city. Horses, carriages, phaetons, chairs, carts, and drays, almost beyond number, abounded. Your market stalls alone at that day would have afforded a fine subject of taxation; for the demand for provisions for your stated and floating population was so great and so long continued, as to render every acre of ground, and every beast of the field, and every fowl of the air, within sixty or eighty miles around you, subsidiary to your market."

"The rapidity with which the borough rose from utter ruin in 1783 to the flourishing condition above described, attracted unusual attention, and the conviction was general that, as it had become so great from so poor a beginning in so short a time, it would continue to be one of the greatest (if not the greatest) commercial towns in the Union."

"Without yielding to the spirit of a *laudator temporis acti*," said a gentleman, alluding to some of the Norfolk people of those days, "and willing to accord to the existing generation all that its merits deserve, I must declare that I have rarely met, either at home or abroad, with their equals. They possessed in an eminent degree what may be called the chivalry of the commercial character, and displayed in their bearing a dignity and grace which looked infinitely beyond an ignoble rivalry and the tricks of trade. One may look long even now in the Northern cities to find the counterpart of the counting-rooms of Pennock and Myers, in the meridian of your commercial renown. I have often regretted that the great merchants of your great epoch, crushed by political events which no human foresight could have anticipated, bequeathed to their descendants no remnant of the wealth which flowed in upon them with every wind and from every shore. But they lived at a period of great political trial. We can, however, emulate their worth, their enterprise, their magnanimous demeanour, and their comprehensive charity.

"It is also delightful to contemplate the characters of the mothers and daughters of that day."

These were days "when," to use the forcible language of another, "one might walk from Norfolk to Portsmouth on the decks of the vessels at anchor in the harbour—when the rich products of the Indies were piled on our wharves, and stored in our warehouses—when our merchants bought cargoes of cotton, corn, and tobacco, and shipped on private account—when Richmond and Petersburg were tributary to Norfolk, and their merchants flocked periodically hither to purchase their supplies—when the business of Norfolk was comparatively larger than that of New York, and really larger than that of Baltimore—when Norfolk, as proud then of her citizens, and as rich in intellect as she was affluent and progressive in trade, boasted a triumvirate at the bar as brilliant as ever entranced a jury, or expounded constitutional law; when our majestic Tazewell adorned the Senate—when the gifted Taylor and Wirt wrestled in the Forum, and surpassed the models of antiquity in elegance of diction, power of eloquence, and splendour of forensic triumph.

* * * * * * *

"The intellectual triumvirate is broken, not demolished; Taylor, the laborious student, in after years the able and indefatigable lawyer; Wirt, the splendid jurist, the captivating orator of the school of Cicero, whose magic eloquence aforetime gave a still deeper tint of loveliness to the shades of Blennerhassett—these sleep well. One polished shaft is still standing to tell of bygone days, venerable with the ivy of age and eloquent of almost classic memories: Tazewell, the astute statesman and retired citizen, yet lingers in our midst."

In the summer of 1807 occurred the wanton attack of the British frigate Leopard upon the Chesapeake, and the seizure and imprisonment of several of her crew upon the allegation that they were British subjects.

The Embargo Act of December 22d, 1807, having become the law of the land, the ports were of course closed; exportation nearly ceased, and business in the towns on the coast was suddenly and sadly interrupted. "In a moment, the commerce of the American Republic, from being in point of extent the second in the world, was reduced to a coasting trade between the individual States."

1809. The embargo law was repealed, and "a ray of prosperity burst through the general gloom."

The Mechanical Benevolent Society was organized this year. In addition to the benevolent objects of this association, there is a provision by which the amount paid in by a member, is returned two-fold to his family after his death. The annual income at this time amounts to about $3000. It was incorporated by Act of Assembly, January 19th, 1811.

The following is the list of the places of amusement and recreation in Norfolk and vicinity at this date, many of which continued for years after:—A theatre, the Wigwam Gardens, Vauxhall Gardens and Baths, Rosainville's Bower, Lindsay's Retreat, Museum Naturæ, and Botanical Gardens.

These were all pretty well attended and sustained. The gardens were frequented on Sundays, and on the evenings of the other days of the week; and they were crowded on public occasions. Not one of these places now remains. This may be some evidence of the improvement in the morals of the community, to whom it is hoped the churches, the family circle, the social evening party, and interesting books, present sufficient attraction to supersede the necessity of any of the above-named places of amusement; although it is not denied that well-conducted gardens, affording the means of innocent recreation, and a pleasant retreat from the noise and bustle of the city, without furnishing the means of, and presenting temptations to, intemperance and dissipation, and encouraging the profanation of the Lord's day, would be a valuable acquisition to the city, and meet with the countenance and support of the public.

The places above alluded to, probably received their principal support from visiters, and from foreigners and other persons connected with the shipping. But our citizens, old and young, the fair daughters of Norfolk especially, feel the want of some agreeable and pleasant place of resort as a promenade. We have no pleasant and inviting parks* or groves here, in which to take an evening ramble, and enjoy the balmy breezes in spring, summer, and autumn times; with cheering strains of

* The public parks of New York City are 10 in number, and embrace a space of more than 170 acres. The public parks in Philadelphia are 11 in number, and cover a large space of ground.

music to calm the troubled, agitated soul after the turmoil of the day; or, at "morning's earliest hour," to listen with delight to the cheerful notes of the feathered songsters of the grove.*

The expediency of condemning the property west of Bank Street, opposite the City Hall, and of filling up the water-lots and Back Creek, between Bank and Granby Streets, for a public square, has been favourably considered by the councils. This would be an improvement of very great utility to the city, and, doubtless, increase the healthfulness, as well as the good appearance of the place.

"The accomplishment of such a work has long been considered a desideratum to the improvement of the city, and, independent of the removal of such an unsightly spectacle from the very heart of the town, it will contribute in other respects to its substantial advancement. We hope that the matter will be taken up in earnest by the two councils, and pressed with energy to its successful completion."

January 11, 1811. Act of Assembly passed, authorizing the corporation to erect lamps for the purpose of lighting the streets.

January 5, 1812. This day was set apart by the Mayor for an expression, on the part of the citizens, of condolence on account of an awful calamity, that had fallen upon the city of Richmond—the burning of the theatre on the night of the 26th December of the preceding year, by which more than seventy lives were lost. Governor Smith, and other distinguished individuals, were among the victims;—a most heart-rending scene, one of those sudden and dreadful visitations that baffles all attempts at description.† The inhabitants of the borough of Nor-

* In the flourishing city of Memphis, on the Mississippi, in Tennessee, there are large natural groves; and, but recently, the wild birds were warbling there, and sporting among the dense green foliage of the tall forest trees.

† The theatre at Capo d'Istria, in Italy, fell, and crushed the performers and audience to death, February 6th, 1794.

The theatre at Mentz was destroyed by fire during the performance, and, on the falling in of which, many were crushed to death, and above seventy burnt, August, 1796.

The first play-house ever erected was that of Bacchus, at Athens, by Philos, B. C. 420. The ruins still exist.

folk, with those of other places, exhibited suitable evidences of their profound sorrow for the mournful event.

The civil authorities, officers of the Army and Navy, the volunteer companies, and an immense concourse of citizens, slowly marched, with solemn music, through the streets. An urn was carried in the procession; the bells tolled a funeral knell, and an appropriate discourse was delivered. The Herald states, that "a more solemn and impressive scene was never witnessed in the borough."

September 5, 1812. A private in Lieutenant Swift's corps of marines, stationed at the Navy Yard, having been sentenced to be shot, for deserting his post while on guard, this was the day appointed for his execution. "The awful moment was announced by the solemn roll of the drum; the delinquent was conducted from the prison, with the usual ceremonies customary on such occasions, and led to the fatal spot where he was to suffer. The whole detachment were under arms, twelve of whom were selected to execute the sentence. When the procession halted, the lieutenant delivered an address, of which the following is an extract:—

"'Soldiers!—An awful scene is now presented for your contemplation. You behold before you one of your comrades, about to pay the forfeit of that crime, which it has been my constant duty to warn you against; he enlisted to serve his country—and deserted. In peace, this is a crime of the first magnitude, and

Theatres were first introduced into England in 1566; opposed by the Puritans in 1633; revived by Charles II., 1660.

"Plays are unbecoming and pernicious pastimes."—Socrates.

"They raise the passions, and pervert the use of them; and are, consequently, dangerous to morality."—Plato.

"They are lascivious vanities and contagious evils."—Plutarch.

"Plays are pernicious, and corrupt youth."—Sir Matthew Hale.

"One play-house ruins more souls than fifty churches can save."—Judge Bulstrade.

"Mr. Macready, the eminent tragedian, now resides at Sherborne, in the bosom of a most interesting family of twelve children. Among many excellent rules for the government of his family, is one from which, it is said, he has never deviated. It is that no one of his children should ever, on any pretence, enter a theatre, or have any visiting connexion with actors or actresses."

its penalty death; how enormous then is the transgression of this man, who has deserted his country in her hour of peril.

* * * * * *

"'The benefit of the service requires that he suffer death, and, in a few moments, he will be launched into eternity! I beseech you, soldiers, to take warning from his fate; fulfil the solemn obligations enjoined upon you, and refrain from the guilty path into which he has wandered to his own destruction.'

"At the conclusion of the speech a solemn pause ensued;—a signal was given, and immediately the engines of death were aimed at the devoted victim;—another pause, and the arm of death was arrested. An officer rushed through the crowd, holding a paper in his hand. It was a *reprieve!*"

CHAPTER XIV.

1813.

War Declared—Warlike Preparations—Battle of Craney Island—Enemy's Fleet and Troops—Dreadful Execution of our Guns—Shameful Depredations of the British—Incidents of the Battle—Letter from General R. B. Taylor—Extracts from the Herald.

Congress having declared war against Great Britain, Norfolk was, of course, from its position, expected to be a prominent point of attack; therefore, a large force was concentrated here, and preparations were made to give the enemy a warm reception, whenever he might find it convenient to pay a visit to the hospitable old borough.

June 22, 1813. On this memorable day Craney Island was attacked by the British, and defended in a manner that reflected lasting honour upon the noble band of heroes who took part in that important battle, as well as upon the State and country at large. It was indeed a brilliant affair. The cool deliberation and mature judgment; the bravery and enthusiasm which were so strikingly manifested on the occasion by our comparatively small force, and the complete success of the day, all united to render this battle one of the most decisive and victorious that occurred during the war.

Craney Island lies about five miles from Norfolk, commanding the inward approach from Hampton Roads; and on its defence depended the safety of the borough, as well as of Portsmouth and the surrounding country. The splendid repulse of the enemy there, doubtless, prevented a more severe and bloody conflict, if not an exhibition of inhumanity and barbarity similar to that which took place at Hampton, shortly after this engagement.

The fortifications of this small island were ordered by Major General Wade Hampton, during his command of this district, and the works were executed under the direction of Colonel Armistead.

The enemy's fleet had come up to Newport's News on the 21st, and were soon in readiness to cover the intended attack of the boats on the following day. The British presented a very formidable and imposing array. There were about twenty vessels, consisting of seventy-fours, frigates, and transports, and an armed force of about 4000 men.

A small battery was erected by the Virginians on the island, mounting one eighteen-pounder, two twenty-four, and four six-pounders. Our force consisted, principally, of about 400 militia-men, one company of riflemen, and two companies of light artillery, one of which was commanded by Captain Arthur Emerson, of Portsmouth. General Robert B. Taylor, the commanding officer of the District at this time, increased this small force by a detachment of 30 men from Fort Norfolk,* commanded by

* This is a circular brick fort, on the north side of the river, and about a mile from the western limits of the city. It has been long neglected, and is fast falling into ruins. Fort Norfolk is situated nearly opposite the U. S. Naval Hospital, the site of old Fort Nelson. These forts were, of course, intended to guard the entrance to the inner harbour. During the war, an immense chain was extended across the river from these two points.

Captain Pollard, of the U. S. Army. Lieutenant Johnson, of Culpeper, and Ensign A. Atkinson, of Captain Hamilton Shields's Company of Riflemen, from Isle of Wight, with about 30 volunteers, were also added, by order of the chief officer. Lieutenants Neale, Shubrick, and Saunders, with about 150 seamen, also joined our force, by the direction of Captain Tarbell, of the U. S. Ship Constellation, then at the naval anchorage, and they acted a brave and noble part in the battle. Captain Emmerson and Lieutenant Thomas Godwin, each commanded a twenty-four-pounder, and the eighteen-pounder was commanded by Captain Rooke, who was at this time master of a merchant-ship—the Manhattan, of New York—then at anchor in our harbour. These three pieces of ordnance were served by men from the Constellation. Lieutenant Howle, Sergeants Young and Livingston, and Corporal Moffatt, separately commanded the six-pounders, at which was stationed the artillery company of Portsmouth. The whole force concentrated at the Island was in command of Colonel Beatty, assisted by Majors Wagner and Faulkner.

"A long pole was got, to which the 'star-spangled banner' was *nailed*, the pole planted in the breastwork, and the stars and stripes floated in the breeze."

About 2600 of the British troops landed at a distance of two miles below the Island, and the action was commenced by that division of the enemy's force. Congreve rockets were thrown upon the Island, from a house on the mainland, within cannon-shot of our battery, and owned by Captain George Wise. Captain Rooke, who was nearest this point, was ordered to fire into the house, the view of which was partially obstructed by a thick growth of trees. A brisk fire of grape and canister-shot was immediately opened upon it; and such was the precision with which the guns were served, that the British were completely routed, with a loss of many killed and wounded; among the former, two of the officers. The eighteen-pounder, served as it was with extraordinary rapidity, and aimed with unerring precision, dealt death and destruction at every fire.* Meanwhile,

* Captain Rooke had been a member of one of the companies in service, but was discharged at his own request, and took command of the ship Manhattan,

the enemy was approaching the island with fifty large barges, filled with soldiers, to the number of about 1500, advancing in regular column-order, led on by the Admiral's boat of twenty-four oars, and fifty-two feet long, with a brass three-pounder in her bow. When Captain Emmerson supposed that they were near enough to be reached by his twenty-four-pounder, he cried out, in a loud, stern voice, "NOW, BOYS, ARE YOU READY?" and the quick response was, "*We are ready.*" "FIRE!" rejoined the brave and enthusiastic Captain; and the battery forthwith opened upon them a dreadful fire of grape and canister. The foremost boats advanced, however, until they grounded, "when so quick and galling was the fire, that they were thrown into the greatest confusion, and forthwith commenced a hasty retreat. Four or five of the boats were sunk, one of them the Admiral's barge; and many others were so shattered that it was with difficulty they were kept afloat."

An eventful moment had come and passed; and exceedingly important interests were involved in the result of this engage-

of New York, which was at that time bound from Norfolk to Europe, with a load of lumber. He was requested by Captain Emmerson to aid in the contest, and consented. While the enemy was approaching the island, it was found, to the dismay of our men, that the ordnance were not in a suitable position, and would prove useless unless removed; and yet it was thought impossible to make the alteration in time. At this crisis, Captain R. asked for a certain number of men, and the work was soon accomplished; the guns were quickly ready for the work of death.

Rooke was a man of astonishing energy and spirit; of unwavering perseverance and dauntless bravery. Some thought, after the fight, that to his efficient services we were principally indebted for the decisive result in our favour. He discovered, on the occasion, a British soldier, probably an officer, up in a tree, making observations, whereupon he immediately took aim, and the unerring shot carried away one of the man's legs.

Captain R. died suddenly, at Key West, Fa., in June, 1834, aged 45. His estimable widow resides in Philadelphia. They had nine children, four sons and five daughters, all of whom are now living, and all, except one, have been married. Five of them reside in Philadelphia, one in Norfolk, one in Portsmouth, one in South Carolina, and one in Texas.

No legal claim can be made upon the Government by his heirs, as he had been discharged when the battle took place. A special appropriation by Congress, would, under the circumstances, meet with the approbation of a grateful people.

ment. The enemy's force was large and formidable; ours, comparatively, as to numbers, inconsiderable. When the firing of the guns announced the commencement of the action, hundreds of our citizens, both male and female, young and old, hastened to the shores on the northwestern part of the town; and as, with straining eyes, they gazed upon the approaching enemy, and witnessed the quick and vivid flashes from the engines of death, their hearts beat with emotion; for there were fathers, and sons, and brothers there. And then, the day might not have been gained, the victory might not have been won, by that gallant band of heroes; and who could tell their fate, and the sad consequences that might have followed a defeat; the distress and suffering that might have fallen with crushing weight upon the inhabitants of the two towns, should the enemy have succeeded in gaining possession of them? But there were brave and powerful men there; and the zeal, activity, and *fury* of the Virginians on this occasion, have seldom, if ever, been surpassed. The execution of the guns was terrible. From the commencement of the firing, till the boats had retreated beyond the reach of the balls, there was almost a constant blaze and one continual roar; while the mathematical precision with which the faithful guns were served, from first to last, was truly wonderful. Every fire appeared to deal death and havoc among the enemy's troops, a number of whom were killed and many were wounded; some were drowned, while others clung to the sinking boats, and cried piteously for help.

A ball from Captain Emmerson's gun is said to have almost cut in twain and sunk the Admiral's barge; some, however, gave the credit to Lieutenant Howle; while others thought that Sergeant William P. Young, with his six-pounder, did the business. It was, doubtless, very difficult to tell which gun did the most fearful execution; although it is very generally conceded, that to Captain E. a large share of the honour of the day was justly due.

The loss of the enemy in killed, wounded, and prisoners was two hundred. The Virginians did not lose a single man.*

* Before the enemy's forces had left the main land, the remaining supply of powder on the island blew up, from some unknown cause, and the sentinel that guarded it was killed. Fortunately, the British troops did not discover the accident.

Here, as in 1775, at the battle of the Great Bridge, fifteen miles distant, not one of the sons of freedom fell—no hero, over whose mortal remains to erect a monument. It is believed, that if a single life had been lost from the ranks of the Virginians, a suitable and enduring memorial would have been speedily raised to his memory.

During the action, Captain Shields's riflemen waded out for some distance, hoping to get within reach of the enemy, but did not generally succeed. Some of our men brought the Admiral's boat, the *Centipede*, to the shore, with a number of guns, pistols, and cutlasses. On board of this barge, one of the enemy's men was found with both legs shot off. Our men carefully wrapped him in the sails of the boat, and took him to the shore, where death soon put an end to his sufferings. The twenty-four pounder, commanded by Lieutenant Godwin, and one of the six-pounders, were disabled by the breaking of the carriages, in consequence of the heavy charges and rapid firing.*

That portion of the British troops that had landed, returned to the shipping in the afternoon, after having committed most shameful depredations, such as "shooting hogs, sheep, &c., breaking furniture, cutting open beds, &c., in the dwelling-houses near which they landed."

The following is an extract of a letter from General Taylor to the Secretary of War, dated July 4th, 1813.

"The courage and constancy with which this inferior force, in the face of a formidable naval armament, not only sustained a position in which nothing was complete, but repelled the enemy with considerable loss, cannot fail to command the approbation of their government, and the applause of their country. It has infused in the residue of the army, a general spirit of competi-

* The descriptions that have been published of this battle have generally been very incorrect. Great injustice has been done to the chief actors. The reader will scarcely believe that such a statement as the following could have been made by one who had the means of furnishing all the particulars. This is an extract from one of the several erroneous accounts.

"Major Faulkner and Captain Emerson, with the brave volunteers and militia, were on the island, ready, no doubt, and anxious to take part in the fight; but the enemy did not come within range of musket-shot, and the battle was fought with three eighteen-pounders, worked by the seamen, and directed by the officers, from the frigate Constellation."(!!)

tion, the beneficial effects of which will, I trust, be displayed in our future combats.

"I cannot withhold my grateful acknowledgments to Commodore Cassin, Captain Tarbell, and the other officers and crews of the Constellation and gun-boats, who have, in every instance, aided our operations with a cordiality, zeal, and ability, not to be surpassed."

The following extract relative to the battle is from the Herald:

"Such a band of heroes as lately united their efforts to fortify and defend the town of Norfolk, deserve the plaudits of their country. It was very fortunate that Governor Barbour and General Taylor were in office at a period so extremely critical; for no men could have exerted themselves more for the salvation of the State. Aid was sent from all parts of Virginia. At every alarm the whole people were in arms. The old and the young were seen at their posts, and each seemed to rival his neighbour in alacrity and zeal. The defenders of Craney Island are entitled to the warmest thanks of every true patriot. The invading enemy was astonished, when he saw his attempts so ably repulsed, and so soon rendered abortive. Thus the great Ruler of the universe frequently permits the valour of a few to defeat the wicked projects of the ambitious."*

CHAPTER XV.

1813.

Anxiety of the Citizens—General Taylor—Fortifications—Forts Tar and Barbour—54th Regiment—Lieutenant Broughton—Orders to March to Slaughter's Field—Excitement—False Alarm—Spirited Remarks of the Herald—Excitement Increased—Mr. Broughton's Statement—The Independents—51th Regiment—Juniors—Artillery—Admiral Cochrane—Militia—Effect of the Repulse at the Island.

GREAT anxiety continued to be felt for the safety of Norfolk, Portsmouth, and the surrounding country, and it was indeed a

* The anniversary of the battle of Craney Island should be celebrated, at least by the gallant volunteers of Norfolk and Portsmouth.

fortunate circumstance that officers so efficient and energetic were in command here at the time. The enemy desired to gain possession of the two towns, and had intended to make a great effort to obtain them. Had success crowned the attack of the British, the consequences would, doubtless, have been lamentable; and the towns once gained, it would have required tremendous exertions, if not a second general conflagration, to dispossess them. Consequently, the soldiers and citizens were required by the officers to be exceedingly vigilant. It was feared that they might land at some point on the bay shore, and proceed by land to the town; in view of which, a redoubt was thrown up, south of Armistead's Bridge, called Fort Tar; after which, other fortifications were erected, with great labour and despatch, near the northeastern extremity of the town, and called Fort Barbour,* the remains of which are still to be seen on the east of Church Street, and south of Princess Anne Road.

We are indebted to the Herald for the following editorial remarks:

"On the day of the attack on Craney Island (June 22, 1813), the 54th regiment, Norfolk Borough, was called out, *en masse*, and the writer of this article (then a Lieutenant of the 54th) was assigned the command of a draft of forty men, to escort the prisoners and deserters from the British (about the same number) to Richmond, to be delivered to the United States Marshal. The militia of the regiment were kept under arms on that occasion some ten or fifteen days,—during which time they were turned out, one bright Sabbath morning, upon an alarm brought to town by a vidette of the guard stationed at Sewell's Point, that the enemy were landing on the shore between them and the mouth of Tanner's Creek. The intelligence came so direct, and was related with so much circumstantiality, that no one pretended to doubt that the enemy *had* landed in good earnest, and would be upon us in two or three hours at the utmost.

"Their orders were to march with all haste to Slaughter's Old Field (ominous name!), about three miles from the city, on the

* A brick-kiln, just ready for burning, being on the line of this work, dirt was thrown over it, and it assisted in forming the fortification. The remains of the kiln were discovered in 1850.

Princess Anne Road, and there wait the enemy's coming (which, no one doubted, would be in less than an hour), and amuse him, while the different regiments around the city were taking up their most advantageous positions for defence. The excitement was great among the women and children in town, and the feelings of their natural protectors, thus compelled to leave them to the fate of war, were none of the pleasantest. They put a good face on it, however, and with a dogged determination to do their duty, they took the dangerous post assigned them. But it proved to be a false alarm."

An officer rode impetuously through the ranks, announcing that the enemy had really landed, and was preparing to enter the town. The drums beat to arms, the greatest enthusiasm was exhibited by many, and the most active preparations were made to receive the hostile army. It was either on this or a subsequent occasion, as we have learned, that the alarm given was intentionally false, to test the readiness on the part of our troops for an attack, and which proved quite satisfactory.

On April 5th, 1814, the following stirring, patriotic, and belligerent editorial appeared in the columns of the Norfolk Herald, and tended to increase the anxiety and excitement, which were already great, among both citizens and soldiers:

"The long talked of expedition which the enemy has been preparing at Bermuda and elsewhere, to come against the *Southern* ports of the United States is now, we may reasonably suppose, on its way hither. Report says, that the armament composing this expedition consists of a large number of ships of the line and frigates; also gun-boats, bomb-ketches, rocket vessels, &c., with all the various engines of death and destruction; and a land force of five or six thousand marines and riflemen! In a few days, perhaps to-morrow, we may hear of their arrival in the Chesapeake, or in Hampton Roads, for Norfolk will certainly be the first point of attack. It would be mere idle boasting in us to say, that the enemy, with a force which he has taken ample time to prepare, and has, no doubt, adapted to the natural obstacles he will have to contend against, will come into our waters merely to threaten and alarm us, and return without attempting anything: such an idea would be absurd. They will assuredly make a desperate attempt to get possession of Norfolk and Portsmouth, but whether they will succeed is by no means so certain. Indeed, let every man, whether citizen or soldier, go resolutely to work, resolved to contend as long as life lasts, to repel the invader or die in the attempt, and it will be morally impossible for the town to be taken. The geographical situation of Norfolk is such that it cannot be taken with its present defences, without the enemy should meet with simultaneous success, from a simultaneous attack by land and water. For let them land and gain possession of the town, unless they have the harbour free for their shipping to come up, they cannot keep it, and to retreat, they would be cut to pieces. And where could they land their six thousand men for the attack, that a complement of two thousand would not cut them up before they reached the town? The nearest point at which they could land would be thirteen miles off, and their road (let them choose which they please), would be principally through almost impenetrable thickets of pine and myrtle, whose thick foliage would afford excellent ambuscades for our riflemen and light infantry. Besides this, we could throw such obstructions in the way of the enemy's march as would, with the co-operation of judicious ambuscades, throw them into disorder and render their capture or destruction inevitable. Upon the known courage and skill of our gallant tars, and the garrisons in the different forts, we may rely with confidence for the defence of the town in the event of an attack by water.

"Again we say, let every man who can carry a musket, or any other weapon that will destroy the enemy, fly to meet him *at the water's edge*, and dispute every inch of ground to the threshold of his own dwelling; and there protect his property and fireside while a drop of blood flows in his veins. Let us fulfil our duty to our *country*, and those dear dependents on our protection, *our wives and children*, and Heaven will smile upon and prosper our efforts. But if we basely fly, or avoid the struggle, contempt and infamy will pursue us to an ignominious grave. Who that feels the honest glow of national pride, but instinctively feels the blush of shame suffuse his cheek at the bare thought of an important and flourishing town, situated in the heart of our country, and at the threshold of the capitol, falling into the hands of an invader? Norfolk once taken by the enemy COULD be held until given up by *negotiation*, or an *act of grace*. But we have said enough. It were treason to doubt that the brave sons of Virginia would not defend their soil and justify the highest expectations of their country."

The following particulars are given by T. G. Broughton, Esq., of the Herald:

"In June, 1812, a new volunteer company was recruited from the line of the 54th, called the 'Independents.' It was officered by Captain Julian Magagnos, and Lieutenants George Lindsay and John Capron. There was no further call upon the 54th regiment, that the writer remembers, after the expiration of the first six months' tour, which was in August, 1813, until the following year, when, probably about the month of March, 1814, the army having been greatly reduced in number, by discharges on expiration of terms of service, our volunteers were again called into service, with the addition of the new corps of Independents, until new drafts could arrive from the upper country. They served a tour of three months."

* * * * * *

"The army at this station (one regiment of U. S. Infantry in the field, and one battalion of Artillery in the forts excepted) was composed of volunteers and drafted militia, from all parts of the State, and, towards the close of the war, from North Carolina. The 54th regiment, Norfolk Borough, was frequently called out, *en masse*, for brief periods, during the war; but the volunteers served for specified terms. The Juniors, Captain G. W. Camp; the Cavalry, Captain Thomas McCandlish, and the Light Artillery, Captain George Ott, volunteered their services at the commencement of the war, but were not mustered into the United States service till the February after, when the enemy having invaded our waters with his ships of war, for the first time, on the 3d of that month, the Governor of Virginia (the late James Barbour), issued his proclamation calling out a military force from the neighbouring and upper country, which continued to arrive by companies, until, towards the close of the month, there had assembled some three or four thousand men.

As fast as possible they were organized into regiments; and although the 54th regiment was exempted from the requisition, with a view to hold them in reserve, with good drilling, as minute men, the volunteer companies before named applied for, and obtained permission to join the regiment which was about being organized.

"In August, 1814, when the expedition under Admiral Cochrane went up the bay to attack Washington and Baltimore, a draft was made on the different militia regiments on the south side of James River, below tide water, for a reinforcement of one regiment. A company of one hundred men was drafted from the 54th regiment, as its quota towards the new regiment; which, when complete, was commanded by Colonel Bernard Magnien, of the 7th regiment, Norfolk County. But the news of the blow having been struck on Washington being received soon after, the whole of the volunteers and militia of Norfolk Borough, Norfolk County, and Princess Anne were called out, *en masse*, and remained in service until about the 23d of October, when the enemy's force having quit the Chesapeake, to prepare for the expedition against New Orleans, they were discharged. Those who served in Magnien's regiment were (as the writer believes) in service some two months and thirteen days; those subsequently called out in the 54th, *en masse*, served about two months. The Juniors, Cavalry, and Artillery, served three tours; the Independents two. The precise period for which the regiment performed service on sundry brief emergencies, have escaped the recollection of the writer."

The quick and decisive repulse at the Island, had taught the enemy a lesson not easily to be forgotten. The castigation, though very severe, they knew to be only a trifle, in comparison with what was to be expected from another and more general engagement; and the brave soldiers at this station had but little further trouble with the chagrined and numerous forces of the enemy.

CHAPTER XVI.

1813—1814.

General Taylor—Officers, &c., of the Army—Colonel Sharp—Major Camp—Lieutenant Ferguson—Captain Capron—Major Maurice, Colonel McConico, Captain Shields, &c.—Parade Grounds—Lieutenant Ball Assassinated—Arrest—Trial and Conviction of a Sentinel—Schooner Tartar Princess Anne Militia—British Squadron—General Parker—Midshipman Hall Killed.

GENERAL ROBERT B. TAYLOR, for some time the chief officer of the District, was an eminent orator and lawyer, as well as a distinguished commander. He was justly regarded as one of the most talented citizens of Norfolk, where he resided, and, in fact, of the State of Virginia, which was "proud to consider him one of her worthiest sons." His polished manners and rare attainments were highly appreciated by his fellow-citizens of the town and adjacent counties.* Having retired from the command of the army at this place, it was transferred to General Parker, on Friday, February 4th, 1814.

The following editorials and communications appeared in the Herald on the ensuing Tuesday:

"We cannot look back upon the term of General Taylor's continuance in office, without adding our mite to the applause, which he has so amply merited and universally received. Appointed to an arduous command, involving the most serious responsibility, at a period truly critical, and without the aid of experience to direct him, he has triumphed over every obstacle; and by his zeal, perseverance, and vigilance, acquired that capability in his new station, which, to a mind less active and intelligent, would have been a work of years. Conscious, however, that the worth and services of General Taylor do not require any eulogium of ours to illustrate them, or impress them more firmly and deeply in the minds of his fellow-citizens, we prefer presenting to our readers the subjoined correspondencies, which we have selected from among many others that have fallen into our hands. Such honourable testimonials of his patriotism and public worth,

* See further description of General T., in another part of this work.

will better illustrate the high estimation in which he was held by those whom he commanded, and their deep regret at his retirement from office:

"'Extract from Adjutant-General's Office.

"'NORFOLK, Feb. 6, 1814.

"'GENERAL ORDERS.

"'The Commanding General has been much pleased with the condition of Forts Nelson and Norfolk; and the Brigade of State Troops has surpassed his expectations in its acquirement of the knowledge of field exercises, and has, in the exercises of the 4th and 5th inst., done honour to itself, and the Brigadier General commanding it.

"'By command,
(Signed) "'JAMES BANKHEAD,
"'Adjutant General.'

"'The citizens of Norfolk and Portsmouth, desirous of offering to General Taylor, upon his retiring from the army, some evidence of the great respect they entertain for him—of the very high consideration in which they hold the patriotic zeal that induced him originally to accept his late important command at this place, and to add theirs to the general and ample testimony already furnished of the activity and skill he has at all times displayed, as well as of the just and proper regard he has continually paid to the civil rights of his fellow-citizens, during his whole period of service here, beg the favour of him to meet them at a public dinner, which they have caused to be prepared at Ducoing's Long Room, on Wednesday next, at three o'clock.

"'LITT. W. TAZEWELL,
MOSES MYERS,
RICHARD BLOW,
J. H. FAWN,
FRANCIS S. TAYLOR,
P. BARRAUD,
WALTER HERRON,
R. E. STEED,
W. T. NIVISON,
WM. CAMMACK,
"'Committee.

"'NORFOLK, Feb. 5, 1814.'

"'GENTLEMEN:—

"'Next to the approval of his own conscience, the most precious reward which a public officer can receive, is the confidence of his countrymen. Judge, then, how deeply my heart is penetrated by the testimony of approbation which the citizens of Norfolk and Portsmouth, the constant witnesses of all my military acts, have condescended to offer me. I dare not appropriate them to myself; it is rather the offspring of their generous regard for good intention than of actual merit. But in this very proportion that my services have been overrated by their generosity, will be my future gratitude to justify the partiality.

"'I accept the invitation,
"'And have the honour to be,
"'Very respectfully,
"'Your obedient servant,
(Signed) "'ROBERT B. TAYLOR.

"'To L. W. TAZEWELL, &c.
"'A Committee on behalf of the Citizens.'

"'CAVALRY QUARTERS, 6th Feb., 1814.

"'GENERAL TAYLOR:—

"'Sir,—Language cannot describe the feelings of the Officers of the Cavalry, in parting from you, as a commander in whose favour they feel so strongly prepossessed. Although their acquaintance is short, and however incapable they may be of judging, they feel an irresistible conviction, that you are eminently qualified to conduct an army to victory, and shed on the American arms that lustre which the freemen of Columbia are entitled to.

"'We feel confidently assured, notwithstanding you have retired from the army, you will not remain an idle spectator in the hour of invasion and danger, but will inspire all around you with confidence and courage. The die seems to be cast—we are compelled to part—may your worth and services be always duly appreciated; you carry with you our warmest feelings and most sincere wishes for your future welfare and happiness, whether in retirement, or in the service of your country.

" 'THOS. HUNTON,
" 'Major Commandant of Cavalry.

" 'WM. R. SMITH, Capt.
JOSEPH SANDFORD, Capt.
NICHOLAS OSBURN, Lt.
E. HUNTON, Adj.
MESHECK LAURY, 1st Lt.
JOSHUA OSBURN, 2d Lt.
JOHN BROWN, 2d Lt.
BENJ. MANABLE, 1st Lt.
SAML. WEAVER, Cornet.
DAVID LOVETT, Cornet.'

" 'NORFOLK, Jan. 7, 1814.

" 'GENTLEMEN :—

" 'Accept my gratitude—'tis the offering of a heart too much enamoured of a soldier's life, to be indifferent to a soldier's praise—your generosity has indeed greatly outstripped my deserts. * * * * * * * In every circumstance of my future life, it will be a precious satisfaction to me that you have deigned to mingle your regrets with those which I experience in retiring from the army.

" 'We separate.—My best wishes go with you. As soldiers, may your standard be always glorious and triumphant.—As citizens, may you be honoured and happy.

" 'I have the honour to be,
" 'Very respectfully,
" 'Your most obedient servant,
" 'ROBERT B. TAYLOR.

" 'To MAJOR HUNTON, Commandant,
" 'The Officers of the Cavalry,
" 'In the U. S. service at Norfolk.' "

Among the officers and private soldiers assembled and in service at Norfolk during the last war with England, there were, in addition to those mentioned, many men who were ornaments to society, and whose great worth of character reflected honour and dignity upon the stations which they were called to fill.

The 9th Regiment was commanded by Colonel Wm. Sharp, "who," said an officer that served under him during the campaign, at Norfolk, "was a gentleman, a patriot, and a chivalrous officer. He was tall; as straight as the barrel of a rifle; and *sharp*, indeed, was the look from his dark eye. I loved him truly, as did the whole of our regiment. He was careful of the health of his troops, and vigilant in all things becoming a good officer and soldier." Colonel S. was highly complimented by Wade Hampton, a distinguished general officer, and the movements of his regiment spoken of in terms of great commendation.*

Major George W. Camp, who acted as brigade inspector, was greatly esteemed by citizens and soldiers as an efficient officer and accomplished gentleman. The rigid and impartial, yet mild, manner in which he required a compliance with the rules, commanded the most profound respect of the soldiery; while his intelligence, polite attentions, and great urbanity of manners, endeared him to his numerous friends and acquaintances, with the strongest ties of affectionate regard.†

Lieutenant Peter Ferguson (now of St. Louis, Missouri), who performed the important duties of adjutant, was a very active and excellent officer. Said a cotemporary, "he could get a regiment ready for the commandant sooner than any man I have ever seen attempt it."‡

* Colonel S. was the father of Wm. W. Sharp, Esq., of this city, well and extensively known as a lawyer of much experience and ability. As a talented and successful forensic pleader, he ranks deservedly high among the members of his profession, and the inhabitants of Norfolk and vicinity. Mr. S. has been for a number of years, the efficient president of the board of directors of the Exchange Bank; having been first elected to fill the vacancy occasioned by the death of Swepson Whitehead, Esq., who was also a lawyer of considerable distinction, as well as a gentleman of great worth of character.

† Father of George W. Camp, Esq., of this city, formerly attorney at law, whose legal knowledge is extensive, and which he communicates with a clearness and readiness, indicative of a strong, well-balanced, and highly cultivated mind.

‡ Brother of F. F. Ferguson, Esq., of this city, assessor and commissioner of revenue.

Captain John Capron also acted as adjutant after Lieutenant Ferguson. "He was prompt in his arrangements, and as quick as a flash."

Among the officers, were Colonel Manning, Colonel A. J. M'Conico, Majors Maurice and Richie, Captain Hamilton Shields* (whose activity, efficiency, and usefulness in directing and supervising the several public works of defence, and whose intelligence and gentlemanly bearing as an officer, rendered him justly conspicuous in the army, and gained for him many friends, and the esteem of the citizens of the borough generally); Captain Taylor, of the Richmond Riflemen; Captain Arthur Cooper,† of the cavalry; Alexander Taylor, of the Petersburg Blues; Courtney, of King and Queen; Magagnoes, of the Norfolk Independents; Marshall, of the Riflemen, from Powhatan; M'Candlish, Jarvis, George Ott, Thomson, Foster, and Graves; Dixon and Smith, Washington County; Poindexter, from Louisa; Woodson, from Prince Edward; Sale, from Amherst; M'Mullion and Dickson, from Rockbridge; Baily, from Shenandoah; Richardson and Cromer, from Frederick; Rowland from Botetourt, Gregory, from Berkeley; Davenport, from Jefferson; Cackley, from Bath; Sergeants Buchanan and Jennings; Lieutenants Newton, King, Powell, &c.

There were also, Colonels Chilton, M'Donald, Coleman, and Parker; Majors Washington, and Hunter; Captains Baker, Quarles, Nimmo, Clark, Gilbert; Adjutants Vincent and Ball; Lieutenants Campbell, Rogers, &c.‡

The first place selected for a parade-ground and encampment was on Briggs' Point, comprising the space bounded by Plume's Cove on the north, Newton's Creek on the east, Marion Street on the south, and Fenchurch on the west. This piece of land was then a spacious and beautiful green. Here the tents were

* Subsequently founder and editor of the American Beacon.

† For nearly twenty years city inspector.

‡ In these statements, the reader may find that the names of individuals are omitted who acted a prominent part in the military affairs of this period. If the name of any officer, however, who was justly distinguished is not included, the omission may be regarded as purely accidental.

erected; and the busy, bustling, and noisy, though monotonous scenes of the camp, were experienced and exhibited for several months. There was another parade-ground in a field near the old Presbyterian Church, corner of Charlotte and Catharine Streets, and there was one on the north of the lot now embraced in the Cedar Grove Cemetery. It included the present Alms-House grounds. The second regiment encamped and paraded on a lot near Armistead's Bridge, and opposite a rope-walk and tannery, then in operation on the west side of the road leading to the bridge.*

During the exciting times, when the soldiery were congregated at this place and vicinity, many interesting events transpired,—quite enough to fill a large volume. But we must pass on without attempting to present them to the reader. There was one circumstance, however, which claims a passing notice.

Adjutant BALL, of the 4th Regiment, and attached to a Rifle Company from Winchester, Frederick County, was a young gentleman of great respectability, and extraordinary promise. He was highly distinguished for his genius, which had been cultivated by an excellent education. He manifested such remarkable talents as an artist, especially in the line of engraving, etching, &c., that he had already attracted the attention of men of long-established reputation in these important and useful departments of artistic skill.

He was on his way with orders from Fort Nelson to Norfolk, in May, 1813, and when about passing the post of one of the sentinels, he was accosted, and accordingly answered as usual. The sentinel, not being satisfied, apparently, with his answer, called him, and he started towards him; whereupon the sentinel fired; and the ball passing through a vital part, he fell,—a victim to an unaccountable intent to murder him thus voluntarily and barbarously. The excitement was tremendous; for he was a favourite with all who knew him; his attainments and gentlemanly deportment had rendered him conspicuously known in the community. The law, however, after some difficulty, was allowed

* An account of the sickness among the troops will be found in another part of the work.

to have its course with the guilty, murderous man. An immense concourse of persons attended the funeral, and there was every manifestation of sorrow and sympathy for the deceased, whose remains were buried in the cemetery at Portsmouth, where a suitable monument was erected to his memory by his fellow-soldiers.

The assassin was tried, and found guilty of murder; but the lawyers obtained a new trial for him, and he escaped with his life to the penitentiary, where he remained for a long term, suffering a punishment which only partially atoned for the dreadful crime he had committed. The death of Adjutant Ball was not only considered a loss to the army, and to his native town, but to the State and the country, to which, it was thought by those who knew him, that his mental ability promised highly important services.

On the night of the 20th of December, 1813, the privateer schooner Tartar grounded on Cape Henry, and bilged. The weather being severely cold, and the wind high, the sufferings of the crew were exceedingly severe. Six of the men froze to death, and many others were frost-bitten.

Towards the close of the following day, the British, after considerable trouble, succeeded in burning the vessel, together with her cargo, consisting of nearly a thousand barrels of flour. A small company of Princess Anne Militiamen kept them off for some time with muskets, although the enemy returned a constant and heavy fire of cannon at the shore. The British squadron at that time occupied Lynnhaven Bay.

1814. "Brigadier General Parker, lately appointed to the command of the army at this place," said a judicious writer of this period, "has resigned, in consequence, we understand, of the promotion over him of younger officers. This step must add to the good opinion already so universally entertained of General Parker; for what officer, who could claim distinction in his profession, would continue to serve under circumstances so degrading and palpably unjust? General Parker, as an old, experienced, and meritorious officer, of courage and talents highly approved, wanted not the splendour of an accidental achievement to light him on to promotion; and if *favouritism* has conferred that on another which belongs exclusively to him, he had no honourable alternative but to resign. There is no one, we believe, who is any way interested in the safety of this place, but must regret the circumstance of General Parker's resignation, though every candid and honourable mind must accord in the sentiment, that he could not do otherwise, consistently with the dictates of honour. Until a new appointment takes place, the command will devolve upon Lientenant-Colonel Freeman."

March 9th. The following melancholy accident occurred on board the Constellation: Midshipman Hall, being in the mizzen-top for the purpose of seeing the top-gallant yards sent down, accidentally fell from thence upon the deck (a distance of a hundred feet), and alighting on his head, was instantly killed.

CHAPTER XVII.

1814—1815.

Market-house, &c., Destroyed by Fire—Carelessness—Inefficiency of Means in Extinguishing Fires—Want of System, Energy, and Engines—Prices Current —Dr. Slaughter's Will—Legacies—Colonel Nivison—Philip R. Thomson, Esq. —His Honourable and Generous Conduct—The Slaughter Fund—American Beacon—Its Founders and Editors—Destruction of the Office by Fire—Contest for the Re-issue, &c.

MARCH 25. A fire broke out in the market-house, which, with fourteen tenements on the square, was consumed. The fire was communicated by accident, in an apartment in the market-house occupied by the watchmen of the town.

The means of extinguishing fires at that time certainly exhibit a very striking contrast to the large and efficient companies, splendid engines, and orderly arrangements, of our fire department, for stopping the progress of the devouring element at the present day. The following account of the fire appeared at the time:—

"It seems almost incredible that a fire should break out in a market-house. Such an event we believe never occurred before; and, in the present instance, can alone be ascribed to the unhappy circumstance of having an apartment in it for the accommodation of the watchmen, through whose cruel neglect the dreadful calamity has been brought upon our town.* It appears that some of the watchmen, previous to retiring from the watch-room, took the ashes out of the stove, and deposited them in a barrel; and, some live embers being among the ashes, they set fire to the barrel, which communicated to the casings of the room. How many accidents of this kind have been produced by this dangerous practice! and still we see there is nothing more common.

* * * * * * *

"It has often been our painful duty to notice the want of means and method at all the fires that happen in our town; but, on this occasion, there appeared to be an uncommon degree of apathy in the crowd, who had assembled rather, it would seem, to gaze at the sight than to render service. But if every one present had shown the best disposition to exert himself, his good intentions would have been unavailing, for the want of means as well as system and regularity. There was no one to direct, and no one to command. The fire-wardens were not recognised, in the general bustle, as possessing any authority, and if they gave orders or directions, they were utterly disregarded. There was one small engine, out of order, and that was private property; about a dozen buckets, and not a single axe or fire hook. Such, in spite of all remonstrance, continues to be the state of things whenever we have a fire; and will still continue, we suppose, until the town is fairly burnt down piecemeal."

The Norfolk Bible Society was organized this year.

October 28. "PRICES, NORFOLK MARKET.—Pork, $10 per cwt.; beef, $10 per cwt.; mutton, 12½ cents per pound; veal, 12½ cents per pound; butter, 62½ cents per pound; salt (home-made), $4 50 per bushel."

* The present watch-house is in the south end of the market-house.

November 23. This is the date of the will of Dr. Augustine Slaughter, who died shortly thereafter. He was a citizen of Norfolk, and a physician of distinction. There are facts connected with the bequest of property in this instance, with regard to the testator, the legacies, and some of the heirs, that are well worthy of a record upon these pages. Dr. S., after having provided for the emancipation and support of his slaves, and making other provisions in his will, appropriated the interest of $3,000 as a perpetual fund for the education of several poor boys in reading, writing, navigation, &c.; said boys to be properly equipped, and bound to the commander of a vessel of war, or some discreet master of a merchant vessel; and their places at school, as soon as vacant, to be filled by others from time to time. This the Doctor intended as his "mite towards fostering our infant navy." The fund was faithfully applied according to his will and desire.

Among several other bequests, he bequeathed to Colonel John Nivison $1,000, as a "small mark of his gratitude for a service he did him, when he was first struck with the palsy, although his ample fortune luckily placed him far above regarding such trifles."

Philip Roots Thomson, Esq., of Culpeper County, was one of the heirs; and to whom he also gave a considerable sum. A few years ago, this gentleman, being in our city, called at the office of an eminent legal gentleman; and, alluding to the particulars of Dr. Slaughter's will, inquired if there was not a technical defect, which entirely annulled the bequest for the education of the poor boys, and which gave *him* a legal title to the sum of $3,000, set aside for that purpose. He was answered in the *affirmative;* and the lawyer, of course, supposed that his object was to secure the money, and thus, sadly and effectually, to frustrate the laudable and benevolent design of his deceased relative. But, instead of this, the attorney was soon surprised to find that such was not his intention, and he had the pleasure of witnessing an instance of generosity, which, though no more than right, is rarely to be met with. He was requested to draw up an instrument, confirming and establishing the devise beyond cavil; thus securing from future difficulty, the execution of the original and benevolent design of the legator, as evinced in his last will and testament. The instrument of writing was, of course, prepared promptly and faithfully, and duly signed, sealed, delivered, and recorded.

But this is not all of that gratifying specimen of strict integrity and honourable regard for the desires of the dead, as well as the rights of the living. He asked his counsel to state the amount of his fee, and was told in reply that, under such circumstances, there was no charge, and more especially as only a few lines were required to accomplish the object desired; whereupon his client threw down several pieces of gold upon his table, which, notwithstanding the repeated refusals of the lawyer to receive it, he would not take back. Having thus consummated his business, he left the office.

Now, this is a case of true and genuine honesty and whole-souled liberality, which it is really refreshing to contemplate in these days of covetousness, when the great and never-ceasing struggle is for mammon, and "the selfishness of the purse" is one of the prevailing sins of the age. There is no incident which we have felt more pleasure in placing upon these pages; and we have chosen to write Mr. Thomson's name in full, that it may be fairly and fully exhibited in connexion with his praiseworthy act, in these local chronicles of the events of the past and the present, as an example worthy of imitation, and which will reflect honour upon him; although, as to the confirmation of the legacy, it was no more than he should have done under the circumstances. But, how many there are whose inordinate love of money, and utter disregard for anything more than strict *legal right*, would have induced them to grasp with unholy eagerness and haste, as a precious treasure, the generous man's dying gift, and the poor boys' fund!

The "Slaughter Fund," as it is called, is still regularly and judiciously applied, according to the will of the generous individual whose name it appropriately bears. There are now among the students of the Norfolk Academy *ten* boys, who are receiving a gratuitous education; and this fund constitutes a large portion of the sum required to entitle them to so inestimable a privilege; and which is rendered more valuable by the fact that we have yet no free schools of a high grade. Let the fund be increased by the bounty of others, who have "enough, and to spare."

April 7th, 1815. At this date, the American Beacon commenced its useful career, under the auspices of Captain Hamilton Shields and Samuel Shepherd, Esq. At the expiration of about twelve months, Mr. Shepherd retired, and William C. Shields, Esq., formerly editor of the Daily Courier, and Mr. Charlton, were associated with the accomplished gentleman first named. In 1834, H. B. Grigsby, Esq., purchased the entire interest, and after occupying the editorial chair with decided ability and success for several years, he disposed of the paper to Messrs. Wm. E. Cunningham,* H. B. Bagnal, and T. F. Boothby. In November, 1847, the office and materials were destroyed by fire; whereupon, the partnership was dissolved, and the two junior members of the firm, Messrs. Boothby and Bagnal, determined to re-issue the paper with the least possible delay. Having engaged a gentleman well known as a talented writer to fill the editorial chair, Mr. Boothby proceeded to Baltimore, where he intended to have the first and several succeeding numbers printed, and sent down daily by the steamer, whence they were to be taken by carriers and delivered to subscribers. But the senior editor of the old firm (Mr. C.) was also anxious to resume the publication of the Beacon; and soon hearing of the intention and diligent efforts of the other party, he was exceedingly desirous that his paper should have the benefit of the *first appearance;* which object he accomplished by availing himself of the facilities afforded by the Advocate† Office, which were offered by the editor of that paper. The Beacon, printed in Norfolk, made its appearance again, one day in advance of the paper of the same name, issued in Norfolk, but printed, as before stated, in another city, to insure the earliest *debut.* Mr. Cunningham having gained the advantage intimated above, his paper was soon re-established, and as extensively circulated and patronised as ever; while the other party relinquished their undertaking, and disposed of their interest to Mr. C., who shortly after associated

* Formerly member of the Legislature from Norfolk Borough.

† Published weekly in 1847–8. See another page.

with himself Richard Gatewood, Jun., Esq. On February 9th, 1852, the Weekly Beacon was issued from the same office. The Beacon was neutral in politics till November, 1851, when Mr. C. announced himself as sole editor, and stated that Whig men and measures would thereafter be supported. This paper is deservedly popular, especially on account of the variety of political, commercial, naval, military, local, and general, information which it usually contains.

CHAPTER XVIII.

1816—1819.

Female Orphan Asylum—Its Founder and Conductors—Its Utility—Buildings—Male Orphan Asylum Wanted—Manual Labour School—Neglected Childhood—First Sabbath School in Norfolk—Union School—Separation—The Sabbath School Cause—Miss M. Tucker—Council—Marine Society—Ward and General Ticket System Compared—Improvements—Stone Bridge—Tobacco Warehouse—Mayor Holt—Lancasterian School—Tobacco Inspection—Norfolk Provident Society—Its Object, Utility, &c.—Act of Assembly—Custom House Lot—The Trip to Baltimore—The Bay Line—Steamer North Carolina—Wonder Booker—Longevity.

January 16th, 1816. Act of Assembly passed, incorporating the *Female Orphan Asylum.*

This association was first known, it seems, as the "Female Charitable Society," and its most commendable object was, "the support and education of orphan girls." It appears that as early as 1807 there was "an Orphan House for female children, on Amelia Street." But we have learned from a reliable source, that the first regular meeting of the present association, was held in a framed building that formerly stood at the northwest corner of Granby and Freemason Streets, and which was owned and occupied, for many years, by the late Francis Butt, Sr.

The society was formed and organized at the instance of the venerable and excellent Bishop Asbury, who may, therefore, be justly considered as its founder. It has long been conducted, and very properly too, by ladies connected with the several Protestant churches, and whose constant and attentive efforts have been instrumental in dispensing many a blessing to the homeless and friendless female orphan. "There is one want," says a certain author, "that none can supply—there is one chord in the heart that answers only to the touch of one hand—there is one magic spell that hangs around the heart in all after life, that none, perhaps, can know and understand, whose lips have been unused to say, *mother*. One of the noblest charities of the human heart is that which provides an asylum for the little ones bereaved." May the smiles of Heaven ever rest upon an institution so necessary, in every large town especially, and whose merciful and beneficial tendency and influence are so strikingly manifest!

The contributions to the society enabled the managers to build a handsome house on Holt Street; which, however, on account of its insecure foundation, gave place, in 1847, to a more suitable and substantial building; and the establishment is still in a prosperous condition.

The propriety of establishing in Norfolk a house for *male* orphans has been frequently urged; and it is sincerely hoped that some enterprising and benevolent individuals will, ere long, take the matter in hand, and give the citizens an opportunity of contributing to the support of such an institution. The indigent orphan *boys* certainly have a strong claim upon the people; and the good that might be accomplished, and the evil prevented by the establishment and proper management of an asylum of this kind, would amply repay all the labour, trouble, and expense, that might be incurred in placing it upon a firm basis, giving it a fair start, and continuing it in its career of usefulness.

These remarks are not made without some knowledge of the number and condition of those who would be the legitimate beneficiaries of such an asylum.

"Some such institution," says a judicious writer, "as a manual labour school for indigent boys—to support, educate, and prepare them for a trade, and make them useful members of society—is sadly needed in our community, and presents strong claims to the attention and action of our philanthropic citizens.

The 'Female Orphan Asylum,' under the auspices of the ladies, has been eminently successful, and the means of rescuing hundreds from starvation, misery, and wretchedness. Let a small farm be obtained in the vicinity of the city, and in a short time it would be supported and maintained from the labour of the inmates of the establishment. A number of subjects are daily running wild through our streets, exempt from all control or protection, engaging in every kind of mischief and vice, and treading that path which must inevitably lead them to crime and infamy. Humanity, as well as a wise policy, demand that they should be removed from their abodes of wretchedness, and placed in a situation where they might be fitted for a career of usefulness and honour. Feed, clothe, and educate them—teach them some useful trade, and instil into their minds the excellence of truth and the beauty of holiness. He, who by his labour causes a blade of grass to grow where it has never grown before, is looked upon as a benefactor of his race; how much more then, should that man be appreciated, who, by deeds of charity, saves an intelligent soul from misery in this life, and perdition in that which is to come."

"There is not a plea on earth," says an observant Christian writer, "so piteous and touching as that cry of neglected childhood—saying, 'Take care of us—watch over us—keep and guard us from the evils that *we* know not of, but that *ye* know—save us from the dark and sorrowful years—teach us betimes what is good—teach us obedience, teach us truth and wisdom, lead us in the way in which we should go.' Oh! the hopes of coming years—shall they all be crushed down in the mire of city vice and vileness? While all other youth is bright and fair, shall *this*, the youth of man alone—be marred and ruined? This poor, crushed childhood—shall it experience a lifetime of misery, ere it blossoms into life?"

> "The young lambs are sporting on the meadows,
> The young birds are chirping in the nest;
> The young fawns are playing with the shadows,
> The young flowers are blowing towards the west.

"But the young, *young children*, O my brothers!
They are weeping bitterly;
They are weeping in the playtime of the others,
In the country of the free."

The first Sabbath School in this place was formed in the spring of this year, by the laudable exertions of a few ladies, belonging to the several Protestant Churches* (the Episcopalian, Presbyterian, Baptist, and Methodist). During the year, three schools were organized, and the union thus agreed to "did not interfere with the regulations or direction of any school connected with it, but was only intended to concentrate the efforts of the friends of the good work, and to provide means to enable them to carry the design into fuller effect."

The report of the Union Schools, in giving an account of their condition, says:

"Two of our teachers have professed religion since they joined, and eight of the scholars. We feel assured that the influence of the schools has been of incalculable advantage both to the children and their parents. Many have been led to the house of God, who have never been there before. We have seen the good effects of our instructions, particularly in the life and death of one pupil. In her last moments, she blessed the Sabbath School as the means of bringing her to a knowledge of salvation, and felt that she could 'read her title clear' to glory."

It was not long after this period that the "Union" was dissolved by mutual consent, and the different denominations established and conducted separate schools, under the management of officers and teachers connected with their respective churches. The cause continued to prosper under the fostering care of those upon whom the management devolved, and it now presents an interesting field of labour for the Christian philanthropist. Hundreds and thousands of the rising race and hope of the coun-

* "It is stated in An Historical Sketch of Sunday Schools in the United States, published by the American Sunday School Union, that 'The first permanent Sunday School organization of which we have any authentic record, was *The First Day or Sunday School Society*. It was established in Philadelphia, January 11, 1791.' A Sabbath School was taught in the house of Thomas Crenshaw, of Hanover County, Va., in the year 1786; and, in the following year, the Rev. John Charleston was converted in that school."

try, are weekly gathered together, for the noble purpose of receiving instruction in those sacred truths, which alone tend to true greatness in this world, and a blessed immortality in the regions of bliss above. No pen can portray, no mind conceive, the benefits resulting to the human race from the benign influence of Sunday Schools.

The Sabbath School cause in this city, in its incipiency, gradual progress, and ultimate usefulness, may be justly considered as being indebted, in a great measure, to the diligent, prayerful, and well-directed efforts of Miss Margaret Tucker, a lady of much intelligence, and of devoted piety, who, with other excellent Christian ladies of Norfolk, in days that have passed, "went about doing good." Indeed, her zealous and self-sacrificing devotion, sound judgment, and generosity, were manifested in her exertions to advance the interests of several other benevolent enterprises; among which we may mention, the Dorcas Society, and the Female Orphan Society. She was emphatically a friend to the widow and the orphan, the poor and the needy, the suffering and the sorrowful; was highly gifted in prayer and exhortation; possessed very considerable knowledge of human nature, and was respected and beloved for her consistent piety and usefulness by all classes of the community. Her works of love are done; her useful career is ended. She has entered the rest above, and enjoys the reward of the faithful.*

On the 27th of January, 1816, an act was passed changing the mode of electing the Council, and adding one to the number. On the 24th of June of every year "seventeen fit and able men, being freeholders," were, under this act, to be elected by ballot or general ticket. From this it would seem that the change consisted in the election by general ticket, as that mode is here for the first time prescribed.

February 7th, 1817. Act of Assembly passed, incorporating the Norfolk Marine Society.

About this time some alterations were made in the government of the town, and a very commendable spirit of improvement ap-

* "And I heard a voice from Heaven, saying unto me, Write, Blessed are the dead which die in the Lord from henceforth: Yea, saith the Spirit, that they may rest from their labours; and their works do follow them."—Rev. xiv. 13.

peared to be abroad in the community. The following extract from one of the city papers, of a recent date, will prove interesting to the reader:

"Until the year 1817, the 'Borough' was divided into eight wards, each electing within its own bounds two Common Councilmen. But about that time it was believed by everybody that it would be a decided improvement to adopt the general ticket system. Experience has shown that some of the wards must often send members to the Council who had no weight or influence, or go unrepresented,—and finally that important branch of the Corporation had begun to be looked upon as little better than the fifth wheel of a coach. It had but little power then, and that little seems to have been exerted very sparingly for the improvement of the town. After the peace of 1815, the citizens began to feel a lively interest in the subject of improvement, and the first step towards action was to change the ward for the general ticket system in the election of Common Councilmen. The first Council, under this new state of things, was remarkable for the number of men of talents and influence who composed it; and they soon commenced the work of improvement by ordering the construction of a stone bridge in Granby Street; the erection of a tobacco warehouse on Town Point; the purchase of a lot ($7,000) adjoining the Court House lot, on which to erect a depôt for the produce of the Roanoke, at a future day; the digging of a mammoth well in the centre of Main Street, and fixing a pair of pumps in it, &c. And besides all this, they effected some salutary changes in the general police of the borough. Indeed, to this day the city is indebted to the first Councils elected under the general ticket system, assisted by that intelligent and indefatigable officer, Mayor Holt, for most of the ordinances by which it is now governed."

In 1852, the ward system was again adopted; the city having been divided into only four wards.

January 22, 1818. Act of Assembly passed, incorporating the Trustees of the Lancasterian School.

January 31st. An act for establishing inspection and storage of tobacco in Norfolk was passed this day.

May 15th. Ordinance passed in Council authorizing a loan

for the erection of a stone bridge over Back Creek, at Granby Street.

1819. Norfolk Provident Society organized. This Association was incorporated by Act of Assembly, passed January 27, 1820. It has proved to be cne of the most useful institutions ever established in the town. After a trial of more than thirty years, during which time its beneficial tendency has been felt in very many instances by the widow and the orphan, it is believed to be in a safe and prosperous condition.

The following brief history of the association, furnished by one of its oldest members, will no doubt be interesting to all who are anxious to make a *post obit* provision for their families, beyond the reach of the ordinary vicissitudes of life:

"In the year 1819, the idea of a society for the purpose of providing a fund for the benefit of the families of the deceased members thereof, was suggested by an individual, on a plan proposed by him. On this suggestion a subscription paper was circulated, which was subscribed to by twenty-two members, who met together in the month of April of that year, formed a Constitution and By-laws for its future government, and obtained a Charter from the Legislature.

"By the terms of their Constitution each member is required to pay $10 at the time of subscribing, under prescribed rules, and to contribute monthly thereafter the sum of *one* dollar at regular stated meetings; for which payments *their families only* should be entitled to receive at their death, after one year's membership, and within three years of their admission, twice the amount of their regular payments; and at any time a member might die after three years' membership, three times the amount so paid in. If the death of a member should occur within the term of one year, the amount paid by him to be forfeited to the Society; but under no circumstances can any member withdraw his contributions, and on a failure of twelve months payment, he ceases to be a member, and all his previous payments are forfeited to the Society.

"It will thus be seen that twenty-two individuals associated and established this society, with a capital of $220 in the month of April, 1819,—now nearly thirty-four years, and it appears by the records that in this time it has contributed to the relief of the families of seventy-five of its deceased members the sum of $31,168 75, and by an accumulation of its members, with semi-annual interest on its investments, it now has a fund of $30,300 invested in 6 per cent. State and City Stocks, together with a balance exceeding $300 to its credit in bank.

"The benefits of such an association must be obvious in a community where the relief it has afforded to many distressed families, in time of their utmost need, is notorious, and this, too, so far differing from ordinary societies for such purposes, as to authorize a legal demand, in lieu of a dependence for a charitable donation."

The following is a summary of the principal Acts of Assembly relating to Norfolk in its early history, and prior to this period:

1680. Act concerning settlements, &c.
1705. Titles to lands, establishment of the town, &c.
1736. Charter and its confirmation.
1752. Charter explained, and privileges enlarged.
1757. Power enlarged, ferries, &c.
1762. Privileges, and limits.
1763. Taxes, watch, and lamps.
1764. Vestry, ministers, &c., E. River Parish.
1766. Trustees, limits, &c.
1769. Confirmation of "An agreement made by Thomas Talbutt."
1772. Taxes.
1783. Powers enlarged.
1787. Charter amended.
1788. Rights, courts, &c.
1789. Seat of Justice removed.
1790. Privileges.
1796. Lotteries.
1798. Provision for the poor.
1801. Docks and wharves.
1802. Charter amended.
1802. Donation of Mr. Godfrey to the poor of Norfolk County.
1803. Charter.
1804. Extension of Church Street.

1804. Norfolk Academy.
1806. Militia.
1806. Flood-gates across Back Creek.
1806. Surveyor.
1806. Hustings Court.
1807. Paving of streets.
1807. Northern boundary.
1808. Hustings Court.
1809. Jurisdiction of County and Corporation Courts.
1810. Ferry to Hampton.
1811. Lamps.
1811. Port Wardens.
1811. Mechanics' Benevolent Society.
1811. Concord Street.
1812. Pilots.
1812. Extension of Bermuda Street.
1813. Removal of obstructions in Bute Street.
1816. Suppression of Small-pox.
1816. Incorporation of Library Company.
1816. Female Orphan Society.
1816. Salary to Mayor.
1816. Election of Councilmen.
1816. Extension of Granby Street.
1816. Commissioner of Revenue.
1817. Extension of Catharine Street.
1817. Norfolk Marine Society.

February 1, 1819. Act of Assembly passed, authorizing the Governor to cede to the United States the jurisdiction over a certain lot of land, in the borough of Norfolk, for the purpose of building a custom-house thereon. The act required a custom-house to be erected on this lot, within the space of five years after the session at which the act was passed; and that "if, at any time thereafter, the said custom-house and public stores shall be suffered to fall into decay, or be rendered useless as to the purposes aforesaid, and so continued for the space of five years, then, and in those cases, the jurisdiction over such territory shall revert to the Commonwealth."*

* At a very early period in the commercial history of this section, applica-

At this period, the trip by steamboat, from this place to Baltimore, was performed in about twenty-four hours; and this was considered a very short time for so long a distance. The steamers that run hence to New York by sea, require less than this length of time to perform the trip; and one of the boats on the Bay Line, now runs the distance, from this city to Baltimore, in a little over eleven hours.

We may remark here, that this line is so well and ably conducted, that accidents seldom or never happen. The boats are very superior, kept in the finest order, and are in charge of officers of long experience, and well-tried skill and judgment. The North Carolina, a very large and splendid new boat, has recently been placed upon this line; and, under the able management of Captain Russell, presents unusual attractions to the traveller, who desires to go north by the pleasant and delightful bay route.

Died, this year, in Princess Anne County, Wonder Booker, a coloured man, aged 126 years. He was remarkable for the strength of his physical constitution, and worked in his master's garden at the age of nearly 120 years. When he was born, his mother was nearly *threescore!* It is stated, as an undeniable fact, that she had arrived at the good old age of 58 years, when she gave birth to a son who was so remarkable for his longevity and vigour of body. She gave him a very appropriate name; and we have thought fit to *book* the *wonder.*

The writer has also been informed of other extraordinary cases of longevity in Princess Anne. The age of one old lady, at her death, was just 99 years, 11 months, and 30 days, requiring only one day to complete her hundredth year. She left a female servant, who is said to have attained the age of 120 years.

tion was made for a custom-house by both Norfolk and Portsmouth, as considerable business was done on both sides of the river. Norfolk was finally selected as the location. The custom-house was long situated on Town Point, prior to the erection of the present building on Wide Water Street.

CHAPTER XIX.

1820—1821.

Navigation Act—Trade of the West Indies—Commercial Distress—United States Bank—Colonization Society—Brutal Murder of Lagaudette—Startling Discovery—Arrest, Trial, Conviction, and Execution of the Murderers—Exciting Scene at the Gallows—Bungling Work—The Murderers and their Victim—Thieves—Highway Robbery—Awful Thunder Storm—A Gloomy Year—Sickness—Terrific Hurricane—The Great September Gale—High Tide—Effects of the Storm—Booth—Day of Humiliation and Prayer—Public Meeting—Navigation Law—Trade of the West Indies Declining.

MAY 15, 1820. On this day the *Navigation Law* was passed; which restricted vessels from bringing the produce of the British colonies to our ports; and from taking in return that of the States. The effects of this law were of course injurious to the commerce of Norfolk. Notwithstanding which, the exportations to the West Indies alone, amounted to $118,000, and the importations in sugar, molasses, fruit, rum, &c., were considerable; but the succeeding year the amount was much less. Norfolk was about the only port at that time on our coast, at which assorted cargoes of produce could be conveniently obtained. Tobacco, grain, flour, meal, lard, fish, and many other articles, required by the West Indies trade, were furnished here at fair prices.

For many years previous to this, Norfolk showed manifest signs of advancement in appearance and in commerce; but a sad reverse in the commercial affairs of the place occurred about this time. Some of the principal merchants were compelled to suspend payment, others failed for large amounts, while some of the small traders were reduced to poverty. There was very considerable interruption to the West Indies trade, and the general business of the place suffered greatly. One cause of the embarrassment and pressure was the liberal accommodations that had been afforded by the branch of the United States bank, which had been established here; very large sums were borrowed, and a heavy business was done. But suddenly and unexpectedly, a reaction was experienced, and the consequences were ruinous, especially to the mercantile portion of the community.

December 26. Colonization Society of Norfolk organized.

March 20, 1821. On this day there was perpetrated in the borough, one of the most inhuman and diabolical murders ever placed upon the dark catalogue of crime. A small and unsightly frame building,* on —— street, was occupied by three men, two of whom were Spaniards, named Castilano and Garcia, and the other, a Frenchman, whose name was Peter Lagaudette. Their appearance was rather strange, and calculated to excite suspicion; although it seems they had attracted no special notice prior to this occasion.

It was said, that a lass who was passing the house on her way to school, hearing loud screams, succeeded in getting a view of the interior through a back window, just in time to witness the bloody affair; and her statement was in substance, that one of the Spaniards, with the violence and desperation of a fiend incarnate, was levelling powerful and deadly blows at the Frenchman, who imploringly begged for mercy, and tried in vain to escape from the murderous hand of the bloodthirsty Spaniard; that he ran up the stairs, shrieking for help, but the

> "Staunch murderer, steady to his purpose,
> Pursued him close."

And that both coming quickly down again, the wretch dealt his victim another dreadful deathblow with an axe, and accomplished his fiendish purpose! Be this as it may, before the house was entered, Castilano and Garcia had both made their escape, and fled beyond the limits of the town. With extraordinary haste and precision, the body of the murdered man was dissected at the neck, shoulders, and knees, and, excepting the head, deposited in a trunk and secreted in the house. The head was not found, and is supposed to have been burned; which supposition was strengthened by a most unpleasant smell about the time at which the murder was committed. They intended, it was said, to preserve the mutilated remains by salting them, and then re-

* The house is still standing (1853).

move them. The excitement and indignation of the citizens on account of the shocking disclosures were very great.

Proper efforts were made as early as possible to apprehend and bring to justice the murderers; and they were arrested at Lambert's Point, about five miles from the city, on the second day after the discovery of the remains, and imprisoned in the county jail at Portsmouth. After an examination, they were duly remanded for trial, at which they were found guilty of "murder in the first degree." They were sentenced by Judge Parker to be hung, and were executed on Friday June 1st.

Castilano, the elder of the two, who was a physician, and who doubtless had

> "O'er the subject hung,
> And impolitely hewed his way through bones
> And muscles of the sacred human form;
> Exposing barbarously to wanton gaze
> The mysteries of nature,"

was sullen and indifferent on the dreadful occasion, and appeared quite undaunted to the last. But Garcia, who was quite a young man, energetically protested against the proceedings, and earnestly declared that he was innocent of the crime for which he was to suffer.

An immense concourse of people from Norfolk, Portsmouth, and the neighbouring counties, witnessed the executions; and the scene at the gallows was painful and exciting in a high degree. Captain Emmerson, the sheriff, one of the noble heroes of Craney Island, and who quailed not at the approach of a powerful, hostile army, is said to have manifested considerable mental agitation, and the executioner was greatly alarmed. Garcia was first executed; and when the hangman was placing the fatal rope about his neck, Castilano told him that he was doing it improperly, and instructed him how to place the noose. His directions were, however, not followed by the affrighted novice of an executioner, and the culprit was slowly choked to death! Castilano, who witnessed, with the crowd, this bungling work, and participated in the general feeling of dissatisfaction that was manifested, requested the privilege of adjusting the rope about his own neck, which was readily granted; and when the platform fell, his death was sudden,—a few convulsive struggles only, and his spirit, too, departed from earth to a solemn tribunal above.

Lagaudette is said to have been a very handsome man, of agreeable, fascinating manners. Castilano, as before stated, was a physician, and, indeed, an experienced surgeon; for the body of the victim was most skilfully dissected. He was a larger, as well as an older man than Garcia, his companion in crime and infamy.

It appears that they were a trio of desperadoes, thieves, and highway robbers; perhaps a portion of a gang who perpetrated other dark deeds in those days. But a short time previously to the murder, the passengers in a stage-coach had been robbed in the vicinity, the lives of the travellers having been saved by the presence of mind and good management of a lady; and these men, it was supposed, committed the act. They had quarrelled over their booty, on the Sunday preceding the murder; and it appears that the two Spaniards concluded to settle the difficulty by killing the Frenchman, and taking each a half, instead of a third, of their ill-gotten spoils.

At the time the discovery was made, large quantities of jewelry, plate, &c., were found concealed in the house, a portion of which was recognised as the property of individuals from whom it had been stolen.

On the 27th of June, an extraordinary and awful thunderstorm was witnessed by the citizens of Norfolk and vicinity. The flashes of lightning were almost incessant for nearly an hour; several houses were struck; the thunder was exceedingly loud; the wind high, and the rain fell almost in torrents.

1821 was a gloomy year. Business was dull; the West India trade declining, and funds growing scarce. There was considerable malignant sickness in one part of the town, during the month of August (in consequence, as there was good reason to believe, of the arrival of a vessel at Woodside's Wharf, from a foreign and infected port), and on September 3d, occurred a most destructive and terrific hurricane.

The great September gale of 1821 is well recollected by many now living. The wind blew with fearful violence; and the storm of that year has scarcely ever had its equal, in the recollection of "the oldest inhabitant." Many houses in Norfolk and Portsmouth were damaged. Some unroofed, and others entirely demolished. Chimneys, trees, and fences were blown down, and several lives were lost. The power of the storm is said to have been truly frightful and astonishing—

> "The winds
> Held oft a momentary pause,
> As spent with their own fury; but they came
> Again with added power—with shriek and cry,
> Almost unearthly; as if on their wings
> Passed by the spirit of the storm."

The tide rose to a great height; the Norfolk Drawbridge was swept away, and the damage to the shipping was immense.

In the summer of this year, Booth, the celebrated tragedian, who had but a short time before, left London, arrived in Norfolk from the island of Madeira. From this place he went to Richmond, and astonished the citizens by his wonderful genius. His appearance, on his arrival there, is said to have been somewhat singular. He was nearly twenty-five, but looked seven years younger, and "wore an old straw hat, and a linen roundabout; and, without the least shadow of pretension, he sauntered along, gazing at everything he saw." He died in the fall of 1852.

Thursday, September 15, was set apart in the borough as a day of humiliation and prayer.

The commerce of the place and the general interests of the community, suffered so greatly from the effects of the Navigation Law, that a public meeting was held on the 21st of December, for the purpose of adopting suitable measures to have it repealed as soon as possible.

The exportations to the West Indies for this year amounted to only $94,384, being $23,616 less than the preceding year.

CHAPTER XX.

1821—1824.

Team Ferry Boat—Steamboats—Reduction of Ferriage—Privileges—Acts of Assembly—Receipts—Competition Needed—Improper Restrictions—Drawbridge—Strange and Alarming Light—Painful Event—Loss of Life—Death of Rev. E. M. Lowe—Arrival *via* Dismal Swamp Canal—Lamented Deaths—City Inspector.

JAN. 19, 1822. A slowly moving teamboat, which had been built to convey passengers across the river, was tried, and found to answer the purpose. The poor blind horses that were used, were transferred, after some eight or ten years, to a more appropriate position on the mud-machine, and steam ferry-boats were introduced, which, after paying all expenses, yield a very considerable revenue to the county.

It is believed that if the ferriage were reduced to two or three-fifths of the present sum (which is five cents), the receipts would be as much as they are now, and perhaps more. There would be more passing across the river between the two towns, which would have a good tendency. The citizens would thereby become better known to one another; and a more social feeling and friendly spirit, calculated to advance the mutual interests of both sides, might be the pleasing result. But this remains to be tested by experience.*

"All ferry privileges are intended to promote the public convenience. There is no vested right conferred by the grant, and it is, at all times, subject to such change and modification as the legislature may, in its wisdom, deem expedient and proper. The convenience and accommodation, not of the inhabitants of a particular district of country alone are concerned, but of a large portion of the travelling public.

* After the above had been put in type, the writer learned that the court of Norfolk County passed an order to reduce the price of ferriage, after the first of January, 1853, to three cents. The court also decided, to run one of their boats from the railroad depot, to transport freight and passengers to Norfolk.

11

"The first act passed on the subject was in 1748. According to the Act of 1757,* the ferry-keepers were required 'to give immediate passage over the said ferries to all inhabitants of the said county, without any fee or reward.' In November, 1766, it was enacted, 'that the justices of the said county of Norfolk be, and they are hereby empowered and required to contract and agree with proper persons, who will give most for the privilege of keeping the said ferries, and to apply the money arising therefrom towards lessening the county levy.' There was another act in 1792; and, by the act of 30th January, 1817, the county court of Norfolk County was authorized to rent or lease it for a term of years. They generally receive $3,000 for it per annum.

"It will be seen that it was contemplated by the act of 1757, to keep up the ferries by a levy upon *the tithable inhabitants* of Norfolk County. Now, the people of Norfolk, of Princess Anne, of Nansemond, and the travelling world, are taxed, one hundred years after its establishment, to sustain a ferry transportation, in order that a portion of Norfolk County, principally interested, may be exempted from all taxation.

"The receipts of the present ferry have been estimated at from $16,000 to $20,000 per annum. The boats are run just so long after dark, as the superintendent of the ferry pleases, and take their own time in communicating between the two towns in the day-time. Passengers and freight are delayed, too, by the stoppages at Washington Point. Competition alone can secure the public convenience.

"On March 24th, 1838, a ferry privilege was granted to the city of Norfolk, but with restrictions. If these restrictions are proper, the new ferry ought not to have been authorized. If the city of Norfolk had an equal right to the privilege, provided the public convenience is promoted, as all must concede it has, the restriction is unjust. If the county ferry has a right to claim from the legislature a protection against fair competition, it has the same right to monopolize the privilege altogether. All such principles have been repudiated by the legislature of this, as well as of other States, long since. They are the avowed foes of all chartered companies, which do not study to promote,

* See page 65.

and actually do promote, the public convenience and accommodation."

July 22, 1822. The new draw-bridge was completed.

On the night of the 16th of September, the citizens were greatly surprised by a strange and very luminous light, that appeared in a northwesterly direction, differing in appearance both from the aurora borealis and an artificial light. Very serious apprehensions, about the destruction of the world, were felt by the credulous.

Exportations this year to the West Indies only $74,303—less than the preceding year $20,081.

1823. On the night of February 2d, a destructive fire took place on the west side of Market Square, during the progress of which a most distressing event occurred. Mr. B. W. Talbot, an estimable gentleman, a native of Baltimore County, Maryland, and, at that time, one of the firm of Allyn & Talbot, merchants of Norfolk, lodged in an upper room of one of the buildings destroyed. Having, as was supposed, retired to bed, every effort to rescue him failed of success, and he perished in the flames. A feeling of horror appeared to thrill every one present, and profound sympathy was manifested throughout the community. Some remains of the body were found, and carefully deposited in an urn; and the most impressive funeral ceremonies were observed on the occasion.

A Mr. Barret, from the county, was killed, and several young men were seriously injured, by the falling of the walls.

February 26. Departed this life, Rev. Enoch M. Lowe, the beloved pastor of Christ Church, in the thirty-third year of his age.

April 28. The commercial portion of the denizens were much gratified by the arrival, via Albemarle Sound and the Dismal Swamp Canal, of the schooner Rebecca Edwards, Captain Burgess, of Halifax, North Carolina, with a cargo of cotton, flour, tobacco, hogs, &c., &c., to Messrs. J. and P. E. Tabb, and J. and W. Southgate. This, it appears, was the first vessel that passed through the canal, with freight for Norfolk; and so advantageous a means of communication with the adjoining State of North Carolina soon proved to be of great benefit to the town. The arrival was, therefore, very appropriately hailed with joy by the citizens generally.

September 7th. Departed this life, Major George W. Camp. On December 7th, just three months later, Colonel William Sharp, a near relative of the former, was also numbered with the dead; and in their deaths, the community felt the loss of two of its most respected, intelligent, and useful members.

June 21, 1824. An ordinance was passed by the Council, providing for the appointment of an inspector of the corporation—salary to be $400; bond and security required in the sum of $1000.

CHAPTER XXI.

1824.

Illustrious Guest—Lafayette's Visit to the Borough—The News Circulated—People from the Country, &c.—Excitement—Anxiety to see the Old Hero—Patriotism—Surprise of the Simple-minded—The Reception—Entertainment—Illumination—Portsmouth—Bonfires—Grand Banquet—Ball in Portsmouth—Ball in Norfolk—Congress—The Nation's Gratitude and Joy—His Character—His Errand—Services in Liberty's Cause—Subsequent Visit.

Friday, October 22d. This was a great day in the old borough; one of the most memorable in its history. Lafayette, the venerable friend of America and of Washington—he who, during the darkest hours of our great struggle for freedom, had been the nation's friend indeed, and then its honoured and honourable guest in its bright and prospering career of glory—having accepted an invitation from the authorities to visit the borough, accordingly arrived on the above day, and we record with great pleasure that his welcome was most "cordial, respectful, and gratifying!"

The news of the visit soon spread from the town to the country, and the neighbouring towns and villages, whose population converged with astonishing rapidity to Norfolk, the centre of attraction. Very many who had been to the great State Festival at Yorktown, followed the hero hither. Boats, in miniature fleets, descended every river and creek that winds its circuitous way to our broad estuary, and were moored fast by the great attracting point. Nearly every road and by-path leading to the town was thronged with the multitudes who were eager to look upon the man whom the nation loved to honour. The old, the young, the grave and the gay; the learned, the ignorant, the white and the coloured—both sexes, each party, every sect—*all* who could, went forth to see him. The pale invalid, scarcely convalescent, but partaking of the general excitement, and reanimated by the common sentiment of patriotism that moved the hearts of thousands, arose from his couch, and tottered out to take a look; and the halt and the crippled hobbled out too, to catch a glimpse at the long-tried and inflexible old friend of liberty, and enemy to tyranny and despotism.

Some of the simple-minded, not exactly comprehending the cause of the wonderful excitement and stir, were somewhat surprised to see nothing more than a fine specimen of nature's noblemen, in the person of the venerated French warrior and philanthropist. But to the reception.

Two pieces of artillery, commanded by Captain George Ott, were stationed, in due time, at the Ferry Wharf; and as the steamboat Petersburg rounded Town Point and appeared in sight, the roar of the great guns answered the double purpose of saluting, in a suitable manner, the far-famed chieftain, and of announcing to the citizens the near approach of their distinguished guest. For some time previously to the salutation, a large concourse of citizens had assembled on the wharf and on Market Square, anxiously and impatiently waiting to witness the arrival of the patriot.

The two volunteer companies, viz., the Independents, Captain Capron, and Juniors, Captain Gibbons, and the two Portsmouth companies, the Rifle Corps, Captain Young, and the Grays, Captain Langhorne, were in readiness at the place of landing.

Captain (late Commodore) Warrington, George Newton, and William Maxwell, Esqrs., composed the committee deputed to receive him. They embarked in an elegant barge to the boat, which lay in the stream, some distance from the densely crowded shore. Accompanied by his suite and his son, George Washington, and amid the long, loud shouts of the enthusiastic multitude, and the louder thundering of the ordnance, the brave old General was landed.

He was received at the wharf by the excellent Mayor of the borough, John E. Holt, Esq., after which, a procession was formed, composed of the authorities, the volunteer companies, the corporate societies, clergy, schools, and the citizens generally. The General was assigned an appropriate position in the ranks, and the procession moved slowly up the Square; while the huzzas of the excited throng made the welkin ring again.

A magnificent civic arch, with a graceful curve, stretched across Main Street from the corner (now Newton's), and presented a truly imposing appearance. It was tastefully hung with evergreens and flowers, and beautified with well-wrought designs, and the words "WELCOME, LAFAYETTE," stood out in full relief.

The children of the different schools were neatly dressed and prepared for the joyful occasion; many of them carrying baskets of flowers, with which they thickly strewed the pathway of the noble-hearted visitor, of whose generous, heroic deeds they had heard and read, and which they had been taught by their parents and teachers to hold in grateful remembrance. This is said to have been a "most interesting and *heart-touching* scene," at which the General was much affected, and he expressed himself in terms of high gratification.

An appropriate address was delivered by the Mayor, standing under the arch, which was responded to in a suitable style by the venerable chief. There was another spectacle of intense interest attending the visit and triumphal march of the honoured and victorious chieftain through the densely crowded avenues of our town. The doors, windows, and piazzas of the houses, were thronged with ladies, "who," says the Herald, "although not equalling in number those who, in similar situations, greeted the arrival of the nation's guest in the larger cities, might, we think, justly claim the palm of *beauty*."

They waved their handkerchiefs, and the benignant smiles from thousands of blooming faces, appeared to thrill again the old hero's heart with emotions of delight, and combined to add another chapter of glory to the interesting and romantic history of his eventful career, and his memorable journey on the happy shores of the great country, in whose behalf he had freely given some of the best years of his useful life; to whose suffering soldiers he had freely opened his purse; in whose battles, near fifty years before, he had bravely fought, and conquered, and spilt his blood.

He was escorted to Mrs. Hansford's boarding-house, a fine building then, but recently erected by Captain Robert E. Steed, at the west corner of East Main and East Streets, subsequently owned and occupied by Purser Fitzgerald, U. S. N., and now by H. B. Grigsby, Esq. With the entertainments and accommodations there, the venerable visiter was highly pleased. At night, the town was most brilliantly illuminated. The citizens of Portsmouth were busy, too, in showing, on the interesting occasion, "honour to whom honour" was due, and that town also exhibited "a blaze of joy." The shores and river, in front of the town, were lighted up with forty-two bonfires, producing a splendid effect.

On the following day (Saturday), the General received crowds of visiters; among whom were, of course, our most prominent and respectable inhabitants. A grand banquet was held in the afternoon, at which there was soul-cheering music, as well as a plentiful supply of the delicacies of the season. The most courteous and respectful attentions were paid him there also by the citizens, and at night Portsmouth gave him a grand ball.

After he had rested (on Sunday) from the fatigue of his journey and reciprocal courtesies, the citizens of Norfolk were ready again, on Monday, to manifest in a most cordial and hospitable manner, the evidences of the lively sentiments of gratitude which swelled their hearts, for the valuable services of the brave and magnanimous Frenchman. At night a splendid ball was given him in the spacious rooms of the new Custom-House (there not being a more suitable place), which were elegantly arranged and beautified for the occasion; and a very large and fashionable assemblage here, again, paid their respects to him and those who accompanied him.

The reception and entertainment of Lafayette were highly creditable to our citizens, and those of the contiguous town. Norfolk, Portsmouth, and the surrounding country, joined heartily in the "spontaneous burst of acclamation and rejoicing" that rung through the length and breadth of the land.

It is gratifying, by the way, to reflect upon the manner in which Lafayette was received, when he visited the happy land which he had so generously aided in becoming free and independent.

As some evidence of the nation's gratitude, Congress very appropriately voted him $200,000, and a township of land, for his ample means had now been greatly reduced by reverses of fortune; and from north to south, from east to west, on a line of travel reaching near 5,000 miles, in city and town, and village and country seat, he was greeted with joy and delight, and ardent wishes for long life, health, and happiness, on account of the benefits he had conferred personally, and by his instrumentality, directly and indirectly. These important services had justly endeared him and his countrymen to the hearts of our people with the strongest ties of affectionate regard. When he left his home and friends, and came to expose himself to the hardships of war for the benefit of an oppressed people, he was no mercenary in search of money and self-aggrandizement. "He was no nameless man, staking life for reputation; he ranked among nobles, and looked unawed upon kings. He was no friendless outcast, seeking for a grave to hide his cold heart; he was girdled by the companions of his childhood; his kinsmen were about him; his wife was before him.

"Yet from all these he turned away, and came. Like a lofty tree that shakes down its green glories, to battle with the winter's storm, he flung aside the trappings of place and pride, to crusade for Freedom in Freedom's holy land. He came,—but not in the day of successful rebellion—not when the new-risen sun of Independence had burst the cloud of time, and careered to its place in the heavens.

"He came when darkness curtained the hills, and the tempest was abroad in its anger; when the plough stood still in the field of promise, and briars cumbered the garden of beauty; when fathers were dying, and mothers were weeping over them; when the wife was binding up the gashed bosom of her husband, and the maiden was wiping the death-damp from the brow of her lover. He came when the brave began to fear the power of man, and the pious to doubt the favour of God. It was *then* that this ONE joined the ranks of a revolted people. Freedom's little phalanx bade him a grateful welcome. With them, he courted the battle's rage; with theirs, his arm was uplifted; with theirs, his blood was shed.

* * * * * *

"After nearly fifty years, that ONE has come again. Can mortal man tell, can mortal heart feel, the sublimity of that coming? Exulting millions rejoice in it; and their long, loud, transporting shout, like the mingling of many winds, rolls on, undying, to freedom's farthest mountains. A congregated nation comes around him. Old men bless him, and children reverence him. The lovely come out to look upon him; the learned deck their halls to greet him; the rulers of the land rise up to do him homage. How his full heart labours. He views the rusting trophies of departed days; he treads upon the high places where his brethren moulder; he bends before the tomb of his FATHER;—his words are tears—the speech of sad remembrance. But he looks round upon a ransomed land and a joyous race; he beholds the blessings, those trophies secured, for which those brethren died, for which that FATHER lived; and again his words are tears—the eloquence of gratitude and joy."

CHAPTER XXII.

1824—1827.

Lieutenant G.—Shipwreck—His Wife and Child—Affecting Scene—Sudden and Singular Death—Mrs. G.—Fire—Court-House and Jail Destroyed—Mr. Taylor and Dr. Slaughter—Court-House—Storm—High Tide—Destruction of Property—New Burying-Ground—Legacy of Elizabeth Crommeline—Exports—Non-intercourse Laws—Mr. Tazewell—General Smith—Trade Declining—Destructive Fire—Christ Church, &c., Burned—Loss and Distress—Countryman Frightened—Reports the Town on Fire—Ordinance concerning the Erection of Wooden Buildings—Lyceum—Its Name—Aristotle's School—Odd Fellows' Hall—Lancasterian School-Room—Interments in St. Paul's Graveyard Prohibited—Mild and Unseasonable Weather.

"In the winter of 1824, Lieutenant G——, of the United States Navy, with his beautiful wife and infant child, embarked in a packet at Norfolk, bound to Charleston, South Carolina. For the first day and night after their departure, the wind continued fair and the weather clear; but, on the evening of the second day, a severe gale sprung up, and towards midnight, the Captain, judging himself much farther from the land than he really was, and dreading the Gulf Stream, hauled in for the coast; but with the intention, it is presumed, of lying-to when he supposed himself clear of the Gulf. Lieutenant G. did not approve of the Captain's determination, and the result proved that his fears were well founded; for towards morning, the vessel grounded.

"Vain would it be to attempt a description of the horror which was depicted on every countenance, when the awful shock, occasioned by the striking of the vessel's bottom, was first experienced. The terror of such a situation can be known only to those who have themselves been shipwrecked. No others can have a tolerable idea of what passed in the minds of the wretched crew, as they gazed with vacant horror on the thundering elements, and felt that their frail bark must soon, perhaps the next thump, be dashed to pieces, and they left at the mercy of the billows, with not even a plank between them and eternity. First comes the thumping of the vessel; next, the dashing of the surge over her sides; then, the careening of the vessel, on her beam ends, as the waves for an instant recede; and lastly, the crashing of the spars and timbers at each returning wave; the whole forming a scene of confusion and horror which no language can describe.

"But awful as is the shipwrecked sailor's prospect, what are his feelings compared to the agony of a fond *husband* and *father*, who clasps in a last embrace his little world,—his beloved wife and child. The land was in sight; but to approach it was scarcely less dangerous than to remain in the raging sea around them. Lieutenant G. was a seaman, and a brave one, accustomed to danger, and quick in seizing upon every means of rescuing the unfortunate. But *now*, *who* were the unfortunate that called on him for rescue? *Who* were they, whose screams were heard, louder than the roaring elements, imploring that aid which no human power could afford them? His *wife* and *child!* O, heart-rending agony!

"But why attempt to describe what few can imagine! In a word, the only boat which could be got was manned by two gallant tars. Mrs. G. and her child and its nurse were lifted into it; it was the thought of desperation! The freight was already too much. Mr. G. saw this, and knew that the addition of himself would diminish the chances of the boat's reaching the shore in safety; and horrible as was the alternative, he himself gave the order,—'Push off, and make for the land, my brave lads!' —the last words that ever passed his lips. The order was obeyed; but ere the little boat had proceeded fifty yards (about half the distance to the beach), it was struck by a wave, capsized, and boat, passengers and all, enveloped in the angry surge. The wretched husband saw but too distinctly the destruction of all that he held dear. But here, alas! and for ever, were shut out from him all sublunary prospects. *He fell upon the deck, powerless, senseless, a corpse*,—the victim of a sublime sensibility.*

* It has been stated that the words, "Push off, and make for the land," &c., were not the last that were spoken by the devoted Lieutenant G.; and that the giving of further orders, when the boat upset, together with the powerful additional mental excitement which it occasioned, in all probability caused the rupture of a blood-vessel, or some sudden and fatal derangement of the heart.

"But what became of the unhappy wife and child? The answer shall be brief. Mrs. G. was borne through the breakers to the shore by one of the brave sailors; the nurse was thrown upon the beach, with the drowned infant in her arms. Mrs. G. was taken to a hut senseless, continued delirious many days, but finally recovered her senses, and with them a consciousness of the awful catastrophe which, in a moment, made her a childless widow."

February. A fire occurred on Main Street, which destroyed the old court-house and jail buildings, which stood at the head of Market Square. They had been, some years before, converted into stores, which were occupied mostly by persons now living. The site of the large block of buildings at the head of Market Square, now owned by the heirs of General Robert B. Taylor, was occupied by this old hall of justice. This property belonged jointly to Robert Taylor, Esq., the father of General R. B. Taylor, and Dr. A. Slaughter. Dr. S., as before stated, died in 1814, since which time the lots alluded to have been the property of the heirs of Mr. T. The old jail buildings were located between the court-house and Talbot Street, on the site on which now stand the houses belonging to the heirs of Thomas Talbot and Tildsley Graham, Esq.; including the large dry-goods buildings occupied by Messrs. Stewart and Jones, and belonging to the respected heirs of Mr. Talbot.

The contracted and incommodious court-house, that was situated on East Main Street (but recently taken down and removed), was built in 1790.

In 1825, there was a violent storm, accompanied with an astonishingly high tide, which almost entirely inundated the lower portion of the town, materially damaging many articles of merchandise, such as sugar, salt, tobacco, &c., and floating away quantities of lumber and fire-wood.

January 8. Act of Assembly passed, authorizing the Common Council to appropriate a piece of land as a new burying-ground.

March 31, 1826. Ordinance passed providing for the establishment of a new cemetery.

July 11. An ordinance passed, providing for the disposition

of legacies, left by Elizabeth Crommeline to Christ Church, and the poor of the borough.

She bequeathed, by will, one thousand dollars for the use of the poor, to be vested in stock, or placed at interest; and the same amount for the benefit of Christ Church.

For the year ending 30th September, the exportations from this port amounted to $219,912, being $19,412 more than those from Baltimore for the same year. The exports from Norfolk were, with a few exceptions, in American vessels. From Baltimore, produce to the amount of $43,174, included in the above calculation, was taken away in British vessels.

This year the effect of the Non-intercourse Laws and commercial restrictive system, existing between the United States and Great Britain, with regard to the trade of the West Indies and the British Colonies, were very seriously felt by Norfolk; indeed, it was highly detrimental to the trading interests of the southern ports generally. The commerce of our town now began very perceptibly to decline; disastrous consequences ensued, as predicted by Mr. Tazewell, of Norfolk, and General Smith, of Baltimore; whose able debates and efforts, with regard to this interesting and important, though complicated, subject, are well remembered by many at the present day.

1827. On the morning of March 9, between one and two o'clock, a fire broke out in a frame workshop, at the southeast corner of Main and Church Streets, where now stands the National Hotel. The shop was occupied by a most industrious and estimable mechanic, a coachmaker and wheelwright, now living.

The wind blew a gale from about south by west. The workshop was very soon destroyed, together with several adjacent buildings on Main Street. But the sparks and even the burning embers, were blown to a considerable distance up Church Street, on which, and on the western part of Mariner Street, the loss was very great. The Protestant Episcopal Church, which stood where the Presbyterian Church now stands, was consumed. It was a large and lofty building. The block of buildings known as Murray's Row, was also destroyed. At this place, Mariner, between Church and Fenchurch Streets, the fire raged with fearful violence.

"It was a fearful night;
The strong flame sped
From street to street, from house to house,
And on their treasures fed."

The flames from the houses on either side of the street, united in one vast column, which towered above the highest houses, strewing the fiery missiles for many rods. The entire northeastern section of the town was menaced by the flames, and it was saved only by the most active exertions of the firemen and citizens. The large and handsome framed mansion, erected by Mr. Plume, and at that time occupied by Walter Horron, Esq., corner of Church and Wood Streets, was set on fire by embers from the church, at a distance of half a mile below, and was also consumed.

Every part of the town was most brightly illumined, and, indeed, the light of the conflagration was visible for many miles around. About sixty houses were burned. The flames, gathering strength and power from the strong wind that blew, filled the citizens on Church and Fenchurch Streets with great consternation and alarm. Many families were deprived of a shelter, and the loss of property was very considerable. It was stated that an individual from the country, on his way to market, on seeing the rapid spreading flames, and the showers of burning embers, concluded that the whole town was on fire; whereupon he turned his horse, made the best of his way home again, and reported accordingly!

March 10th. Ordinance passed in Council, prohibiting the erection of wooden buildings of more than ten feet square and one story high, "on any lot or piece of land lying on Mason Street, as extended from Newton's Creek on the east, to Elizabeth River on the west; or on any lot or piece of land lying southwardly or westwardly of said street."

The immediate cause of the passing of this necessary prohibition, was, doubtless, the destruction of property on the preceding day. The ordinance has been frequently violated, although the penalty is quite severe, viz., $20 for each offence, and $5 for every week thereafter, until the building is removed or taken down. By a recent ordinance, the prohibition extends to all lots south of Bute Street.

March 23d. The Lyceum was opened. This was a neat, one-story building of brick, situated on the north side of Wolfe Street, and intended by the proprietor, Wm. Maxwell, Esq., for public lectures, the meeting of literary associations, &c. The name is the same as that of the place in which Aristotle instructed his pupils in philosophy. By adhering to his relative, Calisthenes, this philosopher lost the favour of his pupil Alexander, and, therefore, removed from Mytilene to Athens, "where he set up his new school. The magistrates received him kindly, and gave him the *Lyceum*, so famous afterwards for the concourse of his disciples."

The Norfolk Lyceum was purchased, in 1839, by the Odd Fellows, and greatly enlarged and improved, a second story having been added, for the purposes of that useful and respectable Order. There are three commodious rooms on the first floor, which are occupied by schools and debating societies.

August 7th. Ordinance passed, providing for the building of a new Lancasterian school-room.

Ordinance passed, prohibiting the burial of persons in the old church-yard of St. Paul's, whose near relations had not already been interred there.

There was no frost in Norfolk or vicinity during the month of October, and in December following there was neither frost nor ice.

CHAPTER XXIII.

1828.

Dry Dock at Gosport—Summer Days in Midwinter—Vegetables, Flowers, and Birds—Melancholy Accident and Loss of Life—Three Midshipmen Drowned—Mr. Hunter's Fortitude, &c.—Snow—Ordinance concerning Fire-wood—Suggestion—Prices — Christ Church—Ministrations — Present Pastor — The Clock—Original Plan—Present Condition—Bell.

JANUARY 1st, 1828. On this day was commenced that extensive and splendid piece of masonry, the Dry Dock, at the Navy

Yard, Gosport. This day was remarkably warm, and on the 5th of the month, the inhabitants found it most agreeable to dispense with fires, except those who could not consent to depart so far from the fashion of the season. Summer clothing was most comfortable; blankets could not be endured at night, the doors and windows were thrown open, many sat in their porches, and enjoyed the evening's balmy air, while numbers of ladies and gentlemen promenaded the principal thoroughfares. Asparagus and other spring vegetables of mature growth were offered for sale in the market. The trees and shrubs budded. The blue-bird, the wren, and others of the sparrow kind, returned and resumed their matin songs. The sweet-scented hyacinth, and the lovely violet, with other gentle spring flowers, bloomed and perfumed the ambient air. The seasons, which

> "Gave warning of the lapse of time, that else
> Had stolen unheeded by,"

appeared almost to have changed their wonted course; for in the month of January, instead of the usual supply of ice and snow, and the chilling breath of Boreas, the air was mild and pleasant, the south and southwestern zephyrs blew, and all nature began to assume the pleasing and enlivening aspect of the vernal time.

On Saturday, April 5th of this year, a most melancholy occurrence took place in the harbour. Midshipmen William J. Slidele, Frederick Rogers, Robert M. Harrison, and Bushrod W. Hunter, were out on a short pleasure excursion, in a sail-boat, which unfortunately capsized, and the three first-named gentlemen were drowned. They were all young men of fine promise, and very respectably connected; and their sad, sudden, and unexpected fate was greatly lamented. The bodies were recovered, and those of Harrison and Slidele were among the first committed to the silent tomb in the new cemetery; whither they were conveyed under very solemn and impressive circumstances, and with every mark of respect for their worth, and sympathy for their untimely death.

Mr. Hunter was rescued from his perilous situation, when life was nearly extinct. He had endeavoured, with uncommon fortitude and presence of mind, to cheer his drowning companions, and encouraged them to continue their efforts to save themselves. He still lives, an ornament to our gallant Navy, to the church, and to society.

On the 7th of April, it snowed considerably; an interval of *two years* having elapsed since any had fallen in the borough or its neighbourhood.

On June 20th, was passed "An Ordinance to amend and reduce into one, the several ordinances concerning fire-wood." Among the requirements of this law, there is one which provides "that the cord of wood shall measure eight feet in breadth, four feet in length, and four feet in height; and that each and every piece or log of wood shall be sound, straight, free from projecting knots, and of full length."

It has been suggested, and perhaps very properly, that the measurer of wood, for house-keepers, should keep a correct daily record of all sales, purchasers' names, prices, &c.

The price of hard wood, per cord, in the Norfolk market, varies, in the spring and summer months, from $2 00 to $2 50; and of pine, from $1 75 to $2 25. In the fall and winter seasons, the price seldom exceeds $3 50 for hard, and $3 for pine; although, in very severe weather, the price has risen to $6, $7, and even $8.

This year Christ Church (Protestant Episcopal) was erected. That beautiful building exhibits, as yet, but little of the usual effects of time. It was built with great care, and was truly a handsome offering to HIM whose exalted name it bears. May it long remain, as it now is, a monument of the liberality of the numerous and highly-respected congregation that assembles within its sacred walls; and of the faithfulness, taste, and skill of its chief builder, Mr. L. Swain. The situation was well chosen; being central, airy, and affording a good view of the edifice from several points.

Its solid walls of brick are well stuccoed; the windows are arched; two massive columns stand at the front of the main entrance and partly support the gable and steeple. On each side of the entry is an ascent to the gallery. This neat edifice stands at the northwest corner of Cumberland and Freemason Streets, and fronts on the latter, being the oldest of three houses of worship, prominently situated, but a short distance from each other, on the west side of the last named street, and which combine to add greatly to the good appearance of the central part of our improving city.

The excellent condition in which this sanctuary is kept, the good order always preserved during service, the devout eloquence of its ministrations, and the sacred and soul-thrilling strains of its choir, accompanied by the solemn, soft, and deep-toned music of a very large and superior organ, combine to render it a peculiarly attractive place of Divine worship.

The clock attached to this building—that large and faithful time-piece, whose long-swinging pendulum has, for a quarter of a century, measured off the fleeting moments—contributes much to the convenience of the citizens, with regard to that which is but seldom, if ever, properly appreciated—

"'Tis folly's blank, and wisdom's highest prize."

Christ Church, for some reason deemed sufficient by the building committee, was not built exactly in accordance with the original plan; of which the steeple was better proportioned than that of the present building, which, it is thought, would have a finer effect, if considerably higher. Both the interior and exterior of the house have been recently painted, and the former improved and supplied with the means of being brilliantly illuminated with gas. The bell of this church is very large and sonorous, having a rich, bold, and musical tone, which is sometimes heard for more than ten miles.

The present devoted and popular pastor of this church, Rev. Geo. D. Cummins, is a gentleman of great ability as a theologian and pulpit orator. Many of his discourses are characterized by peculiar dignity and beauty of style, and energy of delivery.

CHAPTER XXIV.

1828.

Religious Revival—Lieutenant in the U. S. Army enters the Ministry—Talents —Preaches in Uniform—The People go in Crowds to Hear Him—Description of a Camp Meeting Scene—The Young Preacher—Solemn and Impressive Devotions—Extraordinary Sermon—The Preacher's Style, Subject, &c. —Thrilling Interest and Wonderful Effect—Exciting Scene—The Preacher Overcome—Revivals—Melancholy Statement—Pastor of St. Paul's, New York—Other Preachers—Panny Baker—His Success and Usefulness—Affecting Scene—His Death—Presidents—Professors, Editors, &c.—Appropriate Work of Methodist Ministers—Methodism—Principles of Truth do not Change —Men Change—Reformation.

About this period (1827–8), there was an extensive revival of religion in several of the churches of the town, and many others in the neighbouring counties, and, we believe, in various sections of the country. Many of our citizens date their permanent religious impressions and the commencement of a life of piety, from this time.

Some time during this or the preceding year, commenced, in this vicinity, the clerical career of a young gentleman of prepossessing manners, who exhibited commanding talents as an orator, and whose pulpit efforts soon placed him prominently before the public as a successful revivalist, and an able minister of the gospel of Christ, while his fruits were sufficiently manifest, and his trophies sufficiently numerous, to attract the favourable notice and excite the fondest hopes of the church with which he, about that time, united. He was an officer in the United States Army, a lieutenant, we believe, and was then attached to a body of soldiers connected with that branch of the national defence, and garrisoned at Fortress Monroe. He was educated at West Point, where, at an early age, he had received strong religious impressions under the pious ministrations of Bishop McIlvaine, of the Protestant Episcopal Church. At a revival of religion, which he attended in the Methodist Episcopal Church in Hampton, about this period, he was a seeker after a deeper work of grace and higher religious attainments; and he was among the happy number who there partook largely of the divine influences; shortly after which, he joined the Methodist Church. Manifesting very considerable religious zeal, and, as intimated above, decided ability as a speaker; and, moreover, professing to be "moved by the Holy Ghost to preach," he became a member of the Methodist ministry, and promptly engaged in the awfully responsible work of proclaiming the "unsearchable riches of Christ." His preaching soon attracted great attention; for it "was not with enticing words of man's wisdom, but in demonstration of the Spirit and of power." In Norfolk, Portsmouth, Hampton, and elsewhere, even his early efforts were highly commended. His style was pleasing, his delivery fluent, and his language chaste; his voice agreeable and musical, his gestures graceful, and his whole manner in the pulpit exceedingly animated and impressive.* There was not observable, it is true, in the young orator, extraordinary acuteness of reasoning, nor was there any great attempt at deep and learned theological investigation; these were not yet expected. But his illustrations were apt and striking; and his thoughts upon the subjects chosen were expressed in a clear, winning, and graphic manner. Before he finally resigned his commission in the army, he occasionally spoke in undress uniform, and, as may be supposed, he drew very large audiences to hear him.

In 1828, he officiated at a camp meeting, held by the Methodists at "Nimmo's," a place famous, especially in those days, for striking exhibitions of Divine power, in the conversion of sinners, and for the copious outpouring of the spirit of the living God. The location is in the good old county of Princess Anne, about twenty-one miles from the city, and two miles below the court-house, in a section in which the Methodists have long predominated.

* "Let the rising ministry take warning! Awkwardness in the pulpit is a sin; monotony a sin; dulness a sin; and all of them sins against the welfare of immortal souls.

"It is as easy to be graceful in gesture and natural in tone, as to be grammatical."

A discourse, which he delivered at that time and place, is remembered by many living at the present day. It was a quiet, bright, and beautiful Sabbath morning in August. The rudely and hastily constructed board tents, on the "camp-ground," were arranged in rows, forming three sides of a spacious square, amid a magnificent natural grove of oaks and beech, of gigantic growth, whose wide-spreading branches cast a dense shade, which answered well for the protection of the numbers who congregated beneath them, from the rays of the sun.*

These lines of the poet, doubtless, express the feelings experienced by many a devoted servant of God, at that place and on that occasion:—

"God! thy greatness here I feel,
Heeds my heart thy love's appeal,
At thy forest shrine I kneel;
All my sins confessing!

"Here, with strength, my soul imbue,
Light thy altar-fires anew,
Aid me to be pure and true,
Father! with thy blessing!"

The voice of prayer and praise arose, and resounded far down in the deep green woods, where, too, the singing-birds sported and carolled merrily, as if rejoicing in their existence. The winds, as they came in gently from the sea, that rolled along in its might and majesty but a few miles distant, made melancholy music among the thick foliage above; and, at intervals, the murmuring sound of the breaking waves of "old Ocean," that

"Played low upon the beach,
Their constant music,"

mingled harmoniously, though solemnly, with the "moaning echoes of the wind."

The young officer, who had been but recently transferred from the service of his country to the army of the "Lord of hosts"

* That beautiful and extensive grove has long since disappeared. The "woodman" should have spared those trees.

and the "God of battles," and who had united with the "Soldiers of the Cross," to fight in the bloodless warfare against the enemies of his Heavenly King, drew, as may be imagined, a large crowd to hear him on this occasion: a great concourse of people from the town, and from different sections of the surrounding country, were rapidly collecting together.

At an early hour, he seemed in deep meditation, upon the works of God it may have been, as they were there manifested in the charming beauties of Nature, as well as upon the solemn message that he was about to deliver.

At the hour specified for the sermon, a horn was blown; and the seats beneath a capacious shelter, formed by the thick green branches of trees thrown upon a framework of poles, were all quickly filled with people of both sexes, old and young; the females being seated on the right, and the males on the left of the principal aisle, which divided the rows of benches; while multitudes stood around.

The coloured people, who were rapidly gathering too, from all directions, in their shady location a few rods distant, had not yet commenced their loud shouts, nor were they yet sufficiently excited to engage in their frantic dance of joy, while, hand in hand, they formed a ring around the converts; and their melodious, though simple notes of praise, were not yet too distinctly heard to break in upon the impressiveness of the scene; the whole vast assemblage anxiously awaited the appearance of the young preacher, and the commencement of his discourse.

He soon walked from "the preacher's tent," accompanied by several other clerical brethren, and, with a light and graceful step, he ascended the "stand," or pulpit, which was built of rough boards, beneath the dense, umbrageous foliage of one of those tall old sons of the forest,

> "Whose deep-dug roots are twisted around the stout ribs of the globe,
> That mocketh at the fury of the storm, and rejoiceth in summer sunshine."

An appropriate hymn was sung in a solemn tune; and again those "wild old woods" resounded with the voice of praise. The music made there, by thousands of the most charming of all instruments, that of the human voice, mingled and arose in one great volume of melody, swelling out in loud, full, clear tones, while the concordant reverberations were heard around, apparently inspiring the hearts of all with solemnity; calming down, perhaps, the agitated feelings of even the most hoary-headed sinner present, and impressing the mind of the gay and thoughtless with the importance of eternal matters. A fervent prayer was offered at the throne of grace; after which another hymn was sung, and then the preacher arose.

"He glances at the assembly; but, although that glance is momentary, yet it speaks volumes, which those who mark can easily understand. His hearers feel that their best interests are dear to him. They sympathize with the travail of his soul. He opens the sacred volume, and all listen as if God himself were speaking. He announces the subject of discourse, in which all must feel interested.

"In commencing he is deeply serious, although far from being loud and boisterous. The thoughts and feelings which have been confined in his breast at first escape in gentle accents.

"He addresses the understanding of his audience, knowing that they require to be informed before they can be excited; that the way to the heart is through the understanding. His descriptions are clear. His pictures are vivid. His aim is direct. His hearers cannot mistake him. They feel the tendency of his thoughts, and they eagerly anticipate the object at which he is aiming. There is no dry detail; no eccentric starting from the line which his peculiar and solemn circumstances have marked out for him."

The great necessity of a speedy repentance and regeneration was urged; the danger of delaying a prompt, decisive, and entire consecration of the heart to the Great Author of life, and the "Giver of every good and perfect gift;" the wretchedness attendant upon, and surely following a life of impenitence; *the merits of a crucified Redeemer*—the only hope, yet all-sufficient source of safety and deliverance from the impending dangers to which the deathless spirit of man is exposed; the final doom of the lost; the never-ending glory of the redeemed—

"Time gone, the righteous saved, the wicked damned,
And God's eternal government approved."

These, we believe, were some of the most prominent points in the sermon.

"The only effectual method," says Blair, "to become pathetic, is to be moved yourselves. There are a thousand interesting circumstances suggested by real passion, which no art can imitate, and no refinement can supply. There is obviously a contagion among the passions.* And Cicero said, that the instances in which he was most successful, were those in which he abandoned himself to the impulses of feeling." Thus it was now with the speaker, very shortly after he announced the text. He appeared to feel, and doubtless did feel deeply, the importance of his subject; he spoke fearlessly, forcibly, and convincingly, the overflowing sentiments of his heart, and the effect was most powerful, solemn, and extraordinary.

His language was well chosen and appropriate; but the tone of his voice, his looks and gestures, interpreted the emotions of his full heart. "For a while, an almost breathless anxiety prevailed, deeply impressive and solemnizing from its singular intenseness." But this did not continue long, for it was soon broken by the audible and increasing responses from the other preachers and the more devotional part of the auditory; and he had not spoken longer, perhaps, than half an hour, before a scene, such as has been rarely witnessed, began to manifest itself in the assembly.

"As he proceeds along, he seems to gather a mysterious energy, arising not from wiredrawn theory or splendid creations

* The following brief extract will serve to prove the truth of this statement of Mr. Blair, and to convey an idea of the style and manner of a successful preacher of an earlier period in the history of the church.

"Lord save the sinner—*save him!*" he cried, in the highest pitch of his voice. "Death is upon him, and hell follows. See, the bony arm is raised! The fatal dart is poised! O, my God! save him—save him! for if death strikes him, he falls, hell receives him; and, as he falls, he shrieks, 'Lost! lost!! Lost!!! Time lost! Sabbaths lost! Means lost! Heaven lost! ALL LOST!! *and lost for ever!*'

"The effect was so overwhelming that two of the congregation fainted, and it required all the preacher's tact and self-command to ride through the storm which his own vivid imagination and powerful appeal had roused."

of fancy, but from the *clear plain sentiments of truth.** The light which he at first scattered now begins to diffuse heat. He soon becomes an altered man.

"The powers of the world to come seem to take possession of his spirit. He draws the curtain which conceals the invisible. Earth and all its busy scenes vanish. *Heaven and hell are revealed!* Every countenance reveals the light of the one or the gloom of the other. There is not a careless or inattentive man in the place; all are compelled to look in the direction in which he points. He now feels that he has got access to the immortal souls with whom he is surrounded, and he does not fail to improve the precious moment. He urges with divine energy the things which belong to their eternal peace. He presses with resistless eagerness the inquiry, '*What shall I do to be saved!*' He appeals to the conscience in a tone which it dares not refuse to answer. The affections and passions are raised at his command. Love, and fear, and hope, start from their slumbers, and the whole moral being becomes intensely awake."

Tears were seen coursing down the cheeks of many of the listeners, while others turned pale, and trembled, as though their eternal doom had been sealed, and they stood upon the verge of destruction. Men and women shouted aloud; but the speaker's voice, rising almost to its highest pitch, was yet distinctly heard by many whose eyes were intently fixed upon him, and who exhibited evidences of the deepest emotion, which continued until some fell suddenly upon the ground. This, indeed, was a frequent occurrence before he concluded.

It was soon evident that the speaker's emotion was also gaining the mastery; and his energy, excitement, and pious exultation, still rapidly increasing, he was completely overwhelmed by the intensity of his feelings; and he suddenly fell prostrate upon the floor of the pulpit or stand, from which he was removed to one of the tents.

An enclosed space in front of the pulpit, thickly covered with clean stalks of wheat, and furnished with benches, was crowded

* The foundation of all that can be called eloquent, is good sense and solid thought.—Blair.

with kneeling penitents, while others lay at full length upon the straw, and many were to be seen under great excitement, and in attitudes of prayer, in different parts of the congregation. Several were so much affected, appeared so happy, so transported by the divine influence, that the body appeared to be scarcely capable of retaining the spirit; and such rejoicing and cries for mercy, and general manifestations of mental agitation and excitement as took place on that occasion, especially after the speaker himself had fallen, have rarely, if ever, been witnessed since; and it is a well-known fact, too, that this meeting was remarkable for deep, powerful, and genuine religious convictions, and for the large number of hopeful and unwavering converts.

The scene resembled those which were often witnessed during the extraordinary pulpit efforts of the celebrated Whitefield; when, to use his own words, "the whole congregation was alarmed; crying, weeping, and wailing, were to be heard in every direction; many were seen falling into the arms of their friends; and my own soul was carried out till I could scarce speak any more."

May we not appropriately put the question, Why are not such manifestations of God's convicting, converting, and sanctifying power, witnessed more frequently at the present day? Divine power is undiminished; grace as freely bestowed; "Jesus Christ, the same yesterday, and to-day, and for ever."

It may be said of this, as of other kindred religious revivals, that it was all the result of sympathy, or mere "animal excitement,"—a sudden and transient ebullition of feeling, soon to evaporate,—

> "A brightly flashing, glowing fire,
> That burns,—but only to expire."

To some extent, or with some individuals, doubtless, the excitement was transitory; evanishing too soon, alas! and leaving no trace of any real good effect. But, that truly religious impressions, and, in many cases, a most gratifying change from sinfulness to deep, permanent piety, and extensive usefulness, were the happy results, cannot be reasonably doubted,—to the truth of which, the closing hours of life, ay, and many a death-bed scene, have testified plainly and unequivocally. How often, indeed, has the dying Christian joyfully pointed back to a season of religious excitement, resembling, in many respects, that described above, as the commencement of the life of devotion, which enabled him to launch out fearlessly upon the death-stream, triumphing in the blissful hope of entering safely the bright and peaceful haven of eternal repose; leaving a comforting assurance for the consolation of surviving friends, and exclaiming, with his last expiring breath, "*All is well, all is well.*"

The indulgent reader must excuse another allusion to this subject. The writer has heard an individual, a man of intelligence, who heard the discourse described above, and who concealed and stifled his convictions, declare that his refusal to yield then and there, to the powerful influences of the Spirit of God, and to accept the offers of pardoning mercy upon the just and simple terms of the gospel, was the most unhappy incident of his whole history,—a circumstance which has embittered his life for a quarter of a century.

Rev. Martin P. Parks, now of Saint Paul's, Broadway, New York, formerly Professor at Randolph Macon College, Chaplain at West Point, &c., is the esteemed clergyman whose pulpit ministrations, long years ago, are still so well recollected. His devout, though much less impassioned eloquence, has often been heard in Christ Church in this city.

There were several other excellent preachers present on the occasion alluded to; among them were Rev. Bennet T. Blake, Rev. Dr. Daniel Hall, and Rev. John P. Baker, or, as he was familiarly called, "Panny Baker." They were then members of the Virginia Conference, and were generally esteemed for their usefulness, and abundant success as ministers of the gospel. We offer some remarks relative to one of the three whose names we have given.

Rev. Panny Baker, who is well remembered by persons in this city, but especially by many of the good people of that section of Princess Anne County to which we have alluded, was, in some respects, an extraordinary man. Illiterate, homely in person, of an indifferent physical constitution, he was, nevertheless, a man of wonderful faith,—powerful in the place of prayer, or at the seeker's bench; and it is very probable that his labours were more successful, and more signally blessed, than those of any minister who has succeeded him upon that "circuit." His health was early sacrificed to the cause in which he laboured. "Consumption, that sly and deceitful destroyer," fastened its deadly fangs upon his vitals. Pale, emaciated, broken down, perhaps by over-exertion, but "rejoicing in hope," and patient in suffering, he appeared upon the camp-ground; hundreds flocked around the carriage in which he reclined; and as he reached forth his trembling hand, and looked upon the people with an expression of deepest tenderness and concern, assuring them that he should see them no more in this world, and entreating them to meet him in Heaven, whither he was hastening, tears flowed most copiously down many a cheek, and from eyes unused to weeping; while stout hearts, which, perhaps, he had failed to move before, were now made to feel. It has been stated that not one among the hundreds who took leave of him, on that occasion, failed to shed tears freely, and to feel most deeply.

A few weeks thereafter, at the residence of Rev. Dr. Webb, he breathed his last breath, and his pure and happy spirit triumphantly ascended to Him, whom he had so faithfully endeavoured to serve on earth.

We will observe, and, we trust, without incurring censure for indulging in what may be considered an unprofitable digression here, that it has been a source of controversy and regret among some of the members of the Methodist Church, in this and other sections of our State, and elsewhere, that several of its ablest ministers have heeded and accepted a call, to retire from the regular duties of the itinerancy, to act as presidents and professors of colleges, editors, &c.

It is thought, by many judicious persons, to be an unwise policy to deprive the church of the immediate influence of their personal ministrations upon the people—of their ministerial efforts in the "travelling connexion," inasmuch as their present places, as it is declared, might be supplied by local preachers or laymen. It is affirmed that the work of Methodist ministers is to *travel and preach;* "to go," using the words of the founder of Methodism, "not only to those who want them, but to those who *want them most;* to spend and be spent in the work." The pulpits and altars of the churches, the meetings for prayer and praise, the family circle, the couch of the sick and dying, the damp hovels of the wretched, the prison-houses, the cottages of the poor, and the palaces of the rich, too—these, it is thought, constitute the legitimate fields of labour for Methodist ministers; not merely in some particular and favoured locations, but (in its regular turn) in every part of the territory embraced in the jurisdiction of the Conferences to which they belong. But strong and convincing arguments have been adduced in justification of the course pursued by the church, and alluded to above.

There are some persons, who, on taking a glance at the church-going portion of the community, are wont to exclaim, "Methodism has changed." But doctrines and principles, if properly based upon the infallible Word, alter not in their nature. The rise and fall of empires; the heavy, onward tread of hostile armies, sated with the blood, and hardened by the fearful and unavailing shrieks of injured innocence; earth's deep heavings and convulsions; the "crush of worlds;" the ample sweep of unmeasured and immeasurable eternity, all combined, will not suffice, it is well enough known, to produce a change in a single well-established principle of divine truth. It is man, unstable man, that changes, and wanders into error. The delusive effects of sin and satanic agency upon his heart, seduce him into forbidden paths, away from the once adopted and immovable standards of Christian faith. There are many, however, both in this and the other branches of the church militant, "who hold fast the profession of their faith without wavering."

The impatient reader will say we have travelled quite far enough from our proper course; and so, perhaps, we have. But who will declare, after taking a look at the "signs of the times," that some great reformer, with a big, unfaltering heart like Luther's,—firm, resolute, steady to his purpose; urged onward by the all-powerful principle of love to God, and the souls of men,—would not find work to do in orthodox churches of every persuasion, in pointing professors back to the holy standards of faith and practice, which, at the present day, are in too many cases, sadly neglected?

CHAPTER XXV.

1828—1832.

Dismal Swamp Canal—Methodist Protestant Church—Naval Hospital—Snow-Storm—Population—Dr. M'Alpine—Cold Weather—Anniversary Celebration—Procession—Interesting Display—Oration, &c.—Strange Solar Appearance—Insurrection in Southampton—Its Effect—Increasing Commerce—Mayor—Singular Weather—The Cholera—Death of the Mayor—Death of John Tunis, Esq.—His Enterprise, &c.—Philanthropic Remark—Benevolent Idea—Reflections—Riches—Dr. Johnson—Utility of Poverty—Old Methodist Church Taken Down—New Building Dedicated—Dr. William A. Smith.

On Wednesday, December 31st, the Dismal Swamp Canal was completed, and opened for the uninterrupted passage of vessels.

The Methodist Protestant Church was organized this year (1828). The theatre that stood on Fenchurch Street was purchased by that denomination, and converted into a house of worship. This having been burnt a few years after, the present neat building, on Church, near Freemason Street, was bought, and the members still worship there. Rev. John Whitefield is the present able and esteemed pastor.

1829. The Naval Hospital, near the site of Old Fort Nelson, was commenced this year. It is a very large and exceedingly commodious and handsome stone building, finely adapted to the important purpose for which it is intended. The location was well chosen, being healthful, retired, and convenient. This massive structure is a splendid ornament to the harbour, and presents its beautiful and lofty front for the admiration of the beholder on coming up the river, or from the Norfolk side. The strictest order and discipline are observed at the establishment, and its utility at this great naval depot is obvious.

March 19, 21. Great snow-storm.

1830. Population of Norfolk, 9,860.

Died, this year, in Kempsville, Princess Anne County, Doctor James M'Alpine, a physician of great popularity, and remarkable for his skill and success in the treatment of disease, as well as for the deep interest which he manifested in his patients of every class. His death was sudden and unexpected, and the sad news spread with astonishing rapidity through the length and breadth of the county. Old and young, white and coloured, were startled, and greatly distressed by the intelligence; and, indeed, a death has seldom, if ever occasioned more general sorrow in Princess Anne County. A large concourse of persons attended the funeral, and very many gave unmistakeable evidence of their sincere grief for the great loss which the county had sustained.

1831. During the month of January, the weather was exceedingly cold. The usual trips of the old steamboat Hampton, Captain S. Selden, were prevented, on one or more occasions, by the ice, which was of considerable thickness in the harbour; and on the 18th, a severe snow-storm commenced.

The anniversary of American Independence was celebrated this year in a style that far surpassed all other occasions of the kind in Norfolk. The recollection of such an evidence of devoted patriotism on the part of our citizens twenty years ago, is pleasing, especially to those who witnessed the splendid display which marked the return of the fifty-fifth birthday of the nation.

The rising of the sun, on that bright morning, was greeted by heavy discharges of artillery, and, at an early hour, a procession was formed, comprising the different volunteer companies, and a long train of large cars, or carriages, which consisted of plank platforms on wheels. On these, the different trades were represented, and as they passed along, drawn by fine horses, it was truly animating to behold the different mechanical operations, by a judicious and ingenious arrangement, all busily and systematically going on,—the carpenter at his bench, amid the shavings that curled rapidly from his jack-plane; the brick-mason, amid his bricks and mortar, causing the shrill sound of his trowel to resound far and wide; the blacksmith, with his dingy face and brawny arms, his roaring bellows and heavy sledge, causing the sparks to fly, like a "fiery shower," from the glowing bar, and "fall like golden rain around him;" the painter, the hatter, the cordwainer, &c., &c., each in his respective car, was to be seen engaged at his useful and indispensable avocation.

The procession, after marching through the principal streets, halted on Freemason Street, at about eleven o'clock; at which hour, H. B. Grigsby, Esq., formerly editor of the Norfolk Beacon, delivered, in Christ Church, an oration, which was characterized by well-chosen subjects, as well as great strength and beauty of language, combined with superior rhetorical skill, and a graceful delivery. After the conclusion of the address, the procession again took up the line of march. Salutes were fired; fine bands of music cheered the hearts of the multitudes; the government and merchant ships were handsomely dressed with maritime flags; the streets were thronged with visiters from the neighbouring towns and counties, and never in any place of the same size was there a more charming exhibition of female beauty than on that exciting and interesting occasion. But, alas! there were some who mingled in the gay and cheerful crowd that day, that were marked as victims of the dreadful scourge of the succeeding year, then already on its mysterious and rapid course to the western continent. True it was, that some of those, whose hearts beat with the liveliest emotions of pleasure then,

"Ere the twelve months made their round again,"

were reposing in deep sepulchral stillness.

The citizens were much surprised, on the morning of August 13th, by the very strange appearance of the sun. Owing to some change or derangement of the atmosphere of that great central luminary of our system, a very singular phenomenon was exhibited. The sun's disk seemed, on rising, to have changed from the usual brilliant golden colour to a pale, greenish tint, which soon gave place to cerulean blue, and this, also, to a silvery white. In the afternoon, he appeared like an immense circular plane of polished silver; and to the naked eye there was exhibited, on his surface, an appearance that was termed a "black spot." The sun shone with a dull, gloomy light, and the atmosphere was moist and hazy. These phenomena excited much wonder and astonishment among the people. The credulous were induced to believe that some awful calamity was about to happen; and among the various speculations of the more intelligent part of the citizens, none appeared to be satisfactory. It was evident, however, that some were waiting in considerable suspense to witness what would come next.

During this month, came the startling intelligence of the bloody affair in Southampton County. Mounted forces, well armed and equipped for battle, proceeded from Norfolk, Portsmouth, and elsewhere, to assist in quelling the insurrection, and in arresting the deluded and inhuman wretches. The diabolical plans of Nat Turner, and his wicked and misguided followers, were soon effectually defeated, and the ringleaders brought to justice and condign punishment. We refrain from a statement of the particulars of this affair, in which some estimable residents of a neighbouring county came to a violent death, and by which the voice of mourning was caused to be heard in several highly respected families of this city.

The excitement on this occasion was, of course, immense; and no little alarm and mistrust was induced, especially among the female portion of the community, which the lapse of more than twenty years has scarcely sufficed to eradicate from the minds of all. The immediate effect of this insurrection was to tighten the reins of servitude, to cause a more entire subordination to be insisted upon by masters, and to excite a greater degree of vigilance over the movements of servants.

1832. This year, gloomy as are the recollections of it, in some respects, was noted as the beginning of a brighter period in the mercantile history of the town of Norfolk. Commerce began to flourish; the number of vessels, both large and small, arriving in our port, rapidly increased. Although against wind and tide, the old borough now began to move slowly and surely onward in her career of prosperity. To the lumber trade, for which Norfolk has long been noted, a fresh impulse was given; and, indeed, in all the different branches of business a reaction was observable, notwithstanding the sad and fatal pestilential visitation of that year.

Jan. 20. Act of Assembly passed, vesting in the freeholders and qualified voters the privilege of electing the Mayor of the borough.

The weather, during the month of May of this year, in this section of the country, was remarkable for the season. Gentle easterly winds prevailed; and nearly the whole month was humid, cloudy, and dreary. The atmosphere was light and enfeebling, and exhalations floated near the surface of the earth. These circumstances combined to prepare the physical system for the ravages of the approaching destroyer, of whose presence, a few weeks after, the dying and the dead gave painful and unmistakable evidence.

Among the victims of the cholera, during its first visit to the town, there were some valuable citizens, whose sudden departure cast a deep gloom over the community; yet, it must be admitted, that a large majority of those who fell a prey to the dire and mysterious disease, were generally persons of enfeebled constitution, whose health had been impaired by age, protracted disease, or intemperance; or whose habits of life were irregular and uncleanly. Those enjoying a good state of health, who yielded to the effects of the scourge, had prepared the system for it by imprudence in diet; and many of such cases might have been cured, had the nature of the disease been better understood by the physicians. It was a melancholy time, indeed; all appeared sad, many were greatly alarmed, a number of the citizens left the place, and some of the stores were closed.

During the summer of this year, the celebrated Indian warrior, Black Hawk, passed through the town.

October 13th, departed this life, John E. Holt, Esq., who had been for twenty years Mayor of the borough. He was an intelligent and efficient officer, and manifested a lively interest in the welfare of the town.

On the 8th of December, Norfolk lost another valuable citizen, John Tunis, Esq., who was distinguished for his public spirit and usefulness in advancing the local interests of the borough. As an opulent merchant, he was noted for his liberality, integrity, and general information. His plans for future operations, and schemes for the advancement of the town, were extensive and judicious; some of which had already commenced. But, alas! he was called away from the busy scenes of this life, ere he could realize the consummation of his arrangements.

This enterprising gentleman remarked, but a short time before his death, that if his plans should succeed, and he was not often mistaken in his calculations, there would not in a few years be a man or woman in the borough necessarily without employment. "If my abilities were equal to my wishes," said the brilliant Addison, "there should be neither pain nor poverty in the universe." Here was a grand and benevolent idea, but, at the same time, a still more grand impossibility, far beyond the reach of the limited powers of man or angel; and an implied desire of doubtful propriety, even though it could be carried out; for God, in his wisdom, sees fit to inflict pain and poverty on many a noble sojourner here; and the most unmixed, unalloyed happiness, is frequently to be found in the humble walks of life, and even beneath the roof of extreme poverty. Listen, as you pass, at the silent twilight hour, the humble and quiet abode of some devoted, though indigent, old "mother in Israel;" and you hear her chaunting the praises of God. The lonely pious widow, or the devout poor man, far retired from the busy world, amid great earthly privations, is often to be found in the enjoyment of real happiness; as "cheerful as an angel of love on an errand of mercy," and rejoicing in the anticipation of the "rest that remaineth for the people of God." Poverty is sometimes of great utility; "necessity is the mother of invention." Nevertheless, riches are very desirable, and are often the means of usefulness and happiness. Besides, as said the "colossus of English literature,"* who had suffered the inconvenience of indigence, and who had been sorely pressed by circumstances of absolute want—scarcely able to procure the common necessaries of life:

> "This mournful truth is everywhere confessed:
> Slow rises worth, by poverty distressed."

It is this, however, that sometimes lights up the latent or smouldering fires of genius. Poverty and distress often excite the mind of man to action, and nerve him to the performance of what he would not dream of undertaking in prosperous circumstances. And as the strength of the old oak, standing alone upon the mountain side, is often greatly increased by exposure to the fury of the roaring tempest, taking deeper root when rudely rocked by the

* Dr. Johnson.

howling storm-god; so misfortune and distress often combine to render the strong man still stronger.

But the object determined upon by the individual, the date of whose death we record, was considered by him to be quite within the range of possibility, and not beyond the reach of perseverance, and extensive, well-directed personal effort; and a suitable appropriation of ample facilities and large capital, the great essential elements of all vast enterprises. And although the wish implied was limited in comparison with that of the "Christian philosopher," yet it was an evidence of generous impulses and a noble soul, that felt deeply for the welfare of others. Hence the record of his remark here.

The old Methodist church on Cumberland Street was taken down this year, and a very large and commodious house erected, which, in March, 1833, was dedicated to the service of God by the Rev. Wm. A. Smith, through whose instrumentality it was built.

CHAPTER XXVI.

1833—1836.

Public Square—Portsmouth and Roanoke Railroad Company—Extensive Fire—New Buildings—Meteoric Phenomenon—Citizens alarmed—Railroad Stock—Roanoke Navigation Company—City Debt—Railroad Bill passed—Demonstrations of Joy—Sabbath Desecration—Commercial Prosperity—Great Guns and Fireworks—Failure of the Road—Rebuilding of the Road, and its Prospects—Death of General R. B. Taylor—City Inspector—Earthquake—Back Creek—Shipping—Cold Weather—St. Paul's Cemetery—Religious Revival—Almshouse—Another Railroad Subscription.

1833. February 27th. Act of Assembly passed, authorizing the filling up of that portion of Back Creek, on the east of Bank Street, to establish a public square.

April 3. Ordinance passed, authorizing a subscription for stock in the Portsmouth and Roanoke Railroad Company, to the amount of $60,000—twelve hundred shares.

On the night of November 4th, an extensive fire occurred on the south side of Main Street, which consumed some eighteen or twenty old wooden buildings, extending from a few doors east of Market Square to Marsden's Lane. This fire was considered a public benefit. That important portion of the city, including Newton's Row, and the Mechanics' Hall in particular, presents a striking contrast to the unsightly, hip-roofed, sharp top, and rickety hovels that fed the flames on that occasion.

On Wednesday morning, November 15th, the well-remembered meteoric phenomenon was exhibited to the view of those of the citizens who were so fortunate (?) as to be early aroused from their slumbers, and great was the consternation and astonishment of the beholders of the great starry shower. Some fell on their knees and cried for mercy, as if at the eleventh hour, tremblingly expecting the near approach of the end of all earthly things; while others rejoiced in anticipation of the coming of the "mighty angel from heaven, clothed with a cloud, and a rainbow upon his head, and his face, as it were, the sun, and his feet pillars of fire," to swear "that there should be time no longer." A few calmly viewed the strange and sublime appearance, and with profound awe, wonder, and humiliation, adored nature's great Author, patiently awaiting the result.

December 4. The council agreed to a farther subscription to the Portsmouth and Roanoke Railroad stock, of $40,000, being 800 additional shares.

"The city had previously subscribed $20,000 to the old Roanoke Navigation Company, to prolong its existence. The whole of that appropriation was sunk, together with $80,000 more, subscribed by public-spirited individuals, anxious to secure that valuable trade, without stopping to calculate the chances of profit or loss from the investment *per se.* But did the corporation lose its $20,000? No, not a dollar of it. In the place of the defunct Roanoke Company, there sprung up a spirited and thrifty trade with the Roanoke, and other rivers in North Carolina, on individual account, to which the expenditure of the capital of that company had pioneered the way, and the increase of business in the city, and of the revenue therefrom to the coffers of the corporation, sufficed to cover its loss of $20,000 in three or four years, as may be seen by reference to the commissioner's books of that period.

"The increase of the city debt, about this period (1833–4), consisted: 1st, in the subscription of $100,000 to the Portsmouth and Roanoke Railroad Company, authorized by the almost unanimous vote of the citizens; 2dly, an expenditure of nearly $40,000 in getting up a separate ferry; and 3dly, an appropriation, by the Common Council, of $13,000 to prop up the railroad when it was on its last legs. Total, $153,000—out of which there remains, as property, about the sum of $10,000, in a wharf in Portsmouth, and improvements to the corporation ferry wharf in Norfolk. The balance, $143,000, was virtually a total loss, though, in reality, it was offsetted by no inconsiderable increase of revenue from the trade on the railroad, during the seven years of its existence; and the estimated amount of ferry stock ($10,000) has been, for a number of years, producing an income of $1,000 per annum."

1834. On the evening of the 19th of January, came the intelligence that the Portsmouth and Roanoke Railroad Bill had passed. It was unfortunate that the news was received on Sunday; for the Divine injunction, the serenity and calmness of the Sabbath evening hour, and all the hallowed associations inseparably connected with the sacred day of rest, were insufficient to induce a large portion of the citizens of both towns to repress their feelings of rejoicing. It was a close vote, but the bill was now a law of the State; the battle had been fought, and the victory just barely won; and the inhabitants of Norfolk and Portsmouth looked eagerly out, as it were, upon the brightening future, with cheering anticipations of prosperity, wealth, and commercial greatness. So the bells rung a merry peal; great guns announced the glad news for thirty miles around. Several field-pieces had been placed at suitable distances on the road to Suffolk, to which place the information was carried, by successive firing, in a few moments after it was known here. The evening being cloudy, and the air favourable for the communication of sound, the effect of the rapid and consecutive firing was somewhat singular. For many seconds, there was a loud, irregular, continuous roar, very much resembling successive and heavy peals of thunder. Bonfires blazed on the wharves, and in some of the principal streets;—Church Street was brilliantly illumined. Kegs of powder were moistened, and fired along the shores; hundreds of rockets shot forth over the river; and, "for more than two hours, the town rang with notes of rejoicing."

After a succession of insurmountable difficulties, this road became useless, and was abandoned; the hopes of those who had been most sanguine of its success, and of its inestimable advantages to Norfolk and Portsmouth, were blasted; and the evidences of disappointment and gloom then exhibited, are too well remembered to need a record here.* May not the unjustifiable desecration of the Sabbath, on the reception of the news of the success of the bill in the legislature of the State, have been one cause of its rapid downfall? But it has risen again under circumstances calculated to inspire the most confident hopes o complete success, and it will doubtless prove highly beneficial to this community.

April 13. Departed this life, Judge Robert B. Taylor, an eminent jurist, to whom allusion has been, and will hereafter be, made in these sketches.

July 1. Ordinance passed, increasing the salary of the City Inspector to $800.

August 27. Tuesday—between the hours of 6 and 7 A.M., the shock of an earthquake was very sensibly felt in Norfolk and vicinity.

November 25. Ordinance passed, providing for the filling up of Back Creek, above Bank Street Bridge, for a public square.

1835. In the month of January, there were more square-rigged vessels in our harbour than there had been, at any one time, since 1820. Among them were a number of British brigs from the West Indies.

February 10. Exceedingly cold; mercury in thermometer 26° below zero; river frozen over.

* The failure of the Portsmouth and Roanoke Railroad was caused by bad management, over which Norfolk had no control, and which she was powerless to remedy.

February 29. All interments in the old burying-ground (St. Paul's), prohibited from this date.

During this year, there was an extensive religious revival in the several Protestant churches in Norfolk and vicinity.

June 8th, 1836. Ordinance passed, providing for the payment of the contract with Wm. McLain, for the erection of the new Almshouse.

An ordinance was also passed at this date, authorizing a subscription of $50,000, for stock in a proposed railroad from Edenton to Norfolk.

CHAPTER XXVII.

1836.

Centenary of the Borough Charter—Reflections—Centennial Celebration—Procession—Mace—Oration by Wm. Maxwell, Esq.—Hymn—Aquatic Excursion—Fireworks—Serenade—Reflections.

SEPTEMBER 15th. A century had now elapsed since the Royal Charter was granted, and this was a day of very considerable interest in the history of the borough; a day both of rejoicing and serious meditation. The man of reflection could not but go back upon the swift wing of thought, and linger awhile "in solemn contemplation," amid the varied scenes of that long interval, pregnant as it had been with changes, revolutions, and commotions, political and religious, at home and in distant lands; affecting not only the welfare of our town and its residents, but also that of the State and the country at large—involving the highest interests of the vast Western Continent and of the whole world. Kings and crowns had fallen; great conquerors had arisen—had run their course of glory, and returned to the peacefulness of retirement, or ended their days in the dreariness of exile. A check had been put upon the power of despotism. Rivers of human blood had been shed; but anarchy and oppression had given way to the reign of justice; and the darkness of superstition had been succeeded by the brilliant light of truth divine. The edicts of injustice and cruelty had come over the wide and heaving bosom of the ocean; but a manful resistance had been offered; a noble and a glorious compact had been signed; eloquent voices from the Old Dominion and elsewhere had rung out long and loud, and an oppressed people had heard and heeded the spirit-stirring and truthful appeals. A great though unequal contest had commenced, progressed, and ended gloriously for the sons of freedom, in "Freedom's Holy Land." Hard blows had been aimed by the sacrilegious hand of fanaticism at the sacred ties that bind the different members of this great confederation; but thus far the Union had remained "one of many," firm as the Andes in their rocky foundations, and was still dispensing the untold blessings of its example, and the bright light of its influence upon the present happiness and eternal destiny of earth's babbling millions.

A hundred long years had sped on their course, and were lost in the deep oblivious ocean of the past. During their rapid flight, how many of those who had acted their part in life's short drama, had retired, at its conclusion, behind the impenetrable curtain which Death drops between time and eternity! Of the inhabitants even of the town of Norfolk and its vicinity, what numbers had been laid low in their cold and narrow beds, and had long been sleeping the deep, undisturbed sleep of death, awaiting the loud blast of the trumpet that "shall sound!" Two generations had ascended the stage of life, had pressed quickly by, and gone down to the gloomy regions of silence and forgetfulness; and a third was then departing and following on in the beaten track. The old and the young; the most honoured citizen and the least regarded mendicant; the tender babe, the joyous youth, and the strong man in his prime—all, all had been arrested by Death, and forced to submit to the sad penalty to which Adam's sin rendered man amenable. The bright eye of beauty had closed; the cheek of roseate hue had grown pale in death; cheerful voices had long been hushed and forgotten, and forms that had mingled in many a social scene and contributed to its joy, had fallen under Death's cold, palsying touch; all lay concealed beneath earth's teeming surface; and, in accordance with the Divine declaration, were strangely commingling with its dust.

War, pestilence, storm, flood, and fire had done their work of desolation. Norfolk had shared largely in the calamities of the Revolution. Once in ruins, she had, by a noble exertion, arisen again, and with increasing strength and beauty, had already taken a respectable stand among the towns of the Atlantic coast. Many a severe blow had been levelled at the prosperity of the old borough; but all seemed willing, on this auspicious centennial day, to acknowledge that she had right bravely and successfully contended with every difficulty, and, agreeably to the views and declarations of Jefferson and others, was now surely, though slowly, rising in the scale of commercial importance.

These and other considerations were duly regarded, and the authorities and citizens, generally, very appropriately determined that the hundredth anniversary should not pass without a suitable celebration, and the necessary arrangements were accordingly made for the occasion.

At sunrise, there was a salute of twenty-six guns, and the bells rang for service in the churches; whither many of the inhabitants repaired, and most properly commenced the day with the exercises of prayer, thanksgiving, and praise. At half-past eight o'clock, in front of the old Town Hall, a grand civic procession was formed, in which were the mayor, aldermen, and other officers of the corporation; the clergy, the different companies and associations; the schools, and a very large number of the citizens. There was a military parade at the same hour; and the volunteer companies joined the general gathering at the Court-House. The procession was a very large one for the size of the town. Captain John Capron was chosen as marshal, and he manifested very commendable activity and spirit on the occasion. By the assistance of his aids, he succeeded in preserving excellent order. William Maxwell, Esq.,* a distinguished lawyer, had been judiciously chosen as the orator of the day.

* Now residing in Richmond, and editor of the Virginia Historical Register.

The procession marched through the principal streets; martial music cheered the hearts of the moving, animated mass; the stores were closed; very many visiters to the town united with the procession and thronged the streets; the sun shone brightly and the air was balmy; "children and sires," people of all ages and classes, were gathered in large groups, and on every thoroughfare through which the procession passed, in the doors, windows, and piazzas, sparkling eyes, and bright and cheerful smiles, and looks of beauty and words of love, added an irresistible charm to the occasion.

The venerable Thomas Newton, Recorder, acted as standard-bearer: on one side of whom walked Wm. W. Lamb, Esq., Deputy-Sergeant, bearing the "beautiful and bright," though ancient. silver *mace** of the corporation, and on the other, John Williams, Esq., Clerk of the Court, carried the original charter, with its ancient signet. The procession, after quite a long march, halted at the new Presbyterian Church, then nearly completed, which was soon most densely crowded; hundreds, of course, failing to obtain seats or even an entrance within the walls of the building. An appropriate and fervent prayer was offered; after which, the talented and eloquent orator arose, and, in his peculiarly happy style, delivered an address, which was acknowledged to be exceedingly appropriate to the occasion.

His manner was calm and dignified. He had, it is believed, no notes to refer to; his memory required no help, no prompting. There were but few studied periods, and not the least affected attempt at display. Indeed, the speaker was a man of too much experience, taste, and judgment, to essay to edify his hearers with a mere flourish of words at such a time. His address appeared to reach the hearts of his auditors; and while there was not a manifestation even of the mental effort that some had expected, yet, all appeared to be greatly pleased. The orator proceeded with a deliberation and self-possession that

* The *mace* was presented to the corporation of Norfolk by Robert Dinwiddie, Esq., Lieutenant-Governor of Virginia in 1753. It weighs several pounds, and is a beautiful piece of work. It was formerly carried before the mayor on going to court, and in all public processions.

relieved, at the outset, the minds of his auditors of all unpleasant suspense as to the result.

"He touched eloquently upon the old inhabitants of the borough, whose descendants had come up that day to commemorate their work, while their own worth was such as to entitle them to the grateful remembrance of those who will succeed them on the stage of life.

"What added peculiar interest to this part of his address was the circumstance, that the grave-yard, where nearly all the charter-men and our early inhabitants were buried, was in front of the building and of the orator while speaking. He dwelt with great effect upon the Stamp Act, and upon the proceedings of the Norfolk Sons of Liberty, who protested against that measure; and he took occasion to pay a glowing tribute to the memory of Patrick Henry, for his exertions in the House of Burgesses on that occasion.

"He discoursed most happily upon the American Revolution; and when he came to the acknowledgment of the guardian care of the Deity for so many years over our fathers and ourselves—he was *superlatively grand.*"*

* A talented writer, in a description of Mr. Maxwell, written in 1827, remarks as follows: "The principal characteristic of his eloquence is imagination, chaste, sparkling, and luxuriant. It fills the mind with kindling delight and increasing rapture; and the impressions left with the hearer are those which Longinus describes as the criterion of true eloquence; a general and vivid feeling of delight; and an absolute inability to point out the immediate parts of the oration which produced it. In conducting a cause, he often reasons with great ability, but his reasoning is not a chain of dry sophisms and lifeless logic; every step of the demonstration is lightened by flashes of fancy so bright and beautiful, as to show in the strongest colours, and in the fullest light, the forms they were designed to illumine. On some occasions his whole heart seems to *liquesce,* and be poured forth in the streams of eloquence that flow unceasingly from his lips; while his hearers catch the feeling with the rapidity of the electric fluid, and believe, as they retire, that they have felt almost all that eloquence can make men feel. This feeling he hath wrought alike on the learned and illiterate, the nobly great and meanly low, the enemy and the friend.

* * * * * *

"He is a master magician over certain classes of feeling. He pleases and enraptures, but never astonishes his audience. I have seen a numerous auditory now held in silent rapture by his eloquence, and I have seen it again thrown into a universal titter by his resistless ridicule."

The following stanzas, which were composed for the occasion, were sung with fine effect at the conclusion of the exercises in the church:

"God of our fathers, hear us now,
As in thine earthly courts we bow;
Accept our thanks for mercies past,
And blessings brightening to the last.

"Of old, beneath these smiling skies,
Thou bad'st our beauteous borough rise;
And, fostered by thy guardian care,
The scion grew and flourished fair.

"O, be it Lord, thy gracious will,
And it shall flourish fairer still;
And children's children in their days,
As we do now, shall sing thy praise."

In the afternoon, there was a grand aquatic excursion, commanded by Captain Jacob Vickery, aided by Captains James Connick and Thomas Ivey. They procured a number of beautiful barges, &c., of different shapes and sizes—

"The long boat, the jolly boat,
The pinnace, and the yawl;
The skiff, and the sailing-boat,
The fishing-boat and all."

These were soon filled with ladies and gentlemen, sweethearts and beaux, boys and girls, the gay and the beautiful, the loved and the loving,—all as cheerful as they could be made by agreeable company, handsome scenery, and a bright sun, whose golden rays were reflected by the "breeze-ridden ripples" that danced merrily along to the shore, while the soul-thrilling music from the majestic war-vessels in the harbour floated upon the balmy air of that

"Eve of Autumn's holiest mood."

This long line of crowded boats, as they proceeded down the river, presented an exceedingly novel and imposing scene, and, commanded by those gallant men of the sea, who had often successfully crossed the agitated bosom of old Ocean, they returned with their invaluable freight without loss or accident to mar the festivity of the interesting occasion.

At eight o'clock, a hundred rockets soared and exploded over the lively old borough; the closing hour of whose first centesimal anniversary was cheered by a delightful instrumental serenade.

Long will the pleasing occurrences of that day be remembered by many now living. But who, of those that witnessed the first, will be here to mingle in the moving crowd, and mark the interesting circumstances that may attend the second centenary of the charter? All, who lived then, will probably be gone to their eternal destiny, and others will have risen up to fill their places, and perform the complicated task of life; other forms, other faces, and other minds, will be here; and they will think of the few whose memory time will fail to obliterate; but all, of "every nation, every tongue," will be gathered, recognised, and identified, at the last great day of accounts.

CHAPTER XXVIII.

1836—1840.

Presbyterian Church—New Organization—Ministers—Services—Membership—Prices Current—Fire—Distinguished Visiter from France—Pleasing Incident—French's Hotel—Important Commercial Era—Unwise Legislation—Lieutenant Maury's Statement—Ocean Steam Navigation—What Norfolk might have Done—Real Estate—Exploring Squadron—Commercial Convention—Common Council—Destructive Fire—Explosion—Fire in Portsmouth—Loss of Life—Nuisance Removed—Public Square—Buildings—Avon Theatre—City Prison—Norfolk Academy—C. Hall, Esq.—Academy Square—Character of the Institution—The Norfolk and Portsmouth Herald.

October. The New Presbyterian Church was completed this month. That large and commodious house of worship is situated nearly opposite St. Paul's Church, being on the east side of Church Street, a few feet south of the western terminus of Holt.

Street. A tall and handsome cupola, or dome, with a gilt ball of several feet in diameter placed over the apex, was subsequently added to the building, greatly improving its external appearance.

On Saturday afternoon, November 19th, the church was organized, and the members registered; and on the following day—Sunday, the 20th—the house was dedicated, by Rev. Dr. Wm. S. Plumer. The membership is numerous, highly respectable, and devout. This church has been for several years past, blessed with zealous and eloquent ministers, among whom were Rev. Messrs. Cassells and Anderson. Rev. George D. Armstrong, an able and zealous minister, was elected, in the spring of 1851, to fill the vacancy occasioned by the removal of Mr. Anderson to St. Louis.

The good order in which the house is kept, the respectful attention to the accustomed ordinances of worship, the singing, the music of a fine-toned organ—these, with the impressive appeals from the pulpit, have long rendered this church an attractive place of resort for religious worship, especially on the holy Sabbath. These remarks are only in strict accordance with the public sentiment. Another observable feature in this collective body of Christians may not be inappropriately alluded to here. The Presbyterians of Norfolk are remarkably united as a church; the members appearing truly endeared to one another; and while there is also manifested a liberality of feeling and sentiment with regard to other Christians, each member appears to take a special interest in the welfare of his brother or sister in Christ. This is surely a commendable trait in any religious association. But it is no more nor less than a Christian duty, enjoined, not only by the sacred obligations of brotherhood, but by the holy oracles of Divine truth. Nor are these remarks intended as the least possible reflection upon any of the other esteemed associations of Christians, whose piety and prayers have doubtless assisted in securing the blessings of Providence upon the place, and perhaps averted many a calamity, or tended to lessen the force and severity of the misfortunes with which the town has occasionally been visited.

The following are some of the prices current in the Norfolk

market at this period: pork, hog round, 10 to 12 cents per lb.; beef, 10 cents; mutton and veal, 10 to 12 cents; bacon hams, 20 cents; turkeys, in demand, $1 to $1 25; meal, $1; fire-wood, $3 to $5.

March, 1837. A fire broke out at night on the east side of Market Square, near Main Street, and six or eight large brick buildings were consumed, including a fine lofty edifice at the corner, then known as Reilly's. The weather being very cold, the engines were worked with difficulty, and great efforts were required to arrest the progress of the flames. The vacuum caused by this destructive fire, by which several persons sustained considerable loss in goods, furniture, &c., is now filled by Newton's beautiful row, extending south from the east corner of Main Street and Market Square.

On the 19th of April, Norfolk was visited by a distinguished stranger, who has since made no little noise in the world, as the head of the great nation over which he now presides with an ability that even his friends hardly expected. Le Prince Napoleon, Louis Bonaparte, then an unfortunate exile; now Louis Napoleon Bonaparte, Emperor of France, arrived with his suite on this day, in the French frigate L'Andromede, which was accompanied by the Sirene. The Prince was well entertained, during his short stay in the borough, and very appropriately and politely manifested and expressed his grateful sense of the attentions which he received. He was a fine-looking man; erect, dignified, and manly in his person, without possessing, however, as much resemblance, in his features, of his illustrious uncle, as some of his relatives; but in the shape of his head, his shoulders, and his chest, bearing, as is asserted by those who saw and noticed him well, and who were capable of judging, a striking likeness of the great and powerful Emperor Napoleon.

There was one incident of interest, and worthy of note, which took place on the eve of his departure hence in the steamer Kentucky for Baltimore. He noticed a small ornament of gold, a striking resemblance of the great French conqueror, in a standing attitude, which was worn by a young relative of one of our most respected merchants, who accompanied the noble

Frenchman to Portsmouth. He was much pleased, and expressed his satisfaction with considerable energy, on finding that the memory of his world-renowned relative was thus honoured across the waters, and on being informed that there were many here who showed, in a similar way, their regard for the illustrious dead, and who cherished the recollection of the extraordinary and wonderful deeds of the eventful life of him whom God raised up to "break down despotic governments, and humble the pride of kings."

The day on which the Prince arrived, French's Hotel, now the National, was opened; and it is remarkable that this distinguished person and suite were the first guests received and entertained in that large and commodious establishment.

The National Hotel is the largest in the place, and is well adapted to the accommodation of travellers, or permanent boarders. The building covers an area of 7,065 square feet, fronting 152 feet 9 inches on Church Street, and 54 feet on Main Street, standing at the southeast corner of those two thoroughfares. It is five stories high, being the highest house in the city, and contains 84 rooms, including 13 sitting rooms and parlours. There are several spacious passages, and seventy-five fireplaces. At the principal entrance, on Main Street, there is a plain Ionic portico, supported by two columns 15½ feet high. The principal dining-room is 68 feet long, and 27 feet wide. The cistern connected with the building contains 12,500 gallons. The exterior walls are well stuccoed, and painted a dark brown, darker even than the dull, frowning Quincy granite colour first adopted. A coat or two of white, or of some light colour, would have a much more pleasing effect.

A hotel, upon a more extensive plan, is greatly needed in this city, and the erection of one is now under consideration.

This was certainly a most important, or, perhaps, we should say unfortunate, era in the commercial history of our city, and, in fact, of our State. The reader will see, by the following statement, how much Norfolk has lost by injudicious legislation, in one instance alone. Do not all who feel an interest in the welfare of the State, and especially of Norfolk, deprecate, with feelings of mortification and regret, the unwise policy pursued by our law-makers in former years?

"In 1837, commenced the era of Ocean Steam Navigation, though, twenty years before, the South had sent out an *avant courier* from Georgia. The South, however, rested content with the honour of being the first to stride across the Atlantic under steam. For though, at that very time, various conventions were held at the South, binding the merchants of the South, like the oath Neptune administers to sailors crossing the line, 'never to kiss the maid when they can kiss the mistress, unless they like the maid best,' the South stood still; while Great Britain, by means of the 'Sirius,' the 'Liverpool,' and the 'Great Western,' actually and practically demonstrated the great problem of Ocean Steam Navigation.

"Still another opportunity was presented to the South, of entering upon the great race for commercial supremacy and independence, but only to be neglected. France was looking for a port in the United States, from which to establish an opposition line; and it was proposed that the South should take stock, if France would select Norfolk as the terminus of the line. Application was made to the legislature of Virginia to grant only a charter for that purpose, but they refused to grant it; and so it was established at New York, but it was soon abandoned. If the charter had been granted, Norfolk would, at this day, have been the centre of steam navigation for the United States. The lines to the Isthmus would have belonged to Norfolk, and probably, the lines to Havre and Bremen. But Boston got the line of steamers, sent its ships to Liverpool, and recovered all the trade, and more, too, than it had when the steamers first began to ply.

"New York, for ten years, looked quietly on, feeling the way with English capital, as Norfolk might have done with France, until she got the federal government committed for many millions of her steam-ship enterprise; and then she launched her ocean steamers, and now she leads the world in that navigation."

1838. Value of the houses in the city at this time, $2,188,625; and, $2,704,430.

August 18. The Exploring Squadron, in command of Lieutenant Wilkes, sailed from this port.

November 12. On this day a commercial convention was held in Norfolk. There was a large attendance of able and talented delegates, from different sections of our State and of North Carolina. The meetings were held in the Methodist Church, and the session continued for four days. Governor, now ex-President, Tyler, presided with much dignity. Resolutions were passed concerning Direct Trade, Agriculture, and Internal Improvements. Able reports were presented on these and other interesting subjects. The debates were animated and entertaining, and called together a large assemblage of both ladies and gentlemen. The speakers on the occasion were, Messrs. Tyler, Venable, Hubard, James, Segar, Millson, French, Cunningham, Tabb, Southgate, Hayne, M'Farlaine, Soutter, Woodis, Allyn, &c.

1839. "On the 14th of February of this year, an act was passed, increasing (nominally only) the number of councilmen to twenty-six, but requiring them still to be 'fit and able men,' and to be elected in pursuance of the act of 1816. These twenty-six, at their first meeting on the 28th of June, were to elect, from their own body, a recorder and eight aldermen, for one year; that being done, the remaining seventeen persons constituted the Common Council."

March 14. A destructive fire occurred on Newton's Wharf. It broke out in the auction store of Messrs. Nash & Co., which, with several other warehouses, and a large amount of merchandise, was consumed; one or two kegs of powder exploded, causing much fright and scampering, but destroying no lives.

April 3. Fire in Portsmouth, on High Street, nearly opposite the court-house. Several buildings destroyed, including a book store, tin factory, and the printing office of the "Portsmouth Times," John T. Hill, editor. Mr. Godwin, a cabinet-maker, was killed by the falling of a wall.

This year, the cove, which extended east from Bank Street nearly to the southern terminus of Cumberland Street, was filled up, enclosed, ornamented with shade trees, and denominated the "Public Square."

This cove was, for many years, an eyesore to the inhabitants, and was justly deemed a public nuisance. The malaria that arose therefrom, on a hot summer's day, at low tide, was not at all pleasant. View the spot now. That noble structure, the City Hall, standing upon its firm foundation, in the centre of the lot, which rises gradually from Bank, Williams, Cove, and Avon Streets, until it reaches an elevation of several feet above the level of those streets, and immediately over what was formerly the middle of the cove. The green turf, paved walks, substantial and ornamental railing, &c., all tend to form a very striking contrast to the unsightly bog of former days, and present an excellent example of the improving taste of the "city fathers." The Clerk's and Register's Offices, two neat (though rather small) fire-proof buildings, are located nearly in the rear of the City Hall. The site and foundation of Avon Theatre, which was erected this year (1839), and destroyed by fire in 1850, is on the east, or in the rear of the above public buildings. The lot was purchased by the Corporation as the site of the new City Prison, which was completed in 1852. "The exterior dimensions of this edifice are sixty-one by ninety-one feet; the main front wall is thirty-three feet high, including battlements; but is surmounted by buttresses at each corner; and in the centre by a tower forty feet high, in which the great city bell is to be hung. The style is the Gothic of the time of Queen Elizabeth, and shows off the building as if it were of far higher dignity than that of a jail." The cells and other interior arrangements, are well calculated for the purposes intended. The thick granite walls, and heavy iron bars, hinges, bolts, &c., present an appearance of great strength, solidity, and security. Architect, Mr. John H. Sale.

May 25, 1840. The corner stone of the Norfolk Military Academy was laid on this day with appropriate ceremonies. This is thought by many to be the handsomest building in the city. Those capable of judging, pronounce it to be "a perfect specimen of architectural beauty." It is of the Grecian Doric order, the model having been copied from the temple of Theseus at Athens. The length of the building is ninety-one feet, breadth forty-seven. There is a handsome portico at each end, with six symmetrical columns, fronting west on Catharine, and east on

Cumberland Street. The walls are stuccoed in a very durable style. The plan was drawn by Mr. Walter, a celebrated architect of Philadelphia, and the building was erected under the supervision of C. Hall, Esq., an intelligent and opulent bookseller of this city, which is indebted to his taste and enterprise for some of its finest improvements. The situation is most favourable. It stands in its pride in the centre of a beautiful green of about four hundred feet square, bounded west by Catharine, north by Charlotte, and east by Cumberland Street, and on the south by a line extending from the first to the last-named street. The ground rises regularly from the boundaries of the lot to the building, which adds considerably to its imposing appearance. This large and beautiful lot of land, the improvement of which has augmented the value of property in its vicinity, was set apart some years before the Revolution as a church glebe, and was intended for the parsonage of the clergyman who officiated in St. Paul's; but after the Revolution it was assigned to the trustees of the Norfolk Academy.

This institution of learning is well conducted, and stands deservedly high in the estimation of the community, the best evidence of which is the liberal patronage which it enjoys. "A cheering demonstration has been afforded by the annual examinations at the Academy of the efficient manner in which this institution continues to be conducted by its present able and indefatigable professors. The proficiency shown by the pupils under examination, in the several branches of Mathematics, Greek, Latin, French, English, Geography, Astronomy, and Chemistry, evinced their close application to study, and the judicious and skilful course of tuition pursued by their instructors. The specimens of composition are of a high order of merit. Under such successful auspices, we may confidently anticipate that this cherished institution will continue to prosper."

August 13th. The Norfolk and Portsmouth Herald was, on this day, just forty-six years after the commencement of its prosperous career, changed from a tri-weekly to a daily and tri-weekly publication, and we record with pleasure the fact, that the judicious proprietor found the experiment a successful one.

CHAPTER XXIX.

1840—1844.

Commercial Depression—Politics—Prices Current—Population—High Tides—Festivities—General Harrison—Fire—Hailstorm—Walters's Hotel—Judicious Management—Fire, and Loss of Life—Roman Catholic Church—Baptist Church in Portsmouth—Death of one of the Heroes of Craney Island—Death of an Old Citizen—Mayor Delany—Artesian Well, *alias* Market Square Pump—Cisterns—C. Bonsall, Esq.—Supply of Water from Deep Creek—Arrival of Henry Clay—Procession—Festivities—Speeches—Colonel Garnett—The Ladies—Joseph H. Robertson, Esq.—Governor Tazewell—Mr. Clay's Visit to Portsmouth—The Courier—Caterpillars.

BUSINESS, at this period, was in a very depressed state; and while politics was the all-absorbing topic of the day, the condition of the commerce of the place was but little better than it was during the embargo of 1808. Norfolk suffered, as she had before, and has since, from the deleterious effects of legislative restriction to the shipping interests. There were very few vessels in port. Produce was low: flour, $4 25; corn, 35 cts.; bacon, 8 cts.; firewood, $1 75; and staves, "below zero." Population of the borough, according to the census, 10,920; population of the county, whites, 11,280, slaves, 7,845, free coloured, 1,967; total, 21,092.

During the month of November, the tides were unusually and unaccountably high; the wind, at no time during their continuance, blowing above a moderate breeze.

Thursday night, November 19th. There was a brilliant illumination, and a great festivity, on account of the Whig victory which had been gained in the election of the now lamented President Harrison.

December 9th. Drummond's rope-walk destroyed by fire.

December 17th. Hail, from 3½ to 4¼ inches in circumference, fell in the afternoon of this day; great destruction, of course, to window-glass, &c.

January 1st, 1841. Walters's Hotel, now the "City Hotel,"

was this day opened by Bray B. Walters, Esq. The judicious arrangements and active exertions of the gentlemanly and liberal-hearted proprietor have been crowned with success. This establishment is, and well deserves to be, decidedly popular, with both residents and travellers. The tables are well supplied with the various productions with which the Norfolk markets abound, while the numerous apartments and rooms of the house are kept in very neat and comfortable order.

1842, June 2d. Twenty five tenements destroyed by fire, on Little Water Street, Holt's and Woodside's Lanes; boy killed by the falling of a wall.

July 10th. The new Roman Catholic church was dedicated. It is a very handsome building, ninety-six feet long by fifty wide, of the Grecian order. The entrance is by three ascents of granite steps. There is a mitred recess for the altar; and, in the basement, a commodious Sunday-school room. William Callis, architect and carpenter. The Rev. A. L. Hitselberger, a distinguished and very eloquent divine, is its pastor.

July 17th. This is the date of the dedication of the new Baptist church in Portsmouth. It is a neat, handsome structure, of seventy by fifty-five feet; cost, $16,000. Rev. Thomas Hume is the able minister in charge.

June 7th. Departed this life, Captain Arthur Emmerson, of Portsmouth, one of the noble heroes who engaged so unequally, and yet so successfully and triumphantly, with the British at Craney Island, in 1813. He was greatly respected and loved by all who knew his worth of character. His loss was deeply felt and sincerely deplored by his friends and fellow-citizens. He was for a number of years Clerk of the County Court, which office is now filled by his worthy son, Arthur Emmerson, Junior.

July 24. Died on this day, Robert Soutter, Esq., merchant. He was a native of Scotland, but had resided in Norfolk for many years, having long been an extensive and prosperous dealer in foreign and domestic produce. This gentleman was greatly esteemed by a large portion of his fellow-citizens, for his devoted piety, his modest and unpretending demeanour, and incorruptible integrity, which great essential elements of character he had borne throughout his career. A massive and truly beautiful granite monument, standing in the centre of a neatly enclosed lot in the new burial ground, marks his "resting-place." It is the largest and tallest within the limits of that solemn repository. On one side of the base is carved, the word *Soutter*, and on the opposite, "*Resurgimus*."

1843. March. Twelve buildings burned on Little Water Street.

June 24. Wm. D. Delany, Esq., was on this day elected mayor of the borough, and received annually, until 1851, a large majority of the suffrages of the qualified voters. Of his faithfulness as an officer during the lapse of eight years, the decided vote with which he was regularly honoured, even when opposed by gentlemen of acknowledged ability and merit, should be considered the best evidence.

During this month there was issued in Norfolk by the writer and G. W. Shields, Esq., one of the former editors of the Courier, a specimen number of a monthly publication, in pamphlet form, entitled the "*Religious Visitor*," which was to be devoted to moral, religious, and literary information. The number published, the object and plan of the work, were severally commended by the press, but the subscription list did not fully justify its continuance.

This year the pipes of the Artesian well in Market Square were sunk.

It affords a supply, as far as it goes, of tolerably good water, although the name "Artesian well" is very improperly applied. *Market Square Pump* being much more appropriate. "An Artesian well," says Dr. Buckland, "is a well that is *always overflowing*, either from its natural source, or from an artificial tube; and when the overflowing ceases, it is no longer an Artesian well." This pump has nevertheless proved to be a most useful and necessary addition to the means of obtaining water. Much the larger portion of the regular supply is now obtained from cisterns. These are brick reservoirs built below the surface of the earth, and supplied by means of pipes leading from the gutters at the eaves of the houses. The cisterns contain from one or two thousand to fifty thousand gallons, and the water is generally pleasant to the taste, cool, and healthful.

The late C. Bonsal, Esq., is said to have had the first cistern sunk in Norfolk. It was on his lot on Main Street, head of Market Square.

"Several plans to furnish the city with a plentiful supply of water, have been suggested. One contemplates the erection of a tower near the basin of Deep Creek, from which the water would be conveyed by means of iron pipes, passing the southern branch of Elizabeth River above the mouth of Deep Creek, thence in direct line to the Eastern Branch bridge, under which they would pass to a distributing reservoir to be located on some convenient site in Norfolk.

"Another plan is to have an iron steam water boat, capable of carrying fifteen hundred barrels of water, which might be forced by means of steam pumps from the vessel into the distributing reservoir. United States vessels, the Navy Yard, and the commercial marine could also be supplied by this means."

1844, April 24. On this day, Hon. Henry Clay arrived in the city; and on the following day he was received in due form, as the guest of the citizens of all parties.

A procession was formed on Main Street (at the head of Market Square), in the following order:

Music.

Military.

Consisting of the Light Artillery Blues, Captain R. W. Bowden; Junior Volunteers, Captain F. F. Ferguson; Norfolk Riflemen, Captain Dunstan; and Virginia Guards, Captain Lloyd W. Williams.

Corporate Authorities.

Committee of Reception.

Citizens and Strangers generally.

The whole forming a long extended line.

The procession moved up Catharine Street to the residence of Colonel Myers (western intersection of Catharine and Freemason Streets), where Mr. Clay was received in an elegant barouche, and brought into the line of the procession, which proceeded along Freemason to Granby Street, down that street to

Main, and through Main till it came to Church Street, and turning up Church Street passed through Cove, Cumberland, Wolfe, and Catharine Streets, till it came again into Main Street, and thence passed up Talbot Street to Ashland Hall, where it halted amid the roar of a salute of twenty-six guns from the field-pieces of the Norfolk Light Artillery Blues.

At the site on the north side of Ashland Hall (now occupied by an engine house, and the Clerk's and Register's offices, and a portion of the City Hall Square), a spacious arbour was erected, and a collation spread, at the upper end of which a platform was raised for Mr. Clay, from which he addressed the assembled multitude.

"The arbour occupied a space of seventy by one hundred and forty feet, and was formed of a covering of sails supported by three rows of pillars. Five rows of tables, nearly the entire length of the arbour, were set, each table adapted to accommodate two hundred persons in single file; and upon the social system of fire and fall back, thrice that number were enabled to partake of the viands, which were abundantly provided for on the occasion. The interior of the arbour was decorated with national flags, evergreens, and flowers fresh from the forest, in a style highly creditable to the taste and industry of those who had the arrangement of this part of the fete, and attracted the admiration of all. At the upper end of the arbour, and immediately under two of the windows of the Hall, was the platform, upon which Mr. Clay was to receive his welcome from the President of the day, Colonel Wm. Garnett. The Hall was also handsomely decorated, and the letters, WELCOME, HENRY CLAY, two feet in length, were braided against the walls in leaves of laurel; and the spacious room (forty by eighty feet) was devoted exclusively to the accommodation of the ladies, of whom there were at least one thousand within its walls. They were enabled to see and hear Mr. Clay through the windows near which he spoke, the sashes of which had been taken out for that purpose.

Mr. C. was welcomed by Colonel Wm. Garnett, in behalf of the people, in a concise and beautiful address. Mr. Clay's reply was most graceful and powerful, "enchaining and enchanting the minds of his audience by a flow of forensic eloquence and irresistible argument. The speech, as it was delivered, awakened a lively feeling of interest and pleasure, which was manifested by frequent and enthusiastic plaudits from the audience.

"At the conclusion, Mr. Clay, playfully, and in an under tone, observed to those who stood near the platform—'Now I will leave you Philistines, and pay my more willing respects to the ladies.' So saying, he turned and entered the Hall.

"At two o'clock he returned to the arbour, attended by the committee of reception, and the whole company, numbering some three or four thousand, took their places at the tables.

"Among the toasts, the following was prepared by a spirited and beautiful tribute to the illustrious individual who was the subject of it, in a short address delivered by Joseph H. Robertson, Esq., in his own graceful and eloquent manner, during which the sage, it is said, shed tears:

"'Our distinguished guest, Henry Clay; his services in defence of our national honour, in the vindication of the rights of man, and his patriotic efforts during the most alarming domestic dissensions, entitle him to the gratitude of the American people.'

"To which Mr. Clay made a feeling and happy response.

"At three o'clock Mr. Clay retired from the arbour, and in the interval of the time appointed for the call of the Portsmouth Committee (five o'clock), visited Governor Tazewell, who had made him a friendly call on the day of his arrival. It is gratifying to notice this circumstance, as showing that great and liberal minds are incapable of being influenced by party spirit to stifle the kinder suggestions of social feeling.

"At five o'clock, Mr. Clay was waited on by a committee from Portsmouth, by whom he was escorted to the residence of Captain Samuel Watts, and during the evening he was introduced to a large number of ladies, for whose reception the hospitable mansion of Captain Watts was thrown open for that purpose."*

Many joyous and spirit-stirring incidents marked his reception by the citizens of the sister town.

* Captain Watts, of Portsmouth, has very ably represented Norfolk County in the Legislature. He was the Whig candidate for the office of Lieutenant Governor, in 1850. He is justly regarded as a strong man by his party, and stands deservedly high in the estimation of the community as an orator and

The Evening Courier, a spirited penny paper, commenced its course this year, William C. Shields, Esq. (formerly of the Beacon), editor and proprietor. The Courier was subsequently published by Messrs. G. W. & J. E. Shields, sons of the former editor. On the 13th of January, 1851, the name was changed to the "Daily Evening Courier." This useful paper was originally neutral in politics, but for several years advocated, with considerable ability and spirit, Whig men and measures.

It was announced in December, 1852, that from the first of January following, this paper would resume its neutrality in politics; be printed by Mr. James H. Finch, and edited by Mr. R. J. Keeling.

The summer of this year was noted for immense numbers of caterpillars, which destroyed the foliage of the shade and fruit trees, and the vegetables. In many parts of the town and vicinity, these insects were unusually abundant and exceedingly annoying.

CHAPTER XXX.

1845—1847.

Norfolk becomes a City—Objections—Improvement—Effect of a Name—Congratulations of the Petersburg Intelligencer—Lynnhaven Oysters—Conchology, Ichthyology, &c.—Richmond Times and Compiler—Kind Remarks—Sources of Prosperity—Amendments to the Charter—Evidences of Advancement—Court-House in Portsmouth—Methodist Protestant Church Burned—Animal Magnetism—Professor De Bonneville—Severe Storm—Extraordinary Tide—Destruction of Property—Exciting Scene—Loss of Property on the Coast—Lame Boy, Dog, and Cat—Loss of Life—Distressing Scene—Sabbath-School Celebration—Interesting Sight—The Ladies—Addresses—Temperance Reformation—John B. Gough—Remarks—Mexican War—Volunteers—Captain John P. Young—Captain O. E. Edwards.

1845, February 13th. At this date, Norfolk, by Act of Assembly, became a City, and various alterations were made in the

enlightened politician. His speeches are generally characterized by sound argument, superior oratorical skill and energy, and the evidences of extensive reading, careful investigation, and uncommon mental capacity.

charter. The change, though strangely and strenuously objected to by some of the citizens, was certainly a judicious one. It appeared to have a good effect upon the people and the affairs of the place generally.

Mr. Jefferson predicted, it is said, that Norfolk would commence a career of prosperity and importance about this period of its history, and quite sure it is that the business of the place and the general aspect of affairs all seemed to improve; and whatever other causes may be assigned for the improvement, unexpected as it was by many, it was believed that the change in the appellation of the place had no inconsiderable effect both at home and abroad.

> "Some have said, What is in a Name?—most potent plastic influence:
> A name is a word of character, and repetition stablisheth the fact.
> * * * * * * * * *
> And greatest is the power of a name, when its power is least suspected."

The following pleasant remarks appeared in the Herald, shortly after the passing of the legislative act above mentioned:

"We recognise the obeisance of our friend of the Petersburg Intelligencer on the occasion of our promotion to a higher rate (as he deems it), by the legislative act which has made us the 'citizen of a city;' and if he behaves himself, we promise him the first lieutenancy of our ship. It is strange that this incorrigible wag can never turn his thoughts towards Norfolk without letting them run upon *oysters*. From congratulations and good wishes on the event of our said promotion, he whisks off to talk to us about oysters:—

"'By the by, Commodore (quoth he), speaking of turtles—were those 'Lynnhaven pets,' that were sent to Dix at Baltimore, *really seven* inches long? We cannot believe in such oysters until we see them,—and we have no small curiosity about the matter. Not that we care to eat them. Our curiosity is entirely *scientific*, for we have lately been studying a treatise on *Conchology* and *Ichthyology*, with which Colonel Swan furnished us. If we had a bushel or two, we should deliver a highly popular lecture on them.'

"'*Not that we care to eat them.*'—Oh no! The cause of *science* is much more to the *taste* of our philosophic friend of the Intelligencer than a Lynnhaven oyster, *of course!* Really he has such a persuasive way with him, that (as we have before had occasion to remark), like Goldsmith's author, he can 'wheedle milk from a mouse;' but we very much doubt whether he can tickle us into opening oysters for him of the length he speaks of! Such rarities never cross our path; though we are told they are sometimes to be met with; and 'mine host' Mr. Walters, who knows whom to speak to for the best of everything in the eating line, is the only man who could command *such* 'spirits from the vasty deep,' where these *seven-inchers* are said to inhabit.

"We are glad to see the jocularity of the Intelligencer taken up and treated in the amiable vein, and with a judicious disposition to harmonise all rival feelings between the three principal towns of the State, by its neighbour, the Richmond Times and Compiler, in the following article:

"'The old Borough of Norfolk has been declared by legislative act to be a 'city,' and our neighbour of the Petersburg Intelligencer seizes the opportunity to doff his beaver to the worthy editor of the Herald, and tender him his best wishes upon this accession of new honours. This is all right and neighbourly, and we join our neighbour in making a most respectful bow to our friends of the Norfolk press and their fellow-citizens, and tender them our most sincere good wishes for their prosperity, individually and collectively. May the city of Norfolk grow rapidly, and become a great, a very great city.

"'But let us say, in passing, to our friends down there, that the policy of Virginia must be stimulated considerably to make their city what it ought to be, and they ought to help to impart this added energy. They must co-operate with us in effecting a communication with western and southwestern Virginia. Norfolk now has command of the Dismal Swamp Canal and the Roanoke River; and the only remaining source from which she can hope for prosperity, is from the trade to be attracted to James River by this communication with the West. When that communication is effected, and the connexion between the canal and tidewater here made, she will participate with this city in the advantages of the trade thereby acquired. We feel warmly for her welfare. We ardently desire to see Norfolk one of the greatest maritime cities of the Union. Whether this gratification is in store for us, we know not. But this we do know, that if she does not become what we desire to see her through the trade to be conveyed to her wharves from the James River, she cannot by that from other sources. Let her, therefore, join with us in advancing the common interest of Virginia, and of Norfolk and Richmond. Let her discard her misgivings, and let her energies be found in co-operation to effect the grand object which all the people of Virginia should have so much at heart.' "

The following are among the provisions in the amendments to the Charter:

The rights, privileges, &c., formerly vested in the Common Council, to "be vested in two bodies, to wit: the Select Council and the Common Council."

Thirty-seven freeholders to be elected triennially for the Councils, the Recorder, and Aldermen.

The officers of the city to be elected annually in general meeting of the two Councils.

The Recorder and eight Aldermen to be chosen triennially from the thirty-seven persons elected, and with the Mayor, to constitute the Court.

In the intervening years, twenty-eight citizens to be elected for Councilmen.

The twenty-eight Councilmen to elect by ballot, annually, eleven of their number for the Select Council; the remaining seventeen to constitute the Common Council.

Each body to have a president, vice-president, and clerk.

All ordinances to originate in the Common Council; and, having passed that body, to be sent to the Select Council for concurrence or amendment. Amendments to be reported to the former, and, in case of disagreement, the two bodies to assemble together, elect a president *pro tem.*, and the proposed measure to be decided by two-thirds of the members composing the united bodies.

A majority of the members of each body to constitute a quorum, whether acting separately or in general meeting.

The court to appoint only the clerk of the court, the prosecuting attorney, and the constables.

The power over the public property of the corporation, such as lands, tenements, streets, wharves, &c., transferred from the court to the councils.

Sergeant to be elected triennially, on the 24th June, by a plurality of the qualified voters.

The act passed February 13th, 1845, was amended March 20th, 1850, and among other provisions is one, making it lawful for the councils to establish, at their discretion, free schools within the city, and for that purpose build school-houses, and annually assess and levy upon the property and inhabitants of the city to pay for the same.

Of the advancement of the "city" from this time, the increase in real estate to the amount of $122,048, for the year ending 1st February, 1846, is conclusive evidence, as also the increase of tonnage entered and cleared at the custom-house of more than 100 per cent.

The new court-house for Norfolk County, located in Portsmouth, was commenced in 1845.

The site chosen for it is the lot on which the old clerk's office and jail formerly stood. The building presents a front of seventy-eight feet on High Street, and fifty-seven on Court Street; a conspicuous situation, in which it is almost compelled to meet the eye of every stranger who visits Portsmouth. The exterior plan, which was designed by Mr. William R. Singleton, of St. Louis, Mo. (but a native of Portsmouth), is in fine proportion and classic taste. The front on High Street has a projecting portico, elevated fourteen feet from the ground, of four Doric columns, three feet in diameter at the base; after the model of the temple of Jupiter Stator. The Court Street front presents a recess portico entablature, supported by two columns, similar to the portico on High Street. The roof is surmounted by a handsome cupola, supported by eight columns of the Ionic order.*

For the interior, the committee adopted the plan of Mr. Willoughby G. Butler, of Portsmouth. The main floor is elevated

* This has been removed.

fourteen feet above the ground, the basement beneath being divided into rooms for elections, on the right of the entrance from High Street, and for clerk's offices on the left—the latter being entirely fire-proof. The principal floor contains the court room, fifty-seven by fifty-four feet; height of the ceiling twenty feet. In the rear of the court-room are two jury-rooms, each nine by twenty-four feet; and two in front, one on each side of the vestibule, nine by seventeen feet.

"The plan of the jail is exclusively Mr. Singleton's, and shows quite an ornamental front on High Street, while its interior arrangements are designed to be all that could be devised for the security of the prisoners, and the health and cleanliness of their apartments.

"The court-house of Norfolk County was at one time in the Borough; and from thence the seat of justice was removed to the town of Washington (called Ferry, or Washington Point). By an Act of the General Assembly, passed January 20, 1801, it was again removed and located in Portsmouth. The lot and buildings on Washington Point were vested in Wm. Wilson, Robert Thompson, Samuel Hatton, Wm. Godfrey, and Enos M'Coy, Esqs., as Commissioners, who were empowered to sell the same and apply the money arising therefrom to the building of the new court-house, which was finished in 1806, and was just forty years old when the present building took its place.

1845. March 6th. On the evening of this day, the Methodist Protestant Church, on Fenchurch Street, formerly a theatre, took fire, and was destroyed.

June. During this month, a very considerable excitement was produced among the inhabitants by Professor Debonneville, a celebrated lecturer on animal magnetism. His lectures and experiments drew great crowds, and were for several days the principal subject of conversation among many of the citizens, both male and female.

Friday, February 27th, 1846. A snow-storm of almost unprecedented severity commenced on this day, the wind blowing a gale from the northeast.

Saturday, 28th. The snow was several inches deep, and rain began to fall during the day, which continued until noon on

Monday, March 2d, when the rain gave place to hail, which fell rapidly, the wind continuing with unabated violence till midnight, when it increased to a terrific hurricane, which tore off the roofs of buildings, uprooted trees, and demolished fences. The tide soon rose to an extraordinary height. Never since 1825 had it risen so high. Wide Water Street, and the streets, lanes, and wharves below, were completely inundated, and very large quantities of merchandise, such as sugar, salt, lime, &c., were destroyed. The loss of the merchants was estimated at $100,000. West Wide Water Street resembled a narrow river, with high perpendicular banks; and the number of boats passing through this and Commerce Street, Roanoke Square, &c., the bustle among the merchants, and the merry, free, and care-little laugh of the sable boatmen, now and then increased to a loud and joyful ha! ha! as some hapless passenger chanced to tumble overboard, in the cool and briny water; the howling of the storm, and the breaking of the waves against the walls, all united to present a scene of great novelty, activity, and confusion. The shipping in port suffered considerably. Large piles of firewood and lumber were floated away. Drummond's Bridge was swept off, and also a large steam-mill in Portsmouth.

From Cape Henry to Whale's Head, on the coast, the fences, and many of the out-houses, were floated away. Nearly all the cattle and sheep, and immense numbers of hogs, and even some horses, were drowned, numbering in all, according to estimate, about 10,000 head, besides poultry in great quantities. Vessels were driven ashore, and farm-houses were unroofed and blown to pieces. One small tenement, which had been deserted by all its inmates, except a lame boy, a faithful dog, and a cat, having been removed by the tide, the roof and other portions were scattered upon the rolling surges, while the remainder of the building, with its affrighted occupants, who were fortunately provided with a ham of bacon, was driven furiously about by the wind. The hopeless trio nestled closely in a bed, exposed for twelve long hours to the violence of the pitiless storm; but the frail ark of safety was snugly moored among the trees of the forest, many rods above the usual high-water mark, whence the wet and shivering creatures were taken, and properly cared for.

On Nott's Island, in the neighbouring county of Currituck, the loss and damage were exceedingly severe. It was reported, and announced in some of the papers, that several families were swept away, besides immense numbers of cattle.

On Tuesday, the wind ceased, and the swollen waters subsided, when it was truly distressing to behold the scenes of destruction caused by that memorable storm.

July 4th. In addition to the usual exhibition of patriotic regard for the birthday of American liberty, there was a most interesting display made by the different Sabbath-schools of the city.

At seven o'clock, the bells reminded the scholars and teachers that the hour was approaching at which they were to repair to their usual places of meeting. Thence, at about eight o'clock, the several schools—eight in number—under the direction of their respective superintendents, proceeded in regular order to the Academy lawn. Having met and united in one general gathering, the procession marched through some of the principal streets. At the head of each school there was carried a beautifully-painted banner, with an appropriate motto.

It was a charming sight; and the pleasing emotions which it excited were plainly betrayed in the countenances of the crowds of all ages who gazed upon it. The sun appeared occasionally from behind the fleecy clouds that obstructed his rays, (rendering the day unusually pleasant), and looked forth with peculiar brightness, as if well pleased with the holy and joyful scene. The children connected with the Orphan Asylum walked in front.

In that large procession, numbering about one thousand children, of almost every age, from four to sixteen, what a diversity of talent and disposition! The ladies connected with the schools were present, and walked in the procession, thus evincing their devotion to so noble an institution. It was an occasion calculated to encourage the highest hopes of the Christian and philanthropist for the well-being of the rising generation. Might not a great company of ministering angels have hovered in gladness over the cheering scene?

The schools having assembled in the Presbyterian Church,

appropriate addresses were delivered by Rev. Mr. Wadsworth, of the Methodist Church, to the children, and by Rev. Mr. Caldwell, of the Episcopal Church, to the officers and teachers. The remarks of the reverend gentlemen were highly appropriate, and well calculated to inspire all present with an increased devotion to, and interest in, a cause, upon which rest in a great measure the hopes of the country—a cause which has been so abundantly blessed by Heaven, and whose influences, for time and eternity, are far beyond the limited stretch of the imagination of man.

During this and the following years, and, in fact, for several years antecedent to 1846, considerable excitement was produced in the minds of quite a large portion of the community by the Temperance Reformation. The reformed inebriate and talented lecturer, John B. Gough, and others, visited the city, and delivered addresses to large assemblages; very many persons took the pledge of total abstinence from all intoxicating drinks as a beverage, and numbers of inebriates were apparently reformed.

This, it must be admitted, is a useful and a good cause, and its tendency has, to a great extent, been advantageous and beneficial to the community. And yet it cannot be reasonably doubted, that some have exhibited too much fanaticism in their efforts, while much less real good has been accomplished in some instances than was expected. The seemingly reformed have, in many instances, returned to their cups; and hundreds have paid too little regard to the obligations under which they have been placed by the pledge. The effect of the movement, however, upon the rising generation, is considered highly beneficial and quite salutary. One unpleasant feature in the progress of this reformation is, that some apparently pious men, have been led by their devotion to its objects, to neglect their religious obligations—to lessen their attention to the ordinances of the church and the means of grace. The true Christian will, generally, be virtually all that any association, secondary to his church, can require of him; and if he cannot attend to the less important, without neglecting the greater, it is decidedly unwise and improper to engage in the former; hence, it is the opinion of some great and good men, who entertain the highest regard for this reformation, that it should be conducted entirely by non-professors. We venture not, as yet, however, to embrace this view of the subject. Time will be required by many to test its soundness, and we cannot fully agree with the supporters of the theory.

On the 16th of December, 1846, a meeting was held in Ashland Hall, at which patriotic speeches were made relative to the Mexican War. A company of volunteers was soon raised, being composed of young men of the city and county of Norfolk, and of Princess Anne. On the 26th, an election of officers took place, and O. E. Edwards was chosen captain.

January 1, 1847. A company having also been raised in Portsmouth, John P. Young was elected captain. On the 12th, this company went to Richmond, and was suitably received and disposed of by Governor Smith. The company proceeded to Mexico, but was not favoured with an opportunity of engaging with the enemy.

Captain Edwards's company was also offered to the Governor for his disposal, but not being received, the offer was made to the Governor of North Carolina; being again refused, proposals were then made to the United States Government, and promptly accepted. Captain E. having received a commission as captain, in a regiment of voltigeurs, embarked, on March 27th, for Fort M'Henry, near Baltimore; after which, the company proceeded to Mexico, where Captain E. was assigned to the command of the howitzer battery attached to the regiment. During the engagement at the National Bridge, and elsewhere, Captain E. and his company fought with great gallantry. After his return to the city, he was presented, by some of the citizens, with an elegant sword, as an evidence of their appreciation of his brave conduct and distinguished efforts in the service of his country. He has since died in California, leaving a wife and several children, who reside in this city.

CHAPTER XXXI.

1847.

Destructive Fire—Frightful Accident—Boys Burnt—Suffering and Death—Rev. Mr. Beall—Marble Tablet—Virginia Temperance Advocate—Grain Business—High Prices—Unseasonable Weather—Fish—Moonlight Excursions—Prices of Grain—Rev. Mr. Anderson—Indian Corn—Demand from Ireland—Shipments—Sabbath-school Celebration—Rev. Mr. Cummins—U. S. Ship Pennsylvania—Grain and Corn—Death of Colonel Newton—Death of Dr. Moseley—City Hall—Corner Stone—Ceremonies—Oration—Rev. Mr. Hitselberger—New Orphan Asylum—View of the Old Church at Jamestown—Gift of the Norfolk Ladies—Public Buildings—Streets Paved—Spirit of Improvement—Beacon Office Destroyed—Snow and Thunder.

JANUARY 16, 1847. At an early hour, a destructive fire broke out on the south side of Main Street, two or three doors east from the corner of Market Square, which consumed several very valuable buildings, and a large quantity of goods. Newton's beautiful block on Market Square, and the property on the north side of Main Street, were seriously menaced by the flames; but for the very active exertions of the several fire companies of this city, and of Portsmouth, on this as on other occasions, the destruction would have been very great. The loss was estimated at $60,000.

A frightful accident, attended with loss of life under very painful circumstances, occurred after the fire had been subdued. Several boys, among whom were Robert Brown and Barlow Daniel, were endeavouring to extricate, from among the smouldering ruins, a large tin can, containing a quantity of spirits of turpentine, camphine, or other explosive liquid, which had been kept in the cellar of one of the stores destroyed. Just as they succeeded in pulling it out from a pile of hot bricks, it ignited and exploded, scattering the combustible substance in every direction, and simultaneously saturating, and setting on fire, the clothes of the unfortunate boys above named. It was, to them, an awful moment, of the intensest agony and horror. The poor boys were, in an instant, completely enveloped in a thick sheet of glaring white flame, which arose several feet above their heads. No martyr at the stake, nor any act of savage cruelty, had, probably, ever presented an instance of more excruciating bodily torture, so completely enwrapped were they in the fierce, flashing, devouring element, fed as it was by the fiery fluid;—a lamentable condition, truly, for human beings to be placed in. Daniel, who was a sprightly and intelligent youth, ran screaming to the so-called Artesian well, which was within a few rods of the ruins, while Brown, a stout, active boy, of about fourteen, made the best of his way over the piles of rubbish, inhaling the white flame as he proceeded. Happening in the daytime, a number of persons hastened immediately to witness the frightful scene, which words are scarcely adequate to describe. Terror was strikingly depicted in the countenance of every man present. The beholders stood, for a few moments, aghast, with uplifted hands, and uttering exclamations of horror. At first it seemed difficult, and even hazardous, to render assistance. A gentleman, however, had sufficient presence of mind to throw his cloak over Daniel, in his rapid, fiery flight; but he disengaged himself, and, with almost superhuman effort, hurried on to the pump, where copious streams of cold water were quickly thrown upon him. The stores near the ruins were soon emptied of their occupants. Some came with water, others with blankets; one of which was thrown over Brown, the flames extinguished, and the remaining fragments of half-burnt garments removed, after he had fallen upon a heap of rubbish.

Too much pain has already been inflicted upon the feelings of the reader, and perhaps this narrative should end here; but having commenced it, the sad conclusion may be expected. Besides, it may not be improper to show the extent of physical suffering to which the unfortunate creatures of earth are sometimes subjected.

The half-stifled screams of "Put me out! put me out!" thrilled the hearts of those present with indescribable pain, and the distorted and blistered condition of poor Brown's body, and that of his helpless companion in misery, was too shocking to behold, and the reader would sicken at a further detail. The unfortunate youths both received the most prompt and skilful medical and maternal attention; but death relieved them of their sufferings on the following day. They both had widowed mothers, whose emotions of deep, heartfelt, agonizing sorrow must be imagined.

March 10th, 1847. Departed this life, Rev. Upton Beall, formerly of Frederick, Maryland, the esteemed pastor of Christ Church. The members of his charge caused a handsome marble tablet, with an appropriate inscription, to be prepared and placed in the church, on the west wall, near the northwest corner; and they also had erected to his memory, in Cedar Grove Cemetery, a beautiful monument, with an epitaph and significant emblems.

May 15th. On this day was issued the first number of the Virginia Temperance Advocate, a weekly paper, edited by the author of these sketches, and devoted to temperance, morality, literature, health, &c. It was favourably noticed by the press, and well received by the community; the subscription-list included the names of many of the most intelligent citizens in town and country. It was subsequently edited by W. W. Davis, Esq.

A very heavy and extensive grain business was done in the spring of this year; the principal cause of the demand being the scarcity of food in Ireland. A large number of English and American vessels were freighted with corn, flour, meal, pork, &c., &c., and a scene of great activity was exhibited in the commercial portion of the city. Some of the enterprising and more experienced merchants were greatly enriched, while the injudicious and incautious sustained heavy losses. There were some who might have adopted the following lines:

"Of all the days since I was born,
I hate the day I dealt in corn;
And long shall I lament the hour,
When I resolved to trade in flour.
And, what is worse, I've had no ease,
Since buying up the beans and peas.
Alas! how wretched do I feel,
Whene'er I'm told the price of meal.
Oh! had I dealt in pork and lard,
I would not say the times were hard.
But curse upon all speculation,
Which ruined me, if not the nation."

May 21st. Corn was this day quoted at $1 05; fine flour, $10; superfine, $11; family, $12.

During the month of May, the weather was remarkably cool for the season. Fires were comfortable, and overcoats were worn.

So plentiful was the supply of fresh fish in the market, during the latter part of this month, that half a dozen fine large gray trout sold for only six and a quarter cents.

Moonlight excursions down the river in steamboats, to Hampton Roads and the Capes, with music and dancing, became very popular among the pleasure-loving, and the "loved and loving" in particular.

June 11th. Price of corn, $1 15; oats, 55 cents.

Sunday, June 13th. Rev. S. J. P. Anderson was this day installed pastor of the Presbyterian Church.

June 24th. For the quarter ending this day, 750,830 bushels of Indian corn were reported as having been inspected in the city, and all the returns had not been made.

This article of food was now becoming somewhat scarce, even in this land of plenty and of inexhaustible resources. The long, loud cry which came booming, as it were, over the broad bosom of the Atlantic for bread, and which had been so nobly and generously heeded and responded to, had almost imperceptibly reduced the supplies, even in this great corn region, below the mark which prudence might have dictated. Vessel after vessel, laden with this invaluable fruit of the soil, had descended the various rivers, which drain the fertile valleys in our vicinity. The warehouses groaned and cracked beneath the immense pressure of the nutritious substance, and it was transferred in vast quantities to the ample holds of the vessels, which bore it rapidly away before the ocean breezes to the shores of unhappy Ireland, for the relief of the famishing inhabitants of that oppressed island; where the cries of the starving thousands of all ages, first loud and clamouring, then growing weaker and fainter, were still unheeded by many, till they were hushed in death, and the trembling tenements fell in ruins as the spirits ascended to their God.

July 4th. On this day, in addition to the usual display of the military, there was another large Sabbath-school procession, numbering about one thousand children, besides the teachers; all of whom were under the general supervision of Walter H. Taylor, Esq., assisted by Wm. H. Hunter, and Harrison Robertson, Esqrs., whose vigilant attention was instrumental in preventing the occurrence of a single accident to cast a shade of unpleasantness upon the splendid picture. Who that witnessed that scene did not entertain the wish that the numbers of young hearts then beating with life, and love, and joyfulness, might ever be preserved from the contaminating influences and ruinous consequences of sin? Able and eloquent addresses were delivered by Rev. Mr. Hendrickson, of the Baptist Church, and Rev. Mr. Anderson, of the Presbyterian Church.

On Sabbath, July 10th, Rev. George D. Cummins, who had been duly elected Rector of Christ Church, to supply the vacancy occasioned by the death of Rev. Mr. Beall, preached his introductory sermon to a densely-crowded audience. The discourse was very interesting and appropriate, evincing a high order of rhetorical talent, as well as an exalted sense of the dignity and responsibilities of his sacred office, and of his new and important charge.

July 24th. The U. S. ship Pennsylvania—that giant among vessels—moved majestically down from the mouth of the Southern Branch, opposite the navy-yard, to the anchorage off Smith's Point. As an evidence of the great depth of water in the harbour, although the tide was unusually low when the ship was removed, she met with no interruption whatever, but passed steadily along, in silent grandeur, to be a magnificent ornament to our capacious haven. Her dimensions are as follows:—220 feet, lower deck; 217 feet, length aloft; 190 feet, length of keel for tonnage; 56 feet, 9 inches, moulded breadth of beam for tonnage; 59 feet, moulded breadth of beam outside of wales; 23 feet, depth of hold; 51 feet, extreme depth amidships; 3,306 23–95, tonnage; guns, 140; 18,341 yards duck, one set of sails; 14,624 yards duck, bags, hammocks, boat-sails, awnings, &c.; total, 32,965 yards; 11 inches, shrouds; 10 inches, mainstay; 278 feet, mainmast; 110 feet, mainyard; 82 feet, topsail yard; 52 feet, topgallant yard; 36 feet, royal yard; 10,000 lbs. sheet anchor; 1,521 yards main-topsail.

This ship, which cost the nation $800,000, was built at Philadelphia, and is now lying at the Gosport Navy-Yard. She is the largest ship in the American Navy, and the most costly. The only voyage she ever made was from Philadelphia to Norfolk.

July 23d. Corn at this date was quoted at 65 cts., and flour at $6 50, exhibiting a very considerable fall in price within a few weeks.

August 5th. Departed this life, aged 79 years, Hon. Thomas Newton.*

Saturday, August 14th. Dr. Moseley, an eminent medical gentleman of Norfolk, died suddenly, of apoplexy, in his office.

Monday, 23d. The corner-stone of the large and beautiful City Hall was laid this day. The volunteer companies, Free-masons, Odd-Fellows, Sons of Temperance, Rechabites, Druids, city authorities, officers of the Navy, the clergy, and the citizens generally, accompanied by a fine band of music, moved in procession through some of the streets, and then assembled at the northeast corner of the foundation of the intended hall of justice.

A box, containing coins, papers, and other memorials, was placed in a square cavity, hewn out of a large piece of granite, upon which was placed another piece, and on this the thick and solid foundation-stones were laid, there to remain, perhaps, for ages, undisturbed, and concealed from the view of the busy crowds by which it will often be surrounded. An able Masonic address was delivered by Mr. J. C. M'Cabe, after which the Rev. A. L. Hitselberger, of St. Patrick's Church, who was selected as the orator for the occasion, delivered an address, which was characterized by elegance of style, combined with highly appropriate and classical allusions, and patriotic sentiments. "It was, indeed," says the Herald, "one of the most masterly efforts of eloquence which we have ever listened to, and in which the gifted speaker exhibited extensive learning and familiarity with the history and jurisprudence of ancient times."

September 8th. The corner-stone of the new Orphan Asylum was laid, under the supervision of the lady managers of the insti-

* See pages 54, 55, 71, &c.

tution, assisted by John Tunis, Esq., and several other gentlemen. No oration was pronounced, on account of the illness of the person selected to perform that duty.

October. A beautiful token of attachment to the home of their nativity was shown by two Norfolk ladies, then residents of another city, who had lithographed, at their own expense, an accurate view of the ancient church at Jamestown (the first built in Virginia), intended especially, as expressed on the plate, for the Norfolk Female Orphan Asylum.

During this year, several public buildings were commenced, Freemason and other streets were paved, new streets were opened, and a spirit of improvement, such as had not been manifested in the place before, began to diffuse itself.

Saturday evening, November 27th. Beacon office and reading-room destroyed by fire.

Dec. 21. At an early hour it commenced snowing, with a strong wind from northeast. The ground was soon covered to the depth of two or three inches. At three o'clock, in the midst of the violence of the storm, the inhabitants were startled by several peals of thunder, the heavy, dull, and yet loud sound of which, echoed and rolled along beneath the lowering clouds for many seconds after each explosion.

CHAPTER XXXII.

1848—1849.

Southern Argus—Its Peculiarities—Remarks of Bulwer—Methodist Church Destroyed — Destructive Conflagration — Suffering — Insurance — Bethel Church, &c.—Philharmonic Association—Youthful Heroism—Narrow Escape from Drowning—Captain Hamilton L. Shields, U. S. A.—Captain Edward H. Fitzgerald, U. S. A.—New Baptist Church—California—Reflections —Visiters—Internal Improvements—Cumberland Street Methodist Episcopal Church—Unsuitable Location—General Millson—The Cholera—Norfolk Female Institute—Dr. Selden—Gas-Works—New Buildings—City Revenue—Death of M. King, Esq.

January 8th, 1848. On this day the first number of the Southern Argus was issued, by S. T. Sawyer, Esq., editor and proprietor. This paper is very ably conducted, and zealously advocates the principles and tenets of the Democratic party, a liberal system of internal improvements, the interest of the merchants, &c. It also presents, daily, an interesting variety of useful selections, which have rendered it popular as a family paper, as well as a valuable commercial and political journal. There is one peculiarity about the Argus, which is observable by its readers: it seldom notices or copies the particulars of the frightful accidents of so frequent occurrence in various sections of the country, and generally omits those extreme cases of inhumanity, suffering, or cruelty, which occupy so large a place in the columns of some papers. Perhaps this may be the wiser course, in view of the effect which the reading of such accounts has upon the minds of some persons.

"It may be observed," says Bulwer, "that there are certain years in which, in a civilized country, some particular crime comes into vogue. It flares its season, and then burns out. Thus, at one time, we have burking, at another, swingism—now suicide is in vogue; now poisoning trades-people in apple-dumplings; now little boys cut each other with penknives; now common soldiers shoot at their sergeants. Almost every year there is one crime peculiar to it; a sort of annual, which overruns the country, but does not bloom again. Unquestionably, *the press has a great deal to do with these epidemics.* Let a newspaper give an account of some out-of-the-way atrocity, that has the charm of being novel, and certain depraved minds fasten to it, like leeches. They brood over and resolve it; the idea grows up a horrid phantasmalian monomania; and all of a sudden, in a hundred different places, the one seed sown by the leaden types, springs up into foul flowering. But if the first reported aboriginal crime has been attended with impunity, how much more does the imitative faculty cling to it. Ill-judged mercy falls, not like dew, but like a great heap of manure, on the rank deed."

March 2. The Methodist Episcopal Church, situated on Cumberland, near Cove Street, was destroyed by fire. It was a large, handsome, and commodious building, erected in 1832–3; dedicated March, 1833; cost about $18,000; insurance nearly $14,000.

June 14. A fire broke out in the lumber-yard of Messrs. Ferguson and Milhado, the contents of which, and of an adjoining one, belonging to Mr. John Tunis, each containing a very large quantity of plank, scantling, shingles, &c., &c., were consumed, together with hundreds of barrels of pitch, tar, and turpentine, and several very large warehouses filled with foreign and domestic produce. The fire spread with fearful rapidity, sweeping both sides of Woodside's Lane, every building on the south side of Wide Water, from this lane to Fayette Street, and a long row on the opposite side of Water Street. The Mariners' Bethel, a new and handsome Gothic structure, shared the same fate. The flames bursting from the windows and steeple of this building, presented a grand and imposing scene. Many valuable buildings on Fayette and Kelly Streets, including Harris's extensive bakery, were also destroyed. The unsparing element soon reached West Main Street, on which a number of valuable family residences were also laid in ruins. More than sixty buildings, exclusive of kitchens, stables, &c., were destroyed. Great quantities of produce were burnt, including thousands of bushels of corn, a very large amount of sugar, molasses, coffee, cotton, naval stores, several horses, &c., &c. The loss was estimated at $200,000.

Many families were left in a most destitute condition, and excited the profound sympathy of the community. The councils met on the Thursday following; promptly voted an appropriation of $500 for the relief of the sufferers, and appointed a committee to solicit aid in their behalf. Many of the buildings, and a considerable portion of the produce, were insured, although many of the merchants were heavy losers. The Bethel Church was insured for $5,000. Among numerous painful instances of suffering and destitution, we record one only,—that of a mother, with an infant in her arms, and three or four small children gathering closely around her for protection. They had fled from the fury of the flames, having saved only a few pieces of furniture.

On Thursday, the 22d, the Philharmonic Association gave a concert at the National Hotel, for the benefit of the indigent sufferers by this calamitous fire, and the musical entertainment proved to be one of a highly interesting character. The large saloon of the National was crowded by a fashionable audience, who appeared much delighted with the "concord of sweet sounds." A number of ariosoes, rondeaus, duetts, &c., were most admirably sung, manifesting a highly cultivated musical taste and talent, and producing a thrilling effect upon the audience.

This Association is composed of young gentlemen whose native musical genius has been carefully cultivated. Their voices being happily harmonized, the various intonations are clear, full, and distinct; and whether in solo, duett, quartette, or "in full chorus joined," the music swells out *a tempo giusto*, and in strong, deep-toned, and thrilling melody—rising or falling with singular harmony and calm cadence—some of the closing strains resembling those produced by a well-trained instrumental band.

On Tuesday afternoon, July 18th, a son of E. S. Pegram, Esq., merchant, while bathing in the river, was swept off by the current, and in imminent danger of being lost; whereupon, Bryant Ward, aged ten years, a son of Wm. Ward, Esq., immediately swam out and succeeded in reaching his companion, but not having sufficient strength to rescue him, both were soon exhausted, and would have perished, but for the timely arrival of a boat sent to their aid. The little hero remained insensible for some time, and when questioned as to his temerity, replied: "I could not bear to see him drown." A noble example of youthful heroism, well deserving of a record here. He was suitably rewarded by the father of the lad for whom he had freely hazarded his life, and the generous act was deservedly commended by all who were made acquainted with the circumstances attending it.

On Thursday, 20th, an elegant and costly sword was presented to Captain Hamilton L. Shields, of 3d Artillery, U. S. A., a native of this city, as a testimony from his fellow-citizens of their appreciation of his gallant services in the war with Mexico. Captain S. entered the army from West Point, and took part in the siege and capture of Vera Cruz; after which, he was in very nearly every engagement from that place to the city of Mexico, and greatly distinguished himself by his bravery and soldier-like conduct.

Captain Shields received, in 1850, the honourable and important appointment of Judge Advocate of the Eastern Division of the United States Army.

Subsequently to the above presentation, a splendid sword was tendered by the citizens to Captain Edward H. Fitzgerald, U. S. A., of Norfolk, in testimony of their approbation of his gallantry and noble conduct in several engagements with the enemy on the ensanguined fields of Mexico.

August 15. The corner-stone of the Freemason Street Baptist Church was laid in the afternoon of this day. The situation of this beautiful building was most judiciously chosen, being on the north side of Freemason, and east side of Catharine Streets, and at the northeast corner formed by their intersection, which is very near the centre of the city, affording a fine view of the structure from four or more different points.

During a portion of this and the succeeding year, considerable excitement was manifested in the city on account of the extraordinary mineral developments in California; and some enterprising young men and a few of the middle-aged, proceeded hence with all possible despatch to the land of promise—the land of glittering gold; and doubtless they were cheered on their devious, weary way by the bright anticipation of future wealth, honours, and happiness, when in the enjoyment of the great object of their toilsome journey. Some, it is gratifying to record, have succeeded quite well in their expectations; while others, who were unused to the hardships and perils of a long and tedious route, and the privations of a new, unsettled, uncultivated country, became sadly discouraged, and after many a day of disappointment, sickness, and sorrow, returned to the cherished home of their childhood and youth—glad enough, indeed, to see again the familiar faces of relatives and friends, and to enjoy the pleasures and comforts of life. Some, alas, sickened, and lingered in pain awhile; then closed their eyes in death, far, far away from the embrace of friends and the kindly attentions peculiar only to "home, sweet home."

"The spades and mattocks with which they hoped to exhume the buried treasure, have been used for a mournful purpose, and thousands are sleeping their last sleep, entombed among the glittering dust that has lured them from home and family.

"The misery and suspense of the friends and relatives of the emigrants, at home, are scarcely less painful to contemplate than the sufferings of the gold-hunters themselves. The fate of many of the latter will never be known to those they left behind. Among the lists of deaths, the words 'stranger' and 'unknown' frequently occur, and hundreds have died and will die in that far-off land, of whose decease not even these anonymous memoranda will be made. The story of the overland emigration has not been half told. Thousands are yet struggling through the grassless and unwatered plains between the Council Bluffs and California, as the first crusaders struggled through the marshes of Hungary, and their line of march like that of the crosses, will hereafter be known by the graves and bleaching skeletons in their track."

"Gold many hunted, sweat and bled for gold;
Waked all the night, and laboured all the day;
And what was this allurement, dost thou ask?
A dust dug from the bowels of the earth,
Which, being cast into the fire, came out
A shining thing that fools admired, and called
A god; and in devout and humble plight
Before it kneeled, the greater to the less.
And on its altar, sacrificed ease, peace,
Truth, faith, integrity, good conscience, friends,
Love, charity, benevolence, and all
The sweet and tender sympathies of life."

During the last week in December, several members of the Legislature paid a visit to Norfolk and Portsmouth, among whom were Messrs. Burwell of Bedford, Boyd of Wythe, and M'Cue of Augusta. They addressed the people of the two towns on the subject of internal improvements. The principal object of their visit was to direct attention to the Lynchburg and Tennessee Railroad, and the extension of the Louisa Road to the Ohio. They aroused a very fine feeling, apparently, in behalf of those great measures.

Sunday, Jan. 8th, 1849. The new Methodist Church, on Cumberland Street, was this day dedicated by the Rev. J. E. Edwards,

16

the minister in charge, whose discourse on the occasion was eloquent and appropriate. This edifice occupies the site of that which fell a prey to the devouring element on the night of 2d March, 1847.

"The building is of the Grecian Doric order, designed by its architect and constructor, Mr. William Callis, of this city. It is sixty-four feet front, eighty-four feet deep, with an elevation of thirty-nine feet from the level of the street to the apex of the roof.

"The front presents an open vestibule, supported by two handsome columns, of about three and a half feet in diameter, and four bold antæs or pilasters, all supporting a neat entablature, and pediment, in plain Grecian Doric taste. The sides are also ornamented with antæs, and a continuation of the entablature from the front.

"The entrance to the chapel is by two flights of commodious granite steps, fronting the street,—seven on either side, landing on a platform of eight feet square; and six more turning right and left, land on a platform of ten by thirty feet, the front of which is enclosed with a very neat, cast-iron railing, finishing to two ornamented lamp-posts of cast-iron. Three doors in the vestibule open into the chapel, and two lead to the galleries.

"The basement, which is of nine feet pitch, and neatly finished, is divided into a lecture-room, sixty by fifty-seven feet; four class-rooms of fourteen by twenty-four feet (unnecessarily large); and one of ten by fourteen, including the minister's study. There are, also, a wide passage, and the necessary fuel and sexton's rooms.

"The church proper, or chapel story, is about twenty-six feet pitch in the clear. On the lower floor are three aisles and one hundred and twenty-eight seats, which will accommodate seven hundred and fifty persons; the galleries, which are commodious, will accommodate four hundred more, on the sides, beside the front, occupied by the Choir, which will accommodate about one hundred and fifty."

This large and commodious house of worship has been pronounced, by competent judges, to be, both externally and internally, one of the neatest, and most symmetrical buildings in the

State; but while it answers well all the purposes of the numerous membership and congregation, for whose accommodation it was erected (excepting the Sunday-school room, which is rather small, owing to the unusually large size of the class-rooms), it must be admitted that, on account of its unfavourable location, it is comparatively concealed from view. Situated on a narrow street, which abruptly terminates at a row of buildings, a few rods below, and on the south; being immediately opposite another lofty block, and between buildings, which project, on either hand, several feet farther towards the line of the street than its beautiful front, it can only be seen to advantage by standing off, at a very short distance, on the opposite side of the street on which it stands. The burning of the other church afforded an excellent opportunity for obtaining a more suitable site, which was greatly desired, and even insisted upon by some of the members; but there were others who had worshipped for nearly half a century just *there*, who naturally felt a strong attachment to that particular spot, and who, perhaps, deemed a change of location very unwise, if not almost sacrilegious. But, in addition to this, it was found very difficult to obtain a more suitable lot, at a fair price; consequently the present structure (like the former) though in a central situation, is comparatively but little ornament to the city.*

Rev. Mr. Edwards, who served this church the first two years after its erection, was succeeded by Rev. Robert Michaels; and Rev. Nelson Head was appointed for the conference year, commencing Nov. 1, 1852.

April. On the fourth Thursday of this month, General John S. Millson, attorney at law, a native and resident of this city, was elected, by the Democratic party, a member of the House of Representatives from the First Congressional District of Virginia. He was re-elected in October, 1851.

General M. ranks high, among his political friends, as an efficient, firm, and faithful representative. By his talents, close mental application, and diligent attention to his professional

* The writer has been informed that a proviso in the original deed of the ground to the trustees, is to the effect that no other building than a church shall be erected thereon; otherwise the lot will be forfeited.

duties, he rose rapidly in the estimation of his fellow-citizens, as a lawyer, while his urbanity of manners, fidelity, exalted moral and social qualities, and unostentatious dignity of character, command the respect of his constituents. His style of oratory is energetic, forcible, and attractive, yet calm and deliberative, although he sometimes indulges quite freely in a dramatic or theatrical order of declamation. He is justly regarded as an eloquent and able advocate and defender of the leading principles and doctrines of the Democratic party.

An intelligent writer thus alludes to one of his addresses, delivered in October, 1852:

"We have heard many and effective speeches during the present canvass; numerous points urged with vigour and argument deserving the highest approval; but General Millson adds to these usual ingredients of Democratic addresses, a novelty which attracts and absorbs the attention of his hearers."

The qualities which we have mentioned are such as, it is believed, will continue to elevate the General in the scale of populary, at least with his party; and, as he is yet, comparatively, but a young man (about 45), he will probably receive more important honours, than those that have been hitherto conferred upon him by his fellow-citizens.

May 17, 1849. On this day, that fearful disease, the Asiatic cholera, again visited the town, after an interval of sixteen summers. Its attacks were generally much less fatal than in 1832. The alarm was, nevertheless, great among many of the inhabitants; and this, in some instances, doubtless prepared the system for its ravages. The progress of the disease was, in many cases, very readily arrested by the physician, when called in before the patient had begun to sink too rapidly, to yield to the effects of medicine. Some cases terminated fatally, in a few hours after the first symptoms; others lingered a day or two. A few recovered quickly, and others gradually; requiring, in some instances, the lapse of months for the restoration of the system. It proved, as in '32, to be truly a mysterious malady; quite manageable in some cases, in others baffling the highest professional skill; defying the most searching investigation as to its real cause; now, seemingly overcome by some simple and newly-discovered antidote, and anon, pursuing its destructive course, despite all remedies, all attention.

Some persons insisted that it was contagious; others, to the contrary. It appears that there is yet much to be learned about it, by those whose profession may again bring them in close contact with its unseen power. We close now this digression, and leave the subject, serious indeed as it is, for the consideration and study of that invaluable class of citizens above alluded to, among the number of whom, in this region, one, at least, fell beneath its irresistible strokes.

July. The "*Norfolk Female Institute*" was established this month. The principals are Rev. Aristides S. Smith, A.M., and Rev. Leonidas L. South, A.M., gentlemen who have proved themselves to be qualified for their duties; and we state with pleasure that success has crowned their efforts, and the prospects of the Institute are pleasing and favourable. This establishment is justly deemed a useful acquisition to the city, being "designed to furnish to parents and guardians in the South, a school in which they can secure as thorough a classical, English, and polite education as can be obtained in any of the seminaries of the North."

"The buildings are spacious and elegant, and admirably suited for a boarding school for young ladies. They are located in a retired part of the city, on the most elevated spot of ground within its limits. The grounds attached to them are beautifully laid out, and ornamented with a profusion of trees and shrubbery. Embracing, too, more than an entire square, they furnish ample room for both amusement and exercise."

Died, this month, Doctor Wm. Selden, aged 77, a physician who acquired an enviable distinction, and who was greatly esteemed during a long life, sedulously devoted to his profession in this city.

October 1st. The *Gas Works*, having been established by a company composed of enterprising and wealthy citizens, the first exhibition of the lights in the streets and buildings of the city took place on this day.

The works first erected are situated on Briggs' Point, near the eastern extremity of the city, at the southwest corner of Mariner and Third Cross Streets. The retort-house is forty-five by twenty-five feet, built of the best Baltimore bricks, and presents quite a handsome and ornamental front. From the centre of the building an immense chimney springs up, nearly eighty feet high. There are two wings, fifteen by twenty-three feet; one on the east and the other on the west of the main building. Connected with the establishment are two large cisterns, each holding 50,000 gallons. These buildings will be abandoned, another location having been selected on James Street, near Armistead's Bridge, and buildings erected on a much more extensive scale. The works at the new location will go into operation early in 1853, when important improvements will be introduced in the manner of generating the gas, &c.

"When the storm howls, and the tempest shakes our dwelling-place at midnight, it is pleasant to look out upon the city below, all mantled with a silvery light. Here and there, on this side and that, as far as the eye can reach, the friendly lamps are seen, like so many faithful sentinels at their post, keeping watch, while the storm-king threatens destruction on every hand. These lights are like the bright stars that gleam out upon the mariner, when rocked by the billow on the bosom of ocean, amid the shout of the tempest. They cheer many bleeding hearts. Light is pleasant to eyes that are accustomed to weep, and never more pleasant than of a stormy night. Our gas lights confer this blessing upon many who have not the means, otherwise, to command it. Let them burn on quietly and beautifully. We would not have them extinguished to be lighted no more, for any consideration."*

Surplus of revenue over expenditures of city this year, $8,757 50.

December 8. Died on this day, Miles King, Esq., a gentleman who possessed great worth of character, having filled in Norfolk several offices of public trust and confidence. He was some time Captain of the Norfolk Light Artillery Blues, and afterwards filled the office of Navy Agent in this place; he represented the borough in the Legislature of the State; after

* The use of gas for lighting streets was introduced in London in 1814.

which, he was, for years, regularly elected Mayor. In 1843, his health began to decline, and he retired from public life.

CHAPTER XXXIII.

1850.

Internal Improvement Meeting—Delegation from Clarksville—David Shelton, Esq.—Doctor Wilson—Extracts from Interesting Letters—Unseasonable Weather—Launch of the Powhatan—Engines—The Gosport Iron Works—Norfolk Iron Works—Mechanics' Hall—Its Utility, &c.—Avon Theatre Destroyed—Fire in Portsmouth—Cadets of the Virginia Military Institute—Their Visit to Norfolk, &c.—Acknowledgments—Snow-Storm—General Scott—Fire in Gosport—Fruit, Vegetables, &c.—Farms—New City Hall—Location—Architecture—Dimensions—View—New Baptist Church—Description—Ashland Hall—Drought and Warm Weather.

FRIDAY evening, January 11th, 1850, a very large meeting of the citizens of Norfolk was held at Ashland Hall, for the purpose of conferring with a delegation of the citizens of Clarksville, Mecklenburg County, Va., on the subject of a railroad connexion from that town with the Seaboard and Roanoke Railroad, at a point at or near Gaston, North Carolina.

"David Shelton, Esq., one of the delegation, explained in a lucid and forcible speech, the increasing interest which was felt in the Roanoke country in the great subject of internal improvements. The delay and difficulties in the navigation of the Roanoke River, owing to the bad management of the Roanoke Navigation Company, were pointed out, and the speaker announced the determination of those he represented to have a railroad connexion with Norfolk and Portsmouth. 'The port of Norfolk was their natural market, and here they meant to come.' Mr. S. stated the cost of freights to Petersburg and Richmond, and the great tax upon the planters of the Roanoke."

Dr. Wilson, of Clarksville, followed Mr. Shelton in some very appropriate remarks.

An account of the further action of the city, with regard to this and other roads, will be found in another part of this work.

The following is an extract of a letter from Dr. Wm. A. Smith, addressed to the delegates above mentioned, on the object of their mission.

"The road to Clarksville should be the commencement of one, in due course of time, to Memphis, Tenn., to connect with the prospective Government road, through the territories, to San Francisco, in California. The use of steam from thence to China, must result in the introduction of imports from China (tea, in particular) into this country. These must find a shipping port on the Atlantic coast. What point offers the advantages of the port of Norfolk? None; emphatically, none. The best port on the coast, it lies on nearly the same parallel of latitude with Clarksville, Memphis, and Francisco. To talk, then, of allowing that vast portion of this trade that would reach Memphis from Francisco, seeking the Atlantic coast, to wind around by way of Lynchburg and down to Richmond and Petersburg, and thence to sea, when it can be brought in a straight line, varying only three-fourths of a degree from Francisco to Norfolk, is idle in the extreme."*

* Rev. William A. Smith, D.D., President of Randolph Macon College, from whom the above letter was received, is distinguished not only for his extensive acquirements as a theologian, and for his talents as a pulpit orator, but also for his general knowledge and usually correct views of those measures which affect the great commercial and political interests of our State and the country at large. This letter is somewhat characteristic of the man; and it is believed that his judgment in the premises may be relied on.

Dr. Smith is well known in Norfolk, having served the Church here for six or eight years, since his first appointment to this station, which was about the year 1831. About two years subsequently, he met with the sad accident (a fall from his carriage) which rendered him a cripple for life.

In the great religious revival here in 1834–'35, his labours, notwithstanding his lameness, were arduous, unceasing, and abundantly blessed.

He has a mind of great strength and inherent power, and which, when brought to bear upon a subject, especially in a debate, throws upon it a degree of light which generally carries conviction irresistibly home to the minds of his hearers. He is considered a very able logician. His style of rhetoric is original and commanding, his enunciation full and clear, his manner and gesticulation dignified and impressive; and all combine to produce the desired effect upon large and promiscuous assemblages. He is remarkably ready and origi-

"Dr. S. has subsequently presented the matter in a captivating point of view, so far as the city of Norfolk is concerned. With a prophetic finger, he pointed away to California, and told us that the day would come when a long train of cars would roll on, freighted with the rich products of that distant region, for the Norfolk market. The teas and silks of China, even, he thought, would eventually traverse this portion of the North American Continent, seeking a shipping-point on the Atlantic coast, for their final destination in Europe."

We add, also, an extract of a letter to the citizens of Norfolk, from a committee appointed by the citizens of Clarksville:

"A glance at the map of the Roanoke country will satisfy the most sceptical of the importance to Norfolk and Portsmouth of securing the trade of this extensive and immensely fertile region. Ours is a point of extraordinary concentration. Here the Dan and Staunton come together, both navigable for many miles for batteaux; and, within ten or twelve miles, the rivers Banister and Hyco (one running through one of the most fertile regions of Virginia, and the other through the best part of North Carolina), empty their waters into the Dan; both of them being also navigable for many miles. Your Seaboard and Roanoke Railroad, when completed, will run within forty miles of our town. Yours is our natural market; but the supineness of our people, as well as yours, has left us, up to this time, no alternative but to send our

native. Some of his extemporaneous efforts on particular occasions, with but little or no time for preparation, have been marked by extraordinary strength and concentration of thought and oratorical skill. He is a most fearless and spirited debater, discovering and exhibiting, with much adroitness, the weak points in the arguments of his opponent, and possessing the enviable tact of bringing the strongest points of his own argument to bear with great force upon the question at issue. Yet it must be admitted that it requires a deeply interesting subject, or a powerful opponent, to light up fully the fires upon the altar of his vigorous mind. His information, theological, legal, political, and general, is such as to render him peculiarly fit for the responsible duties of his present office, and even to induce the belief that he could, at very short notice, plead with ability a desperate case at the bar, or deliver a learned and eloquent address on any of the great questions that agitate the public mind at the present day. These remarks are in accordance with the views of persons of good judgment, correct taste, and different religious sentiments, who have had sufficient opportunity to form an opinion.

produce to Petersburg or Richmond. Should the road contemplated be constructed, and we be enabled to send our produce directly to Norfolk and Portsmouth, we shall be saved the expense of a tedious and circuitous transportation, and your cities will be flooded with the productions of our hills and our valleys, until you will not have a place to hold them. Besides, should foreign invasion ever again threaten you, our hardy and brave sons will be able to roll down like a mighty flood to overwhelm your enemies. This latter consideration is particularly worthy of your notice."

The greater part of this month (January), was remarkably warm for the season. Some of the fruit and shade trees germinated, flowers bloomed, and nature bore, thus early, much of the appearance of the early spring-time.

February 14th. St. Valentine's day.—The splendid new war steamer, Powhatan, was this day launched at the Navy Yard, in fine style. That vessel is one of the most beautiful pieces of naval architecture ever sent forth from this or any other establishment.

"The launch of the Powhatan was effected at the precise time appointed—in the morning, forty-five minutes past ten—when she glided from her ways into the watery element, with the grace of a swan and the truth of a rifle—without varying a hair's breadth from a straight line. As she measured her length in the water, she kicked off her trammels and took a plunge for the opposite shore, which was vainly essayed to be checked by two twenty-two inch cables, which she snapped asunder like pipe stems.

"It was decidedly one of the best ordered and the most beautiful launches which has ever been witnessed. Commodore Sloat and his officers, Captain Farragut and Lieutenant Glisson, threw open their houses on the occasion, and displayed a generous and whole-souled hospitality—each having provided a profuse and elegant collation, worthy of an occasion which had redounded so much to their credit and proved to them a source of so much real self-congratulation.

"The Powhatan's keel was laid in July, 1847, and she was constructed under the superintendence of S. T. Hartt, Esq., the

Constructor of the Yard (by the way, he is esteemed one of the brightest jewels in Uncle Sam's casket) according to draughts furnished by Francis Grice, Esq."

The engines of this large government steamer were constructed at the Gosport Iron Works, a private establishment of great capacity and powerful facilities for extensive operations, and which was wisely located in Gosport a few years since by A. Mahaffey, Esq., a liberal, wealthy, and enterprising gentleman from Pennsylvania. The boilers alone weigh about 250,000 pounds—cost, nearly $120,000 ; cost of the copper alone, $90,000.*

On the evening of the 14th, the Mechanics' Hall was first opened and lighted for the reception of visiters, and hundreds, of all ages, male and female, comprising many of the gay and beautiful, congregated in the main hall, which is truly a most desirable acquisition to the city. The situation of this building was well chosen with regard both to convenience and ornament; being on the south side of Main Street, the principal thoroughfare, and only a few doors east of Market Square.

The front is of the Tudor Gothic order, presenting a bold and highly ornamental exterior, which is stuccoed and laid off in the most beautiful and durable style; indeed, the finish of the entire building is very creditable to all the workmen, and especially to Mr. John H. Sale, the architect, and (aided by Mr. Samuel Butt), the chief builder. The entire building covers an area of 5670 square feet, being ninety feet long, by sixty-three wide; height, fifty-four feet to the coping of the battlement. The great hall, which is one of the largest in the State, measures fifty-four by ninety feet; pitch, eighteen feet. There are ten rooms on the third floor, and on the first floor there are three large and elegant stores and one office.

The erection of this handsome structure, affording as it does,

* The Norfolk Iron Works, on Wide Water Street, Mr. N. Cory proprietor, are prepared for extensive operations in making and repairing machinery. The ingenious and enterprising gentleman at the head of this establishment has recently enlarged his buildings, and made arrangements which enable him in many respects to compete successfully with other works. His castings and polished work in iron, steel, brass, &c., sometimes very ponderous and complicated, give great satisfaction.

what the people of Norfolk have long felt the want of, a large, well-finished room, conveniently located, for public exhibitions, concerts, fairs, lectures, &c., proves, no doubt, a profitable investment to the large and useful association, whose property it is (The Mechanical Society), and for whose benefit it was erected. The hall has already witnessed many occasions of great interest and animation. Melodious and charming streams of music resound within its walls, the eloquence of the orator has echoed there; many of the fair and lovely have congregated there too. In the brilliant light afforded by the "invisible and combustible fluid," for the burning of which it is well supplied with beautiful chandeliers, there is presented many a lively and deeply interesting scene.

On the morning of the 15th, between the hours of one and two, Avon Theatre was discovered to be on fire. All efforts to save the large and commodious building proved entirely futile, and with the furniture, paintings, drapery, &c., it was in a few minutes, a shapeless heap of ruins.*

Wednesday evening, 20th. A destructive fire occurred on High Street, Portsmouth.

23d. The cadets of the Virginia Military Institute being in Richmond, on the occasion of the laying of the corner stone of the Washington Monument, accepted an invitation to visit our city, and arrived in the Richmond boat in the afternoon of this day, and remained for several days; during which time, they partook of its hospitalities and sociabilities. This large and well-disciplined corps of young men, with its accomplished officers, by their gentlemanly deportment and soldier-like movements, made a most favourable impression upon the citizens, who were highly pleased with the exhibitions of their extraordinary skill as tacticians, upon the parade ground; while the gallant young soldiers from the mountains expressed themselves, in terms of great satisfaction and gratification, with regard to the circumstances attending their visit to the salt-water region of the State, and relative to their reception and stay in the city of

* There was formerly a theatre on the east side of Fenchurch near Main Street. It was a neat, stuccoed building, of moderate size.

Norfolk. "For four consecutive days and nights there was one perfect scene of entertainment and merry making."

The following is an extract of an eloquent and beautiful letter, addressed by the Cadets to Richmond, Norfolk, &c., after their return to Lexington:—

"Lavish as we have been of our thanks, in what vocabulary shall we find words sufficiently warm, glowing, and sincere, to express to you, citizens of Norfolk, our heartfelt gratitude for your hospitalities? Elsewhere, we were received as friends—*you* received us as brothers. Domesticated in your houses, introduced as old acquaintances to your families, surrounded with every attention that fancy could conceive, or friendship execute, we felt that, among you, we were really and truly at home. Ties were formed, which time, destroyer as he is, will smilingly pass by, and leave to brighten in eternal youth; friendships there linked together, which the lapse of years can only render stronger. We know not, ladies of Norfolk, in what language to speak of *you*. We know not how to requite the gentle affability, the kindness which uniformly marked your demeanour towards us. To the volunteers of Portsmouth, as to those of Norfolk, and to Commodore Sloat, and the gallant officers under his command, we must pay our meed of thanks."

April 17. On this day there was a considerable snow-storm. It commenced snowing rapidly, and in large flakes, at 9 o'clock, and continued for several hours. It froze at night, destroying much of the fruit, such as peaches, apricots, cherries, the first growth of figs, &c.

April 24. The city was this day visited by the hero of Lundy's Lane, Vera Cruz, &c. General Scott attracted a crowd of eager spectators, who were naturally anxious to look upon one of the most renowned and successful chieftains the world ever knew. A salute was fired, on his arrival, by the Artillery Blues; and, with his suite, he was escorted, by the volunteer companies, to the National Hotel.

May 1. Destructive fire in Gosport—thirty houses burned.

For the purpose of conveying some idea of the business done here, in fruit and vegetables, at this season, we present the following statement:—On the 17th of this month, six hundred bushels of green peas, and five hundred quarts of strawberries, were shipped to Baltimore. Four hundred bushels of peas were also shipped to Washington. This may be considered a tolerably fair business, for so early a day in a very backward season. An intelligent writer thinks that, "Since the line of steamers between New York and this place have been in operation, the farms, in this vicinity, are more profitable than the mines of the modern El Dorado."

In 1852, the shipments of early fruit, vegetables, &c., had wonderfully increased; a very heavy and profitable business was done.

Wednesday, May 29. The Worshipful Court of the city of Norfolk convened on this day, for the first time, in the court-room of the new City Hall.

This large and handsome building, to which allusion has already been made, occupies a portion of the space formerly intended as a public square; bounded by Bank, Cove, Avon, and Williams Streets. This site was judiciously selected, in preference to that on which the old court-house stood, being more central, and affording a fine view of the building from the harbour. The erection of this beautiful structure, is said to have been "a triumph of mechanical skill." Its walls rest upon solid rows of piles, of sufficient capacity, in the opinion of the most experienced architects, "to sustain any weight of superstructure that could be raised upon them. In this particular, the most important of all, especial care was taken to secure a permanent and immovable foundation."

The length of the building is eighty feet (north and south) by sixty in width. The portico, fronting west, and seen from Bank Street, Granby Street, and the harbour, is supported by six massive columns of the Tuscan order; it is sixty feet long, leaving a recess of ten feet at each end. The cupola adds greatly to the beauty and the bold and commanding appearance of the building, being thirty-two feet in diameter, and fifty-two feet high. A passage, thirteen feet wide, extends through from the front to the rear entrance. On the north side of the passage is the court-room;

and on the south, the mayor and sheriff's offices. On the second floor, and north side, is a spacious room, in which the United States' Court, for this district, is held. The council-chambers and jury-rooms are also on the second floor. The front wall is faced with granite, and the exterior of the others stuccoed in the most durable manner, and made to represent the same kind of stone. The entrance from the ground is by steps of granite, which extend nearly the entire length of the portico. The building also presents a handsome view on the eastern side, where there are, also, handsome stone steps to the entrance. The foundation walls are of granite, and rise from the piles eight feet to the surface of the ground, and thence of hewn stone five feet above. The walls are strengthened, to sustain the piers above, by reversed arches; and a cylindrical brick arch, of elaborate construction, supports the platform and pillars of the portico.

Height of the main building, fifty-eight feet; entire height to the summit of the cupola (from which there is a fine view of the harbour and surrounding scenery), one hundred and ten feet, above which is erected a tall flag-staff, from which, on public occasions, a very large ensign, with the stars and stripes, is unfurled to the breeze. Attached to the lightning-rod, a few feet above the top of the staff, is a gilt vane, five feet long, in the shape of an arrow.

Beneath the principal passage, on the first floor, there is a large cistern, holding about forty-five thousand gallons. The roof is covered with tin. The original plan of the building was drawn by Mr. William R. Singleton, architect, formerly of Portsmouth, and now of St. Louis, Missouri; some alterations were suggested by Mr. Walter, of Philadelphia, which were adopted. General superintendent of the work, Mr. Thomas Constable; carpenter, Mr. Isaac M. Smith; stone-mason, Mr. O. H. Rand; plasterers, Messrs. Holmes and Tarral; painter, Mr. John W. Belote; tin-worker, Mr. G. L. Crow. Cost of the building, including the clerk's and register's offices, about fifty thousand dollars. The piles were driven by the machinery and workmen of Mr. N. Nash, ship-builder. The situation affords an excellent view of the structure from several different points. It is on a line with that portion of Main Street, east of Church, from which the cupola is plainly seen. The view, from the harbour, on the west, and approaching the city, is full, and really imposing. It is seen, also, for a considerable distance, on the Seaboard and Roanoke Railroad.

"The first eight miles of the road (to Bowers's Hill) is perfectly straight; and riding on an open platform, the traveller has the benefit of an interesting perspective view of it as it recedes in the long vista of forest trees on each side; and it is quite remarkable, that the dome of the City Hall in Norfolk stands precisely in the centre of the vanishing point of vision, and continues in full view for four miles, when the projection of the trees gradually shut it in. The City Hall was located without a thought of its relation to the railroad; and its position presenting it as a prominent land-mark and object of vision through a vista of many miles of the latter, is really a curious coincidence."

May 30, Thursday. On the evening of this day, the Freemason Street Baptist Church was dedicated. An able sermon was preached by Rev. Dr. Fuller, an eminent divine of Baltimore.

This is one of the handsomest, and is unquestionably the most ornamental building in the city. It is, indeed, a noble temple of worship,—a splendid monument of human art, and of the taste and liberality of those who have been instrumental in its erection, on so favourable and well-chosen a spot,—the northeast corner of Catharine and Freemason Streets. It is truly an ornament to the city, and would be to any in the Union. It is justly prized and admired by all. That tall spire, shooting up towards heaven, far above all surrounding objects, and observed for miles around, standing forth in its symmetrical beauty—who does not admire it? May it remain there, in its pride, for ages, witnessing the rise of other "tall piles," and the extension of this old town for miles to the north, to the east, and to the west.

"The style of architecture is the florid perpendicular Gothic of the fifteenth century, which, from its beauty of outline, the variety and boldness of its parts, is one well adapted and most appropriate for religious purposes. The design was furnished by the well-known architect, Thomas U. Walter, of Philadelphia. The building, measuring from buttress to buttress, fronts sixty-five feet on Freemason Street, and its length on Catharine Street, including the tower, is one hundred and five feet. The buttresses have a massive appearance, indicative of strength and stability. The tower is one of the best proportioned and picturesque we have ever seen of this style, and we have examined most of the old Gothic edifices in the north of England and south of Scotland. It combines, in a high degree, strength and beauty—is both massive and graceful. Its height from the street is two hundred feet.

"The basement comprises a handsome lecture-room, fifty-two feet square; well supplied with commodious seats, and lighted with gas. In its rear are two spacious rooms, one of them furnished with every convenience for the pastor's use as a library and study room. The other is designed as a committee-room.

"The entrance into the main body of the church is made through a large vestibule, to which we ascend by a series of Connecticut stone steps. On either side of the vestibule are Tudor doorways communicating with the side aisles, and a still larger one of the same order leading to the centre one; on entering which, the eye is arrested by a beautiful prospect painted on the chancel wall, in the rear of the pulpit, forming a recess. 'The groined arches, clustered pillars, tessellated pavement, present the appearance of reality,' and make the recess seem to be much larger than it actually is, until a nearer approach dispels the illusion. The chancel is elevated from three to four feet above the floor, and the front is chastely ornamented with open-worked panels. The baptistery is placed in the centre of the chancel, and on either side of the chancel is a dressing-room. On the main floor are one hundred and twenty-four handsome pews, cushioned, and each capable of seating from five to six persons. The galleries contain about forty pews of different sizes. The fronts are ornamented with open-worked figures in the lancet form, each separated from the other by a pinnacle shaft. The front gallery is furnished with a fine-toned organ, from the manufactory of Mr. George Jardine, of New York. The edifice is also adorned with well-executed coloured windows.

"On the whole, this may be justly deemed the finest and most striking Baptist edifice in the State—a credit to the denomination and to the enterprising society to whom it owes its erection. Their building cost, at least, $35,000."

Rev. Tiberius G. Jones, an eloquent and devoted minister, an able writer, and an accomplished scholar, is pastor in charge of this beautiful church.

June. The councils directed the enlargement of Ashland Hall, for the accommodation of public meetings. For some reason, it was not completed till October, 1852. It is now a large and airy building, with two spacious rooms—the lower one being the hall proper, for public assemblages, and the upper being the head-quarters of the Norfolk Junior Volunteers. The location is on Talbot Street, near the City Hall.

During this month, and a portion of July, there was very little rain, and the weather was exceedingly warm, the mercury in the thermometer often as high as 96°. So oppressive and protracted a drought had not been experienced, perhaps, since 1785. Vegetation suffered much, the cisterns were empty, and the demand for water was great.

CHAPTER XXXIV.

1850.

Steam-Packet Communication—Foreign Trade—Convention at Old Point—Sad Intelligence—Death of the President of the United States—Funeral Obsequies—Oppressive Weather—Tornado—Hon. Henry A. Wise—Internal Improvements—Canal from Norfolk to Albemarle Sound—Surveys—Mrs. Mary B. Johnston—Survey of the Harbour—Stone Wall—New Custom House—Powder Magazine—Church Street Paved—Its Former Condition—Advance in the Price of Property—Dry Weather—Doctor Mallory appointed Navy Agent—His Qualifications—George Loyall, Esq.—Colonel Garnett appointed Collector of the Port—Conway Whittle, Esq.—Seaboard and Roanoke Railroad—Extension to Suffolk—Its Completion to Weldon.

JULY 1st. A meeting of the citizens was held at the City Hall, for the purpose of appointing delegates to co-operate with those of Richmond, Baltimore, &c., who were to meet in convention at Old Point, on the 4th, to consider the plan of establishing a steam-packet communication with Europe.

Eloquent addresses were delivered, appropriate and spirited resolutions were passed, and fifty delegates were appointed.

The convention of delegates assembled, according to appointment, in the spacious ball-room of Old Point Hotel (which was tendered by John S. French, Esq.), at 5½ o'clock, and the subjects of Direct Trade, and a Steam Navigation Company, were duly considered. H. L. Kent, Esq., of Richmond, presided. Able addresses were delivered by Hon. John Y. Mason and Robert G. Scott, Esq., of Richmond, and George Blow, Esq., of Norfolk.

July 10th. The sad intelligence was received of the death of General Z. Taylor, President of the United States. The flags were half-masted, and the bells were rung; and on Saturday, the 13th, business was suspended from twelve till two o'clock, the bells tolled, and a feeling of deep solemnity seemed to rest upon the public mind in consequence of the death of the hero.

July 17th. Stormy; wind east; increasing to a gale by midnight, and continuing with great violence till eight o'clock on the 18th; prostrating a number of trees and fences, and unroofing some houses. The wind changed to the south in the evening, and to southwest at an early hour on the 19th, when, to use the language of an extravagant modern writer, "the orient beams of expanded morning burst asunder the fettering ties of the sombre shroud, which had trammelled the earth in its darkening folds."

In Portsmouth on the 25th, and in Norfolk on the 26th, there were suitable and impressive funeral obsequies, in honour of the successful and illustrious conqueror, who had been suddenly called away from the performance of the duties of the most exalted station that earth affords. In each town, a long procession, comprising the soldiery and very many of the citizens, marched through the principal streets, and an eloquent oration was delivered in Portsmouth by Captain S. Watts, and in Norfolk by T. C. Tabb, Esq.

On the 30th, the range of the mercury in the thermometers

was ninety-six to ninety-seven, and on the following day it stood at ninety-four degrees.

August 23d. A tornado of surpassing violence passed through the southern part of Princess Anne and Norfolk Counties, and several others west of those, leaving destruction and ruin in its track. Stout oaks and slender saplings were alike torn up by the roots, or snapped off at the trunk; the fences were scattered like the leaves of the trees; the corn was levelled, and the fodder separated into narrow, worthless shreds; houses were lifted from their foundations, and the timbers scattered in broken fragments, by the force of the wind. Horses, cattle, hogs, poultry, &c., were driven furiously along; and several persons lost their lives. As an evidence of the extraordinary power of the wind, a plough, standing in a field, was taken up and carried by the wind to the distance of two hundred yards. Those who were within the track of the hurricane,—which was only two or three hundred yards wide,—represent the occasion as one well calculated to appal the stoutest heart; for the crashing noise made by the falling of houses, timbers, trees, and fences, was completely swallowed up and lost in the tremendous and furious sound of the wind, which was heard for miles, like the rumbling of the distant cataract; then increasing to an overwhelming continuous roar, like the breaking of the swollen surges of the great deep against the rocks, or the deafening thunders of Niagara.

On the evening of September 26, Hon. Henry A. Wise, of Accomac County, of whom the reader will find some personal remarks on other pages, delivered, in Mechanics' Hall, a very able and eloquent address on the subject of connecting Norfolk and Portsmouth with the interior, by means of railroads and canals. He alluded, in very appropriate terms, to great works of internal improvement now in progress, and in contemplation. He spoke with startling eloquence, and most convincing power of argument, of the reason that Norfolk is not already a great city, and of the means by which she may become a great southern emporium. The propriety and necessity of the contemplated canal from the southern or eastern branch of Elizabeth River to the waters of North Carolina, and other important improvements, were urged with great energy and clearness.

"One line of communication alluded to, was to commence at the head of the east fork of the south branch of Elizabeth River, a few miles above Great Bridge, from which point a canal, six miles in length, is required to connect with North River, in Virginia, which empties into Currituck Sound, and a canal, only three or three and a half miles in length, will continue the navigation from the lower end of Currituck Sound to North River, in North Carolina, which empties into Albemarle Sound a few miles below. The river and sound navigation, all the way from Norfolk to Albemarle Sound, is never less than six feet in depth; and if the canalling is made sixty feet wide, as is contemplated, the whole route will be the same as river navigation, with the exception of one lock only in the Great Bridge Canal."

The following is an extract of a letter from G. P. Worcester, of New York, who surveyed the route of the proposed improvement.

"By a reference to the maps of my survey, it will be seen that the line of water communication commences at the harbour of Norfolk, and continues up the Elizabeth River to Great Bridge, crosses the swamp by means of canal into North River, continues down the North River into Currituck Sound, through the Sound into a small bay, and crosses a belt of highland by means of a canal, into Doctor's Creek, opening thereby an easy and useful navigation with Albemarle Sound, and its tributary streams. And, it is to be presumed, that after this line of water communication shall be completed, and a line of steam tow-boats in readiness, that boats, carrying the produce from the interior, and the coast of North Carolina, would daily traverse the entire distance from Albemarle Sound to the harbour of Norfolk, with a saving of labour and expense, and without any direct rivalry. And if any conclusion can be drawn from the amount of transportation which must necessarily follow, it must be admitted that this canal, when completed, will not only sustain itself, but make a handsome return for the capital expended in its construction, besides enriching the counties through which it passes, by the reduced cost of transportation which it will effect, compared with any facilities now in existence for that object. From the foregoing data as a basis, I think a canal of fifty feet surface and seven feet depth, with the improvements of the navigation, may be estimated for the following sum."

The estimate specifies the several amounts necessary for dredging, excavating, bridges, locks, &c., all of which amount only to the comparatively small sum of $131,386.

A survey was made by Colonel Crozet, in 1840, of a canal route from Whitehurst's Landing, on the Eastern Branch near Kempsville, to the head of North River. The detailed estimate of the work of cutting the canal amounted, in the aggregate, to $380,000, including excavation, dredging, bridges, superintendence, &c., &c. The following is an extract of Colonel C.'s report:—

"The appearance of the country is very deceiving. It was supposed to be much lower, and the work expected to be much less, than an actual measurement has disclosed. I fear that the estimate here exhibited will disappoint the expectations of some of the friends of the scheme; but it is certainly preferable that they should have a full view of the difficulty before them, than to be taken unawares after having embarked in the enterprise. The difference of the tide in North River and Elizabeth River, the tide in the latter being that of the ocean, and the other regulated by the winds only, will be so small as to produce but an ordinary current on either direction, and, consequently, no locks will be required at the ends of the canal. But a bar may be expected to be formed at the opening into each river, by the oscillations of the waters lifting up the sand into the canal; this is an unavoidable evil in all such canals, and occasional dredging must be expected.

"As regards the object of the canal, it would take a great deal of timber to market to Norfolk, from the extensive swamps of Currituck, Back Bay, and in North Carolina, as well as the common produce of the country, the cultivation of which it would promote and secure. Steamboats, and other crafts, would pass this short route to Currituck, Albemarle, and Pamlico Sound; and this would greatly benefit the commerce of the lower part of North Carolina, bordering on the Sound, and produce to that section of country, a short, safe, and easier way to market than by any other route, and particularly that by Ocracoke Inlet, the only opening now remaining between Pamlico Sound and the Atlantic, and which is not likely to have the fate of the former Currituck Inlet—a probability which favours the project under consideration. It will then be readily seen, that a very extensive country is included in this scheme; but as regards the exact revenue and benefits to be derived from it, I do not think that any person is now qualified to make a statement to be relied upon.

"The extent of the subscription, by the persons immediately interested, will be, I conceive, the surest and most decisive criterion to judge by."

September 27. Departed this life at Lebanon, on Tanner's Creek, the seat of her late husband, Mrs. Mary B. Johnston, aged eighty-six, a native of Philadelphia. She had been a member of the Methodist Church for sixty years, and died in great peace. Her father fell in one of the battles of the Revolution; after which she visited Norfolk; but the only indications of a town to be seen, were immense heaps of ruins, and three new buildings. She came to attend to some business connected with a claim upon the Government, growing out of her father's services, and meeting with Captain John Johnston, formerly well known in Norfolk, they were shortly after married. She witnessed the rise and progress of the town, from its ruins to its present limits and prosperous condition. She was one of the first resident Methodists in this section of the country, having had a distinct recollection of Bishop Asbury, and the first preachers who visited Virginia. A long and capacious room, in which her aged and coffined remains were placed for the performance of the funeral solemnities, was built with a view to the accommodation of the small flock that gathered there in the early days of Methodism; which has since increased from scores to hundreds and thousands. Verily, great works have been wrought, both temporally and spiritually, within the limits of one eventful lifetime.

October 1. The Councils passed a resolution, requiring the appointment of a joint committee to inquire into the propriety of a survey of the harbour, with reference to an application to Congress for the purpose of running a stone wall from Town Point to Fort Norfolk. This was in contemplation many years ago.

Should the work ultimately be accomplished, it will prove a great and striking, though costly improvement to the harbour and to the city.

The General Appropriation Bill passed at the recent session of Congress, very properly made provision for fifty thousand dollars for a new custom-house at Norfolk,—a building greatly needed here, in consequence of the dilapidated condition of the old one, and the anticipated increase in the commerce of the port.

In 1852, the appropriation was increased to $100,000. The site chosen for the building is on the south side of Main, nearly opposite Granby Street.

"The design is by A. B. Young, Esq., Government Architect. The building will front on Main, running back one hundred and thirty-five feet to Broad Water Street, and will be three stories high. The front basement is to be used for a post-office, the entrance to which will be on each side of the main entrance to the first story, which, together with the rest of the building, will be used for a custom-house. A porch extending the whole width of the building and supported by six columns will ornament the front, in the centre of which the main entrance will be. On each side of this entrance, there will be an entrance to the post-office. The structure is to be of granite and is to be finished in a plain and substantial manner, but when completed according to the plan will be one of the most imposing and showy buildings in the city."

An extensive powder magazine is also to be erected by the U. S. Government, at the site of old Fort Norfolk.

October 9th. On this day the centre stone-laying and curbing of Church Street, north of Town Bridge was completed by Mr. R. Dalrymple the contractor—distance, 1166⅔ yards. The improvement was exceedingly necessary and important. This is the principal thoroughfare out of the city to Princess Anne, and a portion of Norfolk County, and yet in wet weather the traveling had been through mud, mire, and water, and in dry seasons, through the dust, which rose in clouds, and was scattered by the winds, to the great annoyance of both travellers and residents. It is now a long and handsome though crooked street, and "affords a wide field for the spirit of progress to pursue the onward work of improvement in. 'To it, then, my masters!' and let us see in the next ten years, the whole of the newly paved division of the street built up with handsome houses, and another application to the City Councils for authority to pave the extended part of Church Street (or Centre Street at it should then be called), from its present terminus to Lindsay's Gardens.

"The appreciation of lots on Upper Church Street goes ahead of everything we have heard of. We might safely say that it averages one hundred per cent.; for in not a few instances, to our knowledge, it exceeds that rate. And yet this is not the result of a spirit of speculation; for those who offer to buy do so with a view to build."

The months of September and October were exceedingly dry for the season. To this date (15th October), there had been no rain for four or five weeks.

November 1. Dr. Francis Mallory, of Elizabeth City County, formerly member of Congress, entered this day upon his duties as Navy Agent at this station, to which he was appointed as successor to George Loyall, Esq. This new appointment appeared to give very general satisfaction, inasmuch as the Doctor is not only well qualified for the discharge of the responsible duties of the office; but he is also a gentleman of great urbanity of manners, whose private character is marked by a happy combination of agreeable social and moral qualities. He is, moreover, an able and zealous advocate of some of those measures which are believed to be well calculated to advance the prosperity of the city.

An intelligent writer thus appropriately alludes to the appointment:

"I am pleased that the office has been bestowed upon the Doctor, than whom Virginia does not possess a purer and more courteous gentleman. Besides, his qualifications for its duties must be of a high order, from his practical knowledge of the Navy, and the interest he evinced in its extension and usefulness while a member of Congress. When removals are made, the intelligent friends of the removed cannot otherwise than feel gratified when the mantle falls on those equally deserving and patriotic—and not on the shoulders of professional office-seekers, and impertinent demagogues."

Mr. Loyall had held the office for thirteen years, during which time he disbursed more than $14,000,000 of the public money without the loss of a cent to the treasury.*

Colonel Wm. Garnett was, during the past year, appointed Collector of this Port, in place of Conway Whittle, Esq. Mr. W. had been in office for a number of years, and was also a most correct and faithful public officer. The present esteemed incumbent, is considered well fitted for the discharge of the responsible duties of the office.

Saturday, Nov. 9th. On this day the Seaboard and Roanoke Railroad (which takes the course of the old Portsmouth and Roanoke road) was completed to Suffolk; and, by invitation of the obliging President of the Company, some five or six hundred of the citizens of Norfolk and Portsmouth made a trip in the cars to the above-named pleasant little town. The track is laid with the best imported T iron, and the road, thus far, is said by those well entitled to an opinion, to be one of the most level and best constructed in the country. This important work was completed, in 1851, to the rich and fertile valley of the Roanoke.

* Mr. Loyall is a gentleman of no ordinary talents. The following remarks respecting his style as an orator, are from the pen of one who had listened to a political speech which he delivered more than twenty years ago.

* * * "His manner was pleasing and impressive; and his action evidently reflected that polish which true oratorical taste and long experience only can impart. His voice is full and its tones are remarkably distinct.

* * * * *

"He advances openly and honestly in the demonstration of his subject. The main object of the investigation is perpetually exhibited to the eye of the understanding, and the hearer follows the orator in the clear and luminous track of his argument, without being confounded by subtile wanderings, or bewildered by needless intricacies. His course is onward; he is seldom fascinated by the golden glitter of an ornament, or beguiled by the fading beauty of a flower; his occasional illustrations do not appear to have been previously culled and collected, and are almost as well adapted for one subject as another; but they spring directly from the one under consideration. Hence, he invariably leaves a distinct and lasting impression on the mind of the hearer."

CHAPTER XXXV.

1850.

New Methodist Episcopal Church—Description of the Building—Workmen—Pew System—Seating of a Congregation—Pews and Free Seats—Dedication—Rev. J. E. Edwards—Membership—Dr. Doggett—Quarterly Review—Labelling the Streets and Houses—Census.

IN November, another house of worship was completed in the city,—the new Methodist Church, situated at the northeast corner of Granby and Freemason Streets, fronting on the latter. It is a very neat structure, of the Ionic order, fifty-five by seventy-five feet, covering an area of four thousand one hundred and twenty-five square feet, and measuring forty-five feet from the ground to the apex of the roof, and thence to the top of the cupola, sixty-six feet, making the entire height one hundred and eleven feet. The front is ornamented by a beautiful and handsomely finished portico, with four large fluted pillars. The external appearance of the church is singular and striking, although improvements could be made in the plan of this as well as other public buildings in the city. There is considerable raised and indented square work on the outside of the walls, which are well stuccoed, showing several different colours. The entrance is by two ascents of granite steps, which rise to a platform paved with hexagonal bricks.

The seats, which are in strict accordance with the "pew system," as it is generally called, have the appearance of rows of mahogany sofas; being beautifully finished, and cushioned with fine black hair-cloth. They form a curve, from wall to wall, of an eighth of a circle. Two massive fluted columns rise from the floor of the pulpit, which is in a recess built in the rear. The pulpit-desk is a neat piece of joinery; and the railing of the altar being handsome figured work, assists in giving beauty and appropriateness to the whole interior. On the first or basement floor, is a commodious Sabbath school-room, besides four class-rooms, a passage, and a stairway.

Architect, J. J. Husband; Chief Carpenter, William Callis; Bricklayer, H. E. Herbert; Painter, B. W. Gatch; Stone-mason, R. Dalrymple; Plasterers, Hall and Brooks.

Without intending our remarks to apply particularly to this edifice, we will observe, that although the pew-seat system has among its advocates some of the most worthy friends and pious members of the M. E. Church in Norfolk, it does not generally meet with the approval of the Methodists here; being considered by some as an innovation of doubtful utility, if not an unwise departure from an established custom. But the objections to appropriated seats, although their introduction appears contrary to the economy of Methodism, as set forth in the Discipline, as well as to the advice of its sage founder, are surmountable here, as well as in England, and in different parts of this country.

The seating of a worshipping congregation is regarded by many persons, even among those connected with the Methodist denomination, as a matter which may, with considerable propriety, be left to the choice of those who are most interested. There should certainly be large and commodious churches in every city, where all may enter and worship, the stranger as well as the citizen, of every grade, in one common, indiscriminate mass; and it will be conceded, perhaps, by all, that the free-seat system has long supplied this want. Yet it appears equally essential that there should be provision made for those who, being permanent residents, and settled in their religious views and feelings, desire particular seats, which they can claim as their own property, for the especial accommodation of themselves, their families, and friends; to which they can go without the embarrassment that often attends the search for a seat in a free church, especially when a strange and "popular" preacher officiates; or on a bright and pleasant Sabbath morning; where they may quietly sit, and in which they may be free from the annoyance during service of crowding, whispering, the fumes, stains, and odious sight of tobacco juice, and from a superabundance of carbonic acid gas; and free from the trouble, after dismission, of a search (sometimes fruitless) for the scattered members of the household, or for the man with the wrong cloak, hat, cane, or umbrella.

But even these difficulties and inconveniences might be prevented, it is thought, at least in a great measure, by abolishing the unnecessary and unreasonable custom of seating the males and females separately; and there are many who are opposed to renting and selling pews, who would not object to the appropriation of particular seats for the accommodation of such families as prefer to sit and worship together. This method is adopted in some places, and works well.

We allude to this question merely as a legitimate subject of local history, and yet without intending our remarks to apply particularly to this city; for it is well enough known that pews have been introduced by the Methodists in their churches in many other places. We will add, that the wisest policy of all religious associations is to carry out those principles in their government which effect the greatest good to the greatest number; which afford Gospel privileges to all classes; which extend the genial influences of the Christian religion alike to the rich and the poor, the high and the low.

We may state, in this connexion, that among the churches in this city that are furnished with pews, or appropriated seats, there are two, in which, although there are some vacant seats, there is seldom a pew for sale or rent. At the present date—December, 1852—all are taken, all appropriated.

It seems necessary that, in every house of worship, at least a small portion of the seats should be free, and their location well designated, even by the words "Free Seats," over the doorway leading thereto. A plan of this kind appears requisite, in view of the accommodation of strangers and others, who may not be able to rent or buy permanent seats. Nor can this plan always be superseded by the attention of the doorkeeper (if there be one) or the sparseness of the congregation. The freeness of the Gospel, the sensitiveness of some persons, the general interests of the Church, and its great and benevolent mission in behalf of immortal souls, may all be mentioned in support of such an arrangement.

The edifice to which we have alluded above was dedicated on

Sabbath morning, December 8th, of this year. An appropriate discourse was delivered on the occasion by Rev. John E. Edwards, the appointed minister for the first two years after its completion, and who was much esteemed by the members of his charge, as a fluent and attractive preacher. During his pastoral charge of the Cumberland Street station for two years preceding the erection of the second church, more than three hundred additional members were received.

A portion of the pews of the "Granby Street Church" were rented December 12th, at which time the membership numbered more than a hundred; to which there has since been a considerable addition.

Rev. David S. Doggett, D.D., an able divine, distinguished for his talents as a preacher, as well as for his superior literary attainments, was appointed to this station for the Conference year, beginning November 1st, 1852. Dr. D. served the church here in 1836–'37. He is now editor of the Quarterly Review of the Methodist Episcopal Church, South, which he conducts with acknowledged ability, and which has greatly increased in popularity, circulation, and usefulness, since his appointment by the General Conference to so important and responsible an office.

During the summer of this year, by direction of the Councils, signs of cast-iron, with the names of the streets, were put up at the corners and intersections, shortly after which, the houses were all numbered.

The following table shows the aggregates of the three classes of population in the City, according to the census of this year, as taken by Deputy Marshall Wing, to which are annexed the aggregate of the same classes according to the census of 1840:

	1850.	1840.	Increase.
Whites, . . .	9,068	6,185	2,883
Free Coloured, . .	957	1,026	
Slaves, . . .	4,295	3,709	586
	14,320	10,920	3,469
1840, . .	10,920	Dec. of free coloured,	69
Increase in 10 years,	3,400		3,400

The above figures exhibit the remarkable result, that while

our white population has increased in the last ten years at the rate of $46\frac{5}{8}$ per cent., the slave population has only increased in the ratio of $15\frac{3}{4}$ per cent.; and there has actually been a decrease of $6\frac{3}{4}$ per cent. in the free coloured population. The aggregate increase of the city population within the ten years, is $31\frac{1}{8}$ per cent.

The census-taker for Norfolk, in 1840, included the officers and seamen on board the Pennsylvania, and other U. S. vessels in port; but in taking the last census, the Deputy Marshal was instructed to pursue a different course; and therefore the actual increase in ten years, of the population, was nearly one thousand more than it appears to have been, according to the above statement.

CHAPTER XXXVI.

1851.

The Daily News—The Weather—Deaths—Caleb Bonsal, Esq.—Commodore Barron—The Chesapeake Affair—Decatur—Correspondence—Commodore Bainbridge—Capt. Elliot—The Duel—Barron severely Wounded—Decatur Killed—Commodore B.'s Social and Official Character—Death of a Venerable Lady—Simon S. Stubs, Esq., elected Mayor—Description of his Honour—Visit of President Fillmore—Gale—The Norfolk Directory and Statistical Register—Its Kind Reception—Acknowledgments—Encouragements—Its Utility—Opinions Respecting Norfolk—Erroneous Impressions Corrected—Notice of the Work—Death of an Old Citizen—Seaboard and Roanoke Railroad—Severely Cold Weather—Fire-wood—Skating—Mineral Springs.

JANUARY 1st, 1851. On this day was issued the first regular number of "The Daily News," T. F. Boothby & C. H. Beale, editors and proprietors. Terms, daily paper, $5 per annum, or 10 cents a week, payable to the carrier. Country or Tri-weekly, $3 per annum, payable in advance.

The character of its editorials, and the judgment manifested in its selections, as well as its typographical execution, give good evidence of the suitableness of its conductors to the important duties which their responsible station enjoins upon them. The "News" is considered a valuable addition to the list of dailies in the city.

"We desire," said the editors, in their first number, "to issue a truly independent paper, and this desire will be sedulously kept in view; unbiassed by favour or affection, undisturbed by party prejudice, we wish to observe calmly the busy scenes and fierce turmoils of partisan warfare; and, if possible, by a word fitly spoken to soften the bitterness hitherto existing between the opposing ranks. At this era in the history of our country, momentous and big with important results, especially do we deem this course demanded by every sentiment of patriotism, by every obligation of duty."

Since October, 1851, this paper has advocated with much ability the measures and doctrines of the Democratic party.

The weather, during the month of January was unusually mild and pleasant for the season, until Wednesday, 29th, when the wind shifted to northwest, causing a very great and sudden change in the temperature, which increased until Sunday morning, following. The weather for three days was exceedingly cold. Ridley's Pond, at the Springfield farm, was frozen sufficiently hard to afford good skating, and the coves of the river were also frozen over.

April 21st. Departed this life, on this day, two of the oldest and most respected citizens of Norfolk, Commodore James Barron, aged eighty-three, and Caleb Bonsal, Esq., bookseller, aged seventy-six.

Commodore Barron was buried on the morning of the 23d, with distinguished military, naval, and civic honours, and Mr. Bonsal in the afternoon of the same day, with the marked evidences of respect, so justly due from those in whose midst he had lived, and whose esteem and affection he had enjoyed for so many years.

Mr. B. was a native of the city of Wilmington, Delaware, and became a resident of Norfolk (pursuing the business of a bookseller and stationer) nearly fifty years ago. Possessing not only the requisite qualifications for business, but, in a high degree, those embellishments of mind and manners which are alone attainable by intellectual culture and refined associations, his career to wealth and eminence was onward and rapid. Other ties than those of business in due time bound his destiny to the community in which he had cast his lot; and in the relations of domestic life he was distinguished by the most exemplary qualities of husband and father. In subsequent years, he filled many places of public trust, and amply justified the confidence of his fellow-citizens by his fidelity to their interest. In all his transactions he was liberal and just; in his conversation he was characteristically sprightly and amusing,—often entertaining and instructive; and all his impulses and instincts were in beautiful harmony with a kind and benevolent nature."

"James Barron, the younger,* was too young to take part in the revolutionary struggle. He did not enter the service until 1798; but by close attention to his duties, and a careful study of his profession, it was not many years before he reached the rank of Captain. In 1807, he commanded the ill-fated Chesapeake. Every school-boy is familiar with the circumstances of her encounter with a British ship of the line, before whose superior metal she was compelled to strike her colours. It is well known that Captain Barron's surrender, after a brief contest, inflicted a severe blow upon our national pride, and under the smarting sense of what was regarded as a disgrace, his character was assailed with accusations, which, of all others, are most degrading to an officer in the navy. The public, ever prone to condemn unjustly, attributed his conduct on that occasion to cowardice; and a court-martial, influenced undoubtedly by the prevailing prejudice, suspended him from his rank for a considerable length of time. For this reason, he had no opportunity, during the late war, of erasing, by gallant deeds, this reproach from his name. All are familiar with the causes which led to the duel, in 1820, between him and the gallant Decatur, which terminated so fatally for the latter. We believe it is a well-authenticated fact, that on his deathbed, Decatur recanted all imputations upon Commodore Barron's courage, and acknowledged that he had taken up a wrong impression with regard to

* He was a midshipman and aid to his father, who was Commodore of the Virginia State Navy of the war of the Revolution.

his conduct in the affair of the Chesapeake. Certain it is, that an impartial posterity has since done him justice. He has gone down to his grave, leaving behind him an irreproachable name, and the esteem and respect of a wide circle of friends."

The following particulars of the duel may not be inappropriately inserted here.

"On the 12th of June, 1819, Barron commenced the correspondence with Decatur, by addressing him as follows:

"'I have been informed in Norfolk, that you have said you could insult me with impunity, or words to that effect. If you have said so, you will no doubt avow it; and I shall expect to hear from you.'

"Decatur replied, on the 17th of the same month, disavowing the offensive expression attributed to him. Two other letters followed, explanatory of the first; the correspondence ended for the time, and Decatur considered it at an end. Nearly four months afterwards, on the 23d of October, Barron again wrote Decatur, complaining of his attempts to injure him with his friends, and considering him as having expressed a willingness to meet him in the field, which he regarded as an invitation to fight, he informed him that he accepted it. Decatur replied in an elaborate and insulting letter; but disclaiming all personal enmity. Finally, after some further correspondence, Decatur left the sole adjustment of the terms of meeting with his friend, Commodore Bainbridge. On the 8th of March, 1820, Commodore Bainbridge was visited on board the Columbus, seventy-four (then lying in the Potomac, preparing for sea), by Captain Elliot, as the friend of Commodore Barron, for the purpose of making final arrangements for the meeting.

"The duel took place at Bladensburg, near Washington City, on the 22d of March, 1820, and was fought with pistols, at the distance of eight paces, or yards, the shortest that is customary. This was done by the seconds to accommodate Commodore Barron, whose vision was defective. On taking their stands, Commodore Bainbridge informed them that he would give the word quickly,—'Present! one, two, three;' and they were not to fire before the word 'one,' nor after the word 'three.' Commodore Barron observed to Commodore Decatur, 'that he hoped, on meeting in another world, they would be better friends than they had been in this.' Commodore Decatur replied: 'I have never been your enemy, sir.' No proposal for reconciliation was suggested. The concerted words were pronounced by Commodore Bainbridge. At the word 'two,' both fired so exactly together that only one report was heard. Commodore Barron fell, wounded in the right hip, according to the announced intention of Decatur, who declared that he would hit Barron in that part of his body. Decatur stood for a moment erect, but was observed to press his hand on his right side. He then fell, the ball having passed through the abdomen. He remarked: 'I am mortally wounded,—at least, I believe so; and I wish that I had fallen in defence of my country.' He was raised, and supported a short distance, where he sank down exhausted, near to where Commodore Barron lay. The latter 'declared that everything had been conducted in the most honourable manner;' and told Commodore Decatur 'that he forgave him from the bottom of his heart.'

"Commodore Decatur was borne from the field to the home of his afflicted family, in the carriage which had conveyed him to the ground. He lingered in great agony until half-past ten the same night, when he ceased to breathe.

"Commodore Barron slowly recovered from the effects of his wound, and was soon afterwards placed by the Navy Department on shore service.

"In social life, as in his official station, Commodore Barron was governed by a high sense of honour, and bore himself with a dignity, courtesy, and affability, which gave a charm to his society. And although of a temperament not to brook the slightest indignity, there was in his nature all the milk of human kindness and benevolence, and the promptings of ardent friendships and enduring attachments, which, when once formed, were held sacred to his latest hour.

"In his family circle he was cherished with unspeakable fondness and affection; and this whole community, in which he was for so large a portion of his life beloved and esteemed, will ever honour and revere his memory."

April 24th. Died, this day, Mrs. Sarah Ingram, aged about ninety-two.

"This venerable lady was descended from the family of Calverts, who were among the early settlers of Norfolk. Her father moving to Philadelphia, married there, and there she was born, on the 22d of August, 1760. In 1773, he returned to Norfolk, and the subject of this notice, a few years after, married Colonel Thorogood, of Princess Anne County.

"The Revolution had then commenced, and the British were overrunning this section of the State. Her husband being actively engaged in the cause of liberty, she was left to provide as she could for her own safety; and she chose to stand her ground at home, her residence then being near the site of the old Pleasure House, at the 'Bay side.' As might be expected, she was not overlooked by the vigilant enemy, who made her house their head-quarters, much to her annoyance, though it gave her no alarm; for she was a sturdy Whig, and resolute in her adherence to her country's cause. Being importuned by the officer in command to write to her husband to take a parole of honour 'not to molest the British troops, on condition that he might go at large unmolested by them,' her reply was worthy of a heroine of the Revolution: '*I would rather see him dead.*' Her firmness and decision of character were suited to the times; but the milder virtues of her sex shone conspicuous, and adorned the society in which she moved. Kind and affectionate in her family circle, she was not less devoted to the duties of charity and benevolence, and her greatest pleasure was in doing good by conferring benefits on the poor and needy."

June 24th. On this day, Simon S. Stubbs, Esq., attorney-at-law,—a graduate of old William and Mary College, and formerly member of the General Assembly from this city,—was elected Mayor.

Of course, Mr. Stubbs is not universally popular as an officer. His Honour does not give entire satisfaction to all. This should never be expected from any person holding such a station. As to the discharge of his duties in his official capacity, it has been said that he is too lenient with the accused and convicted, and in some of his decisions in the Mayor's Court, to incline sometimes to the side of mercy, when the demands of justice are thereby improperly withheld. And yet, in such cases, when the trouble has been taken by impartial persons to ascertain the particulars, his course has been fully justified.

Self-interest, passion, and prejudice, often blind the mental eye, even of the intelligent, when engaged in litigation or legal difficulties before a municipal officer; and then, a nice and just discrimination cannot be made by them between truth and error, or between innocence and guilt; and justice may seem to be wronged by withholding the severest penalties of the law in its strictest construction. Intelligence, thus blindfolded, leads and influences the ignorant, the thoughtless, and the loquacious. Then, the complaint, if not the outcry, is heard against the decisions of the calm, dispassionate, and impartial officer, whose responsible duty it is to sit in judgment upon the conduct of his fellows. Besides, it is a humiliating fact, by no means creditable to human nature, that some persons delight in the punishment of others, and even manifest disappointment if the extreme penalty of the law be not inflicted upon the unfortunate and the guilty. To such persons Mercy ever pleads her cause in vain.

These remarks apply, in some measure, to the administration of the present incumbent of the Mayoralty in Norfolk. His policy is not at all tyrannical. He does not inflict severe punishment when he believes a milder course will have the desired effect upon the accused; when this can be lawfully and safely adopted, and that, legally dispensed with. And, of course, he sometimes errs in judgment, as all others do. Competent as he is allowed to be as a judge of the law, and firm as he has often proved himself to be when he has formed an opinion which he believes to be correct, still, he is probably in a situation that is uncongenial to his feelings and the general turn of his mind. Ever ready to sympathize with the unfortunate, retiring, unobtrusive as he is in his manners, and feelings, too, we should think he would probably prefer to withdraw from the scenes of contention, crime, wretchedness, and human frailty, with which he is frequently and of necessity brought in contact, and with which it is his sworn duty to deal impartially. Yet, without adulation, we may say that he is deemed, by those who know him best, to be a discreet and attentive officer, who is ready to give his decisions promptly, after duly weighing the evidence and all the attending circumstances, in every case of importance that comes before him.

Mr. Stubbs is one of the most unostentatious men in the city, possessing little or no aristocracy; and as to mere pride of office, if he has any, it is in too small a measure to be observable.

Though but little on the shady side of forty, he is a man of much experience in the diversified affairs of life. His sound, discriminating, practical knowledge of a great variety of subjects is, perhaps, inferior to few in the city. This is, of course, much to his advantage as a municipal officer.

As an orator, he could, if he desired it, soon acquire considerable distinction; although, as an extempore or off-hand speaker, we do not admit that he greatly excels. He appears, on some occasions, to lack fire, and a sufficiency of those energetic, quickening impulses, so essential in a public speaker, and which, at a moment's notice, sometimes, thrill the heart, animate the spirit, and excite the popular mind to action. Nevertheless, he certainly has the ability to be very happy in his oratorical efforts; of the truth of which we could, if necessary, adduce very satisfactory evidence.

Finally, as a writer, he is clear and perspicuous. The productions of his pen give evidence of a mind accustomed to close, patient, and careful investigation, with the capacity to grapple with error in defence of the claims of truth, morality, and sound principles.

Mr. S. is a native of Gloucester County, Virginia.

On this day, Millard Fillmore, the President of the United States, who had been for several days sojourning at Old Point, visited Norfolk and Portsmouth. "The steamer Engineer, with the President and his suite on board, reached the wharf at Norfolk at three o'clock, when he was received by the Mayor, Recorder, Aldermen, and City Councils, and under a military escort of the Artillery Blues, Junior Volunteers, and Academy Cadets, proceeded to the National Hotel, where his Excellency and the Secretary of the Interior were introduced to as many of the citizens as could find admittance through the dense crowds which filled every avenue to the audience-chamber. A generous flow of feeling to honour a President of the United States, who, in a trying crisis, had maintained the peace of the country by his steady devotion to the Constitution, regardless of sectional influences, seemed to pervade all classes and all parties; and, indeed, it may be said, at least for this occasion, that the 'monster, Party,' was strangled."

August 25th. Severe storm from the southeast.

A Directory and Statistical Register of the city, edited and published by the writer of these sketches, made its appearance this month. It was very favourably received, quite liberally patronised, and generally circulated. It contains the names, professions, places of business, and residences, of the merchants, traders, manufacturers, mechanics, heads of families, &c., in the city of Norfolk; a list of the public buildings, with their relative position; the names and situations of the streets; a register of the public officers, companies, associations, and institutions of learning, in Norfolk and Portsmouth; an account of the situation, improvements, natural advantages, and commercial resources, of the two towns; officers of the Navy Yard; the steam-packet, railroad, and stage lines and routes; distances to other places; rates of commission, storage, wharfage, and postage; rates and rules of interest and discount; directions about notes; the rivers, bays, mountains, railroads, colleges, resources, and obligations of Virginia; the courts, census returns, public appropriations, qualifications of voters, and law of taxation; officers of the Federal and State Governments; and a variety of other statistical and miscellaneous information, carefully collected from authentic sources.

The very kind reception of this work, the generous disposition manifested by an enlightened community to encourage and sustain it, and the patronage which was readily and ungrudgingly bestowed, placed its author under many obligations, while it proved that no inconsiderable number of the people of Norfolk are ready to foster an object that may appear in some measure worthy of their regard, and which frankly and fairly asserts its claims to their support.

To the respected and intelligent gentlemen at the head of the Press, in Norfolk, Portsmouth, Richmond, &c., for the very polite and complimentary manner in which they were pleased to notice his work—for the strong and significant terms employed in recommending it to the favour and patronage of the community, he tenders his sincerest thanks. Commendations of so pleasing a nature, so beneficial and so efficacious, from those whose sagacity and experience justly entitle them to an opinion, were scarcely expected. Nor should he fail to embrace the present occasion to express himself in terms of respectful acknowledgment, for the many assurances of approbation, and testimonials of commendation, received from other sources, of great respectability and intelligence. He does not choose to affect a stoical indifference to those kind evidences of approval. They are gratifying, and are duly appreciated. Such expressions of approbation are not unfrequently of real value, and often exert a salutary influence upon the efforts of man. Falling upon the ear like the soft and soothing melody of music, they sometimes reach down deep into the heart, and rouse into exertion the slumbering faculties of the drooping soul; while the chilling breath of discouragement often withers, and effectually blights in the bud, the humble effort to benefit society, or even, in some degree, to increase individual happiness. True generosity of soul forms a striking contrast, especially in relation to new enterprises, to the calculating, contracted, and discontented spirit, sometimes manifested amid the diversity of human character, which not only withholds support and encouragement, but seeks to disparage the works of others, and even repines under some circumstances, at their success; a frailty, by the way, which is generally betrayed by its possessor, who rarely succeeds in his efforts to conceal its existence, or to hide his moral deformity from the eye of scrutiny.

It has afforded the writer much pleasure to learn, from many patrons of the Directory, that it has been found useful, especially to men of business, and to strangers visiting the city. It is gratifying also to be apprised of the fact, that it has proved beneficial, interesting, and instructive, to persons unacquainted with Norfolk—its size, government, commercial facilities, &c. Indeed, it was not supposed, until after the experiment, which to some appeared of doubtful utility, had been tried, that it would create an agreeable surprise in the minds of intelligent citizens, even of Virginia, with regard to the seaport of the State.

There are many thinking, practical, and intelligent men, who believe that Norfolk, at some not very distant period in the history of the world, will be a great city. Every person, who thinks upon the subject at all, knows well enough that the place is not what it ought long since to have been. But there are some also who have thought, or who have, at least, appeared to think, that it is far inferior to what it really is, in extent, improvements, business means and sources of wealth, and facilities for extensive commercial transactions. The writer has long been aware of this fact; and, as the circulation of the work is not confined to Norfolk, nor even to the State, it appears that it has tended, in some measure at least, to remove prejudice, correct false impressions, elicit favour, and inspire confidence; and he regards this as not the smallest item in the compensation which he has received, for the labour and pains bestowed upon an undertaking, which, although it has found favour with many, has also been regarded with apparent indifference by, at least, a few, who, it was thought, would be most anxious, for several reasons, to afford their encouragement and patronage.

The following, from a Norfolk paper, is one of the complimentary notices of the work by the Press:—

"It is truly a valuable, and to everybody throughout Virginia, who feels a proper concern in the affairs of one of its chief commercial marts, a manual of much interest and convenience. It is not more desirable from its accurate record of our population, their pursuits and locations, and its judicious arrangement throughout, than as a valuable compendium of the statistics of our city, exhibiting its business concerns, its commercial facilities, public and private edifices, institutions, mechanical skill and enterprise, in their best attractions, and furnishing so truthful a view of the rapid progress and improvements of our beautiful little city, as cannot fail to enlist an interest in its welfare, attract new residents, and inspire all with a conviction that our destiny, as a commercial city, is upward as well as onward.

"Finally, its typographical execution is in the best style of that invaluable art; and the entire work commends itself to the patronage of all our citizens, not only by its intrinsic utility, but as a stimulant to enterprise, industry, and good taste."

Tuesday, November 4. "Died, at his residence in this city, Mr. John M'Phail, in the seventy-eighth year of his age. Born in Glasgow, Scotland, he came, in early life, to this country, and, for more than half a century, had been a resident of this city. Mr. M'Phail took an active part in the formation of the First Presbyterian Church in Norfolk, and, for many years, filled the office of a ruling elder in that church."

Thursday, November 27. The Seaboard and Roanoke Railroad was this day completed to Weldon, N. C.

"The cars left Portsmouth at half-past eight o'clock in the morning, crowded to excess with passengers, and reached Weldon in three hours and a half, running time—distance eighty miles. The train from Wilmington had already arrived with a large number of passengers, from that city and its neighbourhood, who, mingling with their friends from Virginia, a cordial welcome was reciprocated and felicitations were mutually passed on the joyous occasion of opening this new commercial and social medium of communication between their two States."

December. The weather, for a portion of this month, was severely cold, and Wednesday the 17th was the coldest day, so early in the season, within the last seven years, according to those who pay attention to the seasons.

The winter of 1851–52, was the coldest that has occurred here for fifteen years or more. Fire-wood at one period sold as high as $8 per cord. Whitehead's Pond frequently presented a most interesting and exciting scene; hundreds of men and boys being engaged in the delightful exercise of skating, while large numbers of the fair sex gathered upon the shores of the pond, and upon the thick ice, to witness the sport.

Some time during this year (1851), "the congregation of the Methodist Episcopal Church worshipping in the small frame edifice known as 'Zion's Meeting-house,' two miles from the city, on the Lambert's Point Road, caused a well to be dug on their lot. The work was undertaken by Mr. Whitehurst, whose land adjoins the lot a few feet from the spot selected for the well. When he had dug to the depth of about fifteen or eighteen feet, he struck a spring from which issued water very strongly impregnated with alum—so much so as to render it utterly unfit for ordinary use, and it proved to be in reality a bona fide *alum spring*. Such a discovery almost anywhere else would have produced quite a sensation in the neighbourhood, and led to immediate steps to bring it into notice and turn it to account. But here, for the period of nearly a year, it seems to have been regarded almost with indifference, and it was not until the curative efficacy of the water had been tested in some obstinate cases of disease that it begun to attract the attention due to its importance."

"The 'Alum Spring,' as it is called, bids fair to be a place of general resort. All who have drank of its waters—and their name is legion—testify to their wholesome properties, and it is thought by many that the spring will prove a source of great benefit to our city, by attracting persons to spend the summer months here for their health, instead of seeking for that *sine qua non* in the mountains or on the sea-shore. The water contains alum and iron in large quantities—heavy deposits of both are precipitated by letting it stand for a short time, or by heating it; and physicians have pronounced it very valuable as a tonic and remedy in a great many complaints. The spring being on church property, the public are at liberty to go there and drink to their heart's content. The ride is one of the most pleasant in the neighbourhood—or the distance may be walked with ease over a shady road."

A valuable mineral spring was also discovered, in 1851, on the Magnolia Farm, owned by David Jordan, Esq., of Nansemond County. Magnolia is fourteen miles from Norfolk, and about three from Suffolk; and the Seaboard and Roanoke Railroad runs directly past the residence of Mr. Jordan, a circumstance greatly in its favour.

"Professor Stewart, of Baltimore, to whom the test was confided, has pronounced it to be probably one of the most efficient and valuable medicinal waters in the world. It combines the properties of the Saratoga with that of the White Sulphur waters; and may be said to represent perfectly the water of the far-famed Harrowgate Springs. Professor Stewart in his report says: 'I have never met with any mineral water that appeared so highly charged with sulphuretted hydrogen; and when you have a copious spring so easy of access, in our own country, that possesses the qualities of the celebrated Harrowgate Springs of England, I should think it hardly possible that you should fail in obtaining for it the commendation of our most eminent medical men.' "

CHAPTER XXXVII.

1852.

Ordinance—Virginia Bank in Portsmouth Robbed—Conviction and Sentence of one of the Robbers—Cold Weather—River Frozen Over—Remarkable Hail-storm—Destructive Effects—Work on Internal Improvements, &c.—Judge Baker—Clerk of Court—Commissioner of Revenue—Commonwealth's Attorney—Wm. T. Hendren, Esq.—Internal Improvement Meeting—Norfolk and Petersburg Road—Able Discussion—Mayoralty—Candidates—Election of Officers—Objectionable Feature in the Law—City Officers—Councils—Melancholy Intelligence—Death of Henry Clay—Funeral Obsequies—Procession—Oration—The Weather—Death of the Oldest White Inhabitant—New Catholic Church in Portsmouth—Patrick Robinson's Bequest—Death of Billy Ingram, the Oldest Coloured Inhabitant—Incidents in His Life—His Great Physical Strength—Coincidence—Corporation Scrip, in Sums of $100, $50, and $1—Intelligence of the Death of Webster—Wm. B. Lamb, Esq.—Doctor Cowdery—Illumination, &c.—Agricultural Fair—Commendable Display of Agricultural Productions—Premiums—Princess Anne County—British Consul—Line of Packets to New York—Railroad Subscription.

1852, January 1st. On this day, an ordinance called "the Cow Law" went into operation. Cows, which had been allowed to go at large in every part of the city, and get into all kinds of mischief, to the great annoyance of the citizens, generally, and to the women and children, particularly, are now kept in enclosures, or driven without the city limits. It is manifestly a wise and necessary law; in support of which several very good reasons could be mentioned. There are, nevertheless, many persons who pronounce it unnecessary and unjust. The wonder is that it was not passed fifty years ago. The propriety of passing the law was urged in a communication from Mayor Stubbs to the Councils.

Jan. 18. On the morning of this day, it was discovered that the Branch Bank of Virginia, in Portsmouth, had been robbed of a large amount. The entrance was made by means of crowbars, drills, &c., through a window in the rear of the building, and through the doors and bars of the vault to the money, of which the thieves took, in gold, silver, and notes, about $66,000. In September, a man named Rand, of Boston, was convicted of being concerned in the robbery, and sentenced to ten years' imprisonment in the penitentiary. Other persons were arrested, but Rand was the only person convicted. On account of some informality in the proceedings, he was granted a new trial; but he got out of prison and made his escape, as also did one Jack Stevens, who had been confined in the same jail, some months before, on the same charge. At the date of this writing (December, 1852), the money has not been recovered. This, however, does not injure the credit of the bank, which is in a sound and prosperous condition.

On the 23d of this month (January), the Elizabeth River was frozen over from shore to shore, for the first time in a number of years. The ice was not sufficiently thick, however, to obstruct navigation.

April 8th, Thursday. About five o'clock on the afternoon of this day, a very dark and heavy cloud arose rapidly from the west, and soon the inhabitants of Norfolk and vicinity witnessed one of the most remarkable and destructive hail-storms with which this section was ever visited. The frozen balls, as large as marbles, fell in great quantities—the wind blowing from the west. The storm was attended with wind, flashes of lightning, and heavy peals of thunder. Much damage was done to vegetables and fruit; and window-glass to the amount of thousands of dollars was demolished.

May. About the first of this month was issued in the city, by the writer, a work of about one hundred pages octavo, with the following title:

"Norfolk and the Interior; or, Railroads extending from the

Seaboard through Virginia, North Carolina, Tennessee, &c., to the Great Valleys of the West: being a Compendium of Facts and Statistics, showing the Prospective Benefits of Internal Improvements to the Seaport of Virginia; together with Statements relative to the Commerce and Commercial Facilities of the City of Norfolk: to which are added, the Business Cards of Merchants, Manufacturers, &c."

An edition of about one thousand copies was taken by the merchants. The following remarks comprise a portion of a notice of the work by the American Beacon:

"It contains many interesting facts relative to the commercial advantages of our city in connexion with the various railroads that are built, and are to be built, connecting us with the great West and South. All who feel an interest in the prosperity of Norfolk, will find this work exceedingly interesting and instructive, and will be well compensated for the time by reading it."

May 27th. On this day Richard H. Baker, Esq., a gentleman of great worth of character, and high legal distinction, was re-elected Judge of the Circuit Court, an office which he has filled with ability for a number of years. John Williams, Esq., an old and faithful incumbent, was re-elected Clerk of the Circuit Court, and Finlay F. Ferguson, a most efficient officer, was re-elected to the office of Commissioner of Revenue.*

On this day, also, Wm. T. Hendren, Esq., was elected by the people Commonwealth's Attorney for the Circuit Court. He holds the same relation to the Hustings Court of the city, having been elected thereto under the new constitution, June 24th, 1852.

His fellow-citizens have evidently manifested great confidence in his talents, legal intelligence and good judgment, by appointing him to so responsible an office, especially in view of the fact, that he is quite a young man; and it is believed there will be no reason to think that their confidence is misplaced. We may appropriately say, that Mr. Hendren possesses a sufficient amount of talent and experience to sustain the character and dignity of the office. His mind is active, vigorous, and well

* The late William B. Lamb, Esq., a venerable and most estimable citizen, formerly Mayor, long held the office of Sergeant of the city, and his son, Wm. W. Lamb, Esq., has been for years the esteemed and faithful Deputy Sergeant.

cultivated. His educational advantages, and his early opportunities as a lawyer, were such as to bring out and develope the strength of his intellectual faculties, at an early age; and his friends have not yet been disappointed in their expectations with regard to him. Yet, it may be admitted that his mind, like that of many others, who have nevertheless come to judicial distinction, is rather too much after the fanciful, poetic order, to find the most congenial and successful field for mental effort, in deep and profound legal investigation and research.

It is gratifying to observe, that when changes are made in offices of responsibility, which have been long held by able, and faithful persons, young men are chosen, who may justly and fairly assert their claims upon the confidence of all classes of the community.

May 12th. Internal Improvement Meeting, held on Wednesday night, in Mechanics' Hall, in relation to the proposed railroad from Norfolk to Petersburg. It was numerously attended, and its proceedings were highly interesting and satisfactory. The magnitude and importance of the subject under consideration were presented, and the resolutions before the meeting were discussed, with marked ability and sound judgment, by Messrs. Harrison, Robertson,* A. F. Leonard, R. E. Taylor, and others. Mr. L. "delivered an admirable speech, which went largely into the merits of the subject, and demonstrated by incontrovertible facts the certain success and countless advantages which would result to our city from the proposed railroad."

June 24th. Simon S. Stubbs, Esq., re-elected Mayor. The other candidates were Colonel Simon Stone, Major Samuel T. Sawyer, and Captain Wm. D. Delany. On this day the principal officers of the corporation, were, according to Act of Assembly, elected by the votes of the people, instead of being appointed by the Councils, as heretofore.† Owing to a singular and unneces-

* Mr. Robertson was, in October, 1851, elected to represent the city in the General Assembly. He is a young gentleman of strong and active mind, improved by a liberal education. His high moral worth of character, together with his talents and legal qualifications, combined to make him the choice of a majority of the voters of the city, for the above station.

† The votes of the citizens were taken on the adoption or rejection of this law, the majority being in favour of adopting it.

sary provision of the act, requiring the name of each voter to be announced by the Sheriff, with that of the candidate, and then recorded; it was found impossible to receive all the votes. Very many persons were therefore compelled to forego the privilege of voting. This disfranchisement, as may be supposed, gave great dissatisfaction. The objectionable feature in the law will be repealed.

The following are the principal officers chosen by the voters, according to the new law regulating the city elections:

Register, Jos. H. Robertson; Attorney of the Hustings Court, Wm. T. Hendren; City Attorney, Hunter Woodis; Clerk of the Court, John Williams; Assessor, Finlay F. Ferguson; City Collector, Wm. H. Hunter; City Inspector, Cary Fentress; Surveyor, John Williston; Gauger of Liquors, &c., James M. Steed; Keeper of Almshouse, Wm. Hawkins; Physician to Almshouse, Dr. Geo. W. Cowdery; Clerk of the Market, Eli Cuthriell; Wood-measurers, John R. Wyatt and F. A. Johnston; Keeper of Magazine, Chas. W. Constable; Hay-weigher, H. F. Harding; Sealer of Weights and Measures, Thos. R. Lee; Captain of the City Watch, E. Guy.

The following appointments were, according to law, made by the Governor: Inspector of Salted Provisions, Alexander A. Martin; Inspector of Flour, James M. Steed; of Lime, William Loyall; of Naval Stores, Alexander M. Cunningham.

The following are some of the appointments made by the Councils:

Wright Southgate, Chr. Hall, H. B. Reardon, T. G. Broughton, Sr., and Wm. Selden, Board of Health; F. F. Ferguson, Chief Engineer, Fire Department; Jas. M. Steed and D. W. Glass, Assistant Engineers; Jas. Cornick, Jacob Vickery, and Horatio Moore, Port Wardens; Jas. L. Hipkins, J. S. Fatherly, Wm. Drew Roberts, Harbour Masters.

The following gentlemen were on this day elected to compose the Common and Select Councils, according to the Ward system of voting:

First Ward.—J. B. Whitehead, John Williams, F. W. Southgate, R. W. Silvester, W. T. Harrison, N. C. King, G. W. Camp, E. C. Robinson, Josiah Wills.

Second Ward.—Wm. Denby, Sr., G. W. Bluford, W. F. Mallory, Wm. Ward.

Third Ward.—H. B. Reardon, C. Hall, R. Capps, John Dickson, T. G. Broughton, Sr., A. L. Hill, W. D. Roberts, Jr., S. March.

Fourth Ward.—J. G. H. Hatton, Francis Mallory, C. F. Stone, R. H. Chamberlaine, J. R. Spratley, T. J. D. Reilly, W. Phillips.

Wm. D. Roberts, Jr., Esq., was chosen President of the Select Council, and John Williams, Esq., President of the Common Council.

June 29th. On this day was received in the city a telegraphic despatch, announcing the sad intelligence of the death of the great statesman, Henry Clay. The bells were tolled, the flags of the shipping were half-masted, and a general feeling of gloom and profound sorrow was manifested.

July 1st. This being the day appointed for the funeral of Hon. Henry Clay at Washington, business was suspended, and the bells were tolled from twelve till three o'clock.

July 21st. This day having been set apart, at a public meeting, for the city to pay a suitable tribute to the memory of Mr. Clay, the funeral obsequies accordingly took place; and they were of a most solemn and impressive character. The pageant was truly grand; and all parties united in showing their respect for the lamented and illustrious dead. Business was again suspended. The authorities, societies, companies, naval and military officers, &c., with a very large concourse of citizens, including very many from Portsmouth, Hampton, &c., as well as from the counties of Norfolk and Princess Anne, formed a long procession, which, after marching through the principal streets, assembled in the Methodist Episcopal Church on Cumberland Street, where a very able, impressive, and appropriate oration was delivered by Dr. F. Mallory.

There had been but light rains, with long seasons of dry weather, for several years, until about the middle of this month, from which time, for many weeks, it rained heavily; and "more rain fell than during the entire two years previous."

August 19. Died, this day, Mrs. Elizabeth Martin, aged 96.

19

She was the elder sister of Mrs. Ingram, whose death is mentioned April 24, 1851. Mrs. M. was, in all probability, the "oldest (white) inhabitant." Her sight was much impaired, but she conversed sensibly, and walked unsupported about her house, only a short time before she died. From Mrs. M., we obtained some interesting revolutionary details, which, in all probability, would never have been recorded, but for the timely conversations which we sought opportunity to have with this ancient and venerable descendant of one of the oldest and most respectable families of the borough.

A new Catholic Church was commenced in 1851, in Portsmouth, which, at the close of the following year, was rapidly approaching its completion. It is situated on the north side of High Street, on the site of the old building. The style is purely Gothic; and it is, indeed, a beautiful structure. The steeple, which is very handsome and well-proportioned, and a considerable portion of the main building, are plainly seen from the harbour and the Norfolk side, forming a very striking ornament to our sister town. The size of this edifice is 57 by 84 feet; cost $17,000.

In 1809, Mr. Patrick Robinson, an Irishman, bequeathed an estate to the pastor of the old church, which has been recently sold for $7,750, and vested in the new church.

Friday, October 15th. Billy, a servant of the late Mrs. Sarah Ingram, died in this city on this day, at the age of one hundred and seventeen years. "He was a native of Hanover County, Virginia, born in the service of Peter Garland, Esq.; was at Norfolk when it was burnt in 1776, and was pressed into his Majesty's service by Governor Dunmore. He was at the battle of Great Bridge, and remembered all about the siege of Yorktown. Billy was strong, hale, and hearty, even to the day of his death. He was employed as a drayman until he was seventy-five years old, and at the age of sixty-eight could roll a hogshead of sugar weighing fifteen hundred pounds, on his dray without assistance. He was always good-humoured, well-disposed, and scrupulously honest. It is a remarkable coincidence, that for the last sixty years he lived in a family, three of the inmates of which, have died within the last two years, two at the ages of ninety-two and ninety-six, and one at the age of seventy-six."

Saturday, October 16th. The Select Council on this day called up and passed the bill from the Common Council (which had passed that body on the 18th of February last, and been laid on the table in the Select Council), making provision for the issue of corporation scrip to the amount of $20,000, in sums of $50 and $100, bearing six per cent. interest; and $10,000 in sums of one dollar, bearing an interest of one half of one per cent. per annum.*

October 25. On this day, was received in the city, intelligence of the death of Daniel Webster. There was a very general expression of sorrow on account of the loss the Union had sustained in the death of its greatest statesman and diplomatist. The flags of the shipping, &c., were half-masted; and on the 26th, minute guns were fired in commemoration of the illustrious dead. How great, how learned, how wise a man had fallen! But his fame is world-renowned, and he needs no eulogy here. Truly, the writer did not imagine that the demise of both Clay and Webster would be alluded to on these pages, and in one and the same chapter.

November 14. Died, this day, Wm. B. Lamb, Esq., aged eighty-nine, "one of the few remaining patriarchs, whose foundations of future usefulness and distinction, as members of our community, were laid in the last century." He was an alderman of the Borough from 1803 till 1810; and mayor from 1810 till 1815. "Well does the writer remember," says a respected citizen, "with what fidelity and at what sacrifice of time and personal comfort, he discharged the duties of that office (then without emolument), during the period of war, from 1812 to 1815, when the preservation of public order within the town often called him from his family at all hours of the night, and not unfrequently during the entire night. His judicious and energetic course on such occasions was always effective, and his services were duly appreciated by his fellow-citizens.

"In 1815 he was elected President of the Virginia Bank, and continued in that office till his resignation in 1827, when he accepted the office of Sergeant, conferred on him by the Hustings

* At a subsequent meeting of the Common Council, the Committee on Ordinances were directed to bring in a bill to repeal this ordinance, and an amendment thereto, passed November 9.

Court of Norfolk, and which he held at the period of his death—the greater part of the time by the suffrages of his fellow-citizens."

November 20. Died, this day, aged eighty-five, Doctor Jonathan Cowdery, the oldest surgeon, and the oldest officer in the United States Navy. He chose Norfolk as his home and the residence of his family, nearly fifty years ago.

"In all the relations of life, he was a most exemplary gentleman, and will long be remembered and venerated by the citizens of this city, to whom he has been so familiarly and kindly known.

"He was a native of Massachusetts, and after graduating in one of the medical colleges of that State, he entered the navy more than half a century ago, and has faithfully and uninterruptedly served in his useful department, in peace and in war.

"He was one of the medical officers of the frigate Philadelphia in 1803, when that ship, under the command of Commodore Bainbridge, and whilst in pursuit of the Tripolitan corsairs, ran upon a reef and fell into the hands of the enemy. Along with Porter, Jacob Jones, Renshaw, Biddle, Patterson, and other young heroes, who afterwards so signally illustrated the naval history of our country, he was thrown into the prison of Tripoli, and whilst there it was the good fortune of Dr. Cowdery to render important professional service to the Bashaw, during a severe illness; which had also the happy effect of mitigating the rigours of the confinement of his fellow-prisoners. It was an event of much note at the time, and added greatly to the professional reputation of the young surgeon, especially as the medical attendants of the royal Mussulman were wholly unable to relieve their patient. In the war of 1813–'14, and since that time, at home and abroad, his services have been efficient."

November 22d. On the evening of this day, during a heavy fall of rain, the Democrats celebrated their late victory, by illuminating their houses, by fireworks, marching through the streets, &c.

"The houses of the Democracy, were generally illuminated, many with great taste and display of wreaths, flags, and transparencies. Nothing occurred to mar the enjoyment of the occasion, except the heavy fall of rain, and that was not sufficient to dampen the zeal of those who participated in the demonstration."

On the 23d and 24th of this month, the first Fair of the Princess Anne Agricultural Society was held, at the beautiful village of Kempsville. The enterprising farmers of that county deserve much praise for the extensive display which was made on the occasion, of stock, grain, fruit, vegetables, poultry, &c., &c.; and too much cannot be said in commendation of the exhibition of articles of domestic manufacture—the handiwork of the industrious matrons and fair maidens of the county.

"On Tuesday, the first day of the Fair, the committee of arrangements having, by ten o'clock, classified and marked the various deposits intended for exhibition, the judges proceeded to discharge their duties of examining, reporting, &c.

"At twelve o'clock," continues the report of the committee, "the gates were opened for the admission of spectators, and in a short time the whole enclosure presented a very interesting and animated appearance.

"The cattle, both of blooded and of native stock, were very fine; and among those of the blooded stock, were a large number which would do credit to any fair in the country. Praise is richly due to our own citizens, and especially to many farmers of the surrounding counties, who, with much trouble and expense, exhibited largely on the occasion, and contributed much in giving interest and variety to the Fair."

"A large shed, forty feet long, was filled with various samples of the choicest and finest market vegetables, some of enormous size; and it may well be doubted, whether any of the northern agricultural fairs could have competed with us in this branch. The large and fine collection of agricultural implements and machines exhibited by Messrs. March and Borum, of the neighbouring city of Norfolk, deservedly attracted universal attention.

"A house about sixty feet in length was appropriated to articles belonging to the dairy, and the various branches of domestic economy; and the delicacy of the arrangements, and the beauty of the display in this department, excited general admiration, and showed at a glance, without any mention of the fact, that it was under the management and supervision of the ladies.

"This Fair, which, before its occurrence, was regarded by some as a doubtful experiment, has far exceeded public expectation; and its triumphant success should be a subject of rejoicing to the members of our infant society, and to the friends of agriculture in this section of our State. It proves beyond all controversy, that the farmers of the extreme eastern portion of Virginia, have the spirit and the means to present an agricultural fair which can equal, in variety and interest, local exhibitions of the same kind in any part of the country.

"On Wednesday, the second day of the Fair, a ploughing match took place, the address was delivered, and the premiums awarded. The ploughing match, an exciting and well-conducted contest, took place in a neighbouring field, the spectators manifesting much interest in the result.

"The large concourse of spectators having returned to the grounds, the Hon. F. Mallory, himself a practical farmer, who had politely consented, on invitation of the society, to be the orator of the occasion, having been presented to the audience by E. H. Herbert, Esq., the President of the Association, delivered a practical, interesting, and instructive address of about an hour's length, on the subject of agriculture.

"The address being concluded, the President of the Society proceeded to read the award of premiums made by the several committees of judges.

A long list of premiums has been published. We record, with pleasure, that one was awarded to Mr. Edgar Burroughs, of Princess Anne, for an essay on worn-out lands; and another to Doctor Wm. Tatem for an essay on draining. It was found that the best-conducted farms were those of Captain James Cornick, and Messrs. Thomas Ballentine, Wm. S. Wright, Wm. Godfrey, and E. H. Herbert.

The committee on agricultural productions reported that there were four competitors for the best acre of corn, to wit: J. N. Baxter, D. M. Walke, Jonathan Hunter, and Thomas Ballentine; that the product of the first was 87 bushels, the second 72 bushels, the third 68¾ bushels, and the fourth 66 bushels, and awarded the premium for the best acre to J. N. Baxter; for the best acre of wheat to Edgar Burroughs; for the best quarter acre of rutabagas, to James R. Walke, the product being 71¾ bushels of roots, weighing 58 pounds to the bushel.

This is said to be the first fair of the kind ever held in Virginia, and the "eminent success which attended the effort, will inspirit the farmers of Princess Anne and of other counties in this district to repeat it. They have set the ball in motion, and shall it stop here? No! Let it roll onward through every district and county in the State."

"The county of Princess Anne is destined in a few years to become the garden spot of the State. (The same may be said of a large portion of Norfolk County.) Independent of its proximity to navigation and its inexhaustible piscatorial resources, it contains, to the extent of its territory, a larger body of valuable and productive land than any other county in Virginia. In 1852, one of its enterprising farmers realized from eight acres near eleven hundred dollars; and pitched on the same land a second crop, which probably brought him five or six hundred dollars more. Such a profitable yield from the same area of cultivation is hard to beat in any part of the United States. A judicious system of agriculture is now being introduced in the tillage of the soil of this county, and its public-spirited farmers are making every effort to promote improvements in this noble pursuit."

G. P. R. James, Esq., the celebrated English novelist, having been appointed British Consul for Virginia, to fill the vacancy occasioned by the death of Mr. Waring, the former incumbent, arrived in Norfolk this month, and entered upon the duties of office.

Mr. James is "rather below the general stature; stout in person, with a somewhat measured, theatrical walk. He is exceedingly prepossessing in appearance, has a fine, large, expressive eye, commanding forehead, regular features, and is, apparently, about fifty-two years of age."

December. About the first of this month, a new line of packets between Norfolk and New York, was established by some of the merchants of the former place.

On the 10th of this month, the councils, in accordance with the wishes of a majority of the voters of the city, appointed a committee to subscribe $200,000 to the capital stock of the Norfolk and Petersburg Railroad Company, with certain provisions, one of which is, that, if the road is built, there shall be a satisfactory connexion with the Southside Road, at or near its terminus in Petersburg.

CHAPTER XXXVIII.

Opinions respecting Norfolk—Mr. Jefferson's Prediction—Views of Mr. Madison—Unwise Legislation—Internal Improvement—James River and Kanawha Canal—Products of the West—The Norfolk Market—Productions of the Forest—Coal—Railway to the Pacific—Norfolk the Commercial Centre of a large Extent of Country—Coasting Business—The Harbour—The Norfolk and Petersburg Railroad—Its advantages—Surveyor's Report—Convention at Union—New Orleans and Memphis Road—Norfolk the Atlantic Terminus—China and East India Trade—The Consequences—Weldon and Gaston, and Clarksville and Ridgway Roads—Seaboard and Roanoke Railroad—Subscriptions by the City—Arrangements of the Company with the City—Ferry and Bridge Connexion—Trade—City Subscription—Baltimore Steam Packet Company—Wilmington and Manchester Road—North Carolina Road—Charlotte and Columbia Road, &c.—Continuous Lines from Norfolk—Enterprising Men Wanted—Enterprise and Progress—Supineness, Neglect, and the Downward Tendency.

In this chapter we present a few remarks, from our pamphlet on the means, resources, and prospects of Norfolk, and which were originally intended for this work.

Many judicious and reflecting men have entertained the opinion that Norfolk would, at some future day, rival the greatest cities of America. They who felt a deep interest in the welfare and prosperity of our State, long ago expressed their convictions in significant terms on this subject. The views of the gifted Jefferson, whose powerful mind seemed to penetrate deeper in the uncertain future than that of most other men of his day, are familiar to the intelligent reader. The author of the Declaration of Independence, examined the different locations and resources of various sections of this great country, and especially those of his own loved Virginia; and when he declared that Norfolk would be the "great Emporium of the Chesapeake," his opinion had been formed from a knowledge of the advantages of commerce possessed by this particular site. Its deep, capacious, and land-locked harbour, its central position on the Atlantic coast, its mild climate, and its exhaustless regions of back country, south, west, and northwest—these had been duly noticed by the sage of Monticello, and his inference was, that they must, if properly appreciated and improved, render this port the pride of the State, the chief exporting and importing city of Virginia, and of the South.

There was another master mind that turned hitherwards—another distinguished son of the Old Dominion—whom she and the Union delighted to honour—who freely expressed himself with regard to this location. The accomplished MADISON concurred with Jefferson in his views about the facilities of this port for extensive commercial transactions. He declared it to be "*the true interest of Virginia to foster the prosperity of Norfolk, as among the prime objects of her policy.*" But sad to say, Virginia, or rather, her misguided legislators, did not heed these words of wisdom.* They lost sight of the "true interest" of the good old commonwealth, and while other states "fostered the prosperity" of their chief seaports, our law-makers wasted the resources of the State on wild and unproductive schemes, and discoursed most eloquently indeed, upon "abstract questions of political economy," until the chief avenue to wealth and greatness was well-nigh closed, our resources became comparatively dormant, and our treasures passed off to enrich other states. Hence the declination of Virginia from the first to the fourth state in the Union, and from "one-fifth to one-fifteenth of the political power of the confederacy."†

We now give the views of several individuals of experience and sound judgment relative to works of internal improvement and other matters in which Norfolk is deeply interested.

* "The State has expended $20,000,000, principally intended for the improvement of Richmond; and the trifling sum of $190,000 for the benefit of Norfolk, all of which latter sum has been repaid up to this date to $2,357, including the $9,500 they received from the last Dismal Swamp Canal dividend."

† These, and some other remarks of ours on this subject, were copied from a certain work, and erroneously published as the production of another.

"The James River and Kanawha Canal," says a writer of much ability, and of close observation, "will afford a Southern water line of transportation for the heavy products of the West, which must be, for a long period of the year, without a competitor, owing to the ice in the waters north of it. Such articles of commerce as would pass upon a canal in preference to a railroad, would prefer this, for the reason that it would lead to the nearest Atlantic harbour, and consequently the cost upon it would be the least for internal or domestic transportation. A canal boat at Columbus, Ohio, laden with pork, hemp, tobacco or iron, *would greatly prefer going to Norfolk upon this canal*, to passing through the lakes and the Erie Canal, to New York, if the market was as good at the one place as the other, for the simple reason that the distance would be greatly shorter and the navigation much safer from interruption by ice and from the dangers of the lake. *The market would be as good at Norfolk as New York*, because the trade would be intended for foreign nations, and of course the foreign price would regulate that at the port at which it would be purchased for transportation. A common standard would regulate the price at both ports, and would of course render it uniform. It is plain, therefore, that such trade as would prefer water carriage, and as now reaches New York from the heart of Ohio, would find its way to the ocean through Virginia, by means of her canal. But the trade of Ohio, and the West, is not by any means the only inducement offered for the completion of this work. I will hazard the opinion, that the timber of our forests bordering upon the line of the canal, and accessible to it by way of the Upper Kanawha, or New River and its tributaries, will in a few years produce to Virginia a larger sum of money than the whole amount required for completing the canal. I doubt if in America there are to be found such forests for ship-builders as those growing in the section of country referred to. The completion of this work will also open a thoroughfare for the transportation of coal from the prolific mines of Kanawha, Coal, and Guyandotte Rivers to Norfolk, which would make that city the depot whence the whole steam-marine of the Atlantic would be supplied with fuel. The discovery of cannel coal in that quarter of the State, in large quantities, and of the most superior quality, establishes beyond doubt the fact that, with a cheap mode of transportation, the best fuel in the world for steam would be supplied at Norfolk cheaper than any accessible point on the Atlantic border. The coal and timber trade from the western part of our State, would alone make the stock in this canal productive.

"A single glance at the map will present Norfolk as the Atlantic terminus of the contemplated railway to the Pacific, and also as the best point of departure from the United States to Europe and the Mediterranean. She will also become, next to New York, a commercial centre of importation for the West, and southwest portions of the Union, being geographically the commercial centre of a larger extent of country than any other Atlantic city. Her position is pre-eminently advantageous to the whole coasting business of the United States, being in fact the only good harbour on the Atlantic coast south of New York, and more favourably situated than any other port to distribute the agricultural products of the interior along the whole seaboard of the Union.

"The Norfolk and Petersburg Railroad, when viewed in its proper light, and its important bearing upon the railway economy, not only of our own State but of the whole country, cannot but strike the reflecting mind as one of the most essential lines of intercommunication which are now either in contemplation, or under actual construction, 'to unlock those rich treasures so much needed to invigorate the commercial enterprise,' not only of our seaboard towns, and our own back country, but of the whole South and West, from Memphis on the Mississippi, to Cincinnati on the Ohio. It is the last, but by no means least, link in the grandest scheme of internal improvement ever projected in the United States, forming, as it were, the trunk of a gigantic tree, deriving soil for its nourishment at Hampton Roads, and ramifying with its immensely long branches, Western Virginia, Ohio, Indiana, Illinois, and even Missouri; Southwestern Virginia, Tennessee, Kentucky, Georgia, Alabama, Mississippi, Louisiana, and Arkansas; and it may, at no very distant day, thrust one of its topmost leading limbs, even to the Pacific Ocean, while its tap root is insinuating its minute fibres into every European port.

"This road (the contemplated line from Norfolk to Memphis, via Petersburg), will be one thousand and thirty miles long,—of the same gauge throughout, without break—and with only two regular termini; one of them being Memphis and the other Norfolk.

"This one thousand and thirty miles of road will be but a BASE LINE, or trunk, with which twenty or thirty other tributary railroads will unite, and in which they will merge themselves. Most of the tributaries will be of the same gauge; others will be of a different gauge. That I am within the mark, you will at once see when I can mention seven in Virginia alone, that will mingle with the main line. And for all these roads (within certain limits) Norfolk will be the most convenient outlet."

We condense from the Surveyor's Report, the following interesting particulars:

"The survey commences at the intersection of Main and Wide Water Streets (at the Draw-bridge), crossing the Eastern Branch and the County Road in a southerly direction. Three miles from Norfolk, it takes a southwesterly course, and crosses the Southern Branch and the Dismal Swamp Canal, at a distance of six miles from the starting-point; thence a more westerly course to Suffolk, making the entire distance from Norfolk nearly twenty-one miles, which, compared with the distance from Suffolk to Norfolk, via Seaboard and Roanoke Railroad, of eighteen and a quarter miles, is a loss of two and three-quarter miles, which loss is but a secondary thought, taking into consideration the peculiar situation of Norfolk, and the advantages which it is believed will accrue to that city, by this direct communication of her wharves and warehouses with the avenues to the Western trade.

* * * * * * *

"At Suffolk, the line crossing the Seaboard and Roanoke Railroad near the depot, takes a northwesterly direction toward Petersburg, and from this point will compare favourably with any other road in the country in point of directness."

The following remarks are from the report of the delegates

from Norfolk to an Internal Improvement Convention, held in Union, in this State, in September, 1852:

"The undersigned, from a careful investigation and consideration of statistics and other information relating to this important subject, express their belief that, upon the perfection of the great Western line of improvement, from Norfolk to the valley of the Mississippi and of the Ohio, an important trade and travel must ensue, which will not only contribute largely to the treasury of the Commonwealth, but must necessarily inure to the prosperity and great advantage of Norfolk, presuming always that the proper energy exists here to avail itself of the vast resources which will thereby be rendered tributary to our city.

"In concluding their report, the undersigned cannot omit a reference to the solicitude for the advancement of Norfolk, which was very generally evinced by the members of the Convention. The most of them seemed to anticipate with commendable pride, a speedy and permanent connexion with our city,—and were sanguine that the recommendations of the Convention, if entertained by the Legislature, must not only greatly conduce to the development of the vast and wonderful resources of the State, but that, by the same means, Norfolk would be enabled to assume that position as a commercial mart to which her admirable advantages justly entitle her."

"'The New Orleans and Memphis Road, if ever built,' says an intelligent correspondent of the Daily News, 'must terminate on the Mississippi, at Memphis. San Diego or Monterey will be its Pacific terminus, and in the event of the road from Norfolk to Petersburg being built, Norfolk will be its Atlantic terminus. The China and East India trade generally, must pass over the road. What then, I ask, will the consequences be to Norfolk, if some eighty or one hundred steamships (this may seem extravagant to some, but not to you, for you are one of the *progressives*) ply to and from her wharves,—hundreds of thousands of people passing through her yearly,'" &c.

The city of Norfolk subscribed, in accordance with the vote of the citizens, the sum of $200,000 to the Weldon and Gaston, to the Clarksville and Ridgway, and to the Seaboard and Roanoke Railroads; $75,000 being the amount appropriated to the latter.

"In consideration of this subscription, the President and Directors of the Company offered to the city all the facilities necessary to an efficient connexion by ferry with their road, and for the transportation over it of freight and passengers, to or from Norfolk, on terms of fairness and equality."

"If, after a trial of five years, commencing with the subscription by the city of $200,000 to the roads above mentioned, or from the completion of the Seaboard Road to Weldon, the ferry transportation should, in the opinion of the Councils, be found unsatisfactory, the Seaboard Road guarantees to the city of Norfolk a connexion with said road by means of a branch railroad, commencing at the engine shop or outer depot of said road, near the outer limits of the town of Portsmouth, and connecting by means of bridges with the city of Norfolk by the nearest practicable route over the southern branch of the Elizabeth River which may be sanctioned by the Legislature of Virginia.

"To this compact, has been obtained by the Railroad Company, the assent of the Trustees of the town of Portsmouth, as will be seen by reference to their resolutions enclosed to the Committee by the President of the road—thus avoiding future difficulty here or elsewhere, that might possibly grow out of this arrangement between the City and the Seaboard Company.

"By the employment of $200,000 of the credit of the city in the shape of a subscription to these works, our trade and business will reap the same advantages as if Norfolk had expended $1,500,000 on her own account. Others, including states and individuals, have provided six-sevenths of the amount expended, or required to complete the line of improvements from Norfolk to Raleigh and Clarksville, and we are called on to supply the remainder. This the people have directed to be done, provided, in the judgment of the Councils, a suitable arrangement could be made with the Seaboard Road and other interests."

Some time before this arrangement was effected, Norfolk proposed to subscribe $200,000 to the capital stock of the Seaboard Company, as embraced in the estimate of cost, between Portsmouth and the intersection of the Raleigh and Gaston Railroad; and also to subscribe the further sum of $100,000 (or more, if the cost should exceed this sum), to construct a lateral road, according to the report of Mr. Williston, by which this city should connect with the main stem: in consideration that the Railroad Company would keep the lateral road in repair, and transport passengers and freight as cheaply to Norfolk as to Portsmouth, &c., &c.

The polls were opened for the votes of the people to be taken upon this subject, and a considerable majority were in favour of the subscription, with the understanding that the southern and eastern branches of the river should be bridged, and a train of cars should arrive at a depot in the city. The authority to construct the bridges was, however, not allowed by the Legislature—a most determined opposition having been made by Portsmouth—and the subscription was accordingly declined. An arrangement has since been effected with the Baltimore Steam Packet Company, by which the two lines are connected; the Baltimore Company having taken the remaining stock unsubscribed for on certain conditions agreed to by the Railroad Company.

The Wellington and Manchester Railroad is rapidly progressing. This, with the Seaboard and Roanoke, &c., will make a continuous line of eight hundred and sixty-eight miles from Norfolk to Montgomery, Alabama.

The North Carolina Road, from Raleigh to Salisbury, with the Charlotte and Columbia Road, will make a continuous line from Norfolk in that direction.

The Virginia and Tennessee Road, the Nashville and Chattanooga Road, the Memphis Road, with the Norfolk and Petersburg Road (should it be built), or with a connexion between the Virginia and Tennessee and the Clarksville and Ridgway Roads, will form a continuous line from our city to Memphis on the Mississippi.

"The aggregate of lines now made or being made, to concentrate upon Norfolk, amounts to more than two thousand miles of railway," extending through, perhaps, the richest and most productive section of the Union."

But more men of active enterprise, enlightened, liberal, commercial enterprise and zeal, there must be, to make the best of these immense prospective sources of greatness and wealth; let there be a larger number of these; put down sectional jealousies and narrow-hearted prejudices; and let us have wise, impartial, and prompt legislative action and concurrence, and Virginians will ere long be proud of their commerce, of their exports, and of the splendour of their cities. But without these great essential elements of progress, in these days of activity and effort in all other sections, they may dream, and hope, and speculate, philosophise, and elucidate, but all will be in vain; and the commercial tendency of this noble old State, of matchless natural advantages, will be comparatively downward and backward continually.

CHAPTER XXXIX.

Commercial Position—Why Norfolk has not advanced more rapidly—Other Cities—Norfolk and Boston—Virginia and Massachusetts—Formerly Flourishing Commerce of Virginia—Norfolk Waking Up—Internal Improvements—Obstructions must be removed—Produce must find an Outlet at this Port—Means of Access—Products of Virginia, North Carolina, &c.—Improvement apparent in Norfolk—Back Country—Land in the Vicinity—Centralizing Action—Western Trade—Railroads, Steam-Packet Lines, &c.—Effect upon the Commerce of the State—Erroneous Impressions relative to the Storage of Tobacco—Adaptation of the Climate to its Preservation proved—Testimony of the Merchants—The Climate of Norfolk—Warehouses—Inspectors—Merchants—Flour, Wheat, &c.—Means of Access.

It is not surprising that the observant traveller looks around and expresses astonishment at what he beholds here, or that the enterprising and reflecting men of the present days of progress, improvement, and wonderful prosperity, in almost every other direction, should be amazed on taking a contemplative view at what is very generally acknowledged to be, with scarcely an exception, the best commercial position to be found upon the shores of the "whole boundless continent."*

* The contents of this and a portion of the succeeding pages of this chapter, were inserted in the Norfolk Directory, having been taken from the manuscript of this work.

It is an unpleasant and undeniable fact in the history of this noble seaport, that its vast advantages have neither been properly estimated nor developed. In consequence of the formerly unkind spirit and unfriendly policy of Great Britain with regard to our navigation, and the necessarily restrictive measures of Congress in relation to the trade of the West India Islands and elsewhere, as well as the strange and injudicious course of the Legislature of the State, in refusing the necessary encouragement and assistance to, and even placing restrictions and checks upon, commerce; and owing, it must also be acknowledged, to the want of a sufficiently strong and vigorous spirit of enterprise on the part of many of the inhabitants, the prosperity of our port is sadly different from what it should be; its manifest facilities for greatness have been disregarded and neglected, and many enterprising men have been reluctantly compelled to look elsewhere for a profitable investment of their funds, while others have toiled here long without realizing an advancement commensurate with so favourable a position.

Some have laboured entirely in vain; but many able, energetic, and persevering individuals, becoming weary and impatient on account of the indifference in regard to the most important interests, and of the tardiness of the law-making powers in cherishing and appropriating the inestimable gifts of Nature, have gone north, south, and west, in search of a more promising and profitable field of labour. Nor have they sought in vain; for, while there has long been but little regard paid here to the improvement of great advantages and abundant means of wealth, others have failed not to appreciate those which were comparatively inconsiderable. While the people of this section of the Old Dominion have appeared to be satisfied with a slow and gradual progress, and have seemed quite willing to wait and calmly submit to the sad result of delay, towns and cities possessing no advantages over this in regard to location, and, in many cases, greatly inferior natural facilities, have arisen, prospered, and, by a commendable union of industrious personal effort, have long since taken a dignified stand in the nation. It is needless to direct the reader's attention to New Orleans, Boston, Philadelphia, Baltimore, Cincinnati, St. Louis, &c. It is mortifying even to allude to the startling disparity between our city and New York, the great commercial emporium of the North, the South, and the West. But observe, for instance, the contrast, humiliating though it is, presented by the ports of Norfolk and Boston; a contrast owing, in a great measure, to the astonishing difference in the commercial policy pursued by the governments of two States, which admit, by the way, in some other respects, at least, of an agreeable comparison. With the wonder-working power of the eloquence and patriotism of their sons, and the invincibility of their arms, these two old colonies stood conspicuously together in the trying days of the Revolution; and their instrumentality assisted greatly in raising high the undulating waves of public sentiment, until they broke in resistless fury against the strong towers of British tyranny and oppression. Though divided by space, and vastly unequal in size, they battled furiously and fiercely together in behalf of liberty, amid peril, and blood, and death. The one gave to the world John Adams, and other noble spirits of the Revolution; the other produced her Henry, and other fearless men of that eventful period; and they united in calling out America's greatest son to be the chief actor in that long and bloody contest for justice and freedom. May the rude, wicked, and silly attempts of blind fanaticism never prove sufficient to tear asunder the ties of sympathetic regard, made strong by mutual efforts, long past, though well remembered, to cement and build up for time this great national fabric!

Before the commencement of the struggles of the Revolution, Norfolk, as is well known, was an exceedingly prosperous commercial town; and since those "days that tried men's souls," Virginia has justly boasted of her flourishing commerce, her many great ships and wealthy merchants, and rejoiced in the bright anticipations of the future. Behold how far the old Bay State has stridden ahead of the Old Dominion in this respect. How vast the difference now! and how manifest the cause of the almost incalculable advantage which she presents to the world! It is needless to particularize with regard to facts so familiar even to the schoolboy.

But what, we ask, has Nature done for Boston in point of commercial facilities, more than for this identical position? Able statesmen and skilful merchants have answered the question, and the reply is, emphatically, *nothing*—that could not have been readily overbalanced by artificial means, properly employed, and sustained by systematic, judicious, patient effort, and enterprise. But a glance at a map of the country is only requisite to establish the truth of this statement.

Let it be remembered, however, that all of the intelligent and respected citizens of Norfolk and Portsmouth have not remained quiet and passive spectators of the race in which the two adjacent towns have been so sadly distanced. Some have spoken plainly, written clearly and forcibly, and acted a noble part. The result of their efforts has been gradually, though surely manifesting itself; it is already apparent, and it must, ere long, be more plainly seen and more readily acknowledged by all. The scales have at length fallen from the eyes of many who were long and strangely blind to their own interest, as well as to that of the community at large. Renewed vigour and a more enterprising spirit, harmonizing somewhat with the enlightened and progressive movements of the age, are evinced; and although there are some whose years and intelligence entitle them to respect, who still appear to be firmly fixed in their opposition to nearly every innovation, and who are as hard to move as the rocks in their deep-laid foundations amid the heavy breaking surges of the sea, yet the determined and unyielding spirit of improvement is rapidly pervading the community. A few will, of course, object and grumble on to the end of life's short day; but they cannot retard its progress or materially injure its vivifying and cheering influences. A vein of feeling upon the subject is gradually extending through almost every portion of society, and it is hoped it will swell with the life-giving principle of enterprise, until the pulsations shall become stronger and more regular than ever before, and indicate clearly a more healthful state of affairs; and until the very heart of the body politic shall beat with emotion, and rejoice at the bright prospect of blessings and advantages which must inevitably result from the application of the great and never-failing remedies, namely: *individual enterprise, combined with a sound, judicious, and liberal* system of internal improvements—well-established lines of communication southward and westward, concentrating at the seaport of Virginia, as at Boston, New York, Philadelphia, Baltimore, New Orleans, and other cities already named as the great commercial marts of their respective States.

The decree has gone forth, uttered in strong and impressive tones, by the sovereign voice of at least a majority of the people in this region, that Norfolk and Portsmouth must arise and press more rapidly on towards the station they are destined by nature to occupy, with those cities of the world which have come to greatness only by a proper development of their resources for commerce.

Water seeks its level. The course of the aerolite, or other descending body, is towards the centre of the earth. These and other established and well-known laws of nature, cannot be altered; they will remain, doubtless, until old Time himself shall be arrested in his rapid flight, and all earthly materialities shall be changed. But these principles are scarcely more certain and undeniable than the identical and self-evident proposition, that the produce of a country will pass through the cheapest, nearest, and most convenient channels and outlets to the great commercial marts of the world; and that trade will concentrate at those depots which require the least delay and expense, and which offer the best prices and largest profits. Then let all unnecessary obstructions be removed, and open the way for easy, free, and extensive internal communication and transportation. Let the T iron be laid, and the commodious cars roll on through those sections of country which abound with the great staple articles that form so large a portion of the nation's wealth; make the canals almost as free as the waters of our noble rivers; and then, as has been clearly demonstrated in many sections of this great country, with regard to other towns and cities, the long-expected advancement of Norfolk, and every town and village in its vicinity, under the approving smiles of gracious Heaven, will be sure and permanent; and it will be so, notwithstanding the evil forebodings and melancholy predictions of the "croakers" to the contrary.

But where is the city whose commerce is extensive and flourishing, only because it is open to the sea, without suitable means of access for purchasers, producers, and their commodities from the interior? The granaries and storehouses in the rich valleys of Virginia, North Carolina, Tennessee, Kentucky, &c., though less productive than they soon will be, are groaning with corn, wheat, tobacco, cotton, bacon, and other valuable productions. The "fat cattle" that roam and graze "upon a thousand hills," are ready for the markets; salt in immense quantities is furnished at the exhaustless salines; the mines are filled with coal, gypsum, copper, lead, iron, &c., all seeking vent, as it were, from their confinement; and for the want of a suitable outlet in this direction, a large quantity takes a tedious, tortuous, and circuitous course, in opposition to the design of nature, and goes to enrich the merchants and build up the cities of other States, that have done well, 'tis true, to open a communication affording such means of advancement. Fortunately, however, ages of industrious and enterprising toil, will not exhaust the incalculable treasures that lie dormant and undisturbed. Heavy, thick, and extensive forests there are to yield their supplies of timber, and their rich lands for cultivation; immense fields of grain, and pastures with countless herds, afford their annual abundance; the hills, the valleys, the mountains, all invite the efforts of enterprise, and offer their stores of wealth.

On taking a view of the city as it now is, it may truly be said—and it is exceedingly gratifying to remark—that a considerable improvement is presented in its appearance, and which has been going on rapidly during the last eight or ten years. Since the alteration in the title and charter, in 1845, the place has made very perceptible steps onward and upward—a creditable progress in its career of prosperity. Many beautiful public buildings, elegant family residences, large and splendid stores, well-paved streets, and a thriving and healthful population of about sixteen thousand, already suffice to render Norfolk quite a large and handsome city. With a just appreciation and judicious improvement of the natural advantages and favourable position of the port for the most extensive mercantile operations, who can foretell its future greatness, as it would at no distant period be inscribed upon the truthful page of history?

The erroneous, though oft-repeated assertion, that "Norfolk

has no back country,"(!) should never again be uttered. It is but the feeble cry of dull despondency; the language of the short-sighted, uttered in almost unpardonable ignorance, and which might have been applied, with about as much appropriateness, to Tyre of old, before its calamitous overthrow, or that might as well be used now in reference to the densely crowded seaport of the Empire State, the Modern Athens or the Crescent City, the Monumental City or the City of Brotherly Love. That large, quiet, and truly beautiful collection of salt water, bounding the city on the south,—deep, blue, and clear, from the great ocean just below, although it rolls along upon its ample bed, between our city and the interior, is no obstruction to trade, not the least obstacle in the way of the commercial prosperity of the place. It is, of course, as it has been, and as it is believed it will, ere long, prove more plainly to be, the chief source of the wealth and advancement of Norfolk, as well as of the adjacent counties of the southeastern section of the State.

The narrow, level slip of land on the east and southeast, assists greatly in supplying the markets with fruit, vegetables, mutton, poultry, grain, &c.; the beautiful bays, rivers, and deep meandering streams, serving well to furnish ample quantities of the finest fish, wild fowl, and "fat oysters" of the largest size, and the dense forests abounding with oak, pine, ash, hickory, walnut, cedar, beech, gum, sycamore, persimmon, and other useful trees, which afford firewood in abundance, besides the best of timber for the purpose of shipbuilding, &c.

But, as before intimated, it is to the wide domain of the south, southwest, west, and northwest, to the great valleys and plains, the mountains and "hill country" of those immense, exhaustless regions, that the people, at this great natural outlet to the eastern world, must look for the invaluable treasures which a kind Providence has placed at the disposal of the busy millions of the interior.

"Boston, New York, Philadelphia, Baltimore, Charleston, Savannah, Mobile, and New Orleans, have been alone looked to by the States in which they lie as the termini of all the works of improvement in which they have embarked; while Virginia forms an exception to all other communities, ancient or modern, in the struggle for the empire of commerce. We have felt the centralizing action of the Federal Government in favour of New York, and it has tended much to strip us of our foreign trade, since we derived no aid, but rather opposition, from our own State. The seaport of every Atlantic State is more rapidly improving than that of Virginia; and the reason is obvious: they have commenced their lines on the sea-coast, we, at the head of tidewater. They commence at one end and work through steadily to the other; while we begin among the hills above the bars of our rivers, and stop at the mountains."

Let the communication be opened from Norfolk westwardly; tap the great internal thoroughfares, and the produce of the country will flow eastwardly in vast quantities, to benefit the merchants and tradesmen of this, as well as other sections of the State. Cut through the dark and thick old forest wilds, and the towering mountain barriers, too, if need be; let in the bright light of day, bridge the rivers, unite the water-courses, spread out the iron track, to bind, as with a ponderous cable-chain, the East and the West together, and let the unwearied metallic horse be attached to the capacious cars, and strengthened and sustained by the fierce fires of the glowing furnace, throwing off upon the winds that lag behind him the surplus of his resistless power, let him speed on to and fro in his rapid course,—up from these level lowlands, and down again from the rich and splendid undulating country. Send out the conveyances to the Blue Ridge and Alleghany regions, and away down through the magnificent lands of West Tennessee, even to the turbid waters of the old Mississippi, flowing on and foaming still in unabated strength and fury. Send on, with the richly freighted cars, the messages from the seaboard, and the long whizzing trains will return to these shores overburdened with the rich and varied products of the vast and inexhaustible western and northwestern sections of our almost boundless expanse of territory. Here, "where we can stand at our doors and almost hear the voice of the eternal sea, as it thunders upon the beach at hand," let them be exchanged; and hence let them be shipped and forwarded north and east; and by the contemplated Southern Steam Packet Lines from this port to Liverpool, Antwerp, and other extensive marts of the old world, beyond the deep and troubled waters of the ocean. And, as a necessary consequence, capitalists will be attracted hither, manufactories will spring up, labour will be in demand, the limits of the towns will be rapidly extended, and a bright day of prosperity will be witnessed. The influence of Norfolk, in common with other cities, will then be felt and acknowledged, and she will act the part in the commercial, political, and literary world, that will reasonably be expected of the seaport city of Virginia, and be the great central mart of the eastern coast of the Union. The port of Norfolk and Portsmouth will then be a great centre of attraction,—the converging point of trade. All South-eastern Virginia will feel the brightening influence, and share largely in the general benefits to be dispensed. An impulse will be given, not only to commerce, but to the mechanic arts, and other attendants on a prospering community, which, in our happy country, especially, tend to dignify society, and give importance to the name of a people. Then will it no longer be said, to the shame of the good citizens of this old commonwealth, that "Virginia, with a vast domain, whose climate is the sunniest of the sunny; whose valleys the richest of the rich; whose every mountain-side embosoms a store of wealth which the wants and the industry of man can never exhaust; whose thousand streams furnish the water-power for a score of Birminghams and Lowells; which boasts the noblest seaport from the Passamaquoddy to the Rio Grande, and a roadstead that would shelter the shipping of the world; that Virginia, with all these matchless advantages,—with the elements of commercial greatness that might make her the rival of New England, and old England too, has no commerce that can be dignified with the name, and the little she has left is flitting from her grasp, like the vapoury mists of the morning before the chasing beams of the risen sun."

It is quite certain that an impression prevails, in some parts of the interior of Virginia and North Carolina, that the climate of Norfolk is unfavourable for the storage of tobacco, grain, &c. It is said that tobacco will undergo here "the sweating process," as is the case in New Orleans, and other low, damp situations; and that it is consequently hazardous to send it, whether manufactured or in the leaf, to this place. Without a knowledge of the origin of so strange an impression, we say, emphatically, that it is *without foundation.* The statement, by whomsoever made, must have been put forth either through mistake, or with malicious intent; for it is well known that the climate of this identical location is admirably adapted to the storage of this important article of commerce. The observation and experience of years prove, most conclusively, that any assertion to the contrary, is absolutely fallacious. Facts, which cannot be set aside, and living testimony, which cannot be questioned, confirm and establish the truthfulness of what we have stated.

There are merchants, now residing in this city and elsewhere, who have dealt largely in tobacco here, and their testimony is in direct opposition to the idea that this location is not, in every way, suitable to its preservation in a sound and merchantable state. A number of satisfactory statements could be given, but the following will surely suffice to satisfy every unprejudiced mind:

Josiah Wills, Esq., an extensive merchant, and highly-respected citizen of Norfolk, has a tobacco manufactory in Danville, from which manufactured tobacco is sent to Baltimore, Philadelphia, New York, &c., as well as to this city. He has, therefore, every facility of testing the adaptation of our climate to its storage, and of a comparison between this and other locations. He states that tobacco, either in the leaf or manufactured, is preserved in as sound a condition here as in any other city on the coast—that it remains when stored in our warehouses, especially when properly cured and manufactured, without sustaining the least injury.

To illustrate and prove by actual facts, the entire suitableness of our climate to the keeping of manufactured tobacco, Mr. W. says further, that when a portion of large lots put up at his manufactory in March, has been sent in April to Norfolk, and several cities further north, on a careful examination, in the fall, of what remained on hand in each place, the packages of the article stored in this city were found to be in a perfectly sound condition, *and fully equal, if not superior, in colour and flavour, to that sent elsewhere*, at the same time, and under like circumstances.

With regard to leaf tobacco, we are authorized, by the same gentleman, to mention, that a hogshead of the article remained, through some mistake or oversight, in the Tobacco Warehouse, on Town Point, for five years; and, on being opened and examined, the contents were found to have sustained not the least injury—being in a fine state of preservation.

There are, in our city, extensive warehouses, built upon land far enough above the level of the waters of our deep and extensive harbour at the highest tides. The Norfolk Tobacco Warehouse, having been built for the purpose, is well adapted to the preservation of the great staple. There will be suitable and competent inspectors appointed; and whenever it shall come, in quantities, however large, there will be found merchants here, able and ready to manage it to the very best advantage for the enterprising planters of the interior.

This climate is also very well suited to the storage of flour, wheat, corn, bacon, &c.

With regard to the means of access, it is, of course, greatly to the advantage of every city, that these should be convenient, agreeable, and cheap. All suitable efforts should be made to increase the number of visiters, as well as by a display of cheap and valuable wares, and merchandise of every description, to offer tempting inducements to purchasers. The northern cities are well aware of this, and their wise policy has long been to keep down the price of passage and fare, from every section of country likely to be tributary to the centre of attraction. Great are the general and special benefits of such a system; and in those cases in which individual capital and enterprise cannot suffice to present cheap and proper conveyances, companies and associations are formed, and the benefits to be derived from a constant ingress of strangers, of every business and from every direction, are secured. The cost of visiting Norfolk, from almost every point, is, comparatively high. There are many rich and populous regions of country, only a short distance from our city, from which our merchants receive a large portion of their trade—but means should be taken to increase a hundred fold the number of visiters. It would prove highly advantageous to all departments of business—to every interest of the city. It is well enough known, that almost every person who comes to town contributes, in some measure, to its advancement, by an exchange of money for its value. The hotels, the grocery stores, the dry-goods stores, the hardware, book, clothing, and jewelry stores, the fruit, confectionary, and toy stores, &c., are more or less patronised by strangers, who visit the place, whether on business or as a matter of mere pleasure or curiosity, to spend a few days, by way of a change, from the quiet and retirement of country life.

Trade and travel must shortly tend in this direction from the interior of the country. "The great heart of the interior begins now to palpitate and perform its functions in a natural way. It will soon begin to throw off its produce to the great ocean of trade by the shortest arteries of communication." But all suitable efforts should be made to attract visiters from the surrounding country, by water as well as by land, and especially from the shores of the neighbouring rivers and bays accessible by steamers of light draft and light charges; and the result would be pleasing and beneficial, to an extent probably not contemplated even by those who favour the plan.

CHAPTER XL.

Lieutenant Maury—Natural Advantages of Norfolk—Back Country—Supineness of the State—The South—Trade of the Amazon Valley—Line of Steamers from Norfolk, &c.—Para—Clipper Ships—The Wharves of Norfolk—Advantages of the Port—Trade of the West Indies and South America—A. W. Thompson's Scheme—Line of Steamers from Norfolk to Antwerp, &c.—Mr. Thompson's Propositions—Prospective Benefits—Advantages offered by Belgium—Opinions respecting the enterprise—Statements of Mr. Wheeler.

THE following remarks are from a pamphlet, attributed to the pen of Lieutenant Maury, U. S. N., of the National Observatory, at Washington, who has acquired "by his widely useful labours, a transatlantic fame not inferior to the enviable reputation which he enjoys at home."

"Norfolk is in a position to have commanded the business of the Atlantic Seaboard. It is midway the coast. It has a back country of great fertility and resources, and as to the approaches from the ocean, there is no harbour from the St. Johns to the Rio Grande, which has the same facility of ingress and egress, at all times and in all weathers. The waters flowing by it into the sea separate the producing from the consuming—the agricultural from the manufacturing States of the Atlantic slope; and they there unite the channels that lead from the famous regions in the country for corn, wheat, and tobacco to the marts of commerce.

"The natural advantages of the position will be obvious to any one who will compare the back country of Norfolk with that of New York. The country drained by the Hudson is all the back country which naturally belongs to New York. But the back country of Norfolk is all that which is drained by the Chesapeake Bay—embraced by a line drawn along the ridge between the Delaware and Chesapeake; thence northwardly, including all of Pennsylvania that is in the valley of the Susquehanna—all of Maryland this side of the mountains—the valleys of the Potomac, Rappahannock, York, and James Rivers—with the valley of the Roanoke and a great part of the State of North Carolina, whose only outlet to the sea is by way of Norfolk.

"Virginia saw those advantages and *slept upon them.* Nature had placed them there, and she did not dream that man could take them away. But the enterprise of New York has taken them away. The South now wants to regain her direct trade. We do not wish to discourage the effort, great as the odds against Norfolk now are, for we know that there are men in the South who have energy, enterprise, and capacity enough for anything that energy, enterprise and capacity can effect."

After showing how the South lost the direct trade, and the North secured it, and the immense and boundless productions of the Great Amazon valley, the sugar, coffee, tobacco, rice, indigo, cocoa, cotton, barks, spices, gums, and sheep; and some masterly remarks upon "the great king of rivers," the Gulf Stream, the Gulf of Mexico, the Mississippi River, the Carribean Sea, &c. Lieutenant Maury thus proceeds:

"The proposition therefore is, to establish a line of steamers from Norfolk, Charleston, or Savannah, to the mouth of the Amazon.

"Para is the city at its mouth. It has now a population of 15 or 20,000. There is a line of steamers already in operation from Rio to Para.

"From Savannah to Para, the distance is about 2500 miles; from Para, to Rio 2100. The 'Baltic,' would perform the passage from Rio to the United States, or from the United States to Rio, in thirteen days. The time occupied now in going and coming by sailing vessels is ninety days.

"The effect of such a communication would be to turn the whole current of correspondence and travel of the Atlantic Coast of South America, through Norfolk or the North American terminus of the line. No European nation could compete with us for it, for their distance from Para is doubly ours.

"Our present commerce with Brazil and Rio de la Plata is more valuable than our commerce with any of the countries of Europe, except Britain and France. Para, at this time, affords foreign commerce enough to give freight to a fleet of fifty sail. But this is nothing to what it will do when stimulated by civilization, agriculture, and commerce. Of more than twice the area of the Mississippi Valley, that of the Amazon is more bountiful. *There* the labour of one day in seven, is enough to crown the board of the husbandman with plenty. And yet the resources of the vegetable, mineral, and animal kingdoms there, and of man and civilization, still lie almost undeveloped. Commerce, with the ocean for its pathway, the winds for its wings, enterprise for its herald, and wealth, civilization, and Christianity for its attendants and followers, has not visited its shores. Were it but once to spread its wings over the valley of the Amazon, the shadow of it would be like the touch of the magician's wand; its immense resources would spring into life and activity.

"Therefore, let the South *look to the South* for trade and commerce; let her foster by all means in her power liberal commercial relations with a region which has such vast possessions, such countless treasures, such infinite resources to make valuable its future commerce."

Lieutenant M. remarks further, in a letter on this important subject:

"The clipper ships of America, as the new-modelled ships are called, I regard as one of the great advancements of the age. The impressions which they are calculated to make upon commerce, and, through commerce, upon the character of the people, the institutions of countries, and the fortunes of nations, are not less than those of railways and magnetic telegraphs. They are second only to those made by the mariner's compass.

"The average sailing rate of a vessel under canvass, one day with another, upon long voyages, has been considered at about one hundred miles the day. But what do we see in these ships? We see them outstripping steam, averaging, for twenty-four hours together, upwards of eighteen miles the hour, sailing more than eleven hundred miles in three consecutive days, and averaging daily, on the voyage hence to California—a voyage through seas the most boisterous, through regions of the most vexatious calms, and a voyage the most tedious—why, we see the clipper ships outstripping the wind, and day after day, for ninety or one hundred days, averaging their two hundred miles.

"The wharves of Charleston and Savannah are out of the reach of these ships. Those of Norfolk are not; and the considerations growing out of this circumstance are sufficient to turn the scale in favour of Norfolk.

"Measuring the distance by the only true standard time, and taking the mean of the average time under steam, and the mean of the average time under canvass, for the commercial distance to the Amazon, Norfolk, in consequence of her fine harbour and her ability to trade in clipper ships, will be found practically to be the nearest port in the United States to the mouth of the Amazon. By steam, Charleston has the advantage over Norfolk of about ninety miles only; and for the fetching and carrying of that commerce to which this steam enterprise is to give rise, the first rate clipper ships which Norfolk can send out, and which

Charleston and Savannah cannot, will greatly surpass and far outstrip the second and third rate class of ships to which the bars have doomed our more southern cities.

"Therefore, in my judgment, Norfolk is the place. A contract for carrying the Brazilian and South American mails would also assist to build up and sustain this line."

"At the present moment," says another writer, "when steam is revolutionizing the world,—when our own State has at length been awakened from her lethargy, and is entering upon a system of internal improvements with a spirit and energy which will command success and develope her inexhaustible sources of mineral and agricultural wealth,—we beg to call the attention of the citizens of Norfolk, and of all Virginia, to a branch of commerce which is peculiarly our own, and in which we may, with all confidence, defy competition. We allude to the West India and South American trade and mail routes, in which we would have no competition with previously-established lines; or, if they even did exist, we will clearly demonstrate how easily we could supersede them by our peculiar local advantages."

Much has been said and written about the scheme of Ambrose W. Thompson, Esq., an enterprising merchant of Philadelphia, to establish a line of steamers between Norfolk, Antwerp, &c., and of his able memorial to the General Assembly of Virginia. He proposes "to establish a line of first-class steamships, of not less than two thousand tons register each, between the ports of Norfolk, Virginia, and Antwerp, in Europe, touching, in going or returning, at such other ports in England and France as may be desirable;—the said ships to possess great speed and sea qualities, and to be built in such manner as to fit them for any marine or naval purpose.

"He will contribute two-fifths of the cost of construction and equipment of said steamers, and begin their construction immediately, so as to establish the said line at the earliest possible period, provided the State of Virginia shall advance its six per cent. bonds with coupons, having ten years to run, for the remaining three-fifths; the bonds thus advanced to be secured to the State by mortgage on the said ships, accompanied by the policies of insurance, and a contract that the said steamers shall always run from the waters of Virginia. The interest on the said bonds to be paid semi-annually into the Treasury of Virginia and the whole amount of bonds thus advanced to be paid by him at their maturity; but he is to have the privilege of paying them off at any time previous to maturity.

"The State of Virginia, through its Board of Improvement, to have the right at all times to examine into the accounts of disbursements made for the cost of said steamers, and to have the continued right of inspecting them during the term of the State's bonds, and requiring such repairs and improvements made in them as will fully secure the efficiency and value of said steamships."

The Richmond Republican says: "The memorial presents clearly and concisely one of the safest and most thoroughly practical modes of carrying out a great enterprise that we have yet seen; and we trust that no son of the Old Dominion will fail to sustain heartily this effort to give to us a *new dominion* upon the ocean. Let this line but go into early operation, and we shall see all the tributary waters of the Chesapeake covered with active steamboats, developing our internal resources and sustaining the Ocean line. Our main stems of railroads will be extended to the waters of the Mississippi, and through Virginia will pour the commerce of that great valley of the nation."

"The government of Belgium has given assurance that it will co-operate with Virginia, and lend every aid in its power towards the early establishment and permanent support of the line.

"The people of Belgium respond in an equally prompt and promising manner.

"The manufacturers and merchants are desirous to secure a direct import into their country of cotton, tobacco, and other southern produce, that they may in return find markets for the products of their industry and mechanical skill."

This subject is now—January, 1853—pending in the Legislature, having been already favourably considered by the Senate, which passed a bill in accordance with the propositions of Mr. Thompson. In view of the apparent probability that the enterprise would prove successful, we are inclined to express the hope that it may be tried; although it is the opinion of gentlemen of much intelligence and experience, that ten or fifteen years hence would be a more suitable period for the State to advance the sum required by the projector; and that, if undertaken now, the whole scheme, fair as it looks on paper, will result in a splendid failure.

The following are some of the reasons adduced in favour of the scheme, by Mr. Wheeler, of Portsmouth, in an able speech on this subject, delivered in the House of Delegates, in December, 1852:

"We could get the trade, not of Belgium alone, but that of one hundred and three millions of people also, with which Antwerp has immediate communication by railroad, &c.

"In 1838, the United States, with Belgium, had a trade amounting to eight millions of dollars. Supposing that it is successful, and that it will sustain itself, as no doubt it will, what would be the specific advantages? I think eight millions of dollars would be something. This we can monopolize, and Virginia, with all her towns and cities, will rejoice in their prosperity. Besides the advantage of a better market for our tobacco, flour, corn, and wool—of which Belgium consumes so much—we could have in return their manufactures, which are the best in Europe.

"All the cotton trade is at present indirectly freighted from New York to Liverpool; but by a direct commercial line of intercourse, Virginia would realize all the benefits of this, and monopolize the cotton trade; and Norfolk would be the shipping port for all the cotton trade of the United States.

"When the proposed line is established, it will turn the tide of trade from New York to Norfolk; and thence to Richmond, Petersburg, and the different towns and cities of this commonwealth.

"One of the first effects, and an important one too, which this line would produce, would be the lucrative benefits arising from consignment, by which numbers are making fortunes in New York, and these advantages could be had by the people of the cities and towns of Virginia."

CHAPTER XLI.

General Appearance of the City—Buildings—Streets, Gardens, Flowers, &c.—New Baptist Church—Pleasing View—Public Buildings, &c.—Relative Position—Academy—Christ Church—St. Paul's—Eastern Branch—Herbertsville—St. Patrick's Church—Presbyterian Church—Baptist Church—Methodist Episcopal Church—Marine Hospital—Mechanics' Hall—Southern Branch—Navy Yard—City Hall—Portsmouth—Naval Hospital—New Methodist Episcopal Church—Elizabeth River—War Steamers—Craney Island—African Churches—Almshouse—Cemeteries—Cotton Factory—Background—Wooded Lands—Norfolk in 1852—The Situation—Climate—Atmosphere—Norfolk Sunsets—Descriptions—Sunset Scene, by Charles H. Beale, Esq.—Appearance of the City and River from the Outer Harbour—Beautiful Scenery—Location—Productions of the Water, Forests, Fields, and Gardens—The Soil and its Capacity—Grain, Vegetables, Fruit, &c.—Grapes—Land—Sites for Farms.

THE City of Norfolk, viewed from some central eminence, presents to the eye of the beholder a picture, which, though not as exciting as that of some of her sister cities, is one of considerable interest and beauty; producing in the mind very pleasurable emotions. An appearance of neatness, cleanliness, and thriftiness is very perceptible. The streets are, many of them, straight, well paved, nearly level, of convenient width, and in good order. When spring has thrown her verdant mantle over the earth, the view is delightfully varied by blooming and flourishing shade and fruit trees. Flowers of every hue "lift up their delicate hands, and expand their sweet corollas," to delight the eye and throw off their fragrance upon the air.

"There is companionship
In summer flowers; they whisper to our
Hearts sweet lessons of their mission here—
Of love, and gentleness, and every softer grace.
And some, like friends well tried, have followed
Us through every path of life, in this dark
World of sin and grief, to cheer us with an
Old familiar look, or thought, when we were
Strangers in a strange land, or sad in
Some changed house."

The yellow jessamine, the crimson woodbine, the sweet-scented honeysuckle, and other vines of luxuriant growth, entwine the arbours, "mingle their long tendrils, and cling to the white walls of the houses, peeping into the windows and even under the edges of the doorways, as if they love the faces of those who dwell therein," while hundreds of carefully cultivated vegetable gardens contribute to the varied and enlivening scene; and a large number of tasteful and lofty family residences, neatly painted, airy, and commodious, are to be seen in every direction. Many public buildings, too, some of them of great architectural beauty, stand out to view, and lend much to the dignity and beauty of the scene.

We are standing at the base of the principal turret of the steeple of that splendid new temple of worship, the Freemason Street Baptist Church—

> "How reverend is the face of this tall pile!
> *   *   *   *   *
> It strikes an awe
> And terror on my aching sight."

But we look out with delight upon the scene above, beneath, around. We are gently fanned by the breeze that comes slowly in from over the briny waves of the deep blue sea. It is a bright morning in June; the "glorious King of Day" has not yet reached his meridian height, and his rays are not oppressive. The streets, lanes, houses, squares, gardens, trees, flowers, all are before us in pleasing variety. The thick, green foliage rustles to the passing zephyr; the loud, unrestrained voice of the light-hearted school-boy, and the lively, transporting laugh from that group of happy girls, rise above the hum of the passing crowd, and are heard distinctly by the listening ear—

> "How gay in youth the flattering future seems!"

Lightly and cheerily they pass on, full of hope and promise;—may their brightest anticipations be realized! But old Time will travel on, with steady and unfaltering tread; and, ere long, some of the gay and joyful here will say of the hope that now swells the heart with the gilded visions of the future:

"'Twas lovely as the splendid bow
That spans the vault of heaven!
'Twas idle as the pageant show
For infant pastime given.

"'Twas like the moon's ray on the stream,
Reflected bright and clear!
The infant's hand would grasp the beam,
But there is nothing there!"

Who can paint the shade and sunshine, or foresee the joy and sorrow, that they must experience, on their journey through this world of change and disappointment?

With compass in hand,* we now turn the eye from this central position, and look northeast by east, in which direction we have a fine view of the Academy building, and its proportionate dimensions, standing in the centre of its handsome square. East by south, and only a few rods distant, Christ Church shoots up its spire towards the sky. Southeast by east, stands old St. Paul's, amid the slumbering dead. In this direction is seen, too, the Eastern Branch of the Elizabeth, as it glides under the Draw-bridge, and winds along its devious course, greeting Herbertsville† on the south bank, and passing, on either hand beyond, a number of beautiful farms, with their neat farm-houses and cottages half concealed among the trees. In this direction, also, stands St. Patrick's Church, with its chaste front and significant

* See Norfolk Directory for relative position of public buildings, &c.

† Should a free bridge be allowed across the Eastern Branch, and especially if the Norfolk and Petersburg Road be built, the value of property at Herbertsville will be greatly enhanced. Its close proximity to the business part of the city, may induce persons, at no distant day, to establish manufactories, erect buildings, and reside on that side of the river. And as it is a beautiful and pleasant location, from which there is a fine view of Norfolk Bay, or the inner harbour, and of the Southern Branch of the Elizabeth, as well as of the city, it might be a good movement for the proprietors of the property, on this point of land, to lay it off in streets, squares, &c., for a town.

It must be admitted, however, that there is room enough yet, within the limits of the city, for works of enterprise; and unless we soon have more progressive men, a long time it will certainly be before the population of Norfolk will boil over, or "swarm out," like that of some other prosperous places in the world. At the present day, however, much is accomplished in a short time; and a very different state of affairs may be witnessed here, ere many of the present generation shall be resting beneath the green sod.

emblems; and here, too, are presented the towering cupola of the Presbyterian Church, and the neat front of the Cumberland Street Baptist Church. Southeast by south, the Cumberland Street Methodist Church presents its bold and massive proportions. Due south, and over the water, at Washington Point, stands the Marine Hospital,* a tidy and airy structure, half hid amid trees, and surrounded by evergreens and shrubbery. In this direction, we see, also, the Mechanics' Hall, with its showy front and architectural peculiarities, and other handsome buildings. South by west, the Southern Branch, with Portsmouth, Gosport, and the great naval establishment, on its west bank, winds its serpentine way amongst the dense green foliage, to mingle with the juniper-coloured waters of the Dismal Swamp Canal. This is also the direction of the City Hall, which the beholder sees with admiration,—its massive columns, lofty dome, solid walls, and fine proportions,—and awards the meed of praise to the "city fathers." On the southwest, we may look upon the "sister town," exhibiting no mean display of beautiful public buildings and private dwellings. West by south, across the water, and fronting Norfolk, we find that splendid national establishment, the Naval Hopital, an elegantly constructed pile of masonry,—a grand ornament to the harbour, worthy of the noble object for which it is intended, and is so well suited.† West-northwest, stands the Granby Street Methodist Church, its tasteful columns and towering dome overlooking two of the most beautiful streets in the city. Farther on, and in the same direction, Elizabeth River spreads out its deep, broad bosom, floating, in their majesty and pride, some of the most formidable war-steamers, many smaller vessels, and numbers of boats, with their

* The grounds connected with this establishment, and the principal building itself, were greatly improved and beautified by the direction, and under the supervision of Dr. E. O. Balfour, the attendant physician for ten or twelve years, prior to 1849. He merited and received the highest commendation for his kind and skilful attentions to the sick, the excellent order in which the establishment was kept, and the various improvements introduced. His political principles caused his removal, which recently took place, in favour of Dr. Schoolfield, of Portsmouth.

† This is also the direction of the Custom House, and Post Office building soon to be erected, and described on another page.

white sails inviting the breezes; and then on, five miles in the distance, lies Craney Island, the scene of a memorable victory in the last war with England.

In a northerly and northeasterly direction are a number of neat buildings, several African churches, Plume and Company's Rope and Oakum Works, the Gas Works, Cotton Factory, the Almshouse, Cedar Grove and Elmwood Cemeteries, steam saw-mill, farm-houses, cottages and lawns, with a thick growth of pine, oak, and maple in the background, all combining to increase the gratifying emotions, caused by a look at Norfolk as it is in 1852. And it will doubtless be readily admitted, that although the city is situated in a low, level tract of country, where there are no towering mountains to be seen in the distance, nor gently undulating lands and green hills, among which dance along upon the pebbly floor the crystal streams, sparkling in the sunbeams amid fragrant flowers that stoop to embrace the ripples or throw off their soft petals of every hue upon the glassy surface, redolent with the perfume prepared by Nature's own right hand—no startling exhibitions of nature in her wild state—no frowning precipices—no roaring torrents, monotonous murmuring waterfalls nor spangling fountains; yet the situation is pleasant and agreeable, and the inhabitants are certainly in the enjoyment of many blessings, including a delightful, invigorating, and healthful climate.

This location is seldom visited by violent storms of wind, rain, snow, or thunder; and yet it is almost open to the boundless ocean, to which our bold estuary conveys vessels of the largest class in two or three hours.

Perhaps it will not be judged unworthy of remark that the atmosphere of this region is generally very clear and transparent. The disagreeable semi-transparency of the air, often noticeable in some locations, is seldom observable here. We have only a fair share of cloudy and foggy weather. The heavenly bodies generally appear with a peculiarly brilliant and unobstructed lustre, and often give an attractive charm to the dawning or declining day. Sunrise, sunset, and even the solemn midnight hour, frequently present a cheering and delightful sight. Norfolk sunsets have indeed become celebrated, and travellers have left on record some glowing descriptions of their beauty. Said one (after having watched "the unwearied sun" at the closing moments of the departing day, and in concluding a graphic description thereof), "A more gorgeous scene could not be presented to a painter's mind."

The author of these sketches has witnessed many such scenes here, and will record one which was exceedingly striking and beautiful. The disappearance of the great central orb of our system was attended, on that occasion, with a view well calculated to awaken the happiest emotions in the minds of those who witnessed it, and who know how to appreciate the varied attractions of nature. Such a scene is thus fitly described by one of the poets.

> "It is a beauteous evening, calm and free.
> * * * *
> The broad sun
> Is sinking down in its tranquillity;
> The gentleness of heaven broods o'er the sea."

The "expansive forehead" of the great source of light and heat, sank quietly down behind the verdure of the western hills; and then a fleecy cloud that hung in its beauty a few degrees above the horizon, reflected the rays of the departing "King of Day," presenting to the eye of the beholder, the appearance of the brightest and most exquisitely polished gold, changing gradually as they "melted over the verge of the cloud," to a deeper, though less brilliant hue. There was a peculiar transparency in the colour of the adjacent clouds, pictured out upon the broad canvass and by the magic pencil of Nature, which no painter could attempt to imitate with any hope of success. The broad surface of our beautiful river "quivering under the pinions of the evening breeze," scarcely sufficient to waft the lightest bark over its clear waters, reflected, like a great mirror, the hues of the gilded vault above. That beautiful and massive structure, the Naval Hospital, standing in its pride on the opposite shore, gave increasing interest to the view; while that great leviathian of the waters, the Pennsylvania, and other United States vessels on the station, formed a deeply interesting feature in the splendid picture. And now,

"The sun has sunk into his western couch,
And all the rosy spirits of the eve
Are gathered round in bright companionship.
There is a speaking stillness in the calm,
That breathes of holy purity and peace.
Above, the clouds, all silent and serene,
Rest on the waveless azure of the sky
Like spirit isles of beauty, while the moon,
Full-orbed and smiling in her gentle light,
And all the thousand gems whose peaceful sheen
Spreads through infinitude a silvery ray,
Speak noiseless quietude. The bay, at rest,
Mirrors the freighted treasures which it bears;
While deeply pictured in the nether vault
The heavenly one appears.

* * * *

On the earth,
All things seem full of breathing Paradise;
Hope spreads her radiant pinions on the air,
Which floats around the realms of joyousness.
Thought wanders amid flowers of every hue,
Whose breath is full of fragrance. Beauty seems
To have arrayed herself in all her smiles,
To grace the glories of the gladdened eve;
And happiness invites the sons of toil
To share the treasures of her boundless feast."

We have had the good fortune to witness from the same position, still more striking and beautiful scenery attending the closing day, than even that which we have sketched—have "watched the clouds in the western sky, as they formed themselves into festoons of gorgeous drapery;" but this, attended as it was, by the quiet and stillness of the Sabbath eve, was sufficient to calm the troubled emotions in man's breast, and direct the mind in adoration to Nature's great Author.

Charles H. Beale, Esq., one of the editors of the "Norfolk Daily News," is decidedly good at description; and we present the reader with a sketch from his pen of another of our Sabbath sunsets:

"The heavens at sunset, presented one of the most beautiful and brilliant spectacles of sky-scenery that we have ever witnessed. It seemed as if Dan Phœbus had determined to give a parting display of his glories, despite the envious clouds that had veiled his brightness during the day, and to sink in triumph, though suppressed for a time in gloom.

"It was not one of those gorgeous sunsets that we so often see, when the sky is clear, and the whole expanse lighted up with deep and glowing colours of crimson, orange, and gold; but it was more subdued, yet, at the same time, varied, fantastical, picturesque. During the short space of fifteen minutes, the whole aspect of the heavens underwent four changes, all different, but equally lovely. The clouds, which had been dark and charged with rain during the day, towards night melted away into thin vapour-banks, and from the edge of the western horizon to the zenith, alternated with glimpses of the deep blue of the firmament beyond. As the sun slowly sank in the west, a deep carmine suffused the lower space around him, tinging with roseate hues the edges of the clouds which were arranged, row by row, far above; a few minutes more, and they assumed the appearance of drifting snow-wreaths; then a flood of golden light was poured over the whole heavens, which gradually changed to cream-colour, with large spots here and there, like cloud-islands, of deep lake, purple, and maroon. The clouds, too, as they slowly drifted along before the evening breeze, broke into the most fantastic forms, and assumed shapes which the delighted eye could imagine to be veritable air-castles, built, from base to pinnacle, of the most gorgeous but fleeting material.

"But 'all that's bright must fade.' The sun at length retired to greet other lands with his welcome beams, stars peeped out from between the misty veils which sought to hide their modest glances, and, in a few moments, sober, pensive twilight had given place to the dusky mantle of solemn Night, which enveloped things terrestrial in its sombre folds."

We are indebted to the same source for the following correct sketch of the appearance of our city and river from the "outer harbour:"

"We hastened to the upper deck, and, taking a seat on the leeward side of the boat, feasted our eyes on the beautiful panorama spread before them. And, indeed, the scene that presents itself at the entrance of our harbour is a beautiful one; and it is only because we are used to its beauty, that it is not so highly appreciated as it deserves. We had just passed old Fort Norfolk when we gained our post of observation, and, looking behind us, took in at a glance the whole scene. On the left was the city, with its successive rows of warehouses and wharves, the new City Hall just in front, one corner of it hidden by the new depôt for naval stores erected by J. Gordon, Esq.; the spires of the Episcopal and Baptist churches, pointing heavenward, with the cupolas and turrets of others distinguishable among the confused mass of buildings, which, in the distance, seemed to be heaped together without order or arrangement; the town of Portsmouth, occupying the other side, with the Navy Yard beyond, while Washington Point appeared to block up farther ingress, gave to the river the appearance of a small lake surrounded by a city and its suburbs."

The location of Norfolk is also such as to place in reach of almost all the citizens nearly every delicacy in the way of fish, flesh, or fowl, vegetables, fruit, or grain. The land in the vicinity is capable of producing from fifty to one hundred and fifty bushels to the acre, and varies considerably in colour. There are black, gray, chocolate, &c., the greater part of which is easy to drain and cultivate, being well adapted to the culture of corn, peas, oats, clover, potatoes, cabbages, tomatoes, melons, &c. Its adaptation to the growth of apples, pears, peaches, cherries, plums, and other fruits, has also been fairly and favourably tested. Grapes of the finest kinds are also produced, the clusters weighing from sixteen to twenty-four ounces, and measuring ten to twelve inches in length and twelve to sixteen inches in circumference.

There is much uncultivated and unimproved land, which may be had at from ten to twenty dollars per acre; and there are many picturesque and handsome sites for farms within a few miles from the city, both with and without a water front, on the river or one of its several beautiful branches.

CHAPTER XLII.

Healthfulness of Norfolk—The Climate—Erroneous Impressions—Sickness during the War—Malignant Fevers—The Army here in 1813—Causes of Sickness and Mortality—Exposure, change of Diet, Climate, &c.—Intemperance—The Cold Plague—Measles—Dysentery—Bilious—Inexperienced Physicians—Venesection—Injudicious and Fatal Treatment—Calomel—Opium—Water—Clothing—Attendance—Inexperienced Officers—The Citizens—Endearments of Home—Fever in 1821 and '26—"British Spy"—Erroneous Statements—Buffon's Strange Theory—Norfolk on a high Mountain—Sickness in 1852—Injurious Reports—Comparative Statements—Charleston—Average Mortality—Healthful Effects of the Climate—Comparative Table—Coloured Population—Statement of Diseases and Deaths—The Cholera—Longevity—Conclusive Proof.

WITH regard to the *healthfulness* of this location, it is a well-established fact, that Norfolk will compare very favourably, with other cities. The climate, though changeable, is pleasant and salubrious.

The spring and fall seasons are delightfully pleasant, the summers not often uncomfortably warm, and the winters, though formerly quite severe, have, for many years, been comparatively mild and pleasant, if we except that of 1851–2.

The writer is aware, that for a number of years an opinion has prevailed in some sections, that Norfolk is very unhealthy—an opinion well calculated to affect unfavourably the interests of the place. This erroneous impression was caused by the sickness and mortality among the troops at this place during the last war with England, and some cases of malignant fever in the summers of 1821 and '26. Let it be borne in mind that the unhealthfulness among the soldiers was caused by circumstances which would have had a similar effect in other healthful locations. There was quite a large army here, and it was reasonable to expect that among so considerable a number there would be many sick, and that some would die. This would have been the case had they all remained at home. But they were exposed, in summer and fall, to the dews and damp air at night, and to the heat of the sun during the day; and in winter, to the rains, snows, and frosts. Many of them were from the mountainous regions of the State. These were peculiarly subject to the effects of a transition to a damper and heavier atmosphere, at a location only a few feet above the level of the sea. The change in diet and water was also very detrimental to health; while there were thousands whose general mode of life had been such as to render the novel regulations of the camp, particularly injurious and destructive to the constitution. Let it be remembered, also, that quantities of intoxicating liquors, of bad quality, were used, which tended to injure and debilitate the physical system, and to prepare it, according to the opinion of eminent physicians, for the fatal attacks of disease. There was much dissipation among the soldiers.

It is also a well-remembered fact, that the disease which caused the greatest mortality among the troops here, was not at all peculiar to this location. It was the *cold plague*, an epidemic which commenced its ravages at the Canadas, and spread thence, as far south as Georgia. Its symptoms and effects were very similar to those of an epidemic which prevailed to an alarming extent in Northampton County, Va., in 1845, of which three hundred white persons alone, died in a short space of time. This singular and dreadful distemper attacked the throat and lungs; more frequently the latter. It was not understood by the physicians, and hundreds of the soldiers were soon prostrated by its violence, who, after a few days of suffering, were generally relieved by death. The measles and dysentery, which often attack soldiers in camp, also broke out among them; and there were cases of bilious fever too, resulting from the distressing exposure of the troops encamped in the suburbs. It is also a lamentable fact, that the treatment of the sick by the inexperienced young physicians who accompanied the troops hither, was, in a great number of cases, most injudicious, unreasonable, and unsuccessful; and we may add, exceedingly destructive to life. The favourite remedy with those young surgeons or medical gentlemen, those novices in the healing art, was *venesection*, for almost all diseases; and a sad time it was, indeed, for the suffering soldier, when the doctor approached with his lancet—not to his bedside, for beds numbers of them had not. The custom was to bleed often, and bleed copiously. Besides, although the hapless patients were required to swallow large and frequent doses of calomel, opium, &c., while,

> "The summer evening's balmy air,
> Felt hotter than they well could bear;
> And tearless was the fiery eye,
> And the hot throat was parched so dry,
> That every *drop* they *dared* to sip,
> Seemed lost before it passed the lip,"

they were nevertheless allowed, according to the cruel custom of that period, but a scanty supply of the cooling beverage of nature. Even water, which the sinking system so much required to restore its functions, was denied them!

Many unfortunate and distressing circumstances combined to ruin the health, undermine the constitution, and destroy the lives of the troops that were stationed here. The clothing of many of them was utterly unsuited to the climate. Their food was mostly coarse and common; when sick, they were poorly attended, and instead of being carefully nursed, were, in many cases, sadly neglected. There were no suitable and properly-furnished hospitals, where the invalids could receive such treatment as was necessary to the restoration of health.

These unfortunate circumstances, so unfavourable to the health of the militia-men especially, could not easily be prevented. There were large numbers here; the officers were inexperienced; many of the citizens had left the town, and those that remained were unprepared and unable to afford assistance, except to a limited extent. Those who could render aid and comfort, offered it freely; they threw open their houses, and did what they could to help the sick. But there were numbers who could receive no such assistance from the private residents. Added to all this, they were far away from the endearing associations of home, and deprived of the peculiarly tender care, watchfulness, and sympathies, to be received there only. To some of these causes, and perhaps, in many cases, to all of them combined, the illness and fatality were justly attributable on the occasion alluded to.

With regard to the cases of malignant fever, which occurred in 1821 and '26, it is a well-known fact, that they were confined, almost exclusively, to a small portion of the town, which has since been greatly improved. Indeed, it was the opinion of able physicians, that the disease did not originate here.

It seems that the remarks of the accomplished author of "The Letters of the British Spy," about the "annual visits of the yellow fever" to Norfolk, how appropriate soever his observations may have been on some other subjects, were erroneous and unjust; and more especially since they appeared in the fifth edition of the work, which was published in 1813, "with the last corrections of the author." The last "visit of the yellow fever," as an epidemic, to Norfolk, in the eighteenth century, was in '95; and the first in the nineteenth was in '21; so thinks one of the oldest and most eminent physicians of this city. The remarks of the author of the "Spy," on this subject, contain about as much truth, though not as much poetry perhaps, as Buffon's strange theory, of which he speaks in the same connexion, including the recession of the waters from Hampton Roads and the Chesapeake; their beds becoming fertile valleys; and the conversion of the "sickly site of Norfolk" "into a high and salubrious mountain!" The able writer alluded to, may not have intended thus to inflict an undeserved injury upon Norfolk, the most important and flourishing commercial town in his State, at the period at which he wrote; but his book was extensively circulated, and extensively read; it outlived its distinguished author —it still exists—is still read and admired, while he lies quietly in the stillness of the grave; and its influence upon the minds of its readers, and thus indirectly upon the welfare of our town, may have been, and still may be, deleterious to no inconsiderable degree.

Several fatal cases of sickness, resembling yellow fever, occurred in the fall of 1852. The summer had been exceedingly wet—more rain fell here in July and August, as before mentioned, than had fallen for the two whole years preceding. Considerable sickness was therefore expected in this section. Nevertheless, with the few exceptions named, the general health of the city was nearly as good as usual. But the cases of fever in the lower part of the town, which assumed a malignant character, were attributable to the arrival of vessels from infected ports. Cases of the same kind, and owing to the same cause, have occurred in Philadelphia, Boston, and other cities farther north. The quarantine laws will probably be enforced hereafter. Some of our physicians, if not all, advise this course. It was not ascertained, in regard to the cases here at this period, that there was any existing local cause. There were about fifteen deaths during the months of September and October, said to have been caused by the disease called yellow fever. Surely no person with common sense, can say that this was any other than very small comparative mortality, in a population of about sixteen thousand; and yet, false, silly, and most injurious statements were made relative to the existence of sickness here. It was most industriously spread abroad, that the yellow fever was "raging in Norfolk." "It is dangerous to go there," said the reporters, "for the inhabitants are dying off like sheep with the rot!" or words to that effect. Meanwhile the cheerful countenances, the ruddy cheeks, and healthy active forms, and bright eyes of the thousands of citizens that thronged the streets, gave pleasing evidence of the general healthiness of the place, and that the business of the doctors had not increased to the alarming extent represented. Let us pursue this subject a little further. The writer has been informed, by a medical gentleman, who had the opportunity of making a correct calculation, that there were about a dozen deaths. From another reliable source, we learn that there were seven fatal cases in September and eight in October. The disease first made its appearance in a family living in the vicinity of a wharf, on Town Point, at which there was a vessel from a port where the disease existed; and the greater portion of the cases occurred in the same part of the town, or its vicinity, while those who were attacked elsewhere, had been in what was called the "infected district." Now, in this portion of the city there was no sunken lot, no bog, no filthy dock, nor decayed vegetable matter, calculated to engender disease. Whatever may have been its condition twenty-five or thirty years ago, Town Point is now (1853), for the most part paved, built up, and kept cleanly, and free from odious exhalations or malaria; while as much cannot be said of other portions of the city, which were entirely free from the presence of the disease. Thus it appears, that if the quarantine laws had been enforced in the fall of 1852, we should, in all probability, have heard nothing of another "visit" of the yellow fever, which, while we are compelled to admit its existence, spread so slowly, and to so limited an extent, that we may safely say, the climate of Norfolk is utterly unsuited to the dissemination of the disease. But compare the mortality in this city with that in Charleston, at the same period, where nearly fifty died weekly. We mention this fact with sincere regret, and entertaining the hope that the proverbially beautiful and hospitable seaport city of the noble State of South Carolina, may never again be visited with the fatal disease to which we have alluded. Although the population of that city, is perhaps, three times as great as that of our city, still, the comparison is evidently a favourable one, so far as our climate is concerned. Norfolk never was as sickly as it has been represented to be; but whatever causes may have tended to induce the idea of its great insalubrity, in former days, it is well known and acknowledged, that for more than a quarter of a century past, the official statements of the average mortality here, confirm the truth of our remarks, with regard to its healthsomeness, beyond all successful contradiction. The inhabitants, generally, and more especially, those who take exercise in the open air, look well, and enjoy good health; and a change of residence from other places to Norfolk, is well known to have resulted, in many instances, in improved health. Old constitutional diseases and chronic afflictions have frequently disappeared after a short residence here. Indeed, the salubrity of the district, for miles around, is said to have greatly improved within the lapse of twenty years.

In regard to the health of the city, a few other facts will now be presented bearing upon the subject. Let them speak for themselves; and even the prejudiced, if any there are, must admit the truth of the position taken. The following table, showing the average annual mortality, is derived from authentic sources:

	PER CENT.
Norfolk,	1¾
Philadelphia,	2½
New York,	2¾
Baltimore,	2½
Boston,	2¼
New Haven,	2½

Here is, certainly, a favourable comparison, and an enviable evidence of the healthiness of the place. Our bills of mortality also compare favourably with those of the cities of Europe, as well as of our own country; which fact, when it is recollected that we have a large coloured population, must be a satisfactory proof, not only of the excellent health of the place, but also of the good condition of that portion of the inhabitants.

The number of deaths in Norfolk, from June 1, 1849, to June 1, 1850, was 364:

Males,	174	Whites,	186
Females,	190	Coloured,	178
	364		364

Deaths in June,	85
" " July,	79
" " August,	45
" " September,	31
" " October,	16
" " November,	11
" " December,	18
" " January, 1850,	16
" " February,	14
" " March,	22
" " April,	11
" " May,	16
	364

The above statement exhibits a number far above the average mortality for a year; for, it will be observed, that those months are included (June, July, and August) during which the cholera prevailed in the city, and of which a large proportion of those who died in those months were victims.

Three of the above number died of the effects of burns; six were drowned; two died of the effects of drinking cold water when over-heated; seven of intemperance; of apoplexy, eight; casualty, five; and of old age or natural decay, five.

There were four above 90 years of age, seven above 80, seventeen above 70, twenty-seven above 60, twenty-three above 50, forty-three above 40, and fifty-nine above 30; under two years,

88. Non-residents, who died in the city during the year, are also included in the number.

Many of the inhabitants, as is shown by the above statement, live to a very old age. There were, a few years since, in one family alone, on Bermuda Street, five individuals—three white ladies and two coloured servants, one male and one female—whose united ages amounted to 403 years, averaging 80 years and 7 months each! They were all raised in or near Norfolk, and had lived together on the same premises for more than fifty years. The oldest was the coloured man, aged 95. In December, 1840, there were residing in the town eight persons of the highest respectability, whose aggregate ages made 669 years—averaging 83 years 7½ months! There are many persons here who have passed the age of three score and ten, and a number of octogenarians, both in the parlour and the kitchen. There was a lady of respectability, who died in 1852, aged 96, who had enjoyed almost uninterrupted good health, and whose intellectual faculties were in a sound state a short time before she died, and who did not require the attendance of a physician for more than sixty years.

We add here, merely as a somewhat singular fact, that there is in this city a woman of colour, aged 88, who, in 1850, had *never* required the attendance of a physician, having never been seriously sick. She had lost only one tooth, which was occasioned by a cold many years ago; and her eyesight was as good as ever, being able to sew on fine work, and to thread a cambric needle! The duties of her vocation were laborious and constant, requiring much walking; but being very active, faithful, and industrious, her labours were cheerfully performed.

Very many other cases could be added, of extraordinary age and protracted good health, and strength of mind and body, among both sexes, white and coloured, including even some centenarians.* But, perhaps, enough has been said on the subject; and the facts adduced afford, it is believed, sufficiently decisive proof of the salubrity of the location; and these remarks, of course, apply with equal force to Portsmouth and the adjacent country.

* John Guffee, a slave, died here in 1836, aged 120, and Billy Ingram in 1852, aged 117!

CHAPTER XLIII.

Buildings—Sites for Farms—Excursions to Old Point, &c.—The Ladies—Their Beauty, &c.—Attachment of the Citizens to the Place—Hospitality—Intelligence—Morals—Sabbath Schools Mechanics—Churches—Order—Sunday Markets—The Sabbath—Its Violation—Should be kept Holy—The Appointment Necessary to Man—Its Enemies—Its Services.

An intelligent writer of another State, has alluded, in appropriate terms, to the many beautiful public and private buildings in the city, to the handsome and picturesque sites for farms and villas just without its limits, and on the banks of the river and its circuitous branches; and to the frequent opportunities for delightful excursions to Old Point, the Capes, &c. He also pays a suitable tribute to the most attractive of all earthly objects. "I am pleased," he remarks, "with the social character of the place, and the *ladies in particular*. They are whole-souled Virginians. As regards beauty, intelligence, and other necessary accomplishments, they are second to none." Herein consists, doubtless, the principal and most interesting of all the attractions here, as well as elsewhere,—the "beauty, intelligence, and accomplishments" of those on whom the happiness of man and the welfare of communities so greatly depend,—whose encouraging smiles, and winning charms, whether in the relation of mother, wife, sister, daughter, or friend, are always among the chief delights of life and constitute the imperishable and indestructible cement of the sacred family compact, and of society at large. What a Northern letter-writer says in relation to the women of the South, applies very well to the ladies of this section. He states that he was "particularly struck with their beauty of form,—their symmetrical and harmonious figures. In this, they excel Northern women. Many of them dress with exquisite taste, very richly, but seldom gaudily or with any display of tinsel. The proverbial affability and urbanity of the Southern character, finds its fullest development in the women. The Southern lady is naturally easy, unembarrassed, and polite. You may go into the country where you please, from town, village, and post-office, —you may call at the poorest house you can find, provided you don't get among 'croakers,' and, whether you accost maid or matron, you will always be answered with politeness, and treated with spontaneous courtesy."

"The citizens of Norfolk," says an observant writer, "have ever shown great attachment to the place, and rarely departed from it to reside elsewhere without reluctance, and, in many cases, with the disposition to return. A comparison of the names and families for fifty years past, shows this fact very plainly. We may go almost a century back, and the truth of the remark is still more apparent."

Like the other towns of the Old Dominion, Norfolk has long been proverbial for the obliging and hospitable disposition of its inhabitants. There is here, and has long been observable, to some extent, a dignified tone of character, combined, in many instances, with literary attainments, and commercial, political, and general intelligence.

"No city in the United States," said one who possessed every opportunity of judging correctly on the subject, "has better morals than Norfolk. There are nine churches opened every Sabbath for divine worship, and the citizens very generally observe the day religiously. Opportunity is also offered for religious instruction in the Sunday Schools, which are well attended, and superintended by excellent officers and teachers, and well supplied with extensive libraries."

The same writer also observes:

"There is no town in the United States that can boast of a more orderly, moral, and industrious class of mechanics, and none who are better clad and housed, and in the enjoyment of more of the comforts of life than, our Norfolk mechanics."

There are now fourteen instead of nine churches open on the Sabbath, and the erection of others is in contemplation. It is, indeed, a pleasant sight to witness, on the holy day of rest, the multitudes repairing to the different sanctuaries of God, to hear the "glad tidings of salvation."

The inhabitants are an order-loving people. If the place has ever been disgraced by a mob or riot, the fact has not come to our knowledge.

The custom of holding Sunday markets in the city during the summer months, to which it may not be inappropriate to allude here, is, however, certainly a violation of the Divine injunction respecting the sacred and merciful institution of the Sabbath; and the practice is very reasonably objected to by many reflecting citizens. The alteration of an excellent ordinance, passed in 1849 (which prohibited traffic on that day), so as to allow the desecration of the Sabbath by the holding of the public market, has given very considerable dissatisfaction. It is insisted that there is no absolute necessity in the case, and that the custom is an infringement of the Divine command. Every person, rich or poor, who has a suitable regard for the day, and desires to keep it holy, could, with a little management, make all necessary provision on Saturday for the following day, especially if Saturday evening markets were held, as in Baltimore and some other cities, and which was formerly the custom here. Sunday marketing necessarily leads to bad consequences, and causes much unnecessary labour in fishing, killing and preparing beef, poultry, &c., gathering fruit and vegetables, and the additional fatigue of horses used in conveying articles to market. The violation of the fourth commandment by societies and communities, as well as by individuals, has always been followed, soon or late, by visible evidences of the displeasure of a just and merciful God; and this particular aspect of the subject merits the attention and careful consideration of those in whose hands are, to a great extent, entrusted the welfare and destiny of the city.

"Were this to be the last stroke of our pen," said an able divine, "and we had reached the last moment of our life, we should employ both the one and the other in enforcing on our readers the divine injunction, 'Remember the Sabbath-day, to keep it holy.' For, if the threatenings of God are to be believed, if all history is not a lie, if it be notorious that genteel Sabbath-breakers are totally destitute of Christian experience, and if the confessions which the profligate have made in our jails and on our gibbets cannot be invalidated, then the face of the Lord is set against those that turn the Sabbath into a day of pastime or of gainful toil. And, on the other hand, if the promises of God are true, if the concurrent voice of sacred and profane history is to be received; if the testimony of righteous kings, just judges, godly bishops, and the holiest men in all lands, is entitled to credit; and if the joyous experience, the domestic happiness, the sanctified prosperity, and the peaceful and triumphant deaths, of myriads of God's people, are to be regarded as evidences of his favour, then it is demonstrated that God loves, honours, and saves, all those who 'Remember the Sabbath-day, to keep it holy.'"

John Richard Farre, M.D., of London, a physician of great eminence, made the following remarks, with others of equal force, before a committee of the House of Commons, on the observance of the Sabbath:—"Researches in Physiology, by the analogy of the working of Providence in nature, will show that the Divine commandment is not to be considered as an arbitrary enactment, but as an appointment necessary to man. This is the position in which I would place it, as contradistinguished from precept and legislation. I would point out the Sabbatical rest as necessary to man, and that the great enemies of the Sabbath, and, consequently, the enemies of man, are all laborious exercises of the mind or body, and dissipation, which force the circulation on that day on which it should repose; while relaxation from the ordinary cares of life, the enjoyment of repose in the bosom of one's family, with the religious studies and duties which the day enjoins,—not one of which, if rightly exercised, tends to abridge life,—constitute the beneficial and appropriate service of the day." Let it be remembered, then, that a suitable regard for the Sabbath is among the most important requisites in any community, inasmuch as it tends to strengthen the foundation, uphold the pillars, and render more symmetrical and attractive the splendid social fabric of enlightened Christian society.

CHAPTER XLIV.

Commercial Facilities—The Navigation—The U. S. Ship Pennsylvania—The Harbour—Streets, &c.—Wharves—Public Buildings—Churches, Banks, Schools, Papers, &c.—Companies and Societies—Packet Lines—Marine Railways—Manufactories—Wealth, Usefulness, and Influence—Merchants, Warehouses, Capital—Commercial Experience and Ability—Improvement—Railroads, Steamships, &c.—Commercial Advancement.

THE facilities for commercial operations in Norfolk, as before stated, are very great. The warehouses are large, commodious, and well adapted to the storage of produce. The water front is spacious, well sheltered from the northern and eastern winds in winter, and open to the southerly and southwesterly breezes in summer. "The navigation is not obstructed by ice for a single day once in half a century. The great ship Pennsylvania, the largest vessel in the world, is now riding at her moorings, within a stone's throw of the shore, and, if equipped for service abroad, could be at sea in a few hours without the aid of steam. The eastern and southern branches of the Elizabeth River, in uniting, form the harbour of Norfolk—a basin some four miles in circumference, with a width of seven-eighths of a mile. The City of Norfolk occupies the northern and eastern shore, with a water front more than two miles in extent; while Portsmouth, Gosport, and the Navy Yard, range along the southern and western banks.

"The outlet is sufficiently capacious, and yet the harbour, in sailors' phrase, is so 'land-locked' as to afford entire security to vessels of every class, from the small oyster boat to the ship of the line. The bottom is composed of stiff mud to hold the anchor, and is free from sand bars, rocks, and all other obstructions. A fine anchorage extends from the basin down to the roads, distant seven miles; indeed, the harbour of Norfolk may be said to terminate only at the point where Hampton Roads is merged into the Chesapeake, being composed of an inner and outer haven, where the fleets of the world could lie in perfect security in all kinds of wind and weather, ready to embark on their ocean voyage, whenever the mariner chooses to lift his anchor and spread his sails to the breeze."

There are in the city about one hundred and thirty-five streets and lanes, very many of which are well paved. There are also about a dozen squares, courts, &c. The wharves extend from Town Point on the west to the Drawbridge on the East,—nearly one mile,—are forty in number, and mostly in good order.

There are about 60 public buildings, including 14 Churches,* Mechanics' Hall, Ashland Hall, the City Hall, Norfolk Academy, &c.

The number of Banks is 7; Hotels, 5; Seminaries and High Schools, 9; Daily Papers, 5, with which are connected Tri-weekly do., 3, Weekly do., 3; News and Reading Rooms, 2.

There are 5 Fire Companies, 2 Volunteer Companies, a Canal Company, Drawbridge Company, Insurance Company, Gas Company, Telegraph Company, and Hotel Company; a Mechanical Benevolent Society, Seamen's Friend Society, Provident Society, Humane Society, Female Orphan Society, Philharmonic Society, Concordia Society, and several Debating Societies. The secret societies are: The Masons, Odd-Fellows, Sons of Temperance, Rechabites, United Mechanics, Druids, and Red Men.

There are regular steam-packet lines from Norfolk to New York, Philadelphia, Baltimore, Washington, Richmond, Hampton, Old Point, Eastern Shore, Matthews, &c.; stage line to Edenton, Elizabeth City (N. C.), &c. There are three Marine Railways and Ship Building establishments,† extensive Iron

* 2 Protestant Episcopal; 3 Methodist Episcopal, including 1 coloured; 1 Presbyterian; 5 Baptist, including 3 coloured; 1 Catholic; 1 Methodist Protestant; 1 Mariners' Bethel.

† It is especially worthy of note, that the dock-yards of Mr. Nash, Mr. Ferebee, and the Messrs. Graves, of Norfolk, with their well-constructed marine railways, afford great facilities for building and repairing vessels of every class. And some of our merchants have had in contemplation the construction of a dry-dock, of ample dimensions.

Messrs. Page and Allen, of Portsmouth, are very extensively engaged in ship-building, and have acquired celebrity in this important line of mechanical

Works, Carriage, Furniture, and Cotton Manufactories; Cordage and Oakum Works, &c., &c., at which work can be done as well and as cheaply as at the establishments of the northern cities. The capital invested in Manufactures is about $570,000, and the probable annual product $1,140,000. Real Estate about $5,000,000.

There are here, as well as elsewhere, instances in which industry, fidelity, and persevering effort, amid discouragements, with small pecuniary means in the beginning, have been amply rewarded with wealth, usefulness, and influence. The population of Norfolk includes individuals whose business capacity and commercial information will, it is believed, compare favourably with those of other cities. A gentleman of intelligence and observation, in alluding to the various facilities for trade,—our deep river, extensive wharves, spacious and well-built warehouses (more than enough to store the produce of the Roanoke Valley), the large capitalists, rich landholders, &c.,—calls attention to the fact, that by far the greater part of a million of money was, within a few weeks, subscribed by the citizens, to form part of the capital of an independent bank, before the charter was granted. He alludes also to our able professional men, as well as to merchants of skill and experience, who have been devoted to commercial pursuits from their boyhood,—regularly trained in the school and counting-room for extensive mercantile operations. And yet "the wonder grows," that Norfolk should even now begin to advance in wealth and importance. Truly, the greater wonder should be, that she has not long ago given evidences of a more mature growth; that her progress in the onward march of improvement has not been much more rapid. The truth is, there has, for a long time, been too much talk and too little action. But, thanks to the energy and enterprise of some of the knowing and influential gentlemen of this and other communities, we hear now of additional railroads and canals, large packet ships and ocean steamers; and they are

pursuit. A splendid clipper-built ship of 1,500 tons, the largest vessel ever constructed south of New York, will be launched from their yard, and, probably, careering on her rapid course upon the ocean waves, before the close of the spring of 1853.

spoken of in good earnest and with commendable zeal. Some of these enterprises, of great prospective benefit to Norfolk, Portsmouth, and vicinity, have already been commenced; and, now that the public mind has been turned to the subject—now that strong men are beginning to shake off the shackles of lethargy, and are determined to take hold of and urge forward to completion, these means of wealth and advancement, no opposition, from any source whatever, will be sufficient, it is believed, to prevent success. And it is hoped the bright day is not very distant, when commerce and her attendants will flourish here according to the original design of nature. But, there are some who object to all schemes of advancement, who grumble at every praiseworthy attempt to redeem the place from the charge of slow movement and supineness, to which it has been amenable.

CHAPTER XLV.

Talent and Literary Taste—Light Reading—Cheap Literature—Its Injurious Tendency—Evidences of Literary Capacity—Literary Works—Mr. Maxwell's Poems—Letters by a South Carolinian—H. B. Grigsby, Esq.—Dr. Alexander Whitehead, an Accomplished Teacher and Scholar—Beautiful Inscription —C. A. Rodney—Thomas Blanchard—His Ode on the Death of Washington —"Rosehill," by a Virginian—Poems by Quilp—"I Hear thy Voice"—"A Child's Burial."

It is quite reasonable to suppose, that in a city as limited in size even, as Norfolk, there should be manifested no small degree of talent; and that in a place where the culture of the intellect is generally quite well attended to, and the advantages of a liberal education are much appreciated, there should be a considerable share of literary taste; although it may be remarked here, with regard to the education of youth of both sexes, that there is not sufficient effort put forth, either by them or their parents, in many cases to bring out, cultivate, and mature, a taste for solid and useful literary pursuits and acquisitions.

There is, also, among the young, as well as those of mature age, a vast deal too much of light, chaffy reading here, as well as elsewhere, at the present day.* Numbers of either sex are leaving the schools, and passing out upon the stage of active life, with fair promise, and often with striking evidences of mental capacity, which, if properly cultivated and encouraged, might reflect honour on the place and prove a blessing to the country. Sketches, essays, dissertations, &c., in prose and poetry, of solid merit, would be frequently written, put in the form of books, and sent out to aid in enlightening and evangelizing the world. But instead of this, the youthful mind, just ready to bloom forth into strength and beauty, is, alas, too frequently diverted from the pursuit of useful knowledge and real wisdom, by the injurious and debilitating, aye, and demoralizing cheap literature of the day, from the presses of the Northern and Eastern cities of our own country, as well as from those of England and elsewhere—reprinted, "got up" in the cheapest and most saleable style, and published (the trashy stuff is) to the world, to satiate the morbid appetite of thousands—

"Oft crammed full
Of poisonous error, blackening every page;
And oftener still of trifling, second-hand
Remark, and old, diseased, putrid thought;
And miserable incident, at war
With nature, with itself, and truth at war;
Yet charming still the greedy reader on,
'Till done, he tried to recollect his thoughts,
And nothing found but dreaming emptiness."

There are many individuals in this City and vicinity who can write well, and who do occasionally give abundant evidence of their capacity in this respect. Suitable incentives and practice only, are required to mature the taste and judgment of many who hesitate to give publicity to their productions. The papers of our City, and the literary periodicals of other cities, occa-

* "It produces a feverish imagination, prevents the improvement of the mind, unfits it for the pursuits of business, induces a dislike to religious subjects, benumbs the conscience, and prompts to deeds of licentiousness."—*Dunn.*

sionally contain very pleasing testimony of the truth of what we have stated.

But literary works, both in prose and poetry, whose authors are, or were formerly citizens of Norfolk, have passed through the press. It is not our purpose to notice all of them, but it may be considered as coming within our plan to allude briefly to several.

"The Poems of Mr. Maxwell,"* said an intelligent and observant writer, in 1827, "have attained higher celebrity abroad than at home, and in New England than 'in his own, his native land.' He is eminently successful in imitating the nervous energy and innocent simplicity of Goldsmith; but though he were in all respects nearly his equal, he could not complain of neglect, when the modest worth of the son of Erin is disregarded by the vitiated taste of the day, and his sympathetic tenderness eclipsed by the mock-heroic 'Border Tales' of Scott, and the splendid phrensies of Lord Byron. His 'Walcott' and 'Columbian Bards' are excellent of their kind; and I cannot refrain mentioning, for the honour of Virginia, that his Poems were highly approved by one, whose approbation Byron, in his proudest glory, would have been delighted to possess, by Roscoe, himself a fine poet, and the author of the Life of Leo X., and Lorenzo de'Medici."

"Letters by a South Carolinian." Norfolk, published by C. Bonsal: Shields and Ashburn, printers, 1827.

These Letters are well known to have emanated from the pen of Hugh B. Grigsby, Esq., of Norfolk.† They were written when he was quite a young man, and contain most excellent descriptions of several distinguished citizens of Norfolk, &c. They gave unmistakable evidence of the talents which the author is so generally known to possess.

Mr. G.'s able conduct of the "American Beacon" has already been alluded to. His style is bold, lively, and clear—remarkable for correctness and perspicuity. It is regretted that he should have so early vacated the editorial chair. We find it conve-

* See pages 203 and 204.

† Mr. G. is the son of the late Rev. Benjamin Grigsby, a distinguished and devout Presbyterian minister of this city. He was an able preacher, a devoted pastor, and an accomplished gentleman.

nient to make some extracts from his very interesting work. These will answer very well to convey to the reader's mind an idea of his nice, discriminating judgment, as well as the high order of his descriptive powers.

"Of Dr. Alexander Whitehead," remarks the able writer, to whom we have just briefly alluded, "who has passed from the memory of most of the existing generation, one who sat at his feet, and who appreciated his great learning, may fitly say something. He was a Scotchman by birth, and emigrated in early manhood to Norfolk, where he taught the Latin and Greek languages with great success. He was no common scholar; for he not only taught elementary and critical parts of the learned tongues with the strictest fidelity, but expatiated on the felicitous diction, the noble sentiments, and chaste imagining of the higher Latin and Greek classics, with a skill and eloquence that James Moon and Andrew Dalzel would have heard with admiration. The writer of this article has seen him in his old age relish the sly jests of Lucian, and smile at the playful conceits of Anacreon, and he has seen him weep, as, mindful of the loss of a lovely daughter, he read in the first book of Iliad the touching story of Brisses.

"He wrote Latin with great facility and with uncommon elegance. The beautiful inscription on a silver vase, presented by the citizens of Norfolk, thirty years ago, to Cæsar A. Rodney, of Delaware, for his magnanimous defence of the late Commodore Barron, was from his classic pen. Such a scholar the fashion of modern education has not produced, and may never produce. He reached the age of seventy, and, although his latter years were embittered by the loss of a lovely daughter, and by a torturing disease, which gave him but a small respite from actual agony, he bore his burdens gracefully, and died the death of a Christian. Even in such adverse circumstances the love of literature never forsook him; and when a friend would visit him in his confinement, and be almost overcome with the sight of his sufferings, a casual remark would sometimes lead him into a discussion of some topic on morals or literature, in which his fine genius would display itself in all its original brightness, and his knowledge of the classics appear in all the freshness and buoyancy of his earlier years. When he left Norfolk to attend the University of Edinburgh, he was accompanied by his pupil, the late Doctor Hodges, and, perhaps, by Dr. Wm. B. Selden; or, at all events, the late Dr. S. and he, were at the University at the same time, and were, for many years, associates in the practice of physic."

Thomas Blanchard, Esq., formerly a citizen of Norfolk, was "a ripe scholar, a fine classic writer, and a gifted poet." His Ode on the Death of Washington, written January 1st, 1800, shortly after that lamented event, and published in the Herald, "created quite a sensation at the time; and such was its popularity, that the editors found it necessary to publish a second edition of it to answer the public demand—which is saying a great deal more for the literary taste and patriotic feeling of that day than could be claimed for the present, in our community."

We take pleasure in presenting a portion of it to the reader, who will appreciate its merits, and award a suitable meed of praise for so creditable and able an effort, on a subject at once solemn, impressive, and deeply interesting.

TO THE MEMORY OF GEORGE WASHINGTON.

GENERAL OF THE ARMIES, AND FIRST PRESIDENT OF THE UNITED STATES OF AMERICA.

"Procul, O procul! este profani."

Let no obtrusive, no unhallowed eye,
On which the rays of virtue dimly beam,
Let no cold mind, fashioned by common themes,
No breast, that glows with a patriot zeal,
Presume to violate the peaceful verse,
The pious offering to a Hero's shade.

I dare (since some must dare) to send abroad,
On every saddened breeze that sweeps the earth,
The plaintive accents of a general grief.
Then rising upwards from the vale of tears,
Essay, with rapid step, to mount on high
To the raised summit of the hill of praise.
But e'er the task begins, I lowly bow

Not to some storied Muse or fabled God,
But with raised mind, fixed eye, and eager thought,
I bend to Him,
Who from the mountains of omniscient light,
Drew a strong ray, and lent it to the earth.
I ask some pitying spirit of the sky,
To bend in silence o'er the honoured theme,
To guide the pencil and direct the strain.

For thee, lost Washington, the new born Babe
Wears on its tender form the dress of woe;
For thee, the Infant shows its feeble arm,
Bearing, for thee, the emblem of the tomb;
The Child, spurning the sports of early life,
Weeps, while its mother reads the tale of death;
For thee, the Virgin rends her sunny robe,
And veils from day the radiance of her eye;
Pensive along the pebbled beach, the Youth
Muses in thought profound on deeds of thine;
For thee, the Matrons pour the piercing strain,
And tell the stranger, their great Son is dead;
For thee, the Warrior piles his useless arms,
And waits in silence, for the word—Depart!
For thee, great Chief, the Fathers of the land
Suspend their labours, and their minds unstring;
And sad Columbia sits, her bow unbent,
Her darts all scattered, and her quiver broke,
And sends incessant on the passing winds,
The sorrowing tidings on to distant worlds.

* * * * *

Ye blest companions of his early years,
Who saw the youth fast ripening into man,
Lend your glad praises to his spotless morn.
Virgins and youths, if e'er you hope to lay
Your hearts, high beating, to the breast of love,
Join in the chorus of my grateful verse.
Ye veteran bands, brave partners of his toil!
Who drove through frost and fire at his command,
Through all the changes of eventful war,
Sound the loud clarions to your General's praise,
The great "conductor" of your lightning arms.
Ye Sires! who frame the law, and ye who judge,
Rise from your seats, and on the Hero's tomb
Plant with your reverend hands the honoured wreath,
Rich decked and woven by a Virgin train;
And let the land, from all its mountains, send
A general echo, to the great applause,
Till the long peal of praise, America,

Rolls o'er thy cloud-topped hills—sounds through thy woods—
Floats onward with thy streams—surrounds thy shores—
And, sweeping o'er the wide Atlantic waves,
Resounds the plaudit through the Eastern World!

Whether thy spirit, Washington, sits high
In the full centre of a dazzling orb,
Or risen far beyond the roll of stars,
Rests in the radiance of eternal light;
Whether it wanders through celestial space,
Or sits with seraphs on the hills of heaven,
Deign, with propitious eye, to view the land
That bears with reverence every mark of thee,
And from the "unknown regions of the sky,"
With wonted kindness, shield Columbia's sons.

"Rosehill," by a Virginian, which was published about twenty years ago, was generally ascribed to the pen of Thomas C. Tabb, Esq., a talented lawyer of this city, and at this time a member of the Senate of Virginia. This work attracted considerable notice, and was read with a very good degree of interest. It is a pleasant, smoothly written tale, of a moral tendency. A vein of piety runs through its pages, and it contains many beautiful passages. It was favourably noticed by some of the leading reviewers of the time at which it appeared.

"The Bridal Ballad and other Poems, by Quilp," appeared in 1846. Quilp is the fictitious name adopted by Richard Halstead, Esq., of our city. The collection contains evidences of very respectable poetic talent; although some of the stanzas will not bear the test of criticism. The following are among the pieces, and they are taken without very particular care in the selection. There are others of equal, if not superior merit.*

* The design in this feature of this work was principally to notice talent or instances of intellectual capacity, and to furnish specimens as evidence thereof, with but little regard to other considerations. This part of the task, though not unpleasant, was not found to be the least difficult, and it is hoped the intelligent reader will not find it the least interesting department of the work.

I HEAR THY VOICE.

BY QUILP.

I hear thy voice burst from the whispering grove ;
  In every star, thy image pure I see ;
The warbling birds that wake their lays of love,
                Bring thoughts of thee.

It matters not, where'er my pathway lies,
  On the green earth, or o'er the surging sea—
Where'er I wander, my sick, longing eyes
                Are full of thee.

The music tone of trembling tenderness,
  That wraps the soul in voiceless ecstasy ;
The sighs that soothe the bursting heart's distress,
                I breathe for thee!

When twilight fancies fill the shadowy air,
  And memory holds her pensive revery ;
When eyes are moist in pity and in prayer—
                Remember me.

A CHILD'S BURIAL.

BY QUILP.

Pale and lifeless, pale and lifeless,
  On her lowly bier she lies ;
Form all faded—darkness shaded,
  Where were erst her beaming eyes.
Where's the beauty once flung round her ?
  Where's the heart we loved so well ?
Hark! a spirit-voice is answering
  Sweetly—though insensible :

"Brother, weep not ; sister, sigh not ;
  Father, mother, dry your tears ;
Bend not o'er my bier, I lie not
  Where this mortal part appears.

"Let it perish! 'tis but ashes,
  Falling on the parent bed—
Look aloft and bless thy Saviour,
  That thy little child is dead.

"Days of sickness, nights of anguish,
These were mine from early birth;
Would ye have me longer languish
On the pitiless cold earth?

"Ponder! think upon my spirit,
Where it sits enthroned above—
Ponder! souls like mine inherit
Happiness, and life, and love!

"Then, sweet brother, dearest mother,
Father, sister, have no fears—
They who die to live in heaven,
O, remember not with tears!"

Pale and lifeless, pale and lifeless,
On they bear her to the tomb;
Hearts that wring with keenest anguish,
Shudder o'er the cold grave's gloom.
Sods are shovelled o'er her coffin—
Will their sound be soon forgot?
Strangers pass, but they, her kindred—
How they linger round the spot?
Cold and lifeless, cold and lifeless,
With old mother earth she lies;
But a bright, new star is added
To the pure celestial skies.

CHAPTER XLVI.

Ladies of Talent—Contributions to the Press—The Female Mind and Poetry—"Dreaming," by Fanny Fielding—Extracts from the writings of another—Nature's Teachings—The Phantom.

AMONG the talented and educated ladies of Norfolk and vicinity, there are several whose productions have been extensively read and admired. Some excellent pieces have recently appeared in the papers of the city. The lines that next follow are certainly not without merit. They contain much of true poetic feeling and spirit,—breathing, as it were, lofty and ennobling sentiments. The intelligent reader requires no further comment from us. They will be read with interest by those who appreciate refined literary taste and genius, glowing with pure and pious thought, and containing evidences of the deep and pleasurable emotions of the fair author's heart.

"The fondness of the female mind for poetry," says an able contributor to the gems of literature and the beauties of sentiment, "renders it important that we should have female poets. A greater misfortune could hardly befall it, than to be compelled to gratify its love for the tasteful and sublime at the shrine of many poets of our sex. Thankful are we that they have gone abroad and gathered their own poetry amid the affluence of nature. The birds of golden plumage have sung with them, and the fragrant flowers have breathed perfume upon their censers. If they have spoken in a still, small voice, that voice has been heard, where the earthquake and the storm would have been disregarded."

The name appended to the following is fictitious.

DREAMING.

BY FANNY FIELDING.

I am a dreamer, yet I would not give
One fair creation of the mystic spell
Which Fancy, in her sweet philanthropy,
Weaves for the recreation of her child,
For all the more substantial toys that please
The craving spirits of the world at large.
I would not thus exult, yet would persuade,
My fellow-man to trample under foot
The money-loving spirit of the age,—
To break his bonds, and wash from off his hands,
The dust of ledgers, which, mayhap, in time
Will form a barrier around his heart,
Unyielding still, though all good influence
Be brought in might to bear upon the foe.
I am a dreamer. Let me not exult,
But rather thankful be that the great book
Of Nature, with its rich embellishments,
Lies e'en within my reach, and let the thought
Lead my glad heart from thence to Nature's God,
In grateful praise for all the beauteous things
Which people this fair earth; and more than this,

That in each dew-gemmed flower that scents the air,—
Each bird that carols gaily in the morn,
Each star that gems the azure vault of heaven,
Each rustling leaf that whispers me to sleep,
He has made me a friend, and sweet converse
We ofttimes hold together. Beauteous world!
Still changing, yet lovely in its change.
I am a dreamer, and the soft Springtime
Is fraught with many a sunny phantasy,
And beautiful creation to dispel
Clouds which might cast their shadows round my heart.
Iris-hued Spring! thy fragrant breath awakes
Sweet visions of bright promise and delight,
Promise that though the winter of the grave
Enwrap each fragile flower of human mould,
A brighter Springtime cometh, when each bud
Untimely blasted shall revive again,
And bloom immortal in sweet Paradise.
I am a dreamer. Stars of Summer night,
I owe ye much that in the quiet spell
With which your gaze has charmed my very soul,
I learned to dream of heaven wherein ye dwell.
And I have fancied that each fleecy cloud,
Flitting across the midnight quiet sky,
Has borne upon its frail and shadowy form
The image of some dear departed one.
I am a dreamer. O, ye Autumn winds,
What tales of mystery ye tell to me.
Of Time and Death, I hear ye whispering
In every leaf that rustles 'neath my feet.
But they are beautiful, these Autumn leaves,
And oft when gazing on their brilliant hues
I have bethought me of the Christian's end,
Who, having well performed his mission here,
Grows beautiful in death, as the halo
Of that bright land to which he hastens on
Kindles new lustre in the fading eye,
And sheds a glow celestial on his brow.

And Winter nights, shall I forget ye now,
While thus recounting all the kindly things
To which I owe my debt of gratitude?
Shall I forget ye, with your howling winds
Lulling the soul to dreamy slumberings?
These, and Earth's snowy winding-sheet without,
Within, the ruddy glow of social hearth,
Rivalling smiles and glances not less bright.

And when deep midnight sobered all the scene,
Closing bright eyes in slumber's sweet repose,
By the dim ember-light I've sat me down,
Among the cushions of some antique chair,
And watched the shadows flickering on the wall.
These have I oft invested with the forms
Of angel visitants, and fancied me
That their sweet mission was to guard the sleep
Of youth and innocence, and to bestow
The gift of peace upon our household band.

Who would not be a dreamer? God of Heaven!
If loving all the lovely things of earth,—
Adoring the good, praising the beautiful,
And hearing Thee in all things, be to dream,
Grant, in thy mercy, that the spell remain,
Until I may my reverie exchange
For all the blest realities of Heaven.

The following extracts evidently show that the writer is endowed with mental qualities which give promise of literary distinction. Her contributions are readily published in some of the most ably conducted and widely circulated magazines of the country. Her writings, in both prose and poetry, are various, and, in some cases, voluminous. There is real beauty in the stanzas that follow; and, we may add, that they have been highly commended by critics of celebrity. The writer exhibited, at an early age, a talent for poetic composition, which has been diligently cultivated. She graduated at the Patapsco Female Institute, Maryland, in 1850; since which time, she has been studiously engaged in those commendable literary pursuits, that are calculated to improve, invigorate, and mature, those faculties of mind to which some of her writings have already borne testimony.

NATURE'S TEACHINGS.

BY M. H. B.

Go, gaze upon creation, man,
Her every form and feature scan;
* * * *
Each stream, each flower, each little bird,
Whose sonnet sweet so oft is heard,

As borne upon the evening breeze,
That softly murmurs through the trees;
List to the voice of evening star,
Which shines in heaven's dome afar,
Its scintillations soft, though bright,
Upon the sombre shades of night;
Its lustre beams in form so mild,
It e'en delights the little child.

Go, then, at morning's rosy dawn,
And walk upon the verdant lawn,
While moistened yet with mists of night,
And gaze upon the beauteous sight,—
Each spire of grace with dew-drops clear,
All trembling in the morning air,
A thousand crystal pearls display,
More brilliant than the diamond's ray.
List to the birdling's artless song
As on light wing it soars along,
Rejoicing in the light of day,
And blithely skimming on its way.
See how the clouds of rosy morn
Do smile in beauty at its dawn;
And mark the rising sun, how bright
He, in his glory, sheds his light
On opening flower and dancing stream!
See how his rays do brightly beam
Upon the earth. The seas, the lakes—
All nature, of the boon partakes.

Go then at sunset's holy hour,
When Solus doth so gently lower
His face beyond the western hills,
And busy hum of mortals stills—
Tinges the clouds with crimson hue,
Presenting to the ravished view
A sight sublime, to fill the mind
With wonder and delight combined.
Go where the mountain waves roll high,
And lift their snow-caps to the sky;
Oh! can a sight more beauteous be
Than the wide, boundless, deep blue sea,
With waves all fringed with silver bright,
While bathing in the moon's pale light?
The sea! it is the siren's home,
Who oft from coral cave doth come,

With silvery harp, attuned to sing
A lay to make the ocean ring;
The glad waves break in surges bright,
And sea-nymphs dance in wild delight.

Look at the pearly summer showers,
Which give new life to with'ring flowers;
Look Nature through—earth, sea, and skies—
And thus the voice of Nature cries:—
'Twas God, who made the earth so fair,
And decked it with such beauties rare;
His wisdom over *all* presides,
His providence for all provides;
The meanest worm that creeps the land,
Protected is by His own hand;
The smallest bird that skims along,
And warbles forth an artless song,
Hath one to guide its little wing,
And tune its artless tongue to sing.

* * * * *

He treads upon the boisterous deep,
And lulls the raging waves to sleep,
Upholds creation by His power,
And on the wings of every hour,
Sends forth some token of his love;
In Him we live, we breathe, we move.
Should we not then that God obey,
And seek to do His will each day?
He is to us a father kind,
To Him be all our powers resigned,
Love, mind, and strength—all, all be given
To Him who reigns o'er earth and heaven!

THE PHANTOM.

BY M. H. B.

'Twas midnight's calm and holy hour;
The night wind fanned the tender flower,
And earth in quiet slumber lay,
Until the blush of dawning day
Was seen amid morn's roseate hues;
When flowers laden with the dews,
Enamelled mountains, fields, and dales,
Shed their sweet perfume o'er the vales,

Our ravished senses to regale—
How sweet such fragrance to inhale!

* * * * *

A youthful one, in slumber deep—
Her very soul did seem to sleep;
She was alone—yet not alone—
For God beheld her from his throne;
He watched her while she gently slept,
And angels 'round her vigils kept.
But list! she hears a gentle sound,
Which echoes through the air around;
She opes her eyes, beholds a sight,
And lo! it is an angel bright!

Behold! a Spirit clad in white!
And robes of heaven's purest light
Fall gently down in graceful folds;
And, in its pure white fingers, holds
A casket of the finest gold,
With gems whose worth can ne'er be told.
And soon a golden key revealed
The gems which this bright case concealed

* * * * *

The Spirit now the casket fair
Unlocked, and showed her jewels rare;
She gazed upon them with delight,
Those costly gems so pure, so bright,
While radiant smiles lit up her face,
All full of Nature's charm and grace.
And then the kindly spirit said,
Of heaven thou art a favoured maid;
These gems, tho' bright, are not so rare,
As thine own native jewels are.

* * * *

Unwavering and unerring truth,
Hath e'er attended all thy youth;
Oh! may this gem be never sold
For beds of pearls, nor mines of gold!
Remember that this gem is worth
Far more than every gem of earth.
Yes! Truth in all its purity,
Is virtue's best security;
This ægis of sincerity,
From vice can ever keep thee free.

* * * *

The Spirit closed the case of gold,
When she her secret thus had told;

But midnight's past! 'tis blushing day!
And fields are clad all bright and gay!
The maiden now shall see no more
The Spirit which she saw before;
'Twas but a dream! a phantom bright!
A fancy picture of the night;
But truth this vision will impart
To every understanding heart.

CHAPTER XLVII.

Poetic Pieces, by A. F. Leonard—Song of the Emigrants—Ode to Solitude—Byron Walthall—The Stag Hunter—R. James Keeling—Song to the Sea Wave—Old Settlers' Church at Jamestown—W. W. Davis—Lucubrations—The Hopes of Love—S. S. Dawes—Tribute to Mr. Clay—An Hour among the Flowers.

THE pieces which we shall next present, are from the ready pen of Abram F. Leonard, Esq. Possessing a mind naturally strong and vigorous, with a liberal share of poetic talent, as well as a decided literary predilection, and having enjoyed superior advantages in his early mental training, and subsequent intellectual development and scholastic culture, it is not surprising that he should have devoted a portion of his leisure hours to poesy, and that he has been a valued contributor to some of the leading literary journals of the day. He has written ably on a great variety of subjects. The space which we allot to these specimens will admit, however, of but the two annexed articles, which, though they may be unfair criteria, are nevertheless sufficiently beautiful, smooth, and forcible in expression and sentiment, to afford gratifying evidence of the author's prolific fancy and pleasing style of composition.

SONG OF THE EMIGRANTS.

BY A. F. L.

[WRITTEN FOR A DUTCH AIR.]

Swift flies the bark o'er the bounding sea,
Columbia's shores are seen on the lee,
And the emigrant's song is a song of glee,
To the land of the brave and free!

They stand in a group on the open deck;
Nor have they a fear of tempest or wreck,
Though the distant shore is yet but a speck—
The land of the brave and free!

And these are the notes of the cheerful choir,
Of the smiling boy, and the manly sire,
Of the mother's voice, and the maiden's lyre,
And the lover brave and free:

"We have left the vales of our native home;
Far from our altars and hearth we roam,
And we sail through the ocean's wreathing foam
For the land of the brave and free!

"'Twas sad to quit our forefather's land,
To bid adieu to the sorrowing band;
But hope waved on its beckoning hand
Towards the land of the brave and free!

"Oh! long have we tossed on the restless deep!
And our watching eyes would often weep;
But we'd dream in the silent hours of sleep
Of the land of the brave and free!

"Of the land where peace and plenty reign,
Where no despot binds with his iron chain,
And freedom dwells in each holy fane
In the land of the brave and free!

"Welcome the spot where our wishes lie;
Bright beams the face of her azure sky;
Here will we live, and here we'll die,
In the land of the brave and free!"

ODE TO SOLITUDE.

BY A. F. L.

Where dwell'st thou, Solitude?
Upon the desert waste?
Where scorching sands around are spread,
And not a leaf uplifts its head;
Is thine abode there placed?
Dost there thou brood,
In silent mood,
And scan the bustling world—strange mass of ill and good?

Or dost thou sit, entranced,
Upon the lonely main,

Gazing into the teeming wave;
The traceless and unsculptured grave,
Where, sought on earth in vain,
The sailor sleeps
On pearly heaps;
And, far above, the air Æolian vigil keeps?

Or dost thou love to dwell
Beneath the prairie's sky;
To listen to the zephyr's notes
As slowly o'er the grass it floats,
And moves in music by?
Where thou canst view
Each varied hue
That tints the painted flowers, and seems thy glance to woo.

Or is thy presence found
Within the hermit's cell?
Dost hover o'er his mossy bed,
And glide where'er his steps are led?
Dost, guardian-like, impel
His thoughts to prayer
And holy care,
That may his striving soul for happiness prepare?

No! these are not thy seats,
Though thou dost sometimes rest
Upon the lone, unchanging plain,
Or on "old ocean's" vast domain,
An unattended guest;
Far, far from these
Thy mansion is;
To dark and drearer seats thy pensive spirit flees.

I gaze upon the stars
When night, calm, solemn lowers:
When silence spreads her gloomy wing,
And casts a shade o'er everything,
Yet feel not then thy powers;
Each twinkling ray
Bears me away
In flight of busy thought, far from thy shadowy sway.

But when within the breast
There is a painful void,
Which some dear object gone has left,
Some enterprise of hope bereft,
Or long hours unemployed—

Then yields the soul
To thy control;
And sadly quaffs the gall of grief's o'erflowing bowl.

And when from home I rove,
Amid the bustling crowd,
Though animation lights each face,
Though joy inspirits every pace,
And laughter's voice is loud;
I cannot see
One smile for me;
Unknowing and unknown, I am a thrall to thee.

I do not love thy rule.
The hart loves not to feel
The huntsman's shaft impierce his side,
And deep within his vitals hide
Its searching, pointed steel;
To pine away
With slow decay,
In unseen agony, to death a wretched prey.

Then farewell, Solitude!
Thou procreant of woe!
I would not have my peace dispelled;
Nor more beneath thy sway be held;
Gladly I bid thee go!
Farewell to pain
With thy sad reign;
With joy I hail my loved Galeta once again!

The stanzas which next follow, are by the late Byron Walthall, of this city, a young gentleman who possessed no moderate share of talent as a writer of both prose and poetry. It is believed that if his life had been spared, he would have acquired an enviable literary fame. His early death was greatly lamented, especially by those who knew his worth, and the readiness with which he composed pieces that have been extensively read and much admired for their strength and force of style, and for their correctness and beauty of description. But he has gone, we trust, to attune a golden harp to nobler strains above. The verses which follow, are not equal in merit to many of his productions, but they present a tolerably good example of his energetic style.

THE STAG HUNTER.

Bound away, my gray steed, with the silver-white mane,
Like a cloud in the gale, we will fly o'er the plain;
Tho' the steeds of my comrades be fleet as the wind,
Or the stag that we chase, we will leave them behind.

There's a wall, which is raised on yon rocky hillside,
There's a ditch in yon field, it is slimy and wide;
But we pause not for these, we have leapt them before,
And one spring from thy light feet will bear us safe o'er.

Yonder cliff we must mount, tho' as white as the snow,
The bones of a charger are there scattered below;
'Tis the spot where Guy Lambert was thrown in the chase,
And 'tis there that they dug him his last resting-place.

Tho' the bones of that charger look ghastly and white,
And the pale ghost of Lambert is seen there at night,
They will not appal us, we'll scale the steep crag,
And we'll bound from its crest like the strong-footed stag.

Thy broad breast is heaving, but thou dost not yet tire,
And thy bright eyes dilating, shoot forth a wild fire,
While the foam that is cast from thy sides as we pass,
Falls like snow-flakes around on the dew-covered grass.

Bound away, bound away, my gray steed, we have thrown
Every huntsman far out, and we now ride alone;
How thy iron-clad hoofs, as they strike the hard ground,
Wake the echoes that sleep in the valleys around.

* * * * * *

I will win his proud antlers, and then I will come,
As a victor with trophies, to bear to my home:
But I'll pause in the vale, where the buds are most fair,
And I'll cull a wild wreath for my love's raven hair.

The author of the following lines evidently possesses genius as a poetic writer. His pieces, generally, give evidence of originality, good taste, and excellent descriptive capacity, and they consequently obtain admission in some of the best conducted periodicals.

Southey remarked of the author of the hymn called "Wrestling Jacob," that he would have been sufficiently celebrated as a poet, without the trouble of composing another line, after that production; and Professor Longfellow said, that those touching stanzas, by Duganne, entitled "The Lament of the Widowed Inebriate," commencing,

> "I'm thinking on thy smile, Mary,
> Thy bright and trusting smile,"

were enough of themselves to "immortalize any poet." And remarks to the same effect have been made by other critics, relative to particular productions of certain other writers. Now the reader need not suppose that we are very strongly tempted to use such terms of praise relative to any pieces introduced here, from whatever source they may have come. If they merit similar commendation, let it proceed from others. We are willing, however, to hazard the opinion, that if the following lines were the result of the author's first and only attempt, they would be quite sufficient to produce a favourable impression. And the same remark will apply to several pieces upon the preceding, as well as the following pages. The rhyme in the seventh stanza, it will be observed, is faulty and objectionable; but the general sentiment and merit of the lines, nearly, if not quite, atone for this defect. The second and the last divisions of the piece, especially, contain much of the true spirit of poetry. The metaphor of the wave "rousing up the sea-boy to die, while dreaming of his cottage home," is certainly very striking, though not more so than that of "a shroud of foam gathering on the brow" of the breaking wave, soon to be "no more." These lines have creditably passed the scrutinizing eye of those whose literary taste and judgment are extensively known and acknowledged.

SONG TO THE SEA-WAVE.

BY R. JAMES KEELING, OF NORFOLK.

Wave of the ocean waste! canst speak to me?
The winds are sinking to their caverned rest;
The day's last beam hath faded o'er the sea,
And glorious stars are mirrored on its breast!
Wave of the deep blue sea, let's talk awhile.

We know that thou hast heard the fearful moan
Rise upward with the drowning sea-boy's cry;
And e'en while dreaming of his cottage home,
Far, far away beneath a golden sky,
Thy careless voice hath roused him up to die.

We know, too, thou hast dashed, in fearful glee,
O'er the proud argosies that crossed thy way;
Hast felt the winds in revel wild and free,
Sweep round thy form, and curl thee into spray—
And yet thou wanderest here, child of the sea.

But tell us of the ocean dead, thou wave—
Say, do they sleep in calm and quiet now?
Do thy wild brothers hold their restless rave
Around each form, and o'er each marble brow?
Or do they sleep the slumber of the grave?

In the dim palaces of ocean's caves,
Where the sea maiden weaves her coral wreath,
Are there no sighing winds and moonlit waves?
No flashing stars that tremble far beneath,
Lighting the sea-tomb with a quenchless ray?

Methinks thou'rt murmuring now,—Beneath the seas
There is a scene more beautiful than ours;
Whose gorgeous palaces and coral trees,
Imbedded 'mid rich gems and pearly flowers,
Smile like the visioned Paradise of God.

And there, amid that strange and gorgeous home,
Roam the freed spirits of the ocean dead;
Far from the strife of earth, alone, alone;
With a green canopy around, o'erhead,
'Mid the wild music of the sea they dwell.

Stray child of ocean, art thou weary now?
Cease thy wild moan, thy life will soon be o'er;
A shroud of foam has gathered on thy brow—
There, thou art breaking on the silent shore—
Wave of the deep blue sea, thou art no more!

The following lines will perhaps be thought, by some readers, superior, in several respects, to the above; though we should decide otherwise.

LINES

SUGGESTED BY GAZING UPON THE RUINS OF THE OLD SETTLERS' CHURCH AT JAMESTOWN, VA., AND THE DECAYED TOMBS IN THE IMMEDIATE VICINITY.

BY R. JAMES KEELING.

Old monument of ages past, lone champion hoar and gray,
Thy aged walls are falling fast to ruin and decay;
A stranger gazes on thee now with eyes bedewed with tears,
And marks, upon thy aged brow, the work of bygone years.

Thou standest not as thou hast stood in days long past and gone,
Ere yet the storms of passing years had swept above thy form;
Ere yet the ivy vine had learned to bind thy shattered crest,
Or swallow-bird to build on thee her frail and lonely nest.

Long years have rolled above thee since, amid the wildwood glen,
Thy ancient form was reared, in times that tried the souls of men:
And sire, and son, and savage foe, since then have passed away:—
But thou, though ruined, standest now, majestic in decay.

And where are now the few who reared thy form in other days,
And made thy humble aisles to ring with pealing notes of praise?
I ask, ye woods and hills around, I ask ye, where are they?
And wood and hill give back the sound, "All, all have passed away."

And thou, old temple of the Cross, art standing all forlorn,
Here, in thy deathlike solitude, with none thy fall to mourn;
The noble James is rolling by, the music of whose surge,
When blended with the night-bird's cry, must be thy funeral dirge.

Farewell, old timeworn sentinel, lone watcher of the dead,
And you, ye blooming wild-flowers, that wave above each head;
Farewell! ye all may live to breast the storms of many a day,
Yet know that, with the things of earth, ye too must pass away.

The following stanzas, by William Wallace Davis, Esq., attorney-at-law, of this city, were taken almost at random from a collection of poems of which he is the author. They are sufficient, however, to confirm the favourable opinion entertained by many, with regard to his contributions to some of the periodicals of the day. His poetic attempts embrace a variety of subjects, measure, and style; and the rapidity with which he composes is remarkable.

LUCUBRATIONS.

BY W. W. D.

Thoughts of the Past, the happy Past,
Are crowding on me now;
Shadows around by moonlight cast,
Shadows by Luna's radiance cast,
Like Stygian spectres hurry past;
To Somnus' rule I bow.
The night, the night is waning fast:
I'm thoughtful, thoughtful, now.

The hopeful days, the happy days,
Long past, are present now;
On lovely forms once more I gaze,
On forms beloved I fondly gaze;
My lips are moved in silent praise,
To beauty's shrine I bow;
Hope sheds its brightest, lightest rays:
I'm happy, hopeful, now.

The vision flies, the vision flies;
The real is present now.
The moon deserts the starry skies,
Diana leaves the starry skies;
Darker, ghastlier shadows rise,
Dew-damps are on my brow;
A hopeless lot before me lies:
I'm joyless, joyless, now.

A gleam of day, a gleam of day,
Paints the horizon now;
Night's sable pall must pass away,
Night to Aurora must give way;
But shadows round my heart will stay,
Clouds rest upon my brow.
Hope sheds for me no dawning ray:
I'm cheerless, cheerless, now.

THE HOPES OF LOVE.

BY W. W. D.

Go, call the stars from the azure zone,
Call Ocean's treasures all thy own;
And if the stars submit to thee,—
If treasures come forth from the sea,—
    Then, and not till then, believe,
    The hopes of love will not deceive.

Go, bid the mountain and the hill
To crumble, and the valley fill;
And if no chasms wide are seen
The frowning monuments between,
    Then, and not till then, believe,
    The hopes of love will not deceive.

Beneath Niagara place thy bark;
It's watery wall, its power, mark;
And if the ship ascend the fall,
Or if no power's in that wall,
    Then, and not till then, believe,
    The hopes of love will not deceive.

Go, bid the river stay its course;
Go, bid the tempest stay its force;
And if the river heed thy will,
Or if the tempest thou canst still,
    Then, and not till then, believe,
    The hopes of love will not deceive.

We shall introduce next in turn, some specimens from the pen of another resident of our city, who, though he has for years been a valued contributor to the papers, and has embraced in his very creditable poetic efforts many interesting subjects, is only known to a very limited extent as a writer for the press. These pieces show well enough that he might, with considerable propriety, have been less modest with regard to his contributions. Every one who has literary taste, will find occasional intervals for its indulgence. Often, while attending to the peculiar duties of his vocation, the man of business, who has the mind for the more exalted pursuits of literature, forms his plans, arranges his thoughts, and then embraces the first opportunity to retire a while from his merchandise, his books, his customers, and his dollars and cents, to commit them to paper. These casual and hasty attempts sometimes possess real merit, and please more than the studied periods, and careful rhyming, of one with less genius, who devotes whole days and nights to arranging, altering, and transcribing his empty effusions.

AN HUMBLE TRIBUTE TO THE "CHAMPION OF THE FREE."*

BY S. S. DAWES.

Fell Death a sad and guilty deed has done,
That fills Columbia's grateful heart with woe,
For now, alas! he's doomed her favoured son
To seek repose, the silent sod below.
With lightning's bound, the gloomy tidings run,
And e'en the winds with mournful cadence low,
Doth seem to murmur as they loiter near,
"For him that's gone, bestow one tribute tear."

He loved his country, dearly as his child,
And ne'er withheld his fond parental aid;
For oft when dangers raved like whirlwinds wild,
And dire alarms and strife each heart dismayed—
'Twas but for him to chide with wisdom mild,
And, lo! their restless fury quick was stayed:—
When Peace for flight prepared and all looked drear,
None lured like him, the gentle maiden here.

Illustrious Clay—the good—the wise—the just—
Through evil and through good report the same—
Tho' now thy form be nought but mould'ring dust,
Through time will live thy great immortal name,—
Secure from ling'ring years' avenging rust,
A star thou'lt shine on glory's scroll of fame,
And be remembered as some sage or seer,
Whose like on earth will ne'er again appear.

* If we mistake not, the brave sons of Greece and of Bolivia, during their late struggle for liberty, awarded to Henry Clay the title which stands at the head of these verses.

AN HOUR AMONG THE FLOWERS.

BY S. S. D.

One balmy morn we wandered forth, with spirits blithe and gay,
To list each warbling chorister attune his matin lay:—
To see upon the fragrant mead the rose and lily fair,
And Flora's congregated hosts that had assembled there.

The harebell with the violet, in sweet profusion grew,
And with them bloomed the buttercup, who quaffed his fill of dew.
In close commune the hollyhock—the hedge-row's gaudy pride—
Seemed to the poppy whispering love, that languished at his side.

The sun arose in majesty, and cast his light afar,
And ev'ry flower that caught a ray held on its leaves a star.
His dancing beams shone bright upon the winding stream and lawn,
And kissed the reverend trees which seemed to welcome in the morn.

The variegated lilac,—the hawthorn, and the yew—
Each strove to catch his kindly glance, and render homage due:—
The crocus and the marigold which spangled o'er the glade—
And, too, the gentle mignonette, its meek obeisance paid.

Uniting with sweet songs were heard the melody of rills,
And startled echoes from each grove resounded from the hills.
Diffusing odours on the air the Zephyrs gently blew,
And slumbering mists which lingered still with one accord withdrew.

The browsing lambs were seen to frisk delighted on the green,
And mazy rings which fairies formed revealed where they had been.
All prankt in nature's varied hues, the landscape and the sward,
Unto the yearning eye appeared as if just formed by God.

Aside we turned, perchance to muse and moralize on man,
Whose earthly object seems to be, to form, create, and plan:—
Tho' fraught with vain ambitious skill, his art can ne'er portray
The vermeil tints which tinge the rose, nor Heaven's burnished ray.

CHAPTER XLVIII.

Other Specimens—Original MSS.—Literary Taste in Norfolk, &c.—Composition by a Lady—Interesting Subject—Beautiful Sketch—Seminole War—Burial of the Soldiers—Funeral Solemnities—Beautiful Specimens of Penmanship—The Author—The Burial of the Gallant Dead—Solemn Occasion—The Indians, and their "Flowery Home"—Exhumation of the Dead in the Wilderness—Procession—The March in the Wilderness—Dade's Massacre—Indian Warfare, and their Deadly Hate—The Soldier's melancholy Fate—Impressive Funeral Obsequies—Military and Civic Honours—Burial Place—Reminiscences—The Soldier's Rest—Prayer of a Presbyterian Minister—Eloquent Eulogy of a Catholic Priest—Reinterment and Solemn Closing Scene—Music among the Tombs at Midnight.

MANY additional literary specimens could be presented, which are creditable alike to the head and the heart; and we might gratify the curiosity, and interest the mind of the reader, by inserting a number of others from the original MSS. at our disposal. But it is, perhaps, already well enough known, that there are in Norfolk, Portsmouth, and vicinity, persons of both sexes, possessing a good degree of literary taste, with cultivated, penetrating, and well-balanced minds, and ripe judgment; and who, when occasion requires, wield their pens with considerable ability. We shall, however, enrich and increase the interest of this department of our work, by adding thereto one more selection, which is from the pen of a young lady, a native of our city (and daughter of a venerable, highly respected, and intelligent native citizen), who composed this and many other prose and poetic articles of decided merit, while finishing her education at Mount Holyoke Seminary, where the facts in the following sketch were communicated to her by letter.

The subject of this beautiful piece of descriptive composition, is one of considerable importance. Indeed, it constitutes a gloomy chapter in the history of our glorious Union, which will be read with melancholy interest, by all who appreciate the varied military and political events of the past. The mind of the reader—as he peruses this beautiful sketch, containing, as it does, lofty sentiment, touching pathos, and other evidences of talent and good taste in the art of composition—will be thrown back a few years to the troublesome and vexatious Seminole War, and its attending circumstances of peril, hardship, privation, and death to many a brave soldier, in the swamps and everglades of the "flowery land." But the subject is the burial of the soldiers, who had honourably, though prematurely, fallen in that singular and perilous contest with the warlike red men of the "sunny South." Their withered, mutilated remains were carefully gathered up, and conveyed to St. Augustine for interment. A long row of wagons, heavily laden with the crumbling dead, and drawn each by six horses, came forth from the swamps and florid valleys; and, with funeral ceremonies well befitting the solemn occasion, they were consigned to their last quiet resting-place. But we should withhold the description from the reader no longer. We must add, however, that the manuscript of the young and esteemed author, is remarkable for the neatness and beauty of the penmanship. More admirable specimens, in this as well as some other respects, have seldom been seen by the writer, than those from which this selection is made. But, alas! she, too, is numbered among the dead, the early dead. The fair hand that traced these lines lies motionless, cold, and still in the damp, dark confines of the grave; she, too, using her own impressive words, "is now mute and passive in the stirless slumber of death." Her earthly career is ended, her race is run—and

> "What though short thy date?
> Virtue, not rolling suns, the mind matures.
> That life is long which answers life's great end."

"THE BURIAL OF THE GALLANT DEAD.

"It was the morning of the 15th of August, 1842, in the city of St. Augustine. The bells of the churches were resounding with slow, deep-toned funeral peals, and a solemn silence rested on the crowds which thronged the streets. That day was a day of solemnities. The six years' conflict with the savages within their own borders, was ended. The flowery home the red man loved so well, and fought for till his last hiding-place had been sought out, he had at last yielded, and turned his steps toward the setting sun. And now the dead—the gallant men who had gone forth to meet the foe, and had fallen beneath their arrows—were being returned to a more honoured burial. The wilderness had been explored; and, amid the lone swamps and everglades, the grassy hillocks, marked by inscriptions in the bark of the forest trees which shaded them, had been opened, and the dust of those who had been laid there brought forth.

"The dead had come by sea and land; on the bosom of the placid river, across the sandy plain, and through the tangled paths of the wilderness the freight of death had been transmitted by the corps of sorrowing comrades. Pilatka, the outpost, on the banks of the St. John's, which had heard the last farewell note of the bugle as they marched out into the heart of the forest, was the rendezvous for their return. Day after day had the slow-moving wagons brought in the voiceless dust until all who had gone out had been returned—the death-roll was completed. On this day they were to be committed to the grave within the walls of St. Augustine, with the solemnities due to brave men. They had gone out with the sound of stirring music in their ears, and their country's glory waking up brave purposes in their souls, and quelling the gentle rising of affection which lingered around the hearth-stones and the scenes they left behind them. They went out, too, with flags gaily fluttering in the blue air, with burnished arms and tinselled trappings glittering in the sunlight, with plumes nodding to the summer breeze; and they had plunged into the forest depths with unfaltering steps. But there alas, they had met death in almost every form. Sometimes as unconscious of danger, they were treading its mazy paths, the bullet whizzed in their ears, the dark shades became instinct with life, and from behind the trunk of each majestic tree, death came and ushered many an immortal spirit into the presence of its God. Or when they had halted on their weary way at evening, had made their quiet encampment for the night beneath the magnolia's shade, while the evening star was looking down upon them in its beauty, and gentle breezes brought the breath of flowers to their senses; while the soothing music of the nightingale, the hum of insects, and the slight rustling of forest boughs alone fell on their ears and lulled them to quiet sleep; and while cheering visions of home were around them, and perchance the voice of the wife or the welcome of the child was whispering in their ear; then the startling war-whoop aroused them to die; and before each strong arm could grasp its ready weapon, the arrow of the savage had reached their hearts. And when the morning came, it found those strong men that, with the setting sun did bow themselves so proudly in the might of strength, mocking at fear and danger, now mute and passive, in the stirless slumber of death; the reeking blood from their mutilated brows whence the savages had severed the flowing locks, bathing the turf which they had made their last pillow.* The cheerful hum of voices which had sounded there in the evening's shade was still, and the deep quiet which reigned there was undisturbed. The destroyer had left no mark behind him; the crushed blossom or the parted bough gave no sign of his retreating footsteps. The golden chain glittered on the manly breast, and the low tick of the watch amid the stillness of death, told that deadly hate, such as the red man only can cherish, had done the deed.† Thus had they met their fate; and for days perhaps, the scorching sun shone on them in its unpitying glare; and the dews of evening fell on their mangled forms, until at last from a distant post a band of comrades had found them, and opened for them a hasty grave, and committed them in sorrow to earth's cold bosom. And at the posts in the wilderness, some fell under diseases engendered by the burning suns and humid swamps. Or perchance, when death overtook them, they were directing their steps across the deceitful everglades with their thoughts on the trembling earth beneath their feet, and knew not that the wily light-footed savage was around their path, singling out his prey. And when their steps grew weary, the sure bullet, or no less certain arrow, did its work. The death-mists settled over their eyes, and the weary ones sunk down to repose, which should remain unbroken.

*   *   *   *   *

* Dade's massacre.

† The wily foe did not disturb the watches and other personal effects of those whom they slew.

"And now, on this bright morning, they were returning whence they had gone out. And there were waving plumes and glittering armour, and music too. But, ah, how different the notes which hailed their return! The wailing bugle, the muffled drum, and the shrill fife, blended in mournful cadence the solemn dead march; while the slow-tolling bells of the cathedrals struck sadly on the still summer air. The crowd that thronged the streets looked on in deep and solemn silence. Mournful and imposing, indeed, was that great funeral train. The long array of soldiers, the escort of the dead, moved on with slow and measured step; their arms reversed, in keeping with the plaintive wailing of those mournful strains. Sorrow marked their brows, as if thought dwelt wearily on their fallen comrades. Then came that long train of wagons, laden with the dead, covered with flags,—our country's stars and stripes,—which had come down from the blue air to enfold the victims of her strife. A poor reward this, for the light of life, and the hope of immortal spirits.

"The scene, to those who looked beyond the pomp of gaudy trappings, and steeled their reason against the influence of sense, spoke of death and eternity. But there were those on whom worldly associations had power, whose souls were steeped in the magic charms of glory; who regarded more the glistening of worldly honour than the pure glory of celestial things. But to every heart it spoke. The soldiers moved with restrained step; the pall-bearers,—men of noble mien, clad in military uniform, —passed along with measured tread, and downcast eyes. They had held companionship with the fallen in the flush of life. Thought dwelt sadly on their fate. The men of God, too, were there. The Catholic priest, with flowing robe and the holy cross on his breast,—perchance he murmured the mass that should be said for the souls of the departed. The erect form of the simply-clad and devoted pastor of the Presbyterians was there. Episcopalians, too, men of prayer and faith, who, in soul, contrasted the peace-giving doctrines of the gospel with man's strife-breathing policy.

"They moved through the city, and passing down to the banks of the river, they halted where the dead were to find their last resting-place. It was a pleasant place for the soldier to sleep. The bending cypress waved over the bed of many a fallen comrade; and the blossoming turf, and touching inscription on the marble that rose over them, showed that stranger hands and hearts had not performed these last kind deeds. On the right was an orange grove, and here the morning sunbeams sparkled on the green foliage, with their perfume-breathing blossoms and golden fruit, in all their dew-bathed freshness. Just beyond were the barracks, the military home of our country's sons. This spot, now occupied by the barracks, is linked with many a romantic legend of the days when the Spaniards held possession of the walls of the city. A convent once marked the place; the vesper-bell had once chimed out over these sweet waters at evening; and the fresh breezes had kissed the pale brow of the devoted nun. Within its dark and damp dungeons, the impious heretic had dragged out the days of a wretched life, consigned there by judges, whose council-place is the secrecy of barred doors, and midnight darkness; and whose decisions fiends have whispered in their ears. The fame of this sacred spot reached across the waters; and a thrilling story is told of a company of nuns who left the walls of their convent, in the pleasant island of Minorca, to provide a residence here. The voyage was readily accomplished, and the ship had approached near the borders of Sandy Isle. The perfumed breath of the soft air had reached the senses of the wearied ones as they came on deck, and looked forth on these walls, where they were to find a home. The tolling bell came on the silence of the evening air, bringing hallowed associations of their island-home in the Mediterranean. The morning came, and saw that ship, instead of being safely moored in the harbour, fixed in the hidden sand-bank; her masts bending abjectly to the waves, which swept mercilessly over her. The midnight hour had heard the last wail of those pure-hearted, though misguided creatures. But the old convent, like all things earthly, had numbered its days; and these barracks upreared themselves in its place,—a home for the defenders of the soil. And gallant men now walked in these fragrant shades, and breathed in the refreshing breezes that came from the leaping sea; while at evening, instead of the vesper-bell, the martial bugle and life-stirring drum resounded in those quiet shades. And where the sombre dress of the veiled-face nun alone met the eye, were the gay uniforms; and the star-spangled banner floated over the roof in place of the stern, naked cross.

"Where, then, would the soldier love so well to sleep, when felled by death, afar from his childhood's home, as by the side of that orange grove where he had so often wandered; where the familiar notes of the bugle and drum should come on the evening air; and the stone which marked his grave should awaken daily remembrance in the heart of his comrade. For too often the soldier thinks little of his other rest than that which earth can afford. He cares little how or when he meets his end, so that dishonour rests not on his name, and he finds an honoured burial.

The long procession entered the burial-place, and wound along the smooth path, among the stony monuments and simple slabs, which told that the green turf they marked covered brave hearts. Touching and pleasant was the evidence of those deep and strong ties which unite hearts that know not the stronger bonds of Christian love. No changing friendship was that which bound those manly hearts; but enduring as the bands of honour, and sweet to the eyes of friends from distant homes was the sight of that smooth turf, and these blossoming shrubs and waving trees. Many a time had the funeral train entered this quiet spot, and often had the peal of musketry resounded amid the shades; but never had it witnessed a scene like this.

"They halted beneath a grove of cypress, where the martial host, after their last march, were to rest. Three pyramidal monuments, on the polished marble of which the chisel's touch seemed fresh, pointed out the deep, dark vaults which were to receive the dust. Those heavy boxes, enveloped in their banner-palls, were removed, and placed reverentially on the green turf beside the vault. Near them was the little band of kindred, who had gathered from distant portions of the Union to witness the interment of their loved and lamented ones. By the dead were the pall-bearers, with their brows uncovered. On one side was the dense phalanx of the military; on the other clustered the great multitude which St. Augustine and the land around had poured out.

"As the eye rested on that great throng, thought dwelt on the resurrection morn, when, at the trumpet's sound, the dead shall spring to life, thick peopling earth's surface.

"The notes of bugle and drum had ceased; and there was deep stillness, such as could better be felt than described. Then the Presbyterian minister advanced, and lifted up his hands to pray. The dead, a great company, were at his feet; around was breathing life; and his voice went out clear and distinct in the solemn silence. The slight waving of the boughs—God's breath alone—mingled with man's in that moment. He prayed for the living, that man might learn a lesson of his own mortality; that he might remember that, like the breathing harp, his voice should sink in silence; that, as the summer leaf, so his glory should fade. He prayed for the mourners, that were near, and those afar in their desolate homes, whose eyes should never fall on these withered forms at his feet, whose ears were never again to be greeted by their familiar household voices. He prayed for the land; that the clarion of war might no more sound within her borders; that the dove of peace might rest on her banner. He prayed for the dark Indian, who had gone to the setting sun; that the gentle influences of the Gospel, in its harmonizing power, might come to his savage heart. He prayed for that fair land, the red man's former home, that it might become the heritage of a people who should delight to know God. He prayed that, as a people, we might be humbled in the dust for our sins; that love to our neighbour might unite the hearts of this people together for ever.

"Then a Catholic priest, a man of eagle eye, and with a tongue of stirring eloquence, pronounced the eulogy of the gallant dead. He told how, in all ages, the fire of patriotism had glowed in noble hearts; how the sacred shrine of liberty had been honoured by offerings of earth's noblest sons; how the mountain's side and the depths of the valleys had drunk their blood in every region of this wide earth. He told how, in that dark mountain-gorge of Thessaly, the devoted few of the strength of Greece had dared death; he told how the Romans, with unquailing eye, had met the hosts which, like clouds on the wing of the tempest, came down upon them; and he told how the standard of liberty had been reared in our fair land by our fathers' undying bravery. And, pointing to the ashes of the unburied dead, he said, the immortal spirits had now fled from earth; he told how these men had gone out and met the savage, and had given up their lives; and how nations brought destruction on themselves; how their graspings were quelled by the hand of destruction; and well might he have pointed at the difference between the policy of men who defended their dearest rights of liberty, and that which is to gain, let it cost what it may. But his full tones were subdued to a gentle strain, as he spoke of their last groan in the wilderness,—of death unseen by pitying eye. The burial service was then read by him who had often with them committed their comrades to the grave; and those touching words never sounded more solemn:—'Dust to dust, and ashes to ashes!' Their full voices had often responded; but there they were—*dust!*

"Again the voice of the Presbyterian minister was heard in solemn prayer, committing that great multitude to the God of the living. The last 'Amen' was spoken; and then did the dark earth receive her dead out of sight. They had made their last remove. When the last one had been quietly deposited, the roll of death was called; one name after another was spoken, but no response came up from the voiceless dust. They had all resigned their posts; they were free. No more, at morning or evening, should they answer to their names. Then the last act only remained. The volley of musketry was discharged. The smoke-wreaths curled up slowly among the boughs, and the last echoes of the solemn peal died slowly in the distance; but it could awaken no thrill in the hearts of the sleepers. They can hear no sound, till the peal of the last trump shall awaken the myriads in earth's bosom.

* * * * *

"It was midnight. Unbroken stillness reigned in that burial-place. The multitude that a few hours since had thronged its portals, had all passed away. The moonbeams fell softly beneath the still dewy scene. The holy stars looked gently down on that hallowed spot. No leaf whispered. But low, sweet, unearthly strains of melody suddenly sounded out around the vaults on the soft air; then rose to a wild, thrilling strain, and died away in plaintive harmony. Like the voice of angel-harps, it rapt the soul, raising it high above this world. It was the soldier's last, long farewell. They were 'left alone in their glory.'"*

CHAPTER XLIX.

Conductors of the Press in the City—The Editor's Task a Difficult One—Responsibility and Usefulness—Editorial Character—Editors of the Daily Papers of Norfolk and Portsmouth—Francis H. Smith—Captain Thomas H. Williamson—The Different Professions—Ex-Governor Tazewell—Form and Motion—Countenance—His Mind—Oratory—Astonishing Power of His Eloquence—His Manner—Indifference to Forensic Fame—His Political Principles—Compared with Pinkney—Pinkney's Violent Style—His Mind—Exalted Talents of these Two Distinguished Men—Mr. Tazewell at the Present Day—Intellectual Faculties Unimpaired—General Information, and Readiness to Communicate—Intellectual Superiority—Able Original Papers—Varied Intelligence.

We have already taken occasion to allude, severally, to the conductors of the press in our city; some further remarks, however, in a general way, may not be inappropriate here. We, therefore, venture the assertion, without any inclination to indulge in blandishment or fulsome adulation, that the average ability of the respected gentlemen, who hold an editorial relation to the several papers of this city and Portsmouth, will compare favourably with that of the same number in other cities. How much soever we may be disposed to particularize, it would, perhaps, be somewhat imprudent to do so. Place each member of the editorial corps here, under like circumstances; give to all the same facilities, the same experience, and then a particular and separate description might be attempted with some certainty of justness and correctness. An editor has a most difficult and

* One of the United States bands of music that accompanied the procession repaired to the vaults at midnight, and played a number of solemn and melancholy airs around the remains of the dead, as a last sad tribute to departed friends and fellow-soldiers.

responsible task to fill. An able, impartial, and consistent conductor of a public journal, may well and fairly assert his claims to the respect of all parties and every class; for such a one is, indeed, a great advantage to society at large, and a greater blessing, especially, to the community in which his paper circulates, than he is always supposed or allowed to be.

"An editor," said one capable of judging, "should be perfectly independent of all cliques, factions, and influences, political and ecclesiastical. He should have moral courage to speak the truth, at all times and under all circumstances." As to the question, How near the editors and publishers of the daily papers of Norfolk and of Portsmouth approach this high standard, we shall leave it with an intelligent and impartial public to answer.

We may appropriately mention, in this part of our work, Francis H. Smith, A.M., the able Superintendent and, also, Professor of Mathematics of the Virginia Military Institute; late Professor of Mathematics in Hampden Sidney College, and formerly Assistant Professor in the U. S. Military Academy at West Point; author of the American Statistical Arithmetic, &c., was born and reared in Norfolk.

Captain Thomas H. Williamson, a mathematician and a professor of distinguished ability, also, at the above Institute, is a native of this city; and we could mention the names of others of acknowledged merit, but we pass on.

It is quite well known that there are residing in the city, in Portsmouth and vicinity, gentlemen of ability in the different professions—some of long-established reputation, and others whose career of eminence has but recently commenced. No special reference may be expected from our pen, and to particularize might be invidious. But there is here a distinguished, venerable man, to whom a definite and somewhat extended allusion may be reasonably expected—one of the renowned sons of old Virginia, who, in days that have passed, attracted and enchained the attention of thousands by his eloquence—the powers of whose mind were splendidly exhibited at the bar of justice, and whose voice has often resounded in the national halls. *Ex-Governor Littleton W. Tazewell* is, of course, the eminent individual to whom we refer.

"Whoever regards his tall, spare form, and the unusual, yet dignified, motion of his limbs, his expressive countenance, his elevated forehead partially shaded by light grayish hair, curling negligently down his neck, his eyebrows (when he is speaking) arched, as if the blue eyes beneath were gazing at a distant prospect, his cheeks furrowed by long-continued and abstract meditation, his lips remarkably thin and well-formed—whoever regards his entire countenance—placid, yet firm; agreeable, yet not jovial—will intuitively conclude that he is a man of no ordinary cast.

* * * * * * *

"What is the principal feature in the mind of Mr. Tazewell? I answer, argument—strong, convincing, overwhelming argument. He selects his premises with exquisite ingenuity, and with such honest caution, that the hearer is so gradually and imperceptibly seduced, as almost to decide against the concurrent testimony of experience. When speaking, a smile occasionally lightens his countenance, which, while it pleases the audience, is the unerring death-sign of the argument of his opponent.

"He is, figuratively, a monarch in the empire of mind. Fancy, with her beauteous train, is the neatly-attired handmaid, not the ruling mistress of his intellect. Her power is secondary; reason in its pride is the ascendant. When he enters the lists in the defence of truth, the specious guises of error are torn aside, each secret subterfuge is exploded, and truth appears in fascinating colours. His ingenuity, however, in making 'the worse appear the better reason,' is indeed wonderful. In one moment, he can, by the strength of his genius, raise a diminutive molehill into a towering mountain, and, in another, reduce it to its original nothingness, as occasion may require. But there is no arrogant supremacy in his manner; no unfair garbling of another's argument in his reasonings; no insulting superiority in his triumph. He is mild and persuasive; he concedes the fullest force to the arguments of his opponents; and he then proves, with a coolness which no provocation can affect, and with a dexterity peculiar to himself, that, in the present case, they have no power whatever; and when fortune has smiled upon him, when the laurels of victory are thick around him, he dashes them from his brow with an indifference, equalled only by the zeal with which other aspirants after forensic fame would collect and preserve them.

* * * * * * *

"His whole political life has shown a strong and untiring zeal in defence of State Rights. He regards the General Government as the *creature*, and not the *sovereign creator* of the States; and believes that its efficacy is injured, whenever it transcends the limits expressed. He has uniformly opposed the commercial restrictive system; and, in the colonial question, denied the infallibility of the ruling passion of the President, and firmly advised him to meet the act of the British Parliament by a corresponding one of our own.

* * * * * * *

"It has been fashionable, ever since the days of Plutarch, to draw parallels of those who have excelled in the sphere of action. The names of Pinkney and Tazewell have been often enrolled together. The manner of Pinkney was fierce and violent. He often threw himself into the wildest tempest of feeling—the sweat rolling from his brow, and passion burning on his cheek—but it was the undisguised action of his art, not the divine impulse of the soul. The manner of Tazewell is natural, easy, and dignified; kindling in warmth, and rising into action, with a judgment true to nature. The mind of Pinkney sometimes appeared darkened, by the mass of embellishments with which the fecundity of his genius supplied him, and whose false glare frequently seduced him from the strict path of logical accuracy. The ornaments with which Tazewell occasionally decorates his orations, are woven into their general texture; not hung in separate clusters about the web. The mind of the former often resembles the mid-day firmament, when partially obscured by bright and beautiful clouds; the mind of the latter is more like the clear, cloudless azure of the upper sky. In reasoning, both excelled in a comprehensive and irresistible grasp of intellect, and in that mathematical precision, with which the minutest and most remote ramifications of an argument are traced to their legitimate source. Both were frequently engaged in the investigation of subjects which demanded the severest exercise of human genius, and each showed himself equal to the occasion.

Let the public voice, the surest arbiter of eloquence, decide whose triumph has been more glorious, more complete."

The above is an extract of a description of Governor Tazewell, which was written twenty-five years ago, when he rejoiced in the full strength of his mental and physical powers. His dignified form trembles now with the weight of years, but his intellectual faculties appear to have suffered but little from the effects of age. His opinion is now (1853), as formerly, sought and obtained on important and intricate subjects, not only by legal gentlemen of his own City and State, but from abroad. His information on a great variety of subjects is most surprising. He converses as freely, familiarly, and with as much apparent interest upon the various scientific, mercantile, and mechanical avocations, as upon a complicated law case, or some grave question in political economy.

We have embraced opportunities to consult this eminent man with regard to several subjects connected with the history and commercial interests of Norfolk; and on which we had sought in vain to obtain satisfactory information elsewhere. We shall not soon forget our surprise at the readiness, minuteness, and promptness, with which the required information was communicated, nor the pleasure we felt on account of the urbanity of manner, the pleasing, though dignified politeness, which he exhibited during the short interviews. We went prepared to propound several queries, respecting entirely different subjects, and widely different and distant occasions. His answers were all given in a full, clear, remarkably distinct, and definite style; there was no mere supposition, no half-conceived ideas—the circumstances in all their various bearings, direct and indirect, were perfectly well recollected and understood. His mind is, as it were, a great storehouse of the political and historical events of the past; an immense and well-filled intellectual repository, whence intelligence, varied, rich, and valuable, may be drawn at pleasure, or as occasion may require. In the course of his remarks, he casually alluded to some original articles that appeared in the columns of the Norfolk Herald more than twenty-five years ago, on subjects then deeply interesting, and on which the public mind was greatly agitated. They are doubtless among the ablest communications of the kind that ever appeared in that or any other paper, being remarkable for strength of argument, profound reasoning, and the evidences of extensive political knowledge. He was the author, and "Senex" (if we mistake not), is the anonymous signature over which he chose at the time to express his sentiments, and give the public his comments and explanations—clear, just, and satisfactory as they were to many, and perfectly true, as time proved them to be, upon matters which had puzzled other great statesmen on both sides of the Atlantic.

"The lineaments of his mind are no less striking than the features of his face. If a stranger should happen to hear him descanting on commercial topics, he would naturally conclude that his whole life had been devoted to mercantile pursuits. He is an evident illustration of the maxim of Horace, that a wise man is of all trades and professions; '*homo sapiens est sutor.*'"

John N. Tazewell, Esq., Governor Tazewell's only surviving son, is a gentleman of talent, of varied and extensive literary acquisitions, with a knowledge of political matters inferior to but few if any, in this section.

CHAPTER L.

General R. B. Taylor—Eloquence and Success as a Jurist—Extraordinary Powers of Oratory—Graphic Description by a Norfolk Writer—Address to Lafayette at Yorktown—Choice of Virginia—Deportment, Manners, Eloquence, and Military Feeling—Graces of Oratory—Effect upon a Jury—Passion—His Excursions in the Regions of the Beautiful—Indefatigable and Studious Devotion to his Professions—Example—Productions of his Pen—Politics—Chosen to Command the Troops at Norfolk—A Credit to Old Virginia—Diligent Improvement of Talent—Relatives.

THE reader has doubtless heard much of the late Judge Robert B. Taylor, of Norfolk, or, as he was more familiarly called, General Taylor. As a polished gentleman and a soldier, and more especially as an orator, he was very favourably and extensively known. Very much has been said of his extraordinary eloquence and success as a jurist and counsellor at law. Allusion has already been made to the part he took in military matters here during the last war with Great Britain; and the date of his death is recorded on a preceding page. Much might be said of the singular and astonishing effect of his efforts as an advocate at the bar in Norfolk borough, the town of Portsmouth, Princess Anne and other neighbouring counties, in behalf of the unfortunate and often guilty prisoner, and of the influence exerted by his speeches upon his audience; of his enviable power to sway his hearers at will, judge, jury, and all; to convulse them with laughter, or to make them shed copious tears of commiseration for the accused; to thrill the heart with joy or horror, and anon to fasten the conviction of innocence irresistibly upon the minds of the jury, notwithstanding the most energetic efforts of his opponent, and the strongest evidences of guilt. The following extracts are from a description of this distinguished individual, written when he was in the full strength of joyous manhood, by one who was competent to judge impartially of his merits, as well as to present them in a clear and graphic style.*

"General Taylor is about the middle size, slightly inclined to corpulency. His countenance is lighted up with the liveliest and most expressive blue eyes, which reflect the high and chivalrous impulses of the soul within. His head is on the ancient Roman model; and according to Gall, indicative of great powers of eloquence. Nor are these indications false. If the guardian genius of Columbia had selected from the scroll on which the names of her brightest sons are recorded, some favourite champion to address the veteran apostle of Liberty on the mouldering battlements of Yorktown, I do not think that I exceed moderation in affirming that the choice of Virginia would have been confirmed.† His elegant deportment, fascinating manners, and, withal, those brilliant powers of eloquence, heightened by high-

* H. B. Grigsby, Esq.

† General T. was chosen as the orator on the occasion of the great festival at Yorktown, in honour of Lafayette, during his visit to this country. "Generations may roll away, and empires be erased; old Time himself may become gray; and the bright sun be shorn of his glory, ere he again look down on such a festival."

toned military feeling, eminently qualified him for performing the ceremony with corresponding eclat.

* * * * * * *

"I have mentioned that he possessed the light graces of oratory; the alarming start, the ominous look, the significant gesture —all are his; but all these are the mere ministers of eloquence, that stirring inspiration, which, as it were, from heaven, bids them whither and when to move, with resistless magic and overwhelming energy. That his eloquence has often robed the forms of sordid guilt in the rich attire of innocence and beauty, and then bade the tear of commiseration flow over imaginary wrongs; that it has almost swayed some of his audience secretly to indulge the wish that the knife of the assassin, arraigned at the bar, were plunged into the bosom of those who would be so cruel as to condemn him; and that it has anon aroused the undulating wave of the multitude,—there are those of his townsmen who bear eager testimony.

* * * * * * *

"Most orators are rendered eloquent by passion; and, rising in the majesty of genius, march gloriously on. Not so the General. While the passion prevails, his mind appears like a dreadful volcano, vomiting its streams of sulphurous lava in every direction, and which, when the eruption ceases, continues evolving dense columns of smoke,—and finally, all is still.

* * * * * * *

"To listen to the General, in some parts of his speech, is delightful. When his course is unruffled by passion, his excursions into the regions of the beautiful are numerous and striking.

* * * * * * *

"As a lawyer, he is indefatigable. Rising early and retiring late, his whole time is incessantly devoted to his profession; he leaves no document unexamined, no stone unturned, not the most trivial precaution neglected, nor the slightest advantage disregarded, in order to advance the interest of his clients. Few men are more assiduous, none more successful in their profession; herein affording an eloquent lesson to the young lawyers in Virginia."

With regard to the productions of his pen, the same observant writer remarks, in allusion to a report which he composed, as Chairman of the Committee of Schools and Colleges, during a session of the Virginia Legislature, of which he was a member, that it "may vie in elegance of illustration and purity of diction, with any state paper which has for a long time emanated from a legislative assembly."

"Belonging to the old Federal party," says Mr. Pleasants, in his Sketches of the Virginia Convention of 1829, "he had been warmly, and upon principle, opposed to the war of 1812. Yet no sooner was the die cast than his opposition ceased at once. From that moment he only thought of the mode in which he could render his country the greatest amount of service. He had been chosen to command the troops at Norfolk, and during the whole of his service in that capacity, he manifested the zeal, the intelligence, and the activity that distinguish the able commander.

* * * * * * *

"We can say that he was, in every respect, a noble specimen of old Virginia. In person, in manner, and in intellect, he would have been an honour to her in her brightest and palmiest days. In honour, in courage, and in humanity, he was a credit, not only to her, but to the human species. Alas! that so few are left like the men of that golden period of Virginia's greatness."

It must appear quite evident from some of the preceding observations upon General T., that it was not the mere possession of splendid talents that rendered him a great man; not because nature had lavished her choicest gifts upon this favourite child of hers (she has many similarly favoured beneficiaries of her liberal hand); but it was the diligent improvement of them, and the effort to *do well*, whatever duty he undertook, whether as an orator or a writer, a statesman, a soldier, or a counsellor-at-law.

The esteemed widow, and two highly respected and intelligent sons of the General, Robert E. and William E., are residents of Norfolk. Robert E. Taylor, Esq., is a talented lawyer and an eloquent speaker, and has ably represented the City in the State Legislature.

CHAPTER LI.

Henry A. Wise, of Accomac—Interest in the Welfare of Norfolk—Efforts in Behalf of Internal Improvement Schemes—Intellect—Native Genius—Rhetorical Efforts—Style—Power of his Eloquence—Independence—Change of Opinions—Description by an Opponent in Politics—His Voice—Generosity—Social Excellence—His Person—Countenance—Extract from the Southern Literary Messenger—Graphic Description—Style of Speaking—Gestures, &c.—Speech in the Virginia Convention—Convincing Power—John C. Wise, of Princess Anne County—Political Character of the City—Whigs and Democrats—Party Strife and Excitement—Peaceable and Forbearing Character of the Citizens.

Hon. Henry A. Wise, though not a resident of Norfolk, or its immediate vicinity, may, with propriety, be alluded to in these sketches. His name has been mentioned on some of the preceding pages; as he has manifested a commendable interest in the commercial prosperity and general welfare of the seaport of his native state. His powerful voice has been heard, and the effect of his eloquent appeals has been felt in behalf of those important schemes of improvement, which, if carried out, some of them at least must result in great benefit to Norfolk.

He is so well and extensively known, that any account of him here is almost unnecessary. Let some partial description, however, be left upon these pages, of another distinguished son of the Old Dominion; a man, strong and vigorous in intellect, often splendid in his rhetorical efforts, and possessing genius, which "has the power of lighting its own fires." His style of oratory is exceedingly energetic. He is frequently fiery and impetuous, though often very deliberate; yet always at once engaging and enchaining the attention of his hearers, who are now thrilled with the force of his reasoning, the aptness of his illustrations, the variety of his gestures, the clearness and fulness of his enunciation; and anon, they are made to weep by his impressive appeals, or well-nigh convulsed with laughter, by his ready wit, or his extraordinary facetiousness in relating an anecdote.

Many extracts could be presented, to convey to those unacquainted with him an idea of his peculiarities as a statesman, an orator, and a barrister. The following remarks concerning him may be appropriately quoted:

"Henry A. Wise, of Virginia, is one of the most original and independent thinking politicians in the Union. From early boyhood he has always been remarkable for his fearless and courageous self-dependence. No party shackles ever hold him, no ancient usages or prejudices could ever influence his opinions and judgment. It is true he is a progressive and honest man, and must, therefore, frequently have reason to change his opinions; but this he does in an open, honest, frank way, which shows that it is the result of conviction."

"He is," observes another writer, "one of the most nervous and impassioned men in the world, with a voice that rings out, in moments of excitement, like a trumpet call to battle, and a face which blazes in every lineament with fervid feeling. With Mr. Wise, as a politician, we have no sympathy. As a man, he has our profound respect. We have heard from the best authority, anecdotes illustrating the unbounded generosity and self-sacrifice of his nature, such as would read gloriously in a romance, except that they might appear too improbable even for fiction. We have no acquaintance with him, not the slightest, and have never seen him but once, but have reason to believe that, in the scale of social excellence, he has no superior."

But, as it has been truly said, he must be heard to be properly understood and appreciated, and he must be heard, too, when prepared and fully interested in his subject.

Mr. Wise is rather above the medium stature, thin in person, and of slender frame. His countenance is very expressive, and strongly marked, indicating great intellectual power; his mouth very large, and his blue eyes glare out fiercely from their sockets; sometimes, when excited in speaking, they assume an expression of vindictive ferocity. "His face is full of flexibility, and, by the easy play of its muscles, expresses every emotion and passion of the mind. In fact, the whole face speaks, in every muscle and fibre of it."

As he passes along the street, often with the quick, active step of the man of business, he is readily recognised as a person of no ordinary cast; but his general appearance is certainly not such as to produce a correct impression on the mind of a stranger, with regard to his abilities as an orator, or a writer, or of his peculiar social qualities.

There is, in the eighteenth volume of that invaluable and most ably conducted periodical, the Southern Literary Messenger, strict, unsparing, and well-written descriptions of some of the talented men of Virginia, and who were members of the State Convention of 1851. Among the rest, the name of Wise prominently appears. As the reader may refer to the number for June of that year, we shall present only a few brief extracts:

"Face, figure, feature, gesture, flexibility of muscle, limb, voice, and intellect," says the writer, "were called into full play; earnestness of manner, keenness of wit, biting sarcasm, denunciation, unsparing ridicule, anecdote, positive assertion, his own past history and his future hopes, whatever was known and whatever was conjectured, as bearing upon the subject, were all brought out, and flung, wild-cat fashion, in the contest. His style of speaking is a chronic passion; it is always at the height of expression, that voice, feature, and gesture can give. In his impassioned moments, when the force of his words is thus perfectly aided by voice and manner, his arms flung aloft in every variety of unnatural gesture, his face twisting, his voice almost a scream, and his eye glaring with excitement,—at these times his words seem like bullets, dashed and flung with frantic vehemence in the face of his opponents; he speaks concentrated bitterness,—bitter in language, sense, expression, and action.

* * * * * * *

"The effect of his speech on the Basis Question was strikingly evident; and if the true test of an orator is his power to convince a mixed audience of the truth of his opinions, and to carry with him their attention and their opinions, then Henry A. Wise is one of the most eloquent men in Virginia."

He has a brother, John C. Wise, Esq., of Princess Anne County, who, though not as polished a speaker, is evidently a man of lofty spirit, uncommon talent, and excellent judgment.

This chapter will conclude with some remarks relative to the political character of Norfolk, &c.; and we may state, in the first place, that there are in our community but few politicians, or, perhaps, we should say political aspirants, certainly not many vainly ambitious ones; although it is admitted that there is a respectable share of legislative intelligence and sagacity. An observable trait in the character of the most prominent men here of both parties, is a modest, quiet demeanour. But when they are called by their fellow-citizens to act their part in the political arena, they generally acquit themselves with becoming ability and efficiency. The political sentiments of the majority of the voters of Norfolk have long been in accordance with the principles of the Whig party, and, consequently, there have been, for many years, with one or two exceptions, Whig representatives in the State Legislature. At the last Presidential election, however, there was a Democratic majority of twenty-four. And there was, accordingly, great rejoicing on account of the apparent political change in the city; and, probably, there was sufficient reason for the innocent exultation on the joyful occasion. But candour requires us to state that a large number of Whigs did not vote. Whether the same may be said of the members of the other party or not, we are not quite prepared to say. Very certain it is, however, that there was a greater effort made by the Democrats, to swell the number of voters, than by the Whigs. The most casual observer could not fail to notice that there was extraordinary and effective vigilance in the Democratic ranks in obtaining votes. The Democratic party has the ascendancy in Portsmouth, and in the Congressional district.

There is not much of the bickering and strife of mere party; views and principles are firmly maintained; but the clamorous noise, and rabid denunciations of political factions have never prevailed in Norfolk to an extraordinary extent. It is admitted, however, that there has been quite enough of bitter newspaper controversy; and on some special occasions, considerable excitement and a fair show of spirit and animation in political assemblages and processions. Martial music, spirited songs, and enthusiastic cheers, sometimes enliven the occasion, and ring out loud and strong on the evening breeze. But the "sovereigns" always disperse quietly, and depart peacefully, appearing quite willing that each one should enjoy the fullest liberty to express and entertain his favourite opinions and views. On occasions of excitement, reason generally reigns and holds its sway, in opposition to discord and confusion; and a patient submission, a quiet forbearance, have often been observed here, even when demonstrations of violence and bloodshed were seriously apprehended.

CHAPTER LII.

Native Genius—J. H. Whitehurst, of Norfolk, the Virginia Daguerreotypist—Extensive Business—Pictures—Energy of Character—Opinions of Others—Morteotype—Sketch of His Parentage, Talents, Progress, &c.—His Pictures at the Fairs of the Maryland Institute—Premium—His Pictures at the World's Fair—His Mind—Inventive Capacity, &c.—Alexander Galt, Jr., of this City, the Virginia Sculptor—Descriptive Letter from Florence—Triumphs of American Artists—Powers—Galt—Greek Beauty—Correspondence—Bust of Psyche—Bust of Virginia—Promise of the Young Artist—The Bust received in Norfolk—Splendid Specimen—Extract from the Richmond Whig—Evidences of Genius in Boyhood—First Effort—Enquirer—Tribute of T. C. Tabb, Esq.—Particulars of Galt's Genius—Works, &c.—Other Talented Individuals.

We record with peculiar pleasure that this immediate section of Virginia has produced its due proportion of individuals possessing extraordinary native genius as artists; and whose energy of character, close application, and unyielding perseverance in their profession, have already gained for them very considerable distinction, and will ultimately cause their names to be enrolled among those of the masters of the age.

Jesse H. Whitehurst, the celebrated Daguerreotypist, enjoys an enviable reputation, and merits a special notice here. He ranks at the head of the list of artists in his profession; and his celebrity and popularity have already secured for him an extensive and lucrative business, in several of the principal cities of the Union. His pictures are very remarkable for their exquisite finish, surpassing accuracy, and striking resemblance to life. The finest and most delicate touches,—the work of a master hand,—are singularly manifest in all his likenesses.

His life has, thus far, exhibited one of those instances of energy and persevering effort, and consequent success, which it is pleasing to contemplate—an interesting example of that spirited devotion to the chosen sphere of action, which marked the career of some of those worthy men of science whose names have "descended along down the track of time," never to be effaced from the historic page; and the remembrance of whose works will pass on, and on, from age to age.

There is much that could be appropriately said here of Mr. W. as an artist; nor can the foregoing remarks be thought too highly *coloured*, inasmuch as observant, scrutinizing, impartial men, of other sections of the country, have spoken concerning him in terms not less strong.

"Morteotype is a new and beautiful application of Daguerreotype, and is destined to create quite a sensation among the living, if not among the dead. The idea is chaste and novel—the dead are made to live in form, feature, and expression—the tomb-stone gives to the breathing world more than the mere name of the departed—more than can be told by the poet or expressed by the sculptor; a semblance of the mouldering dust that sleeps beneath, when the ghastly remnant of humanity was clothed in flesh, and 'the young blood ran riot in the veins.' The stranger, wandering through our cemeteries, will no longer dwell upon the epitaph of the silent sleeper—but contemplate the features of the one, who once breathed and had volition like himself. The young and lovely will seem to defy the consuming finger of decay, and smile as they were wont in the days of life. The parent can again look upon the features of his beloved child, and forget that it reposes in the silent embraces of the tomb; while the lover can contemplate the features that longest won his heart, and say, 'such was she—but what is she now?' 'Morteotype' is a recent invention of Mr. J. H. Whitehurst, a gentleman who has devoted a great portion of his life to improvements in the art of Daguerreotyping; a young man of extraordinary genius and enterprise. It is the embedding of the sun-created likeness into the stone, and making it impervious to the ravages of time by the use of the peculiar kind of cement, which makes the picture as durable as marble itself.

"If we have been informed aright, Jesse H. Whitehurst is the son of Captain Charles Whitehurst, one of the gallant heroes of Craney Island, and was born in Princess Anne County, Virginia. He is still young, of prepossessing appearance, and urbane manners. At an early age, he evinced great mechanical and artistical talent, coupled with enterprise and ambition. In 1843, the art of Daguerreotyping might have been considered in its infancy; he had foresight enough to see that there was a wide field opened before him. He accordingly visited New York—gleaned what information he could, and, through books and study, obtained knowledge enough of the art to commence for himself—which he did successfully in Charleston, S. C. In the fall of 1843, he opened a gallery in Norfolk, and such was his success that, with his usual 'go-ahead-ativeness,' in January of 1844, he established his celebrated gallery in Richmond. Good fortune still smiled upon his exertions; and such was his triumph over all competition, that he successively opened his branch establishments in Lynchburg, Petersburg, Baltimore, and New York. In 1844, he discovered the rotatory background, an improvement which gives an airy, life-like appearance to the picture. In 1845, he constructed the first perfect skylight in Richmond; this improvement diffuses pleasant and equal light over the countenance of the sitter, and consequently greatly improves the picture. In 1846, he applied galvanism to Daguerreotypes, and by a series of successful experiments proved its utility, when all others failed in its application. To give the reader some idea of the amount of business done by this enterprising young artist, something over 60,000 pictures were sent out from his establishment during the six years that transpired after he first commenced business, giving employment to twenty-three assistants.

"He seldom, if ever, gives dissatisfaction, and never allows a defective picture to leave his gallery. This is the main secret of great success; for every one being pleased, recommendations must come from every quarter. His success in Baltimore has been unprecedented—benefitting him, while, at the same time, it throws business into the hands of his competitors, who are numerous, and some of them extremely skilful. The high finish and rich tones of his pictures, have put everybody in mind of having their likeness taken;. and this newly-created desire does not confine the patronage of the public to him alone, but distributes it among those who have real merit."

At one of the fairs of the Maryland Institute, held in Baltimore, he was awarded the first premium for the superiority of his pictures.

"The English journals, particularly the 'Illustrated London News,' were enthusiastic in their praise of Whitehurst's daguerreotype views of Niagara Falls, exhibited in the Crystal Palace. These views are perfect gems of art, and conveyed a more correct idea of this great natural wonder of the world than our transatlantic friends have ever had before."

The mind of Whitehurst is one of rare and varied inventive capacity; and it would be difficult to conjecture in what direction his genius may hereafter tend, or what further results may be developed by his skill in his favourite art.

Alexander Galt, Jr., of this city, is a young gentleman whose genius, combined with a persevering, studious, and unwavering devotion to his difficult profession, has already placed him prominently before the country, as an artist of great merit and extraordinary attainments. The following letter from Florence shows the favourable auspices under which he is prosecuting his studies:

"I reverence Art, wherever found, as the longing after a better principle; but above all, do I look with pride upon any of its triumphs which belong to America. After lingering in amazement over the glorious achievements of a Raphael or an Angelo, a Canova or Thorwaldsen, it was indeed a gratification to find the genius of our own land so zealously striving to follow in the way thus marshalled. It was, therefore, with peculiar pleasure that I wandered through the studio of Hiram Powers, and gazed upon those marbles, alive, as it were, from his magic chisel. But it is not of him that I would here speak; to swell his fame —of whom the great Thorwaldsen declared, in his astonishment, that, in his fort of busts, there were none superior to him, ancient or modern—would be to paint the lily, or perfume the rose. There are younger men, with promise even as great, but who 'bide the turn of Fortune's wheel.' Many such crossed my path, whom I would love to mention, and, if it might be, bring a thrill of joy to their lone hearts; but occasion and power both would fail me. I must, however, record the name of one of Virginia's most talented children, who, in a future not far distant, will 'link it to a glorious fame.' Need I recall to you young Alexander Galt? He has been at Florence for the past three years, ardently pursuing his noble art. It was my pleasure to make his acquaintance; and I could but admire, from the very first, the manly modesty which pervaded his whole manner. Upon an invitation to visit him, I repaired to his studio in Via Babuino, and passed a delightful hour with the artist and his work. He has boldly entered on that great course which Powers has so triumphantly run, and, if I may judge from the specimens shown, he is destined to rank even beside that famed master. I may be permitted, however, before noticing particularly his morceau, to premise that no part of the human figure is more difficult of conception and execution than the one in question. The human countenance, with all its infinite flexibility of feature and ever-varying shade of expression, presents an obstacle apparently insurmountable. Add to this the vision he must form in his mind of the ideal, so trying a test of his sense of the beauties, without which all Art is dead and inanimate, and you have some faint notion of the extent of his task. In this it was that Powers contended so successfully with the Italian School. Their leading thought was developed in the general outlines, while those delicate traces of the mind, which more often lurk in the smallest line or curve of the face, were left untouched, or committed to chance. The effect, I need not tell you, was flat and insipid. But when a young American presented himself in the Galleries of Florence, and showed them a head so superbly finished that vitality itself seemed to glow in its features, the palm was yielded at once to the stranger.

"It is in this path, then, that young Galt has made his *débût*, and shown himself capable of the highest researches of Sculpture. As I looked upon that bust, redolent as it was with the mildest Greek beauty, it gradually grew upon me, till the appreciation was perfect. Then did I see how youth, sustained only by 'the promised joys of life's unmeasured way,' could pour out for months its whole resources of genius upon this scanty block of marble. The sweetly-knotted hair, the straight and finely-moulded nose and exquisite curve of the short upper lip, so distinctive of the Greek,—the eloquent mouth, the eyes upturned in rapture, the gentle arch of the brow, and the lovely oval of the face,—all announced the true poetry of Sculpture. This is all chiselled with the rarest nicety, and yet nowhere is there visible the smallest hardness or stiffness. And this 'jewelled crown of the body' is set on its basis as lightly and becomingly as grace itself. The swelling bend of the neck, and the rich contour of the shoulders, would do honour to the fairest ideal of a Niobe."

A correspondent of the National Intelligencer, writing from Florence, says:

"His bust of 'Virginia' is much admired; but his 'Psyche' exhibits a decided improvement, and will add greatly to his reputation. There is a pensive sweetness in the expression, a quiet gracefulness in the position, and a true appreciation of the best artistical standard of the Beautiful in the profile and general outline, which cannot fail to win for this work the approbation of every lover of Art. Young as the artist is, he has already made himself known as one of Virginia's most promising sons; and I venture to predict that, with the experience and advantages of study afforded by a few years' residence in Florence, he will be welcomed by the citizens of his native State, as one of whose reputation they may well be proud, and whose kindness of heart and unpretending manners are equal to his talents."

This bust was received and exhibited in Norfolk. It came fully up to the high expectations of the artist's friends. It is indeed a splendid specimen of Art, beautiful to behold—charming to look upon. Norfolk may justly be proud of a son giving such rich promise of future eminence.

A writer in the Richmond Whig speaks as follows of this production and the artist:

"I have just returned from a visit to Galt's 'Psyche,' now on exhibition at the room of the Historical Society in the Athenæum.

"To say that I was pleased would but faintly express my feelings. I was more than gratified; I was charmed; and the more closely and earnestly I studied it, the more powerfully were the magic touches of the chisel exhibited. One by one, beauties before unseen became developed, till at last the wonderful *whole* burst upon me, and I felt that here indeed is a master-piece of Art, here truly is the *embodiment of soul.*

"The works of man are never perfect; but, claiming to possess some taste in matters of this kind, I say with truth, I have never seen a piece of statuary to surpass it. The faultless features, the heavenly expression, the folds of the drapery, that inimitable little ear, itself a study for an hour, have established, beyond cavil, the reputation of the artist.

"But who is Mr. Galt? This question will not be asked twelve months hence. Mr. Galt is a Virginia boy, born in Norfolk. From earliest boyhood he exhibited remarkable talent for sculpture. Amongst the miscellaneous collection usually found in a schoolboy's pocket, is a piece of chalk, for chalking his taw. This was the capital stock on which young Galt commenced business. His penknife was his graver; and many a pretty little figure did he rough-hew out of this coarse material. His next effort was in alabaster. Here genius began to develope itself, till, finally, he aspired to the more elevated art of cutting cameos from the conch-shell; and many a fair bosom amongst his particular friends is at this time decked with the efforts of his youthful labour. Four years ago, he went to Italy, where he is now enthusiastically pursuing his profession. His first effort in marble was a bust of 'Virginia,' which was purchased by the Art Union in New York, and is now on exhibition there, and greatly admired.

"'Psyche' is the second piece, and belongs to a company of gentlemen in Norfolk. He is now engaged on a Bacchante and a Columbus, for gentlemen of Philadelphia and Virginia. His Bacchante was exhibited at the late annual meeting of the Society of Arts in Florence, and Hart and others proclaimed it the best piece at the exhibition."

"It is," says the Richmond Inquirer, "one of the most exquisite pieces of sculpture we have ever seen. The features—very much like those of one of our city belles—are most delicately chiselled, and beautiful, the neck and shoulders perfectly rounded off, the drapery elegant and skilful. Indeed, there is about the bust a beauty, sweetness, and repose, charming to the gaze of every observer. As Virginians, we feel proud of this great triumph in Art of a young native and citizen of our State."

The following beautiful, appropriate, and well-deserved tribute was paid, in November, 1852, to the talents of Mr. Galt, by T. C. Tabb, Esq., of this city, during the session of the Legislature.

A motion had been made by Mr. Tabb to take up and consider the bill authorizing the erection of a statue to Thomas Jefferson, at the University of Virginia.

He said: "Mr. President,—my object in asking the attention of senators for a few moments, is to bring to their notice and consideration a highly-gifted son of Virginia, as the artist of the work proposed by this bill.

"Alexander Galt has been abroad for several years past, diligently prosecuting an artistical education. He has given abundant and unmistakeable evidence of poetic genius and masterly talent, in the lofty and sublime art to which he has devoted his life.

"He was born in the city of Norfolk, and his family are among the most elevated and esteemed of the inhabitants of that place. He gave very early indications of remarkable genius; and such was the moral purity, the attractive modesty, and unobtrusiveness, which distinguished his character and deportment at this period of his life, that he enjoyed, in a singular degree, the confidence and esteem of the community in which he lived.

"While yet a mere boy, his extraordinary genius was displayed in such faithful representations of the human form, and other objects, in the simplest material, and with the simplest instruments, as to excite the surprise and admiration of all around him. With no model for imitation, no master to guide his youthful efforts, he discovered an artistic skill and executed with a delicacy of finish which favourably compared with the works of masters.

"It was soon manifest that young Galt was a genius,—born,

not made; and his father took early measures to afford him the opportunity of prosecuting his noble studies in the classic fields of Italy.

"During his residence in Florence—now four or five years—he has sufficiently distinguished himself to satisfy the expectations of his friends, and has secured the confidence of those who know him best, that, like the eagle, he only wants an atmosphere to fly in; that, upon a work of magnitude and of the greatest importance, he would make the brightest exhibition of high genius, and classic taste and skill.

"At a recent public exhibition of works of Art in the city of Florence,—the usual exhibition, I believe, perhaps the regular annual one,—the palm of excellence and superior merit was accorded to a Bacchante and a Columbus, both from the chisel of Galt;—a compliment that artists alone know how to value, and are willing to strain their genius to deserve.

"Several of his works have been sent to this country, and have been greatly admired. One of his studies, now in this city, has attracted much attention from connoisseurs and amateurs, and is pronounced a work of great artistic excellence and poetic beauty. As the artist of the statue of Jefferson; there is no doubt he will furnish to Virginia a *chef-d'œuvre* of his divine art, and win for himself undying fame.

"I move, sir, that the name occurring in the second line of the bill be stricken out, and the name of Alexander Galt be inserted in its stead."

Mr. Saunders seconded the proposition, and bore testimony to Mr. Galt's desert as a man, and accomplishments as an artist.

The amendment was unanimously agreed to, and the bill ordered to be engrossed.

There are other ingenious, talented, and meritorious individuals in our city and vicinage, to whom it would be appropriate and gratifying to allude here. But our rapidly-accumulating pages now admonish us of the necessity of hastening on to the consideration of other subjects claiming our attention.

CHAPTER LIII.

Why Norfolk has not Advanced more Rapidly—Internal Communication—Sending to the North—Home Manufactures—Direct Trade—Importers—Legislation—Supineness—Prospects Improving—Signs of the Times—New Sources of Wealth and Enterprise—A Sleeping Giant—The Old Commonwealth Arising—Energy—Lethargy—Commercial Position—Climate, &c.—California Gold, &c.—Mexicans and Indians—Eastern Splendour—Consequences of Inactivity—Norfolk Improving—Buildings—Streets—Banking Capital—Authorities—Citizens—Public Buildings.

Although several pages have been appropriated to the consideration of the commercial resources and prospects of Norfolk, the reader's attention will again be directed to some additional reasons why the place has not advanced more steadily, and increased more rapidly in wealth, population, and mercantile importance. The want of suitable lines of communication with the interior has already been alluded to. The practice of sending to the North for almost every description of goods, is highly objectionable, and sadly injurious. Nor can it be avoided under existing circumstances. We are compelled, from necessity now, to get our supplies from the North. And surely our northern brethren deserve great credit for their energy and perseverance. We want more of their indomitable spirit of enterprise and industry here. But it is strange, indeed, that at this advanced period in the history of our State, and of the Union, capitalists have not long since established extensive manufactories here. With regard to direct trade, the reader's attention has already been called to that subject. Norfolk, for a considerable time, enjoyed a high and enviable reputation in this respect. But things have sadly changed. Our merchants possess the means, the facilities, and the knowledge requisite to prosecute an extensive direct trade communication with the cities of Europe, &c. But now, instead of importing foreign commodities by direct lines, they are procured in great quantities from other ports of the United States, notwithstanding the necessary charges for extra commissions, double insurance, and for additional loss in breakage, leakage, &c., &c. Of course it is known that there are here some importing merchants; but there should be many. Here, we have the water deep and wide enough,—the money, and the men of mercantile experience.

Another period of prosperity appears, however, to have dawned. The minds of the people seem, at last, to be directed to the importance of this subject. But a cloud still obscures our commercial prospects. This town, with its unequalled harbour, has contended long with legislative neglect, and with the apathy and supineness of its own citizens. This cloud, it is believed, will soon be dispelled by the rising sun of prosperity. The morning will ere long dawn, and light up this part of the Southern horizon. Some of the old and knowing prognosticators cautiously, but confidently, foretell a long day of brightness and success.

"New sources of wealth and enterprise are of daily development, and the old charge of Virginia indolence is fast passing away. A giant may sleep, and a giant may awake, and, seeing desolation and decay around, by shaking off his lethargy may become a greater giant than ever."

And in view of the protracted supineness of this section in some respects, it may be admitted that a great giant has indeed slept long and profoundly; but it is encouraging, at length, to behold him, as it were, huge, gigantic, and powerful, slowly though certainly rising, shaking off the heavy chains of drowsiness, buckling on the armour burnished and bright, and preparing to enter the arena and engage in the great contest for commercial renown. Let it now be known far and near, that this venerable old Commonwealth will slumber on no longer, amid the noise and bustle of the onward march of others to greatness; the rise and progress of cities and states, and in the glaring light of science and art, with their astounding developments and results.

All real and permanent advancement in the prosperity of a town, is the legitimate offspring of energy of character, and an active spirit of enterprise, sustained by wise and judicious legislative assistance: these are the great prolific parents of success in every important undertaking, and of all great accomplishments. While there are, and have long been, some very striking and creditable exceptions, to the old charge of supineness and a lack of energy here, it cannot be denied that there has, for many years, been a very great want of that indomitable and uncompromising spirit of enterprise, which has invented plans, formed schemes, and wrought wonders elsewhere. A favourable commercial position, internal communication, good climate, rich lands, &c., are not the only requisites to insure the prosperity of a place. Men may starve, if they will, amid the rich and inviting fruit groves of the Indies. Of what avail to the sluggish Mexican was the incalculable abundance of gold, embedded in the soil, sparkling on the hills, gilding the solid rocks, and scattered profusely upon the glittering surface of California? The spirited sons of our glorious Union went and dug, hoed, and scraped up the shining dust, tumbled over the rocks, undermined those old sun-baked hills, gathered up and washed out clean the innumerable particles, chiselled the rugged and towering cliffs, and hooked out the solid metal, fused by deep, internal fires, and belched forth from the bowels of the earth. And still there are numbers hurrying on towards the inviting regions of gold; while the tardy Mexican curses his supineness, and retires, and the careless and ill-fated Indian strides proudly off to his mountain fastnesses to hunt his deer, or descends the deep ravines to spear his fish, satiate his appetite, smoke his calumet, and sleep the greater part of his half-thinking life away, as his unfortunate race has been wont to do, for long centuries that have run their course.

And among those of the old Eastern marts too, who, for a time, lolled in the lap of luxury, and rolled along in Oriental splendour, some there were who lived but to enjoy the treasures that flowed, from the rich districts of country, down the rapid rivers, whose banks were lined with plenty. But, for lack of energy, their rich commerce was attracted to other cities, the arts and sciences were neglected: and then their walls were battered down; the old towers tottered and fell; the gates of brass were broken; the wild-grass grew in the streets and market-places; buildings of surpassing strength and beauty decayed, and fell;

> "Round broken columns, clasping ivy twined;
> O'er heaps of ruin stalked the stately hind;"

and, "at the midnight hour, the owl's long cry still adds to the deep solitude."

But with regard to Norfolk, it is pleasing to record that she is endeavouring to redeem herself from the charge of supineness and lethargy. The old spell is passing off, and many of her people have grown weary of the consequences of delay, slow movement, and dull inactivity. Alluding to our local improvements, said one, who recently took a look at the city, and the indications of an entire change in the old state of affairs:

"We know of no town which presents signs of steadier improvement and progress than Norfolk. Whichever way the eye is turned, the evidences of prosperity are visible. New and renovated buildings, improved streets, and the bustle of business, all indicate a healthy state of things. There is not a section of the city where we do not find buildings in course of erection. The facilities of banking capital and exchange, which she offers to the merchant and planter, must draw to her market, through the new channels now being opened, the products of the country; which trade, will build her up into a commercial emporium. The spirit which now animates her public authorities and population, is adding new impetus to her progress; and if, in connexion with these facilities, her citizens will invest their capital in the various branches of manufactures, her advancement will be rapid and commensurate with the investment."

"Entire new and beautiful streets," says another, "have taken the place of old marshy lanes and alleys. New and capacious buildings have gone up, where, some years ago, were nothing but old shanties and ruins. Among these may be noted a splendid Mechanics' Hall, a superb new City Hall, several large churches, &c. In fact, the place wears a new aspect, and seems to have been thoroughly renovated."

CHAPTER LIV.

Home Manufactures—Northern Establishments—The South—Boots and Shoes —Massachusetts—Farmington, N. H.—Manufacturing Company—Georgia and South Carolina—Money Sent to the North—Stoves, Brooms, Hay, Fruit, &c.—Mortifying Facts—Clothing—Indigent Females—Flour and Meal—Mills—Baltimore, &c.—Profitable Investment—Cotton Goods, Candles, Soap, Paper, &c.—Steam Power—Handsome Sites—Extensive Mills, Manufactories, and their Concomitants—New England—Agriculture, Manufactures, and Commerce—Plough, Loom, and Anvil—Fruit—Hungry Consumers—Milk, Butter, &c.—Cause of New England Thriftiness, Wealth, and Happiness—Enterprise Wanted Here—Norfolk—Progress Elsewhere—Improvements—Great Works—Railroads—Steamers—Cities in the West—Prosperity of the South—Commerce, Shipping, and Products.

We have now some further and more special remarks to offer, relative to the interesting and important subject of home manufactures. The people of the South, as stated on a preceding page, get their supplies of manufactured goods mostly from Northern establishments. Immense quantities of shoes, hats, carriages, wooden ware, candles, soap, starch, paper, meal, flour, loaf sugar, brooms, leather, cabinet furniture, farming implements, &c., &c., are imported from the North and East; all of which could be manufactured as good and as cheap at the South.* But to the North goes the money, in copious streams, as it were, to enrich the already overgrown Northern capitalists, and to increase in splendour and beauty the cities of the Eastern and Middle States. The amount of boots and shoes alone, manufactured in some of those States, to supply the southern and western demand, is really immense, and still increasing, as the following statement, from authentic sources, will plainly show:

No later than 1840, the quantity manufactured in the State of Massachusetts alone, amounted to $15,000,000; in 1847, it was $17,000,000; and in 1849, it reached the heavy amount of $18,000,000!! and it has, no doubt, rapidly increased since that time. "These are pegged, and 'the first man who pegged a

* There are in this city several carriage and furniture manufactories, which furnish work equal, if not superior, to that of the large establishments of the North and East.

shoe in this or any other country,' Joseph Walker, of Hopkinton, Massachusetts, is, we believe, yet alive. The demand for these articles exceeds the supply. Frauds are committed in substituting wood or shingles for leather, in the construction of cheap shoes for the New York market; and in some parts of the shoe, untanned leather is often used. The quarters of kip brogans, as they are called, are sometimes lined with common straw paper, concealed beneath white sheepskin morocco.

"A method of manufacturing boots and shoes, by what is called teams, or a division of labour, has been introduced by Charles D. Bigelow, of Massachusetts, which dispenses with previous training, and makes the workman expert in his particular department in a day or two.

"For one year, it was estimated that the whole number manufactured in the town of Farmington, N. H. (to say nothing of Lynn, Mass.), exceeded 425,000, valued at $300,000. The amount paid for labour, freight, and trucking, was near $90,000. The boxes alone cost $3,000, and required 210,000 feet of boards to make them. There are now six large manufactories, besides some larger ones, all together capable of turning out 600,000 per annum, should the wants of the trade require and the prospects warrant it."

Why could not a company for the manufacture of these articles be organized here? If properly managed, it would certainly pay a handsome dividend. It would require a capital of say $50,000, in shares of $25 or $50 each; with a contingent fund of four or five thousand dollars, for the expenses of machinery, stock, &c.

This business, as will be seen by the following extract from a southern paper, has already been commenced in South Carolina and Georgia:

"Among the different branches of domestic industry daily springing up at the South, there is none that it gives us more pleasure to notice than that of manufacturing our own leather and shoes. In Georgia and South Carolina, there are several small factories established for manufacturing brogans, &c.; and we are pleased to learn, from those engaged in the business, that the demand for their productions is on the increase. The day is not far distant when the Southern States will not only be able to supply their own wants with cotton goods and shoes, but a hundred other articles, for which we have heretofore been dependent on our Northern brethren."

"Let us make a calculation," says a Norfolk writer, "of the sums sent each year from Norfolk to the North. For dry goods, clothing, fancy articles, jewelry, &c., say from $500,000 to $1,000,000. We probably send the same amount for boots and shoes, hats, saddlery, hardware, furniture, stationery, chinaware, &c., and upwards of $1,000,000 more for groceries, and many other articles, including freight and insurance. Now, of all this large sum, the profits of full four-fifths inure to the benefit of the North, and one-fifth only remains with us. Let us suppose that, for the last twenty-five years, we had retained amongst ourselves, of this sum, an additional $500,000 each year, which a moderate degree of industry and enterprise might have readily done, our city and the surrounding country would have had, at the present time, an addition of millions added to its resources.

"Every year we send away our $100,000 for the simple articles of butter and hay; and is it not a mortification to see, every few days, the latter article, for the most part the product of the sterile and rocky State of Maine, conveyed to the surrounding country for the use of our farmers, when equally as good, to my knowledge, can be raised here with very little labour?"

"Consider these things," says a writer in the Richmond Times; "'Just received, another lot of those celebrated Troy Cooking-Stoves.' A heading like the above is not strange to your columns. Does anybody know how many thousand dollars are yearly sent North, from Virginia, for that one article? Have not we as good water-power, as good iron and coal, as they have at the North, or as skilful mechanics?

"'Just received, two hundred dozen Corn Brooms from the North.'

"It is an ascertained fact that half a million dollars is yearly paid for brooms imported into Virginia. Are not the James River bottoms as good for raising broom-corn as the Connecticut? Won't somebody plant a few acres next spring? The crop is said to be worth from fifty to one hundred dollars per acre.

"'Just received, one hundred bales Northern Hay.'

"Is it a fact that Virginia cannot raise hay to feed her own stock? I have seen, even this dry season, at least three tons per acre, on land that, a very few years since, was worth no more than—in fact, as poor a piece of land as could be found in the State. What crop pays better, at from fifteen to twenty dollars per ton?

"'Just received, fifty barrels fine Northern Apples.'

"How many thousands are paid annually for fruit, even in Richmond? The world may be challenged to produce a finer climate, for fruit of any kind, congenial to the climate, than Old Virginia. So it may be said of potatoes, and hundreds of other articles. The above article is not intended as any reproach on our Northern brethren; all praise, on the contrary; and I should be very glad to see them among us and—*fill it out yourself.*"

These extracts convey some mortifying facts, and they apply as well to Norfolk and Portsmouth, as to Richmond; but let the truth be known, and perchance it may cause a spark to fall upon and light up the fires of enterprise and genius that have smouldered here for so many long and tedious years.

"A judicious application of capital and labour to the production of articles of prime necessity in our midst, by keeping the profits of such undertakings among ourselves, awakening industry, and arousing a feeling of self-dependence, has been regarded as the most certain means of advancing the prosperity and happiness of communities. Among the enterprises within our reach, may be mentioned the manufacture of ready-made clothing. It is a business which, of late years, has been carried to a great extent, and must have proved very profitable, or it would not have been so zealously pursued. It is supposed that in our city alone at least one hundred thousand dollars is annually expended in this business. The profits upon these sales pass, to a great extent, into the hands of people of other States, and the labour which it sets in motion and remunerates is the labour of strangers. Do we not owe it to ourselves to make an effort to appropriate the fruits of such enterprises to our own city? As a merely benevolent undertaking, it has high claims to consideration. The manufacture of clothing here would give steady and remunerating employment to a large number of persons, principally indigent females, and relieve distress which cannot be effectually reached by charities, however searching and zealous. To the capitalist it then presents an opportunity of profitable investment, and to the philanthropist an abundant field for doing good."

With regard to the articles of flour and meal, it is estimated that 35,000 barrels per annum are required by our city and its immediate vicinity, while very large quantities are wanted for exportation, and to supply the demand of the surrounding country; which demand would doubtless be greatly increased if there were here extensive mills.

It is a statement that will scarcely be credited abroad, although it is well enough known here, that we have no flour-mills; nor are there even extensive grist-mills, for the grinding of Indian corn, in the city. We state with pleasure, that mills have been put in operation in Gosport, which furnish a large quantity of excellent meal; and Dr. Wm. Tatem's Myrtle Isle Tide Mills, near Gilmerton, on the Southern Branch, also assist in supplying the demand.

Indian corn is generally cheap here, but meal is almost always high. The former is often quoted at fifty-five to sixty cents per bushel; while the retail price of meal is eighty-seven and a half cents to one dollar! The proprietors of extensive mills in Baltimore and elsewhere, often procure their corn from Virginia and North Carolina; and with the addition of freight and other necessary charges, the meal is shipped in large quantities to assist in supplying the demand in Norfolk, Portsmouth, and vicinity. It is hoped and believed that this state of things will not be continued much longer. It must be manifest to a casual observer, that a rare opportunity is presented for a most profitable investment of capital.

But it is very reasonably insisted also, that there should be large establishments here for the manufacture of cotton goods,* paper, loaf-sugar, and other articles already mentioned. It cannot be doubted that there are ample means and facilities for manufactories of almost every description. It is true, there

* A cotton factory is now in operation in this city.

is no water-power, except that afforded by the ebbing and flowing of the tides; but it is asserted by those who are fully competent to judge in the case, that, all things considered, steam-power would be nearly equal to water-power here, where the best of wood is abundant and cheap. There are a number of suitable and handsome sites within a mile of the city; all the necessary machinery and materials can be readily obtained here on fair terms, and there is no real lack of capital for all such purposes.

The introduction of extensive mills and manufacturing establishments, would, in a very great measure, stop the immense drain upon the capital of the place, while hundreds of workmen would be attracted hither, who would require provisions, houses, clothing, &c., and many of whom would become prosperous and useful citizens. An impulse, such as has not been witnessed before, would be given to every department of business. A number of collateral branches of industry would necessarily spring up as if by magic, such as barrel, box, and bag manufactories, and all classes of society would feel the beneficial tendency of so important and agreeable a change in the state of affairs.

"Look at New England," said an able representative in our Legislature, alluding to improvements and manufactories, "how is it that hilly, stony Massachusetts, scarce one-ninth the size of Virginia, exhibits the glowing picture she does of prosperity in all the branches of industry, and of abundant wealth and smiling comfort throughout her borders? It is because *there* agriculture, manufactures, and commerce are beautifully blended; because there is *there* that diversity of vocation which raises up 'rich consumers instead of impoverished producers;' because her consumers and producers are distinct classes, and placed alongside of each other; because the 'plough, the loom, and the anvil,' instead of being antagonistic, act reciprocally upon, and bear bounteous tribute to, each other; because, in fine, by her manufactures she creates throughout her domain a multiplicity of home markets to absorb her agricultural surpluses, large and small, which, after all, is the true secret of thrift.

"But perhaps I shall best illustrate my ideas on this subject by an interesting anecdote which I gathered from an agricultural address, in which is ably enforced this dependence of agricultural prosperity upon manufactures.

"A Mr. Phinney, of Massachusetts, who had reduced to profitable cultivation a piece of land which had been covered with stone, was asked how he was compensated for his pains. 'Pray, my dear sir,' said a friend, 'how do you get remunerated for removing, as you tell me you have, more than a ton of stone for every six feet square of land, now covered with the finest grasses, and orchards of the finest fruits? Where do you find customers to buy, as you tell me you sell $2000 worth of fruit alone in a single year?'

"'Why, sir,' replied Mr. Phinney, 'have we not, besides many other little market towns, 30,000 hungry consumers at one manufacturing village, Lowell, ready to buy all our spare fruit, and milk, and butter, and eggs, and poultry, and vegetables, and our meat, from a pig of four hundred pounds, down to a pint of blackberries?'

"This little anecdote," said the speaker, "solves the mystery, and reveals the secret of Northern and New England thriftiness and wealth. Go to New England, and you do not see, as you do in the Southern States, every body engaged in agriculture. You find one portion of the people producing for the other; one making, the other eating up, the products of the other. There is consequently no over-production, no glut of the market; a just relation is preserved between supply and demand; sale is found for everything at remunerating prices; all have employment, and all are thriving and happy."

All that is wanting then, here, as before declared, is more enterprise—the true spirit and life of business—the real "lightning of the human understanding." Let this irresistible motive power be more fully applied to the mental and physical system of the people, let this all-powerful, life-giving, and wonder-working principle of vigour and force be applied to judicious plans, and these works, and greater than these, will ere long be commenced, and prosecuted in good earnest. And then may it be said, adopting the language of an intelligent writer of the present day, "When Virginia's great Central Canal shall have been completed, and she shall have reclaimed all the solid charms of the 'River of Beauty,' Norfolk will spring up into the New York of the South."

The citizens of Norfolk, it must be admitted, have too long been regardless of their own interests. It is full time now to attempt a change, and to make experiments, at least, in the great work of reform. The dull age of slow movement and tedious delays has passed and gone for ever. Elsewhere,—north, south, east, west,—the noise of ponderous machinery is heard, roaring and clanking, from the dawning day till the latest evening hour. Improvements, upon a grand scale, move on rapidly. Men whiz away through space, like an arrow to its mark, or a bird to its nest. With the rapidity of the "lightning's wing," and the quickness of its vivid flash, they hold social converse with far distant friends; and the enterprising are seeking to make the most of life's fleeting day. Works of extraordinary magnitude are begun, and completed in an exceedingly short space of time. The waters of great rivers and lakes are united by dikes, deep and wide, through dense forests, and beds of solid rock,—lines of railroad stretch out far and long, even towards the secluded abode of the red man in his wildness, who, with the timid deer and the lumbering buffalo will soon start up alarmed at the sharp noise of the steam-horse, as he dashes along in unbridled fury, and they will leave for ever their old familiar haunts. Rocky and towering mountains are tunnelled, gigantic steamers crowded with human freight, and deeply laden with gold and costly merchandise, plough the wide oceans,—splendid cities rise up in the West, and adorn the shores of the great lakes and the "father of waters," while an astonishing impulse has been given, of late years, to commerce, the arts, and the important subject of education, too, in various sections of the great South and Southwest.

"New elements of prosperity are becoming developed in the Southern States, through their internal improvements, and mineral resources, and capacity for manufactures. The Southern States, instead of being tributaries to Northern merchants, shipowners, manufacturers, and mechanics, are beginning to help themselves to the profits of such pursuits. The time is at hand, when New England and New York will,—and even without any non-intercourse laws on the part of the South,—be deprived of the exclusive benefits which they have so long enjoyed in supplying the consumption of the South, with Northern manufactures and fabrics, and conducting for the South all her commerce and navigation. Already, under the operation of reciprocal navigation law, the bulk of the cotton products is carried direct from Southern ports to foreign ports and in foreign vessels. Much is still shipped by way of New York to Liverpool and Havre; but this will soon be prevented by arrangements now in progress with British capitalists and ship-owners. This being done, is it not easy to see that the articles of foreign growth and fabric wanted by the South, will also be brought directly to Southern ports? Coarse cottons, shoes and hats, mechanical and agricultural instruments, the South have begun to supply themselves with by aid of her own labour and capital."

And shall there be still no great manifestation here in Norfolk and Portsmouth, the seaport of Virginia,—no extraordinary bustle and stir,—prominently, beautifully, and advantageously situated as they are? No united attempt to foster industry, and join in those great enterprises, which, if properly managed, must redound to the advancement of all this southeastern section of the State? It is not believed that so humiliating a fact will ever be found on record. The great business of reform has already commenced,—the reform party have the ascendancy, and the opposing powers are too feeble to retard the progress of important works of improvement already begun, or to prevent the completion of others in contemplation.

CHAPTER LV.

Coloured Population—Misinformed Fanatics—Condition of the Coloured People—Fidelity—Preference for a State of Subjection—Reciprocal Regard of Masters and Slaves—Plentiful Fare, Clothing, &c.—Attention, Treatment, Intelligence, Ingenuity, &c.—Venerable Old Freed-man—His Benevolence—Ignorance, Superstition, &c., of the Coloured People—Piety—Easy Life—Sleeping, Eating, &c.—Contentment—Religious Privileges—Marriage Vows—Respect to the Dead—Impressive Funeral Ceremonies—Negro Life in New York—Laziness—Lower Classes—Decrease in Numbers—The Different Classes—Cow Bay—Five Points—Pigs, Cats, Dogs, Rats, and Children—Horrible Condition—Houses—Occupations—Intemperance—Bar-rooms and Sleeping Apartments—Cellars and Filth—Idleness and Theft—"Prigging the Wipes"—Night Orgies—Effluvia—Civic Privileges—Occupation—Frederick Douglass—Menial Slavery in New York—How the Blacks kennel together like Beasts—Accommodations, Furniture, &c.—Wages—Ragged Chimney Sweeps—Pitiable State—The Better Class—Waiters—Private Servants—Their Native Home—Colonization Society—Uncle Tom's Cabin—English Ladies—Unintentional Result.

As the population of Norfolk embraces a large proportion of coloured persons, we may appropriately offer some descriptive remarks in relation to their condition, general character, &c. With regard to the extravagant descriptions and wholesale denunciations, so common in some of the Northern prints, and emanating from misinformed fanatics,—both the observant resident and scrutinizing traveller are struck with the utter inappropriateness of all such vituperation; so far, at least, as the communities of Norfolk, Portsmouth, and vicinity are concerned. Indeed, these remarks apply, in a great measure, to the South generally. The object of the writer, here, is not to advocate slavery, but simply to present an impartial statement of facts.

Our coloured people, the slaves particularly, are generally happy and contented. They are entirely free from those cares and troubles which necessarily grow out of the responsibilities and duties of life, that devolve on those upon whom they depend for support. This statement will apply especially to those who are held in servitude, and who, of course, constitute the principal portion of the blacks here. Very many of them seem as free as any beings on the face of the earth; having, generally, liberal, kind, and indulgent owners, who allow them many privileges and who look anxiously to their welfare, providing for them comfortable lodging-rooms, sufficient clothing, and a full quantity of wholesome food. Although, it must be admitted, that in some instances they are very unfaithful, and sometimes shamefully betray the confidence of their owners, yet, as is well known and acknowledged, there are numbers of cases in which are manifested the most praiseworthy fidelity and devotion to the interests of masters and mistresses. It is also quite observable, that there are not a few who prefer their present state of subjection to their owners, to an unqualified freedom, and whom no inducement which a misguided abolitionist might offer, could tempt to a separation and a consequent self-dependence.* And the strong feeling of reciprocal regard and kindness on the part of owners, is not comprised in any of the fanciful and contumelious descriptions of wild enthusiasts. Many, very many of the more reflecting, intelligent, and observant citizens of the Northern and Eastern States know and admit these remarks to be true.

Very generally, the servants here have excellent fare, and sometimes a superfluity of clothing, and pocket-money besides. The numbers that are employed as cooks, dining-room servants, chambermaids, nurses, washerwomen, carriage drivers, porters,

* "There died lately, in a lower county of Virginia, a mulatto man who was manumitted by his master, and was, under our law, permitted to remain in Virginia. His master had, with his liberty, left him a respectable property, and this man, by industry, accumulated an estate of $25,000. He had purchased his wife, who was a slave, and his children were therefore his own property as well as his wife.

"Falling into bad health, he went to Philadelphia some time during this last summer for medical advice; but learning from the best physicians that his health was worse than he thought, and that he could not live, he wrote to a relative of his old master to come on for him, which this gentleman did, and stayed with him and brought him back to Virginia at his request. He died shortly after his return, and by his last will left all his estate to this gentleman, as well as his wife and children, who are thus the slaves of his friend; trusting, of course, that he would care for them, and provide for them.

"These are notorious and recorded facts, and can be proved if denied; and there are many such occurrences among our coloured people."

hostlers, &c., are well provided for in health and in sickness, and seldom afford a case of bad treatment on the part of the master, or of notable insubordination on the part of the servant.

Among both the bond and the free, of either sex, there are to be found individuals of excellent sense, sincere piety, and disinterested benevolence. There was one, a venerable and pious freedman, whose pilgrimage has ended, the noise of whose dray-wheels was sweet music to the ears of many a suffering occupant of the comfortless and chilly abodes of poverty and distress, especially during the freezing days of winter; as was justly remarked, in substance, by a distinguished citizen. And yet, take them as a body, they are, as may be expected, ignorant, superstitious, and excitable. They appear, however, nearly all of them, to be naturally fond of religious worship, passionately fond of attending church, singing, exhorting, "relating their experience," praying, shouting, &c.; and in very numerous instances in health, and in the trying hour of nature's dissolution, they evince correct views of the Christian religion, and exhibit remarkable cases of entire fearlessness of death; while the sable countenance, and simple, though sincere expressions, give pleasing evidence of the joy with which the hope of a rest in heaven inspires the heart.

Many of the slaves in this part of Virginia live an exceedingly easy life. They labour, it is true, in many cases, well and faithfully; but they sleep soundly, eat heartily, sing cheerfully; being manifestly and necessarily quite unconcerned about their own wants, as well as about those subjects that agitate enlightened society, and the grave questions that often disturb the quiet of the political and religious world. They are allowed, without restraint, to attend church several times on the Sabbath, and often on other days of the week, and worship in their own way, without molestation. In many instances, families of them "hire their own time," occupy a house, and dwell together in peace; pay a commendable regard to their marriage vows (though sometimes imperfectly solemnized), rear their children, perform their family devotions, smoke their pipes and enjoy the comforts of life, besides paying the amount required by their owners, which is seldom extravagant, and often but trifling, sometimes nothing at all. They are generally attentive to one another in sickness, and appear to pay great respect to their dead. They gather together in the house in which lie the lifeless remains, engage in loud singing and praying, often continuing all night; and, after the preaching of the funeral sermon, which always takes place at one of their churches, they follow the "slow nodding hearse" in great numbers—hundreds, aye, and thousands, frequently press quietly on to the last resting-place, where due solemnity is observed; and frequently the welkin rings while the multitude unite their clear and sonorous voices in singing some old, familiar, and appropriate funeral dirge, at the calm, quiet, evening hour, as they commit the body of a faithful fellow-servant to the death-stillness of the grave.

We must now furnish the reader, by way of contrast, with the following extracts of a sketch of negro life in New York, which we take from the columns of The Express, an ably-edited paper of that great city:

"So much has been said, and is still being said, about the glorious and happy lot of the Free Negro, that we have taken considerable pains and trouble to lay before our readers a true statement of the condition of our negro population, and to discover their secret haunts and pursuits, in order to show these ardent philanthropists that there is work enough for them at home without going to the South, where, we think, it would be difficult to point out as much misery and degradation as exists among the black population in a single ward in our city.

"We have spent much time in examining into this matter. We have seen the blacks under almost all circumstances: we have entered their dwellings; we have seen them at work; we have seen them in their drunken revels; we have seen them in their families,—and we have come to the conclusion, that the negroes of New York have made nothing out of the freedom which has been given them. Descendants of the old New York slaves, some of them also refugees of the South, they adopt the idea that they are as good as white men, and act accordingly. They are FREE—they will do as they please, and nothing can make them work but actual starvation, and often not that—and, to live at all, they prey on their fellow-men, and eke out a paltry existence by begging and stealing.

"We do not wish to be understood as including all the coloured people here in this category. There are, probably, in this city, some five hundred, or perhaps even one thousand, bright, intelligent, and intellectual men, who see plainly the evils to which their race is subjected here, and strive daily to persuade them to give up their evil ways,—but thus far without success. We shall touch upon the 'negro gentleman,' in the course of our articles, but at present we shall confine our remarks to the lower classes of negroes, giving a sketch of their condition, socially, morally, and physically; and we commend the details to the attention of a certain class of very zealous philanthropists, who are especially interested in alleviating the condition of the distressed Ethiopian.

"The free negro population of the State of New York, according to the census of 1850, is 47,914, of which number 22,965 are males, and 24,949 females. (Under the head of 'negro' we comprise all who have negro blood in them, from the light Mulatto to the black shining African.) Of these, 13,520 individuals—5,988 males, and 7,532 females—are inhabitants of the City and County of New York. The census returns show that the negro population has fallen off in this State about ten thousand since the last census, in 1840, and when we have concluded our description of the manner in which they 'live and move, and have their being,' we do not think our readers will find it a matter of surprise.

"The negroes in this city may be divided into three classes —the thieves and beggars, the chimney-sweeps and whitewashers, the waiters at hotels and private servants. To each of these classes we will give a passing glance, visiting their resorts, and showing our readers what they really are.

"The thieves and beggars—absolute paupers, who are too lazy to look for work, and too indolent or vicious to accept it if it should be offered to them—mostly rendezvous in the lower parts of the Fifth and Sixth Wards, though they may be found in small numbers in the Fourth, Eighth, and Fourteenth Wards. Their chief haunt is in Cow Bay, a miserable little alley which runs out of Anthony Street, or may be called the continuation of Little Water Street, in the notorious Five Points. This place, though now bad enough, in all conscience, is a paradise to what it was a year or so ago, before the work of reformation in that neighbourhood was commenced by the Rev. L. M. Pease, whose parsonage, and Industrial Home, is but a few rods from the location we are about describing. To look at it in passing from Anthony Street, the ordinary observer would see nothing in Cow Bay but a small, narrow, and exceedingly dirty court, about one hundred and twenty or thirty feet deep, with a row of shabby three-story brick houses on one side, and dilapidated brick and wooden hovels on the other. Pigs, cats, dogs, rats, and children, black and white, wallowing in the mud, or taking their initiatory lessons in rascality together, generally greet the eye the first thing on entering; and what at first sight appears but one court, in the result of an examination proves to be rather a succession of courts—a labyrinth of alley-ways, bordered on all sides with dirty and filthy houses—a hive, sweltering full of human brutes—a small city in itself, teeming with a population altogether of a different nature from those who live but a few blocks from them.

"A stranger should be wary of entering this place without a guide; for so many are the turnings, the dark corners, the high and ricketty stairways, the low and noisome cellars, that, once in, he would be puzzled to find his way out again to the free air of Heaven. This locality is the principal dwelling-place of the negroes; this is where their orgies are carried on; and here they live and die like pigs, and their carcasses are stowed away in some corner of Potter's Field, with about as much respect as would be paid to the carrion of an old horse.

"The houses have generally eight or ten rooms, including the attics and cellars, and in these are crowded not unfrequently two or three hundred souls. The cellars are so arranged that the sidewalk comes up to within eighteen inches or a foot of the wall of the house, and, looking down, one may perceive a deep, dark, nasty trap, into which all kinds of refuse are thrown, and into which, not unfrequently, the inebriated inmates of the courts themselves meet their end. At intervals, reaching from the sidewalk to the bottom of this gutter, are placed ladders, or steps, to give ingress and egress to the animals who burrow in the cellars. The front cellar is usually eight or ten by six feet in size, with a ceiling so low that an ordinary sized man must look out for his hat on entering. One end of this apartment is fitted up with a bar, stocked with villainous compounds called *liquors*, which are sold to the wretched inhabitants for three cents a glass each, as long as they have money, and four cents credit, as long as they have any personal property that the landlord can levy upon for his pay when their money is gone. Back of the 'bar-room' appears another apartment, perhaps a little larger, perhaps smaller, according to the size of the house, and in this kennel are often crowded together fifteen or twenty persons, negroes and white, male and female, adults and children, without any more light and air than what can come in through the door. These sleep together on the same rags—beds there are none—or on the same straw, and rarely or never do the inhabitants of these cellars retire to their rest until they are too much inebriated to remain longer awake, when they lay themselves down, in the clothes which probably they have not taken off for months, and sleep off the fumes of their drunkenness in the midst of the most revolting filth.

"Not unfrequently, in the larger houses, one or two apartments are not all that are to be found in a cellar; sometimes these sinks are two stories deep, or have side branches extending under the courts, and these all, of course, worse than the first. With no floors, or with such as were originally laid, long ago rotten and worn out, so out of repair that whenever it rains the filth of the gutter and courts is washed down to make part and parcel of the heap the wretches sleep upon; never cleaned out from one year's end to the other—these noisome holes are not fit habitations even for the vermin which swarm in them; and yet here these creatures, who call themselves men and women, and who would feel themselves insulted were a white man to call them 'niggers,' drag out their miserable existence.

"During the day, the inhabitants of 'Cow Bay' and its 'courts' and 'alleys' keep themselves pretty quiet; they only step out to get their three or four cents' worth of gin, and then burrow themselves in their dens again. If the day be clear and the sun warm, large numbers of full-grown negroes, men and women, may be seen lolling over barrels in front of the 'groceries' on the corners, listlessly dangling their legs, smoking those villainous nuisances—short, black pipes—or lying asleep full length on the sidewalk. As long as it is daylight, the police do not disturb them, unless, which is not unfrequently the case, they detect those who are awake, or pretending to be asleep, in 'prigging the wipes' (*i. e.*, stealing the handkerchiefs), or begging alms of the passers-by. If they succeed in getting anything undetected, it is instantly pawned, or spent at the bar of the nearest rum-hole for gin and tobacco. Others seat themselves on the curbstones of more reputable streets, and hanging an 'I am blind' about their necks, sit out the day, with their hands stretched out before them, awaiting the chance coppers of the wayfarer, to be spent in the Five Point dens of iniquity at night. Others, again, will lounge around the market-places, slyly stealing whatever they can put their hands upon, from a potato up to a pocket-book. And thus the negro thieves and beggars spend their days.

"At night, as soon as it is fairly dark, the particular locality we have endeavoured faintly to describe, assumes the appearance of a swarming hive. Every cellar, alley, attic, and court, pours out its quota, and the dusky populace crowd the gin cellars and dance cellars, where they spend what they have begged or stolen during the day. There are but three or four of these dance cellars now in full operation, though, formerly, there was one under almost every house. From sixpence to a shilling is charged for admittance to these holes, where, in their filth and misery, the half-drunken darkeys dance till they are tired, and then call at the bar, which is always convenient, for drink. In another room, not known to all who go to these places, is the shuffle-board, the dice-table, and the policy-agency, which generally glean the few pennies the negro has left. Male and female alike participate in these revels, in the hottest as well as the coldest weather; and when they are gathered together, in the full tide of the dance and the game, the effluvia and *toute ensemble* of the scene can be better imagined than described. When they are drunk, or have been 'cleaned out,' they are pushed into the street, where they may be stumbled against, asleep on the sidewalk, half in an alley-way, half out, or altogether in the gutter, at all hours of the night. The station house could not hold the quarter of these wretches, thus found every night; consequently, those whose only offence is sleeping on the sidewalk, are generally roused and sent on their way, but no sooner has the officer passed by on his beat, than they lie down again, and sleep till the next patrol comes around, and so pass the remainder of the night in a series of constant alarms. If, however, they resist the officer when told to go home, they are shut up for the night in the station house, and sent to the Island for vagrancy the next morning.

* * * * * * *

"A negro is an *inhabitant* always, but not a *citizen* in New York, nor entitled to a single civic privilege, until he is the possessor of real estate, over and above his just debts, to the amount of $500; consequently, there are very few negro citizens. Until a negro is a citizen he cannot take out a license to drive a hack, a cab, or a cart—consequently we see very few negro drivers, unless in the livery of servitude, on the box of some rich man. A negro inhabitant merely, cannot take out a license of any sort—yet we find hundreds of cellars where negroes, in defiance of the law, sell liquor—liquid fire—without a license. We find no negroes behind stalls in our markets. We find few, or none keeping store. We find none at the carpenter's bench, the blacksmith's forge, the ship yard, the foundry, the printing office—unless we except, indeed, the half-dozen that Frederick Douglass employs in the office of his abolition paper, because he could not get a white printer to work for him. In fact, we find negroes at no employment which is usually followed by white men—consequently the negro, if he works at all, is driven to those menial offices which no white man, who deserves the name—and who could keep himself from starving by doing anything else—would perform. Thus we find the best of them, who boast of their freedom from servitude to Southern masters, voluntarily becoming, for the smallest stipends, slaves in fact to a greater degree than they were while yet in bondage. We do not find them here following the higher branches of labour, as they do in the South. They cannot here till the soil, nor labour in the workshop, but they clean the mud off their white *master's* boots, they rub down their white *master's* horses, they sweep his chimneys, and whitewash his stables, draw his water, and hew his wood, and, in their highest estate, drive his carriage! Can any one inform us in what respect the Northern slave is superior to the Southern?

* * * * * * *

"We have ourselves seen, in a six by eight attic room of a house in Thomas Street, between West Broadway and Hudson Street, two entire negro families, containing thirteen individuals, male, female, young and old, who in that small kennel, with only one window of six panes of glass, ate, drank, slept,—indiscriminately, men and women together,—cooked, washed and ironed (for the women generally help to support the family, by taking in washing), and in fact, transacted all the business of a household. How thirteen individuals could pack themselves to sleep comfortably in a room, six by eight feet, seemed incomprehensible to us, until we saw it done. Not only did they cover the floor, but moveable shelves, which during the day time were let down parallel with the wall by a hinge, were at night time, when the negroes wished to 'turn in,' propped up, and, having a raised edge to keep the inmates from tumbling out,—with the clothes worn by the sleeper during the day thrown on the shelf to make it a little softer than the hard side of a plank,—they declared they had capital accommodations. Table they had none, chairs they had none, but the sleeping shelves, when a table was wanted for eating or ironing, answered every purpose, and the floor, or half a dozen camp stools, that could be shut up and stowed in a small space, answered for the seats.

"A good whitewasher, when business is brisk, can earn from fifty to seventy-five cents a day; but there are some negroes of more enterprise than their fellows, who act as boss whitewashers, and can always have a gang under their control to do any large job that may offer. These bosses are paid by the job, and pay their underlings by the day, taking care to beat them down to the lowest possible farthing.

"The chimney-sweeps are not so fortunate. The poor creatures strike us as being full as miserable as their brethern, the beggars and thieves, even if they are not so wicked. Constantly begrimmed with soot and smoke, and carrying the dirty implements of their work on their shoulders; their clothes—rags rather, for we never saw the sweep who was not ragged—torn, dirty, and hanging in strips; their hats battered, and scarcely hanging together; and their melancholy cry of 'sweep ho, sweep,' as they shuffle through street after street, looking in vain for a job—invest them with the most miserable air, and causes them to appear (in our eye, at least), objects most supremely to be pitied. They live in the cellars of Church Street, York Street, St. John's Lane, and some parts of Thomas Street, and a few of them we have known on the Five Points. Their apartments are like themselves—wretched, dark, dirty, black, and noisome."

The Express also gives an account of the character and habits of those who compose the better class of coloured persons in New York,—the waiters at the hotels, the private servants, &c., and regrets that these form only a small portion of the negroes of that city.

These humiliating facts were given to the public late in 1851, and it is truly hoped that the miserable and humiliating condition of the unfortunate African, thus described, has since been improved in that mighty city. The extracts we have made, it will be admitted, are sufficiently distressing to contemplate; but the reader may be assured that we withhold the darkest part of the frightful picture, because the refined would shrink from it with amazement. Minds unused to the contemplation of such depths of degradation and wretchedness, would experience too deep a thrill of horror.

Of course, there are places where free negro life presents a less degrading aspect than that which is so graphically sketched by the able writer quoted above. But, we say, when the coloured man is freed, let him be sent to his native and appropriate home beyond the waters of the ocean; to those green and fertile shores,

"Where Afric's sunny fountains
Roll down their golden sands."

There only, he may be "free and equal;" there only will he properly appreciate his freedom, and feel independent. Emancipate the slaves, and whether they find a home at the north, south, east, or west, they are, and ever will be, looked upon as an inferior race, and they will be, virtually, the humble menials and dependants of the white man, or worse. It rejoices the heart of their true friends to know, that, under the direction and influence of a great, benevolent, and philanthropic enterprise, noble barks are bearing them on, in large numbers, before the free breezes of heaven, to the land of their fathers, where the light of divine truth, and the comforts and blessings of civilization, may be realized and enjoyed without hindrance or molestation.

With regard to the author of "Uncle Tom's Cabin," and its fallacies, we merely present a few extracts from the views expressed in the "British Army Dispatch," which are in accordance with those of very many reflecting and intelligent men in England, and in the Northern and Eastern sections of the United States, as well as at the South:

"We believe it to be devoid of truth, principles, and reality, and that its tendencies are highly mischievous, and detrimental to the interests of mankind. In saying this, we entirely acquit its author of evil design, wickedness, or intended falsehood.

* * * * * * *

"We say this one-sided representation is creating mischief between Great Britain and the United States, which nothing can remedy, no treatise obviate, no statesmanship avoid."

Of the recent movements of some respectable, though misguided English females, in regard to American slavery, the same able and judicious writer says: "The sickly interference of our fine ladies, many, nay, most of whom would shrink from the contact of a dying needle-woman on their door steps, and daily pass unheeded the miseries of thousands of white women, is an excess of folly and hypocrisy that will be the curse of freedom throughout the world."

It is quite probable, by the way, that such efforts as those alluded to, will have an unintentional and salutary effect upon suffering humanity. Indeed, it appears that such a result has already begun to develope itself. The withering rebukes that have been elicited from various quarters, accompanied with descriptions of wretchedness, woe, starvation, and ignorance, that almost rend the stoutest hearts, are gradually producing a feeling of disgust from every direction for those who have portrayed the hardships of the negroes of the south in terms generally so fanciful and untrue to life. The effect may be to withdraw the public mind from the imaginary sufferings of these, to the real and untold sorrow, woe, and degradation of thousands at the North, and of immense numbers of the whites in England and elsewhere; and the tendency may be to induce the true philanthropist to direct his benevolent efforts towards the alleviation of wrongs and oppressions where they exist to the greatest extent, and in mournful reality.

CHAPTER LVI.

Portsmouth—Further Observations—View from the Norfolk Side—Act of Assembly Establishing the Town—William Crawford—Wooden Chimneys—Directors and Trustees—Advancement—Plan of the Town—Streets—Buildings—Sociality, Hospitality, &c.—Portsmouth in 1806—Trade with the West Indies—Advantages—Navy Yard—Dismal Swamp Canal—Intercourse—Bridges—Wharves—Merchants—Population—Houses—National Establishment—Improvements—Mayor and Council—Description of the Site, &c.—Harbour—Why the Town has not Advanced more Rapidly—English and Scotch Merchants—Revolutionary Spirit—Gosport Iron Works—Management—Position—Capacity, &c.

It has, of course, been observed that, in the preceding remarks, frequent allusion is made to Portsmouth, to which much of what has been said with regard to Norfolk applies with equal force. But the reader's attention will now be invited to some further observations, more particularly relative to the sister town over the water, standing there on the opposite shore, and presenting quite an agreeable view from the Norfolk side, stretching along the banks of the main stream, and extending for some distance around on the southern branch.

Portsmouth was established a town by Act of Assembly, in February, 1752,* on the land of Wm. Crawford; and in 1763, the limits of the town were extended, by adding the lands of Mr. Veale.

The following Act was passed by the General Assembly, held at the College in Williamsburg, in February, 1752, in the 25th year of the reign of George II., "of Great Britain, France, and Ireland, King, Defender of the Faith," &c.

"An Act for establishing the town of Portsmouth, in the County of Norfolk, and to prevent the building of wooden chimneys therein.

I. "Whereas it hath been represented to this Assembly, that William Crawford, of the County of Norfolk, gentleman, hath lately laid out a parcel of land, on the south side of Elizabeth River, opposite to the town of Norfolk, into one hundred and twenty-two lots, commodious streets, places for a court-house, market, and public landings, for a town, by the name of Portsmouth, and made sale of most of the said lots, to divers persons who are desirous to settle and build thereon speedily; and also that the said town lies very convenient for trade and navigation:

"II. Be it enacted, by the Lieutenant-Governor, Council, and Burgesses of this present General Assembly, and it is hereby enacted by the authority of the same, That the said piece or parcel of land be, and is hereby constituted, appointed, erected, and established, a town, in the manner it is already laid out, by the said William Crawford, in lots and streets, to be called by, and retain the name of Portsmouth, and that the freeholders of the said town shall, for ever hereafter, enjoy the same rights and privileges which the freeholders of any other towns, erected by Act of Assembly, in this colony, have and enjoy.

"III. And be it further enacted by the authority aforesaid, That it will not be lawful for any person whatsoever, to erect or build, or cause to be erected or built, in the said town, any

* The precise day on which the law passed is not positively known. It is supposed that the enactment took place on the 22d day of February, 1752; or, as some have it, on the 11th of February, 1752, old style, which time is equal to the same period. But Portsmouth became a town, actually under the new style.

wooden chimney; and if any person shall presume to erect, or build any wooden chimney, contrary to the directions of this Act, it shall and may be lawful for the sheriff of the said county, and he is hereby required to cause such chimney to be pulled down and demolished."

The following is an extract from an Act passed in May, 1763, eleven years after the institution of the town, by which the first Board of Directors and Trustees were constituted and appointed, and their powers defined.

"And be it further enacted by the authority aforesaid, That Andrew Sprowle, George Veal, Thomas Veal, Charles Steuart, Humphry Roberts, Francis Miller, James Rae, David Purcell, and Amos Etheridge, gentlemen, shall be, and they are hereby nominated, constituted, and appointed, directors and trustees of the said town; and they, or any five of them, shall and may, and they are hereby authorized and empowered, to survey and lay off the said adjacent lands into lots and streets, and to make from time to time such orders, rules, and directions, for the regular and orderly placing and building the houses in the said town as to them shall seem expedient; and that in case of the death, removal out of the country, or other legal disability, of any one or more of the directors and trustees before named, it shall and may be lawful for the surviving or remaining trustees to elect and choose so many other persons in the room of those so dead or disabled as shall make up the number of nine; which trustees so chosen shall, to all intents and purposes, be vested with the same power as any other in this Act particularly nominated and appointed."

The growth of the place, like that of Norfolk, has been gradual; its prosperity sometimes very apparent and rapid, and again almost at a stand, if at all perceptible. The town is regularly laid off in squares. The streets (forty in number), cross at right angles, lying about east and west, and north and south. Many of the thoroughfares are very wide; affording ample space for carriages, drays, &c. There are several handsome and commodious public edifices, including the Town Hall (a description of which has already been given), Oxford Hall, eight handsome churches, a bank, Masonic and Odd-Fellows' Lodges, &c. There are also many fine and commodious stores and private dwellings, a number having been built during the past year.

The inhabitants of Portsmouth have long been noted for their animated sociability, hospitality, and public spirit. "The population embraces men of great worth of character, good judgment, sound discretion, native talent, and enlightened experience. Many worthy descendants of worthy sires survive to grace the places which they have vacated."

"In noticing Portsmouth," said Mr. Simmons, in his Norfolk Directory, published in 1806, "which is situated opposite to Norfolk, much cannot be said of its commercial relations, in a distinct respect; the business of both places being, in a great degree, connected. It, however, carries on no inconsiderable trade, chiefly to the Antilles, and has several square-rigged and other vessels belonging to the port. In addition to its natural advantages, which are equal to those of Norfolk, it has of late acquired some collateral benefits, to wit: the establishment of a Navy Yard at Gosport, the removal of the County Court to the town, the opening of the Dismal Swamp Canal, and the erection of good drawbridges over both branches of the river, which facilitate an intercourse with Norfolk much more than the ferry: —these may certainly be esteemed acquisitions. Yet a more important advantage will be derived from the improvements now making on the wharves and wharf-lots, both by its own merchants and some opulent ones of Norfolk. This town (Portsmouth) is said to have contained, ten years ago (1796), three hundred houses, and seventeen hundred inhabitants; at present (1806), there are about seven hundred houses and three thousand inhabitants. The advantages and improvements of Portsmouth promise, though not a rivalship with its sister town, a reasonable hope of its rise and advancement from its former comparatively non-important state."

Portsmouth includes Gosport and Newtown, about a quarter of a mile distant on the south, and connected by a causeway and bridges. At the great national establishment at Gosport, a large number of men, varying from twelve to fifteen hundred, find employment, much the greater portion of whom, with their families, reside in Portsmouth. They receive their pay in gold, semi-monthly, and, as a matter of course, circulate a large amount in the town for supplies of every description; although Norfolk comes in for her share in the general distribution.

The spirit of improvement is getting abroad afresh in Portsmouth, as well as in Norfolk; and it is believed that when the Seaboard and Roanoke Railroad, shall be connected with other great works of internal improvement, already progressing, and when these shall be completed, this pleasant and agreeable town will, in common with Norfolk, grow with astonishing rapidity.

There are two well-edited daily papers in Portsmouth; the Transcript, by D. D. Fisk, Esq., and the Democrat, by H. E. Orr, Esq.

On the 3d of April, 1852, the voters of Portsmouth, according to Act of Assembly, elected a Mayor and Common Council. John S. White, Esq., was duly chosen mayor or chief magistrate of the town, and the following gentlemen were elected Councilmen: Wm. R. Woodend, Chas. L. Cocke, Thos. Moran, Wm. H. H. Hodges, R. A. J. Thompson, Harrison Ferebee, John Vermillion, H. J. Phillips, John Lash, Caleb Nash, Collin Reynolds, John L. Porter, and Wm. D. Schoolfield.

Mr. John L. Porter was chosen President.

The site of Portsmouth was admirably planned, and is well suited to answer all the requirements of an extensive and flourishing commercial city; and some of the citizens insist that it was intended to be what Norfolk now is, and much greater, in wealth and importance. Portsmouth has the advantage in regard to the width and regularity of the streets, and is upon the better side of the river, in some respects; although the Norfolk side, perhaps, affords to the shipping greater security and shelter from storms, and it is more comfortable and agreeable for landing and discharging cargoes, especially in the winter season.

It is surprising to some persons, that Portsmouth should not have advanced rapidly after the Revolution, and continued greatly in the ascendency; having had, for six or seven years, no rival on the opposite side of the river; Norfolk having been destroyed by fire. But the improvement and rapid increase of the former place were prevented by some of its injudicious, though zealous

28

and patriotic, residents. At the time of the destruction of Norfolk, there were not a few commission-merchants and agents from England, Scotland, &c., extensively engaged in shipping and commerce in the borough. Many of these desired to re-commence business, and settle in Portsmouth. In this, however, they were sadly disappointed, having met with great opposition from some of the most influential citizens, whose enthusiastic Revolutionary spirit and inveterate hatred for the tories were exceedingly unfavourable to commercial operations by persons whose political sentiments were not known to be in strict accordance with their own. Some of the Scotch and English factors and traders, on visiting the town, were treated very repulsively, and even required to leave at short notice. Of course, it was greatly to the interest of the proprietors of the lots on the Norfolk side to offer facilities to those who desired to re-engage in commercial pursuits; and the spirit of opposition not having been so rabid on this side of the water as to destroy all regard to personal interest, Norfolk soon began to rise from its ruins, and at length acquired the ascendency over Portsmouth in point of wealth, population, and commercial facilities, which she has steadily maintained to the present day.

The GOSPORT IRON WORKS, A. Mehaffey, Esq., Proprietor, is an important acquisition to Portsmouth and Gosport, and, indeed, to this section of Virginia. This establishment, though already noticed in this work, claims a further allusion. It is very extensive, and is conducted in a most judicious and liberal manner. All kinds of iron machinery are finished here in the most beautiful style. Steam engines, from a small size to the largest, most ponderous, and powerful; castings of every description, in iron, brass, copper, and lead; and every variety of rough and polished work, wrought or cast, of beautiful workmanship, and astonishing accuracy, neatness, and durability, are all furnished with great despatch at these works. From two to three hundred men are employed, and the probability is, that a larger number will be required. The position was very judiciously chosen, and the establishment must attract an immense quantity of work and be well sustained. The generous and gentlemanly spirit which characterizes the conductors of this extensive concern, is often spoken of in terms of great commendation, and constitutes one of the surest elements of its prosperity. The great engine of the Powhatan, as before mentioned, and other heavy machinery for the U. S. Government, requiring ripe judgment, extensive experience, and great ingenuity, as well as mathematical accuracy and correctness, were constructed at these Iron Works; and other extensive contracts are now in progress.

CHAPTER LVII.

Falls of Niagara—Natural Bridge—Laurel Hill, Harper's Ferry, &c.—Want of Curiosity and Interest—Objects of Attraction—Dry Dock—Old Point, Hampton, &c.—Seashore—Rivers—Farms, Lands, Flowers, Birds, &c.—The Chesapeake—Princess Anne—Kempsville—Digressions—The Ocean—Roads—London Bridge—Bridge over the Thames—Reminiscences—Legends—Romance—Branch of the Lynnhaven—Random Lines—Nature's Music—The Songsters of the Field and the Grove—Nature's Harmony—Grave-Yard—Trees—Current—Associations and Recollections of Youth—Local Attachments.

It has been stated that there are persons living within a few miles of the Falls of Niagara who have heard, for many years, the deep, continuous thunders of that stupendous cataract, and yet, who have never been sufficiently moved by curiosity to visit that sublime work of nature! There are persons living but a short distance from the Natural Bridge in Virginia, who have never gazed in wonder and awe at that splendid exhibition of Nature's masonry, its immovable parapet of rocks—its gigantic arch, thrown by the God of nature across the wild and awful chasm, reaching full fifty-five feet higher than the Falls of Niagara, than which it is still more an object of profound, inexpressible wonder. And so also it may be said of those residing near Laurel Hill, and the "river of beauty," and Harper's Ferry, that grand and exciting scene, and a thousand other splendid exhibitions of nature, besides the numerous magnificent works of art in the country. There are individuals living near them, who, for lack of interest in them, for want of curiosity, or from some trifling cause, will not enjoy a view calculated at once to enlighten and elevate the mind, give to man correct notions of himself, inspire him with humility, and direct his thoughts above, to Nature's Author, the infinitely good and wise Creator and Benefactor. These remarks are applicable to individuals residing in Norfolk, Portsmouth, and neighbourhood. There are many here who have never visited the various interesting and attractive points in the vicinity of the place of their nativity. There are some who know but little of them, while others are scarely aware of their existence.

There is a gentleman, with some pretensions to intelligence, who has been a resident of this city and vicinity for more than twenty years, and who has travelled considerably on business, but who has never been up James River, who has never visited the beautiful village of Smithfield, who has never seen the singular fortification of the Rip Raps or Fort Calhoun, who has seen the healthful and hospitable town of Hampton but twice, and who has never seen Lake Drummond; and doubtless there are others to whom the same remarks may apply. There are intelligent ladies, long since upon the shady side of forty, who were born and reared here, who have never seen that strong, extensive, and beautiful piece of masonry, the Dry Dock, and other extensive works of art at the U. S. Dock Yard, on the opposite side of the river; and doubtless there are others, of either sex, of whom the same may be said. Some have never been to Old Point, or witnessed the splendid and soul-inspiring scenery of the sea-shore; while others have scarcely ever crossed the Elizabeth. How many there are who have never made an excursion up the western, southern, or eastern branch of this wide river; who know but little of the general appearance of the country, the farms and farm-houses, the forest trees, and luxuriant undergrowth, the meandering water-courses, the timbered lands, the swamps, the reptiles, the wild flowers, and the singing birds! But few, comparatively, are aware that "our woods and fields are full of wild flowers of every colour and shade; some of which are splendid in appearance, and would adorn the finest garden, and that an excellent herbarium might be formed, with only that amount of trouble which would produce recreation." How few, comparatively, have, upon some bright morning in spring or summer, taken a pleasant ride from the noise and bustle of the city in a northerly direction, down the Sewell's Point Road to the charming shores of the bold, capacious, and picturesque Chesapeake, or taking an easterly course down the Princess Anne Road, crossing the level piece of land embraced in the eastern portion of Norfolk County, thence on in the former county through the pleasant and hospitable little village of Kempsville, ten miles from the city, at the head of the eastern branch,* and still on towards the ocean. We propose to conduct the reader, in imagination, along this route, and if we should linger, as it were, and recount a few incidents of the past, in connexion with some localities on the way, we bespeak his clemency for the digression.

The Atlantic Ocean, that object of surpassing interest, is approachable from Kempsville by two different roads, and by another about a mile below that village. Perhaps the most pleasant, though not the shortest route, is that in the direction of the old Eastern Shore Chapel. Six miles from Kempsville, by this road, is London Bridge. Ten or twelve farm-houses, within a range of half a mile, together with a store, post-office, sawmill, &c., in the immediate vicinity of the bridge, entitle this pleasant location to the name of village, as it is sometimes denominated.

The thoughtful traveller, when he arrives at the bridge, will be reminded, though only by name and contrast, of the gigantic structures of iron and stone, that span the Thames at London, whose tremendous arches, and deep-laid foundations of solid masonry, defy the utmost force of the swollen current, and re-

* The Legislature granted a charter for a canal to connect the head waters of the western branch of the Lynnhaven and the eastern branch of Elizabeth River at Kempsville.

"This little legislative lift of internal improvement in the tidewater region was put in for by the worthy delegate of Princess Anne, James S. Garrison, Esq., and the estimated cost being only $12,500, the legislature most magnanimously admitted the reasonableness of the application, and passed Mr. G.'s bill, with the usual provision of a three-fifths subscription by the State. The canal cannot exceed a mile in length, while important advantages will accrue from it in the transportation to the Norfolk market of valuable timber and immense quantities of fire-wood, for steam as well as domestic purposes, heretofore too remote for overland conveyance; and it will, no doubt, lead to important results by the extension of the traffic in those celebrated bivalves of the waters of Lynnhaven, so highly and universally esteemed for their incomparable flavour and relish."

A survey was made by Mr. J. Williston, a skilful engineer of Norfolk, who estimated the cost at $27,000, and the work, it is thought, will be indefinitely postponed.

main uninjured by the convulsions of nature, or the ravages of Time's noiseless hand, while thousands, and tens of thousands, of the busy populace of England's wondrous city, cross and recross by day and by night.

The bridge is built over a narrow stream, that winds along its serpentine course northwardly about five miles, to the quiet and beautiful Lynnhaven, and mingles its swampy waters with those of that picturesque river, or exchanges them for the clear, briny fluid of the capacious Chesapeake.*

Connected with the village of London Bridge, we remark, by the way, are many old reminiscences—

> "Old remembrances of days,
> When on the glittering dews of orient life,
> Shone sunshine hopes;"

and some familiar, though unpleasant, legends,—ay! and touching romances in real life,—engraven too deeply upon the writer's mind ever to be obliterated, and to which he is somewhat inclined to allude here. They may not, however, justly claim the reader's attention now; and yet longer let them remain, therefore, among the unrecorded, though well-remembered events of the past.

> Here mem'ry still is wont to dwell,
> And gather up the words that fell
> In tones of kindness, joy, and love,
> From those who now are safe above.
> Here fancy still delights to rove
> In flow'ry dell and vocal grove,
> Where oft at early morn was heard
> The varied song of the mocking-bird;
> Where sung at night the whip-poor-will
> Among the trees "upon the hill;"*
> While softly fell the moon's pale beam,
> Reflected by that flowing stream.

---

* London Bridge Creek, or Lynnhaven Creek, as it is sometimes called, has a shoal, or mud-flat, two or three miles below the bridge. If this place were dredged, which is quite practicable, vessels of small size could go up to the bridge.

* More properly the banks of the stream; but "on the hill," "up the hill," "down the hill," &c., were familiar expressions, in other days, at this locality.

The same tall pines on the old hill's verge
Sing on their mournful funeral dirge.
For ages yet may those old trees
Repeat the music of the breeze;
Withstanding all the tempest's might,
The light'ning's pow'r, the insects' blight,
And lift their heads, both green and tall,
'Till Nature's God shall bid them fall!

The same old spring just "down the hill,"
Now overflows and bubbles still
In summer morning's balmy air,
In noontide heat, or evening fair,
While Night's mild queen looks through the trees
That rustle to the evening breeze,
You still may go the cup to fill,
From that old spring below the hill,
With water sweet, and cool, and clear,
That overflows and bubbles there.

The same old stream pursues its course,
Nor loses yet its wonted force;
The winding of that stream appears
As graceful as in other years;
Its briny waters ebb and flow,
And rise and fall as years ago,
When anglers, who lie cold and still
Beneath the sod "upon the hill,"
So often from those waters drew
The flutt'ring perch in the old canoe.

There yet the wild-duck feeds, and plays,
And looks around, with cautious gaze;
And there she lifts her beauteous wing,
And soars away, the timid thing.
There stands the heron, grave and still,
And watches long his crop to fill;
There yet the blackbird's soothing song
Trembles the sedgy shore along;
And there the child still runs to see
His tiny boat ride gracefully
The rippling wave, before the breeze
That murmurs through those green old trees.

'Tis pleasant still on summer day,
Down that old stream to sail away
To old Lynnhaven's beauteous bay,
Where wind and water hold their sway,

And hear the music of the sea
Resounding softly o'er the lea;
And watch the sea-gull sailing slow,
And sailing swiftly, high and low,
Now screaming loudly in the breeze,
Her voice commingling with the seas;
Then, with a plunge, surprise her prey,
And rise triumphant from the spray.
'Tis charming still upon the shore,
To hear the sea's deep, constant roar;
The birds, the waves, the air, the breeze,
Harmonious join, the mind to please.

But upon the green banks of that gracefully winding tide-water current, we may linger awhile, at least in imagination. Here we would stop and listen to the solemn, familiar music of the viewless breeze; to the sudden flutter of the silvery perch, as it bounds in the sunshine; to the plaintive voice, the low, tremulous call of the turtle-dove, "floating at intervals through the shivering foliage, the very soul of sound and tenderness;" the sharp whistle of the partridge; the shrill cry of the king-fisher, as he darts with unerring aim upon his prey; the soft, rich, and lively song of the black-bird, as he rides, delighted, upon a pendulous branch by the margin, and just over the ripples of the flowing stream, imitable only by the high-spirited mocking-bird, whose notes, varied, astonishing, and unequalled, ring out clearly and merrily from the grove,* and the sweet carol of the lark "warbling upon the wind, raising its note as it soars."

* "The powers of imitation of these birds have not certainly been overrated. When in the right humour they will imitate all sorts of sounds, even to the crowing of a cock. If they do not succeed well the first time, they will repeat the effort, always gaining in correctness, until they master the subject—sometimes with exact truth, sometimes failing to render the notes perfectly.

"But it is as *composers*, not as *imitators*, that the mocking-birds most command our admiration. There appears to be no end to their powers of combination. There is a variety and strange contrast in their song, that would be sought for in vain in any of the sounds presented for their imitation. Sometimes they will begin low down on the scale, working up the gamut, stopping here and there to throw off ad libitum variations, then starting again, always ascending and repeating the same process. Sometimes they begin at the top of their scale and descend in like manner. At one moment they will touch a

"Ethereal minstrel! pilgrim of the sky!
Dost thou despise the earth, where cares abound?
Or while thy wings aspire, are heart and eye
Both with thy nest upon the dewy ground?
Thy nest, which thou canst drop into at will,
Those quivering wings composed, that music still."

"Nature, daughter of the Eternal, whatever may be the jarring of man's evil propensities, thou hast no discord—thy

note, repeat it several times with a greater or less degree of emphasis, and then they will flat or sharp the same note after the same manner.

"It would require the pen of a good musical composer to trace out in a faithful description, all the phases of their song. We have often followed out forty or fifty different arrangements. Within this limit (that of our memory) we could pronounce with certainty, that the same song had not been repeated. We are persuaded that there is scarcely any limit to their combination. The lark, doubtless, surpasses them in the gushing joyousness of his note—the thrush, nightingale, and perhaps other birds, in liquid sweetness. But in the variety and combination of notes, in compass, and flexibility, and marvellous facility of execution, the mocking-bird bears away the palm. Nature furnishes in the feathered tribe, voices of all descriptions that—

'Warble their wood-notes wild,'

and by way of an excusable simile, they may be said to resemble in their peculiar characters those of certain *prima donnas*. The mocking-bird, like the matchless Catalani, unites all styles, with a compass that comprehends every note, from the purest soprano down to the deepest contralto. The bird is aptly named, and its voice is wisely adjusted to its task. With sweetness alone, it would be unable to render its great variety of intonations.

"Its prelude is to rise slowly with expanded wings, and sink back to the same spot, its head hanging downwards. Its action now corresponds with the varied notes of its music. If the notes are brisk and lively, it describes in the air a number of circles, crossing each other, or it ascends and descends in a spiral line. If they are loud and rapid, it, with equal briskness flaps its wings. Is its song unequal, it flutters, it bounds; do its tones soften by degrees, melt into tender strains, and die away, in a pause more charming than the sweetest muse, it gently diminishes its action, and glides smoothly above its resting-place."

"I sing! I sing! in the leafy bower,
At the dawning blush of morn,
When dew-drops gem each open flower,
And another day is born.
And my carol of joy is so light and free,
As I sit embowered in the old oak tree,
That the forest is full of my echoed glee."

realm for ever resounds with lofty melodies, which come to the heart, amid the battle of contending passions, like music amid the pauses of the storm." Here we would ramble awhile, among these old cedars, "moaning to the blast," and these

> "Thundering pines,
> That bend reluctant to the tempest's wing."

"whose branches sometimes become mighty harp-strings, which, smitten by the rushing tempest, send forth grand and incessant harmonies, now anthems, and anon dirges." And when the sky is clear, and the beams of the summer morning's sun have banished the darkness of the night, they cast their shade over a sacred and secluded spot, where lie the mouldering earthly remains of some of the "loved and loving," awaiting that solemn day of reckoning, on which "the trumpet shall sound and the dead shall be raised."

Until the ushering in of that day of days, let the music of Nature be heard in that quiet little nook; the winds their solemn dirges and mournful ditties sing by day and by night; the feathered songsters of the grove, at each returning spring-time, renew their songs of innocence and joy; the gentle wild flowers burst forth and blush in beauty still. Let those old trees be spared, and over that spot their daily shadows throw; and the winding current, with its graceful curves, continue its alternate journeys—passing out to the deep estuaries of old Ocean, and returning again; adding another feature of interest to the scene, till the rapid stream of time itself shall be ultimately and irrevocably lost in the great ocean of eternity.

How tenaciously do some minds cling to the recollections of childhood and youth! How vividly and indelibly are the gay scenes of early days, long past and gone, painted upon memory's tablet! Every meandering, rippling stream, and grassy hill, and favourite haunt of childhood's sunny hours; old trees with their gnarled branches, and every winding pathway through the dense and shady wood,—all these are still to be seen by the mind's eye, as they, in their turn, come up in the imagination. We dream, too, of the music of the grove, the melancholy murmurs of the wind, and see again, as it were, the works of nature as we saw them in their brightness and beauty in other days, ere affliction and corroding care had left their blighting effects upon the heart. And alas! how plainly too are the scenes of sorrow, and the melancholy occurrences which occasionally darkened the bright prospect, pictured on the mind, never to be obliterated!

Restless and anxious, man may wander far from the scenes and friends of his youth; but "there's no place like (his early) home." It is not in the power of time nor distance to sever the tie of fondness, or to erase the indelible marks made upon the young mind by the events of early life.

"There are some persons," observes a certain writer, "who affect to disparage local attachments—that singular and almost inexplicable affection for a particular spot of ground—and, foremost among these, is the brilliant but sophistical Bolingbroke, in his celebrated Reflections on Exile. But, for my part, I have never been able to yield to that cold-blooded, heartless, and palsying philosophy which would sacrifice the generous instinct of feeling to a beggarly calculation of a profit and loss account. I acknowledge the depth and sincerity of local affections."

CHAPTER LVIII.

Incidents of Other Days—Gentleman Waylaid—Desperate Conflict with the Highwaymen—The Criminals and the Death Penalty—The Old Store—Unfortunate Inebriate—Notorious Josiah Phillips—Mingo—Capture and Trial of the Outlaw—Sentenced to the Penitentiary—Shot on the Road to Norfolk—Baptist Church—Preacher—Old School-house—Teaching—Public Schools—Martin Luther on Education—Lynnhaven Bay, &c. — Old Eastern Shore Chapel—Oaks—Old School-house—Events of the Past—Schoolboy Days—Faithful School-master—Scholars—Variety of Talent, Occupation, &c.—Premature Deaths—Early Associations—Great Parting Frolic.

Before we proceed farther on our journey, we will detain the reader still longer, by the relation of some incidents that happened at this place in other days.

On a pleasant and beautiful morning, more than twenty-five

years ago, as the daylight entered the window of a small room under the moss-covered roof of a certain time-honoured farm-house, a stranger might have been seen, calmly and quietly reposing in the embrace of "tired nature's sweet restorer." But there was blood upon his face, and upon the bed! and this plainly revealed the fact, that wounds had been inflicted upon his person. The stranger was a young man of respectability, who had left Norfolk the evening before on a visit to the residence of a friend, to witness and join in celebrating the alliance of one of Eve's fair daughters with the man of her choice. When nearly at the close of his pleasant journey, he passed an old shanty at London Bridge, where rum was sold, and his appearance attracted the attention of two stout negro men, who, nerved by strong drink to desperate, dark, and bloody deeds, planned an attack upon him. Being of a bold and fearless disposition, his only weapon was a penknife. While quietly pursuing his way, the rascals approached him, and one, with a rail taken from a fence, struck him down from his horse. Not having been seriously disabled, however, by the blow, and being a man of much activity and strength of nerve, he was not entirely unprepared for the villains, and a terrible scuffle ensued. Strange to say, he was not even seriously wounded, and succeeded in driving off the robbers, who took with them his saddle-bags, which contained, perhaps, but little more than a change of clothing. His principal misfortune was, his failure to attend the wedding.

The men were arrested, convicted of the crime, sentenced to be hung, and were executed. The youngest (whose name was George, the property of an esteemed citizen of Norfolk), a valuable fellow, in some respects, and rendered credulous, no doubt, by the effects of liquor, was a victim to the daring villany of the other. He finally acknowledged his participation in the deed, admitted the reasonableness of severe punishment, but was horror-struck at the sentence of death, and pleaded earnestly for his life. He became penitent, and before he was "swung off," appeared to have overcome the fear of death.

Jim, the elder partner in the affair, several times escaped from confinement, but was also executed, some months after the death of the other. He manifested no signs of a preparation for his ignominious end, and was apparently ushered into eternity without the pardon of his accumulated crimes.

These two unfortunate men lived in the immediate vicinity of the old grocery. They were there, and, no doubt, under the influence of liquor on the night of the commission of the iniquitous deed; and perhaps the death-penalty was wisely inflicted to deter others from such daring attempts upon life and property, as it appeared to have a salutary influence upon the coloured population of the county.

We shall briefly allude to another circumstance, which we can never forget, and which deeply impressed our mind with the dangerous consequences often attending the use of intoxicating liquors.

> "It was an eve of autumn's holiest mood,
> And all the winds slept soundly—
> Now and then the aged leaf
> Fell from its fellows, rustling to the ground,
> And as it fell, bade man think on his end."

All was still—scarcely a sound arose to break the deep silence which reigned around, save perhaps the low melancholy murmuring of distant thunder, announcing the approach of a gathering storm-cloud in the west. Suddenly, however, the "loud ascending" voice of an unfortunate inebriate was heard in the distance, and then it grew louder, and as he came nearer, the wild scream, at the highest pitch of his voice, resounded in every direction, while the rapid tramp of the horse on which he rode, but too plainly told the danger of his situation.

On the bridge above named, his horse fell, while running, and the wild screech of agony which immediately succeeded the roar of revelry, was caused by the breaking and mangling of one of his limbs in a frightful manner.

We could present the reader with many particulars relative to the notorious and outrageous Josiah Phillips, and his banditti, whose depredations on life and property spread terror and consternation in some parts of Norfolk and Princess Anne Counties, in Revolutionary times; and to the murderous Mingo, of a later period, a free negro, who, after the commission of many a heinous crime and deed of blood, and after eluding for many months the vigilance of his pursuers, was finally surprised and taken in his bed at night, while asleep (his gun within his reach), imprisoned, convicted, and sentenced—to the *penitentiary!* Of course, the people of Princess Anne were dissatisfied with this astonishing result of his trial, produced by the wonderful power of forensic eloquence. A well-devised and successful plan was promptly formed to shoot him on the road, while being conveyed to Norfolk for transportation to the State Prison at Richmond; and the soul of the hardened criminal was accordingly hurried into eternity, probably without a moment's warning, and his body unceremoniously deposited in a hole hastily dug by the roadside, about seven miles from the city. And we could tell of other unpleasant and dreadful occurrences, that might interest the minds of some, but we forbear.

Leaving the bridge, and passing on in a northeasterly direction, about the space of an eighth of a mile, we arrive at the London Bridge Baptist Church, in its pleasant location on the west side of the road, in which has been delivered many an eloquent and faithful sermon, and with which is pleasingly associated, among others, the name of the intelligent and modest Smith Sherwood; for several years its devoted pastor, prior to 1830. This church (which is situated with the side instead of the end towards the road) has recently been put in good order, by its members, who have the religious ascendency in this part of the county.

Here, too, is the contracted and now dilapidated and deserted old school-house, in which many have learned, by sad and painful experience, the difference between two governing principles in school-teaching, viz.: the fear of the rod, and patient instruction encouraged by kind words and mild reproof—except in obstinate cases.

We should not fail to remark, that one of the most gratifying and encouraging sights to be seen, in passing through this country, is the numerous public school-houses that are dispersed throughout its length and breadth. The common school system, which was but recently put in operation here, met with considerable opposition by the voters; but it is now considered as permanently established. How sure it is that it will work to the incalculable advantage of almost every interest of the community;—and how certain that a much more pleasing state of affairs would now be presented, had these free schools been introduced fifty years ago!

A judicious system of public schools has also been introduced in Norfolk County, including Portsmouth. There has been much talk and newspaper discussion on the subject of establishing them in the City of Norfolk. But all to no effect, as yet.

"The prosperity of a town," said Martin Luther, addressing the magistrates of Wittemberg, on the subject of education, "does not consist in amassing wealth, erecting walls, building mansions, and the possession of arms. If attacked by a party of madmen, its ruin and devastation would only be the more terrible. The true well-being of a town—its security, its strength—is to number within it many *learned*, *serious*, *kind*, *and well-educated citizens*."

Proceeding a short distance farther, we may wheel off to the left, taking the route that leads to Lynnhaven Bay and River, so long and justly celebrated for superior fish, oysters, and wild-fowl; and Broad Bay, Linkhorn Bay, Long Creek, the Desert, &c.; or, from London Bridge, we may take a northerly and easterly course, passing the old chapel two miles below, with its thick walls, sharp roof, arched windows and doors; and its fit companions in age, those gigantic oaks, standing in their pride, lifting their tall heads high in air, and reaching out their long and green-clad arms afar, as if to guard the old structure from desecration.

The old school-house has long since disappeared; but could those old trees relate the events of the past, now fading fast away in the dim distance, but still occupying their place on memory's altar, and preserving their identity among the rest in the unfathomed depths of eternity's great ocean, they might tell of

"Childish games and school-boy feats,
And youth's gay sports, and earnest vows of love,
Uttered when passion's boisterous tide ran high;
Sincerely uttered, though but seldom kept."

And of the diligent instructions, strict discipline, kind persuasion, ay, and severe corrections, too, of a well-known man of books,* who had been there—the critic, the scholar, who lives to see some of those who feared him, but who, perhaps, rarely hated him, engaged in the grave and complicated pursuits of manhood.

But where are they *all?*—where *now* are those who were *then* gay and light-hearted school-boys and school-girls, elated with the brightest hopes of the future? Some of them, but very few reside in Norfolk; others remain still amid the rural charms of their native county; others are in distant lands; some are careering upon the surging billows of old Ocean, and battling manfully with the wild fury of the howling storm-spirit, to sustain our national honour or to enrich our shores. Their chosen vocations in life were various, as were their talents and dispositions. Some have been, and still are, prosperous and happy—others unsuccessful and unhappy. The roseate blush upon the full cheek of beauty has faded; the vivacity of youth has given place to the gravity of manhood. Many have passed away. The ungentle winds of misfortune blew upon some, and, unable to contend long with their blighting influences, they withered and fell. Of the number, some of the strongest have fallen—early and prematurely fallen—beneath the stroke of death, and have long slumbered in the silence of the grave. The minds of those who now live, and whose eyes may trace these lines, will be involuntarily and irresistibly carried back to the sunny days of youth, and how many associations will be recalled! They need not to be reminded of a thousand interesting occurrences, among which was the last meeting we all had with that eccentric teacher; that great feast, which he provided for his scholars; the sports, the games, the revelling, the noise, the waste of gunpowder, devouring of turkeys, fruit, sweetmeats, and cakes; in short, that great parting frolic at the old Eastern Shore Seminary.

* William Roberts, Esq., formerly an accomplished instructor of youth; subsequently representative from Princess Anne County in the General Assembly, and now a magistrate and skilful farmer of said county.

CHAPTER LIX.

The Ocean Shore—Sublime Scene—The Music of the Sea—The Minor Key—*Miserere*—The Sea in a Calm—Its Power and Immensity—The Ocean in a Storm—The Mountain Waves—Spirits of the Deep Riding on the Billows and Howling in the Foam—The Sea Personified—Mariners—Dangers—Perils of Ocean—The View from the Land—Sublimity of the Scenery—A Ship at Sea—Becalmed—A Storm-cloud Rises—Wind and Ocean at War—The Ship and Passengers in Danger—The Ship Engulphed—The Calm—Height, Velocity, and Force of the Waves—Distance from Each Other—Irresistible Strength—Influence of the Sight—Beautiful Extract—The Sandy and Wave-beaten Shore—Reflection of the Light—Sun and Moon—Fiery, Sparkling Gems—Mountain Scenery—The Boundless Deep.

We will travel on, now, to the shore of the blue and boundless ocean, of which, how grand, how truly sublime, how extensive is the scene! Leaving the main road, and passing below the wooded lands, the wide, immense, and almost immeasurable expanse of the ever-rolling waters, with the beauteous azure vault reaching down and embracing the troubled surface of the deep, fills the soul with wonder and admiration.

"It is the sea, it is the sea,
In all its vague immensity,
Fading and darkening in the distance!
Silent, majestical, and slow,
The white ships haunt it to and fro,
With all their ghostly sails unfurled;
As phantoms from another world
Haunt the dim confines of existence!"

You pass down a gentle declivity, crossing a narrow tract of loose, coarse sand; and as you approach the agitated waters that roar and roll before you, stretching far, far away, and hear the music of the waves, and the shrill cry of the sea-bird as she "stoops to lave her wing in the cooling flood," the mind becomes wholly occupied with the extent, grandeur, and beauty of the scene. Descending below "high water mark," and standing upon the sandy surface, beaten hard and smooth by the billows, the beholder looks out with straining eyes, "far as sight can

29

pierce;" the heart beats with emotion, and a strange, overpowering, indescribable feeling comes over the soul.

> "Great Ocean! strongest of creation's sons,
> Unconquerable, unreposed, untired,
> That roll'dst the wild, profound, eternal bass,
> In nature's anthem, and made music, such
> As pleased the ear of God!"

Who can listen without interest to the loud, rumbling noise of the surges as they roll along in their power, and lash the sandy shore! At a distance it is a murmuring, broken, half-melancholy sound.

> "Lonely and wildly it rose,
> That strain of solemn music from the sea,
> As though the night air trembled to disclose
> An ocean mystery.
> Once more the gush of sound,
> Struggling and swelling from the heaving plain,
> Thrilled a rich peal triumphantly around,
> And fled again."

Upon the beach it is a loud, continuous roar, and "sometimes the waves of the ocean respond, like white-robed choristers, to the thunder bass of the sky, and so make creation's grand oratorio."

> "Shout to the Lord, ye surging seas,
> In your eternal roar;
> Let wave to wave resound his praise,
> And shore reply to shore!"

"The noise of the waves is in the minor key, plaintive, sad. This is creation itself, giving proof of the Apostle's assertion, 'All creation groaneth and travaileth in pain together.' She feels that the curse is on her, cold and heavy on her heart; and longing for deliverance, she gives utterance to her ceaseless, deep, and heart-rending *miserere*. And she will continue to do so until the Lord bid her assume the major key, and himself give the key-note; and then the spheres above, and the redeemed hearts and retuned voices will raise everlasting hallelujahs."

"Perhaps," says a brilliant writer, "we have seen the sea reposing in calmness. Its ample extent and glassy smoothness, seeming almost to rival the sky expanded above it; its depth to us unknown; the thought that we stand near a gulf, capable in one hour of extinguishing all human life—and the thought that this vast body, now so peaceful, can move, can act with a force equal to its magnitude—inspires a sublime sentiment. Perhaps we have seen it in tempest, moving with a host of mountains to assault the eternal barrier which confines its power. If there were, in reality, spirits of the deep, it might suit them well to ride on these ridges, or howl in this raging foam. We have seen the fury of little beings; but how insignificant in comparison of what we now behold—the world in a rage! Indeed, we could almost imagine that the great world is endowed with a soul, and that these commotions express the agitations of its passions. Undoubtedly, to mariners, hazarded far off in the midst of such a scene, the sublimity is lost in danger. Horror is the sentiment with which they survey the vast flood, rolling in hideous steeps, and gulfs, and surges; while, at a distance, on the gloomy limit of the view, Despair is seen to stand, summoning forward still new billows without end. But to a spectator on the land, the influence which breathes powerfully from the scene, and which consciousness of danger would darken into horror, is illuminated into awful sublimity by the perfect security of his situation."

"In the dim distance," says another, "we see an 'oak leviathan,' the production of that genius which is the distinguishing characteristic of the human mind, floating in pride of strength upon the bosom of the deep. Ay, there she is, a huge, though not unwieldy mass; a giantess of the waters, daring, as it were,

'The elements to the strife.'

She is becalmed; her white wings hang heavily upon the burdened mast, and the pilot, anxious once more to greet the inmates of his happy home, is impatient of delay. The merry voice of the jolly sailor 'trembles along the bosom of the sleeping wave.' Anon a 'spirit moves upon the face of the waters,' and a speck, just emerging from under the horizon, now no larger than a man's hand, spreads, as it travels towards the zenith, and soon overshadows the 'blue above,' while the 'blue below' mirrors its blackness. The God of the universe exhibits his power and his presence; and wind and ocean, by an unseen hand, are arrayed, each against the other, and contend, like infuriated demons, for the mastery. That monument of man's immortal mind, driven rapidly before the tempest's breath, can illy breast 'the war of elements,' and on she whirls to certain perdition; onward, onward she is borne; though

> 'The strained mast quivers as a reed,
> And the rent canvass fluttering strews the gale,
> Still she moves on.'

The moment of destruction is at hand;—hark! the timbers creak, and part; and now, high above the voice of the winds and the hoarse growl of the fretted billows, the wild shrieks of despair burst from the lips of the hopeless, helpless beings who throng the deck of the sinking bark;—another instant, and the echo of that deafening and agonizing shout has died upon the ear of the listener;—the sea yawns, and the floating castle is engulphed like a piece of driftwood in its vortex, and man and his work, are alike

> 'In one vast burial blent.'

The puissant arm of the Most High is here, but nature's great Creator subjects to his will the workmanship of his hands; and scarcely have the ill-fated voyagers upon the great deep been launched into eternity, than He who commands all things whispers, 'Peace, be still;'—the dire combat is at an end, the conflict of the elements ceases, the mountain waves of the lashed ocean subside, and the hoarse bellowing of the rude north wind, dies away into a gentle murmur;—all nature seems hushed in repose. 'What manner of man is this, that even the winds and the seas do obey him?'"

> "Anon thou smooth'st thy brow, and with a song
> Of mournful sweetness murmurest through thy caves;
> Or with soft music, and the kiss of peace,
> Greetest the sunny shore, and brightly smil'st.
> Organ of nature! whence thy ceaseless roll?"

The mean height of the highest waves in a storm, is about forty-three feet above the level of the hollow. After a storm of thirty-six hours' duration, they have been known to average thirty feet, from ridge to hollow. When they meet with an immovable perpendicular obstruction, they sometimes rise in immense masses of water, to the height of *one hundred and six feet above the level of the sea!* They travel with astonishing velocity, propagating their motion at the rate of thirty or forty miles per hour, and exerting a force equal to *three tons per square foot!* Five hundred and fifty-nine feet is the probable mean distance of the waves from each other, or from crest to crest. "The water does not advance with the wave, but the *form* only —the water rising and falling in the same place, except at the beach, where it becomes really progressive, because it cannot sink, and therefore falls over forward."

"When we see a column of water, at least thirty feet in height, advancing with the speed of a railroad train, we can readily imagine that its force is almost irresistible.

* * * * * * *

"These results are astonishing; and it is no wonder that in the encounter with such a force, the largest ships are but toys, and wood and iron almost as fragile as glass. Nothing but stone can be expected to resist such a force, and that must be as firmly fastened as the ledges on which the waves spend their fury. 'Hitherto shalt thou come, but no farther: and here shall thy proud waves be stayed.'"

Reader, have you ever stood upon the ocean shore, and looked out freely upon that broad and heaving bosom; and as you gazed, and wondered, and admired, felt how insignificant is man and how inconceivably powerful his Maker? Surely it must be, to all who can feel, a most exciting and inspiring scene. The feeling of solemnity and awe which it produces cannot be described. Every one is more or less moved, on beholding this mighty creation of God. Some are humbled, and feel like falling low upon the sand, and adoring Him who "rulest the raging of the sea;" some appear lost in wonder at the stupendous scene; while others are highly excited, and are ready to shout aloud, like a distinguished female author, who says:

"How happy I was to behold the beautiful sea once more; to be once more wondering at and worshipping the grandeur and loveliness of this greatest of God's marvellous works! How I do love the sea! My very soul seems to gather energy and life and light, from its power, its vastness, its bold, bright beauty; its fresh, invigorating airs; its glorious, triumphant, rushing sound. The thin, rippling waves came like silver leaves, spreading themselves over the glittering sand with just a little, sparkling, pearly edge.

* * * * * * *

"Close along the shore, the water was of that pale, transparent green colour, that blends so delicately with the horizon, sometimes, at sunset; but out beyond, towards the great deep, it wore that serene and holiest blue that surrounds one in mid-ocean, when the earth is nearly as far below as the heaven seems high above us.

"For a short time my spirits seemed like uncaged birds; I rejoiced with all my might; I could have shouted aloud for delight; I galloped far along the sand, as close into the water's restless edge as my horse would bear to go. But the excitement died away, and then came vividly back the time when last I stood upon the sea-beach at Cramond, and lost myself in listening to that delicious sound of the chiming of waters."

It is pleasant to chase the retiring wave, and gather the variegated shells and pebbles thrown up from the fathomless depths. But to look upon those surges, long and high, rolling gracefully and majestically in from the distance to the shore, spreading their foam, and spending their power there, is well calculated to make a deep and lasting impression upon the reflecting mind. And to behold the cloudless sun or full-orbed moon, rise, as it were, from that vast watery bed; and the glittering spangles of every hue scattered far away upon the ocean's agitated bosom, is also a highly interesting sight—"like an infinite multitude of little fiery gems, moving and sparkling through endless confusion; or like brilliant insects, sporting—all intermingled, and never tired or reposing—the most vivid frisks."

They who have had the pleasure of seeing the grand and

splendid scenery of Harper's Ferry; who have seen the craggy, frowning cliffs near Cumberland; and from Laurel Hill and vicinity, have been favoured with a view of the magnificent scenery, thrown around by nature's hand in every direction, rolling, towering, diversified, and beautiful as it is; who have gazed with delight, far over those mountain barriers, upon many a charming, winding stream, and sparkling, murmuring waterfall; many a wide and wildly-rushing river,—acknowledge that they have never witnessed any work of the Creator which has excited so many thrilling sensations, as the boundless, fathomless deep.

"Dash on, ye ever restless waves;
Roll on, thou mighty sea!"

CHAPTER LX.

Chesapeake Bay—Its Beauty—Discovery—Opinion of Mariners—Delightful Trip—Night Scene—Lynnhaven Bay—Lynnhaven River—Fish and Oysters—The Inlet—The Channel—The Tides—Bottom—Singular Tradition—The River of Chesapeake—Pleasure House Creek—Adam Keeling, Esq.—Dike—New Inlet—Branches of the River—London Bridge—Trading Point—Kempsville—Long Creek—Broad Bay—Linkhorn Bay—Fish—Beautiful Scenery—Transparent Waters—The Desert and its Inhabitants—Old Fort—Remarkable Changes—Church Point—Parish Church Submerged—Grave-Yard—Reflections—The Grave-stones—Name Deciphered—Inroads of the Water—Probable Causes—The Winds and Tides—Donation Church—Parson Dixon's Donation—His Eccentricities—The Old Church Dilapidated—Ladies' Fair—Remarks of Mr. Broughton—Rev. Anthony Walke—Dick Edwards—The Old Cemetery, &c.—Baptismal Font—Silver Goblet—A Venerable Trio—Indian Mound or Fort—Blackbeard's Treasures—Witch Duck—Complaint of Luke Hill and Wife—Grace Sherwood, the Witch—Searched by a Jury of Women—Strange Verdict—Poor Grace Ducked—Subsequent Difficulties—Graceless Affair—The Name Lynnhaven.

Chesapeake Bay,* of which the reader has already observed occasional remarks, is considered by travellers to be among the

* Chesapeake is said to be derived from the Indian, signifying Mother of Waters, the parent or reservoir of all the great rivers emptying within it.—*Steth.*

most beautiful and interesting collections of water in the world. "It was discovered by some of the first colonists of the island of Roanoke, and Raleigh had enjoined it upon one of his own expeditions to settle within its shores; and it is not improbable that the ships of some of the early voyagers may have ploughed its waters."

The following extract will serve very well to convey to the mind of those who have not seen this bay, an idea of its magnificence:

"The trip from Baltimore down the Chesapeake, in the fine steamer Georgia, was a delightful one. I have often heard old sea-captains, who have traversed almost every known sea, lake, bay, and river in the world, speak in the most exalted terms of the noble Chesapeake. As a bay, it has no equal, not even in that of Naples, all things considered. I know of no more delightful trip, especially in the summer season. Mine, on this last occasion, was particularly so. I emerged from the confines of a hot, murky city, and was soon out upon the broad blue waters, with an exquisite breeze, which came up with invigorating freshness from the silver waves. Night came on, and her azure curtain, gemmed with myriad stars, was drawn over the expanse above. A little while longer, and the pale moon, with her full round modest face, peered up the eastern horizon. She looked like a sylvan queen gently blushing to take the place of her lord and master, who had just sunk from his majestic career behind a golden halo.

"A scene on the Chesapeake, thus changing from noonday to gray eve, thence to dim twilight, and deepening into the soft azure of a summer's night, is truly inspiring alike to the poet and painter, as well as invigorating to health, and renovating to the finer feelings of sentimentality and romance."

Lynnhaven Bay is a portion of the Chesapeake, at its southern extremity, and lies between Cape Henry and a point at Little Creek Inlet. The waters of the Chesapeake here make a graceful curve into the land; and the view, to the north especially, is extensive, and very beautiful.

Lynnhaven River is, also, a truly beautiful collection of water, which extends into Princess Anne County from the bay. It has long been celebrated for the finest fish, especially the hog-fish, sheep's-head, spot, trout, &c. As for Lynnhaven oysters, their celebrity has extended throughout the Union, and probably reached the Eastern Continent.

The present inlet to Lynnhaven is of modern origin, as we shall presently show. It is now very shallow ; indeed, there is a sandbar across the entrance, which affords at high tide only about four and a half feet of water, excepting a channel some ten or fifteen feet wide, and from about four to six feet deep. At low tide, the inlet is only knee deep, excepting the narrow channel; and its transparent waters are of course forded with great facility. The channel, inside of the bar, varies from twelve to twenty feet in depth; in some places it is very narrow, and the ebb and flow of the tides therein are rapid, probably from four to six knots per hour. And it is quite worthy of remark, that the egress or ingress of the tides is in some places scarcely perceptible outside of this narrow channel, the water on either side being sometimes comparatively still and very clear and smooth during the ebb and flow of the tides, presenting, we should think, an appearance similar to that occasioned by the passage of the waters of the River Jordan through the middle of the Sea of Galilee, if the accounts of a certain traveller relative thereto be correct.

The bottom of Lynnhaven River is, for the most part, composed of loose brownish sand, which is constantly moved about by the force of the tides.

We have heard strange traditionary statements about Lynnhaven River, some of which are very absurd, and would be found difficult to substantiate. It has been said that this beautiful stream is of comparatively modern origin ; that persons now living, probably knew the individual, who, by having a ditch or drain cut through his lands, caused the existence of this deep and clear river, or a large portion thereof; that the water flowing rapidly through this dike gradually wore it away to a deep and ample river-bed ! This is, of course, all a mistake, a simple impossibility. It is sufficiently evident, that the River of Chesapeake, or as it is now called, Lynnhaven River, existed when the country was discovered. We will mention a circumstance, however, whence doubtless originated the tradition about the ditch.

Until about the period of the Revolutionary war, the inlet to the waters of Lynnhaven, was the Pleasure House Creek, running in from the bay at the site of a building known as the Old Pleasure House,* about two miles west of the present inlet. Adam Keeling, Esq., one of the former and most respected residents of that beautiful section of Princess Anne, situated on Lynnhaven River, desiring a shorter connexion by water with the Chesapeake than that afforded by the creek, which from his section was a very circuitous route, caused a dike to be cut across, from the two nearest or most convenient points on the neighbouring shores of the river and the bay. This proved greatly to his advantage and convenience in fishing on the bay shore. Another object in opening this canal, was the more readily to secure his fishing-boats, &c., from the incursions of the enemy. The water running rapidly out at ebb tide, and in at flood tide, through this narrow dike, it was soon enlarged. The current gradually undermined the trees, and cleared away the sand, the under-growth, and all obstructions, until a wide channel was formed, now known as the Lynnhaven Inlet—the other entrance having been long since closed, in consequence of the opening of this artificial passage which is the only inlet or outlet for the waters of the river and its tributaries.

Lynnhaven River has several branches, one of which we have already alluded to, and which has its source some three or four miles above London Bridge, which bridge is about five miles above the mouth of the creek. Another branch takes its course towards Trading Point, in the direction of Kempsville; and the third is Long Creek, a deep, blue, and beautiful stream, which glides rapidly along upon its sandy bed, and unites Lynnhaven with Broad Bay; thence it takes its course on to Linkhorn Bay; also very handsome collections of water. These reservoirs, as well as the Lynnhaven, abound with the finest fish, oysters, and wild fowl.

It would well repay a trip from afar to view the scenery of this

* Formerly a popular place of entertainment, belonging to a gentleman named Nimmo. It was burned by the British in the last war.

locality. The waters are very clear and salt, having the deep greenish colour of the ocean, on account of their proximity to Chesapeake Bay and the Atlantic. The view from some points is extensive, and very interesting; but more remarkable for serenity and openness, than for abruptness or wildness; although the scenery is in some places varied by the rugged and sterile appearance of the sandhills of the Desert. This occupies a considerable tract of country, and abounds with deer, foxes, bears, wild hogs, wild cats, raccoons, snakes, &c.

An old sand fort was accidentally discovered some years ago upon the banks of Lynnhaven River, by a venerable gentleman of this city, while on a fox-chase. It appears that it had been thrown up and used to prevent the entrance of hostile parties into a creek, which has since been filled up with sand.

Remarkable changes are exhibited along the banks of this beautiful river, the water having made inroads upon the land on the west shore, and retreated from that on the opposite. This is perceptible in a remarkable degree at Church Point, the site of the old Parish Church and graveyard. The old church has long since fallen to ruins; indeed, no vestige remains to mark the identical spot which it occupied; and strange to say, the old graveyard has also disappeared! The remains of those who were interred there, now lie low beneath the sandy bed of the river; and over the stones which mark many "a couch of lowly sleep," rolls on the cool, clear flood of the Lynnhaven; and when the Archangel's trump shall give out its pealing sound, those who were buried in the bosom of the earth, under the green sod upon the river-bank, will come forth from the waters. How deeply, how strangely, how securely buried! The green sea-weed may grow rankly there, and entwine around those old gravestones, and the finny tribes may come up from the bay and the ocean with each flowing tide, and hold their pastimes over those graves and among those stones; the shrill cry of the seagull is heard there; and flocks of playful wild fowl feed and flap their light wings upon the smooth cool surface of the river, but no

——— "living statues there are seen to weep;"

and most truly, indeed, may it be said, too:

"Afflictions semblance bends not o'er (the) tomb."

A tall man may wade out to this submerged burial-place, and feel with his feet (the water up to his chin), the gravestones and their inscriptions.

An eminent resident of our city has done this, and even deciphered one of the names of the dead, whose remains were there interred. The name is Pallett, and is that of some of the old and formerly well-known inhabitants of Princess Anne.

And now a question may very naturally be raised, with regard to the cause of this apparent advance or rise of the water upon the land, and beyond its former mark. Has the water risen, or the land sunk? The writer is, perhaps, unprepared to answer satisfactorily, either to the reader or to himself. We will say, however, that as the graveyard was upon the shore most affected by the action of the waves, during the prevalence of the north-east and east winds of the coast, the banks of the river may have been thereby displaced. The action of high tides has probably had a similar effect. The accumulation of sand, on the opposite shore, has also been very great, and is indeed very remarkable.* Besides, the inlet from the bay, in addition to being more shallow, is also said to be narrower, now, than it was many years ago, probably on account of the rapid accumulation of sand displaced by the winds and waves; and it has, therefore, become too small for the entire reflux of the tides, as formerly. The consequence is, the waters of the bay commence to rise some time before those of the river have fallen to the level of the former. The bay soon rises, however, above the level of the latter, and forces its waters rapidly through the inlet, thus prematurely causing, of course, what is called flood tide in the river. This may be, in some way, connected with the changes which are apparent along the banks of the river.

After the original parish church, at the Point, became dilapidated and useless, or was destroyed, a site was chosen about three-quarters of a mile from the former, and another church

* In some places the lowlands, formerly very valuable for grazing, have been covered with sand, and rendered useless for this purpose.

was erected. The location is on the road leading to the Bay Shore, and three or four miles from Kempsville. This church accidentally took fire, and was consumed; after which (1735) another was built, a few rods distant therefrom, and is now known as the Old Donation Church, so called on account of the donation of a farm, in its vicinity, from Rev. Robert Dixon, one of its pastors, for the education of eight children. This farm is also known as the "Donation."

Parson Dixon, by the way, was an eccentric, and, in some respects, a remarkable man. He required a rigid compliance with the rules of the church; and, in order to make the members punctual in their attendance, he adopted the plan of fining all the absentees. He taught a school at the church, and was exceedingly strict; so much so, that he was a perfect terror to his pupils.

The Old Donation was suffered to become sadly dilapidated, after the erection of the Episcopal Church at Kempsville. Sacrilegious hands stole the bricks with which the aisle was paved, tore away a portion of the pews, demolished the window-lights, &c.; and the bats and owls took up their abode there. The fair daughters of Princess Anne made a commendable and successful effort, at the Agricultural Fair held at Kempsville in November, 1852, to raise funds to repair this ancient church.

"About the year 1815," says Mr. Broughton, "after having remained a long time neglected, and serving as a shelter for the beasts of the field, it was repaired, and again opened for public worship, when it received the name of the 'Donation Church,' as a tribute to the memory of its venerable pastor, Rev. Robert Dixon, who, dying about the period of the breaking out of the Revolution, bequeathed his beautiful farm, about a mile from the church on the Kempsville Road, to the county, as a donation, the income from which was to be appropriated to the education of a certain number of poor orphan boys. This farm was called the 'Donation' to the present time. Originally the church was designated as the 'Lynnhaven Parish Church,' but, after the Revolution, it more generally went by the simple appellation of the Old Brick Church.

"The church, however, after being repaired was only occupied for a few years, when it was left uncared for, and doomed once more to decay and ruin; from which condition a benevolent spirit is now making an effort to rescue it.

"More than half a century ago, the Rev. Anthony Walke ministered the Word of Life in this venerable sanctuary, according to the forms of the Episcopal Church; and some of the aged inhabitants, who were of his congregation, still remember his mild, clear voice, and solemnity of manner in reading the church service. They remember, too, the grave and important air, with which good old Mr. Dick Edwards, the parish clerk, uttered the responses and pronounced the amens. Mr. E. was a man of many callings, among which was that of auctioneer, and his style of crying at sales was inimitable. And they remember, also, the decent and orderly demeanour of the congregation, in their best Sabbath-day attire. Even then there was a recognised distinction of social rank, and the rich style of the gentry, or quality, claimed priority of the humbler class in decent homespun, which was tacitly conceded. All were impressed alike, however, with the duty of attendance upon the Sabbath appointments of Divine worship in the good old parish church."

"Time," says another, "has been busy with his ravages on the church and cemetery. A few trees only remain to mark the spot where the dead repose, and the winds sighing through their branches, sing their only requiem!

> 'Far from the madd'ning crowd's ignoble strife
> Their sober wishes never learned to stray;—
> Along the cool, sequestered vale of life,
> They kept the noiseless tenor of their way.'

"Not a family in this section but has a relative or friend resting here. The great, the proud, the humble and lowly, all have met here on terms of equality. It is strange, indeed, that such a spot should be thus neglected, and the venerable church allowed to come almost to ruin. To our mind (and we are not proof against woman's eloquence), its antique appearance, its historic interest and associations, plead with an eloquence which, though mute, is not less irresistible than that of the ladies engaged in its behalf.

> 'Old plains have a charm for me
> That new can ne'er attain.'

"We hope to see the ravages of old Time stayed, the venerable church and cemetery adorned and beautified, its ancient walls, and the surrounding wood, made vocal with the 'pealing anthem' and the 'note of praise.'"

The old parish font, or baptismal-vessel, belonging to this church, is also a remarkable relic. Hundreds of the good people of the county have stood before its ample basin, to receive the holy sacrament of baptism. This, and a large silver goblet for the communion service, or sacrament of the Lord's Supper, were presented by Colonel Maximilian Boush, an estimable gentleman of Princess Anne County, some of whose descendants are now highly respectable residents of this city.

The Donation Church, Eastern Shore Chapel, and Pungo Chapel, as they are called, form a trio of venerable old relics of antiquity; and thousands of the dead and the living have assembled to worship within their solid, though ancient, walls, and to kneel at their altars. It is hoped they may all be hereafter kept in good order, and supplied with faithful pastors, to dispense the lifegiving word of truth to those of the present generation, and of others yet to come.

There is, in the vicinity of the site of the old Pleasure House, a large and remarkable *mound*, supposed by some to have been thrown up there by the Indians. It may contain numerous relics of the tawny inhabitants of the woods, whose wigwams were erected, and whose blazing fires were built for their revelry and pastimes along the beautiful shores of the Lynnhaven. It is now only thirty or forty feet high, and about one hundred and fifty feet long. Within the recollection of some of the old residents, it was very considerably above that elevation; some say it was more than one hundred feet in height. The origin of this mound, or, more properly, this old fortification, is involved in mystery. There is some reason to doubt that it was the work of the red men; but when, or by whom erected, who can tell? Its appearance is at once singular, novel, and astonishing. There it stands in its loneliness and grandeur, deserted and useless, rising majestically from its moat, far above the adjacent lands, bearing upon its ridges and slopes old oaks and other noble forest trees that have braved, unbroken, the storms of several hundred winters. Who tells its origin—who knows its design—who can describe the men that were garrisoned there? Time has swept them away, as well as the remembrance of the object of their fortress, as also all possible necessity therefor. It extends across a narrow point, forming one side of a triangle, that was formerly surrounded by deep water. Who can declare that this was not one of the places of retreat and defence of Blackbeard, the notorious brigand and pirate, and his fearful gang of hardened, bloodthirsty freebooters, with their treasures of gold, jewelry, precious stones, and untold wealth? Should this old rampart be excavated and examined, it might disclose hoarded spoils and ill-gotten gains, to the amount of millions. This singular fort is on the land belonging to the heirs of the ancient and wealthy Thorogood family. Yankee curiosity and enterprise may yet be brought to bear upon this interesting old relic, and bring out the hidden treasures, if they are there.

We offer next some remarks relative to "Witch Duck," which is the name generally applied to a beautiful country seat on Lynnhaven River, about twelve miles from Norfolk, and now the property of John Hipkins, Esq., of this city. The following remarkable facts will throw some light upon the origin of its singular name.

In 1706, on complaint of Luke Hill and wife, Grace Sherwood, of Princess Anne County, was arrested on the charge of being a *witch*, and by a decision of court it was gravely required that she should be *searched* by a jury of *women*, who accordingly performed the task, and decided and reported that she was "neither like them nor any other woman they knew of." She was then by her own consent, put to the test by a good *ducking* "in an inlet making up from Lynnhaven." This is, of course, the place so well known by the name of Witch's Duck, or Witch Duck. She was subsequently confined, by the direction of the court, in the county jail for trial. What final disposition was made of poor Grace we have no means of ascertaining; certain it is, however, that independently of the ducking, she was sufficiently tormented by legal indictments, and a long and tedious course of law.*

Some of the facts in this extraordinary case we are constrained to withhold, as being unfit for the eye of the refined reader. Take it altogether, it was certainly a very *grace*-less affair for the eighteenth century.

With regard to the beautiful name, Lynnhaven, we offer a few remarks. It is probable that the first syllable was originally disconnected from the last two, thus: Lynn Haven; and this name was, perhaps, given on account of the resemblance of the waters which we have described, to those of the Ouse (near its falls), in Norfolk County, England, on which the town of Lynn—Lynn Regis, or King's Lynn—long celebrated as a corn market, is situated. Some point on the shores of the Lynnhaven may possibly have been thought of by the early settlers as the site of a town to be called Lynn; and Lynn Harbour, or Lynn Haven, would have been an appropriate name for the adjacent waters.

CHAPTER LXI.

Further remarks about Lynnhaven River—Sandbar—Winds—Removal of the Bar—Stone Wall—Sound—Speculations—Fresh Water—Rivers, &c.—Fish and Oysters—Epicures—Health—Canal—A Novel Change—Currituck Sound—The Inlet—Maritime Productions—Fishing—Dismal Swamp Canal—Embankments of Sand—Destruction of Fish, &c.—Sickness—Lamentable Change—Loss to the People—Superstition—Recession of the Waters—Lynnhaven.

We now present a few additional thoughts or suppositions, relative to Lynnhaven River.

In the first place, then, the sandbar at the entrance is no doubt caused by the winds in the winter, and during a portion of the fall and spring months, which have a sweep of more than a hundred miles down the bay, especially from the north.

* When persons were on trial for witchcraft in New England, they were set at liberty on confessing themselves *guilty*.

Again, artificial means might probably be employed, with singular effect, upon the waters within this shallow and narrow entrance. For instance, if the bar could be removed, and its re-formation prevented, so that the tides could freely ebb and flow with those of the sea without, the rise and fall of the water would be much greater within. Or, if this shallow inlet or outlet, which is only about three-quarters of a mile wide, were entirely crossed and obstructed by a stone wall, which could be built at no great cost; or, if it should be closed by the banking of the sand, a very considerable inland sea might be formed; for it must be recollected, that the tributaries of Lynnhaven drain quite a large section of country, comparatively. The waters of the smaller bays mentioned, would probably be considerably raised, and the sedgy, boggy portions of the creeks and coves might be deeply covered with water.

Now, with regard to the effect of damming up the mouth of the Lynnhaven, we have said that a sound might be formed—such as may have existed there before, at some period—rising, by the draining of the country, to a considerable elevation along the banks of the streams. This, however, could be regulated by the height of an embankment or wall at the entrance.

The narrow, muddy streams might be changed to navigable rivers, for it is probable that the accumulation of water would be much greater than the evaporation.

The writer advocates no such plan as the above; but simply alludes to a scheme which appears practicable, and which might be attended with rather astonishing results, although bad consequences might also ensue, sufficient to counterbalance all the advantages.

Epicures, take the alarm! Good-bye to Lynnhaven fish, oysters, and canvass-back ducks, when the waters of the sea shall cease to ebb and flow through that shallow inlet. And as to the effect upon the health of the country, we leave that matter for the consideration of the doctors.

With regard to another inlet and outlet for the new-formed lake, we need only mention the proposed short canal from the eastern branch of the Elizabeth to the western branch of the Lynnhaven.

The reader may fill up the outlines of the picture, for the distant future. He may think, if he chooses, of pleasant villages, and handsome farms and farm-houses, all along the green margin of the artificial lake or sound; of hundreds of sail-vessels and steamboats loading along the shores, for miles, with corn, potatoes, vegetables, fruit, timber, fire-wood, and other productions of the country.

We next proceed to allude briefly, in this connexion, to Currituck Sound, a portion of which is in Princess Anne County, and the remainder in the adjoining County of Currituck, North Carolina; and which may be compared, in more respects than one, to Lynnhaven River.

Currituck Sound, until some twenty or twenty-five years ago, had a short, narrow inlet; sufficiently spacious, however, to admit of the inward and outward passage of the waters of the ocean, as well as the entrance of small vessels. It is said to have been quite as celebrated, also, for superior maritime productions as Lynnhaven. Its shores were very remarkable for extensive fishing operations; and, during the fishing season, presented scenes of great activity.

Some time after the opening of the Dismal Swamp Canal, which diverted the waters of some of the tributaries of this sound, an abatement of the waters, especially in the northern portion of that great fishing reservoir, was soon perceptible—their outward passage being much less rapid, and proving insufficient to clear away the embankments of sand which the waves of the ocean were gradually throwing up at the inlet. The consequences, of course, were, the entire blockade of the entrance to the sound—the discontinuance of perceptible tides—the gradual change of the water from salt to fresh—the wholesale destruction of the fish, oysters, crabs, &c., and the infection of the country for two or three years with malaria, causing much fatal sickness in the vicinity. A lamentable change, truly; a sad loss to those who owned the valuable fishing-grounds on the banks of the sound, and to the country for many miles around, on account of the annual supplies of fish, &c., being cut off from this, hitherto, unfailing source. But so it was, and it could not be remedied.

Some of the superstitious residents of the country regarded the whole affair as a visitation of Providence, or, in other words, a judgment upon the people; for the fisheries are said to have often presented scenes of extraordinary debauchery and immorality.

There is also observable a gradual recession of the waters of this sound, from the shores reaching farthest north.

Now, from the cause and effect in this case, a lesson may be learned with regard to Lynnhaven. Although the proposed canal, to extend to its waters, might not have a tendency similar to that of the Dismal Swamp, yet, independently of this, it appears to be apprehended, by some persons, that at no very distant period, Lynnhaven River may really share a fate, or exhibit a change, not unlike that presented by the formerly celebrated Currituck Sound.

CHAPTER LXII.

Old Point—Place of Resort—Distance from Norfolk—The Name—Fortifications—Castle Calhoun—Appearance—Rip Raps—Hotel—Sea-Bathing—Amusements—Grove—Cottages—Music—Promenade on the Battlement—New Hotel—Virginia Ocean House—Buildings—Parade Ground—Live Oaks—Troops—Ordnance—Ocean Scenery—Northeaster—Terrific Scene—Storm—Hampton—Captain Smith—Indians—Kecoughtan—Battle in the Revolution—Attack of the British in 1813—Barbarous Deeds—Disgraceful and Infamous Conduct—Cockburn—Beckwith—General Taylor—Summer Resort—Hospitality and Moral Character of Hampton—Prosperity—Churches—Afton House—The Barrons, &c.—Elizabeth City County—Soil—Inhabitants—Population—Yorktown—Splendid Scenery—Old Church—Foreign Commerce, Wealth, and Power—Neglect—The People—Captain Anderson—York River—West Point—The Capital—Cornwallis's Surrender—Cave—Burial-Ground—Hugh Nelson—Nelson Family—Hole made by a Cannon-Shot—Northampton and Accomac—Eastern Shore—The Land—Appearance of the Country—Society, &c.—Horses and Carriages—The Ocean—"Accawmacke"—Indians—Eastville, &c.—Hon. A. P. Upshur—Accomac—Hon. H. A. Wise—Drummondtown—Chincoteague—Splendid Scenery—Cape Charles—Southern Watering-Place.

Old Point Comfort, the location of Fort Monroe, is a very popular place of resort in the summer months. It is distant about 16 miles from Norfolk, and 2½ from Hampton. It was named Point Comfort, in 1607, "on account of the good channel and safe anchorage it afforded;" and the word *Old*, was added to distinguish it from New Point Comfort. The fortifications here are upon a truly grand scale. The strength, beauty, and extent of the establishment, and its admirable adaptation to the important purposes of the national defence, combine to render it the most important fortress and military station in the Union; indeed, it is among the greatest in the world.

Between Old Point and Sewell's Point, and opposite to Fort Monroe, at a distance of nineteen hundred yards, is Castle Calhoun, or the Fortress of the *Rip Raps*. The two forts (Monroe and Calhoun) would "present immense batteries of cannon at an approaching hostile ship." The latter is upon an artificial island, made by throwing over rocks, at a depth of twenty feet. "The present aspect of the place is rough and savage; the music of the surrounding elements of air and sea, is in keeping with the dreariness and desolation of the spot."

"The shoal water, which, under the action of the sea, and re-acted upon by the bar, is kept up in an unremitting ripple, has given the name of 'Rip Raps' to this place." The foundation of Castle Calhoun was laid in 1826.

At Old Point there is a splendid hotel, kept in excellent style; the tables, during the summer months, are plentifully supplied with the choicest viands, among which may be named the best of fish and oysters, which, with the superior facilities for sea-bathing and the delightful ocean breezes, the novelties and attractions connected with the fort, the convenient distance to Norfolk, Richmond, Washington, Baltimore, &c., unite to concentrate a large number of visiters there during the summer season in search of pleasure, and for the purpose of recruiting impaired health. "Detached from the building, are extensive billiard saloons, bowling alleys, and pistol galleries, for exercise and amusement, and commodious bathing-houses; the groves of trees in the front and rear of the house, afford an abundance of shade; vegetation has taken a fresh start at the Point. A short distance from the hotel, are two ranges of neat cottages, enclosed, beautified with vines, flowers, trees, and shrubbery, almost obscuring them from view. On three nights in the week, the rich strains of the splendid Garrison Band, fill the air with dulcet sounds, harmonizing with the exhilarated feelings of the listener. On these occasions, a promenade on the battlement of the fortress gives life and vigour to the entire system."

> "How sweet the moonlight sleeps upon this bank!
> Here will we sit, and let the sound of music
> Creep in our ears; soft stillness, and the night,
> Become the touches of sweet harmony."

Preliminary arrangements are being made for the erection of an extensive hotel on the beach, not far from the fortress at Old Point, to be called the Virginia Ocean House.

Within the fort are the necessary buildings for the accommodation of the officers; and also, a beautiful parade-ground, partially shaded by live oak trees, which are found no farther north than this particular spot. One or two regiments of troops are generally garrisoned here. The heavy discharges from the fort, when the officers of the Ordnance Department are testing the strength of the guns, are often heard at Norfolk.

"Perhaps there is no place upon the Atlantic coast where the exciting play of wind and water may be seen to such an advantage as at Old Point. The long, frantic procession of billows dashes into the Chesapeake with a fury that is indescribable. During the last summer we happened to witness, from this spot, the full energy of a violent northeaster (the same which drove the bark Elizabeth upon Fire Island), and it was a sight to remember. The scuds of rain, that you could see approaching with a rapidity beyond the flight of the swiftest bird, the flakes of foam upon the beach, the sudden darkness that occasionally came athwart the sky, the Titanic violence of the waves, combined to form a scene at once of beauty and of terror. At such a time it is not desirable to go out in a sail-boat. Indeed, we passed across Hampton Roads in a small steamer, during the fiercest of this gale, and though we had a capital opportunity to observe the wild magnificence of the angry elements, we were very much of opinion with the Englishman who got wet at Niagara, that "certainly it was very well in its way, but that, on the 'ole, he preferred looking at an hengraving of it in the 'ouse."

Hampton, the shire town of Elizabeth City County, is distant eighteen miles from this city. The site was visited by Captain John Smith and others, in 1607. Burk, one of the historians of Virginia, says: "While engaged in seeking for a fit place for the first settlement, they met five of the natives, who invited them to their town, Kecoughtan, or Kichotan, where Hampton now stands." It became a town in 1705. Hampton was attacked by a British fleet, during the Revolutionary war, and was invaded during the last contest with Great Britain. In October, 1775, the place was bravely and successfully defended by a well-disciplined rifle company, assisted by the inhabitants.

"After the British fleet had been so signally defeated in their attempt on Norfolk and Portsmouth, in June, 1813, by the gallant defence of Craney Island, they proceeded to attack Hampton, which was defended by a garrison of four hundred and fifty militia, protected by some slight fortifications." Perkins, in his history of the late war, says: "Admiral Cockburn, on the 25th of June, with his forces, advanced towards the town in barges and small vessels, throwing shells and rockets while Sir Sidney Beckwith effected a landing below, with two thousand men. Cockburn's party were repulsed by the garrison, and driven back behind a point, until General Beckwith's troops advanced and compelled the garrison to retire. The town being now completely in the possession of the British, was given up to pillage. Many of the inhabitants had fled with their valuable effects; those who remained suffered the most shameful barbarities. That renegade corps, composed of French prisoners, accustomed to plunder and murder in Spain, and who had been induced to enter the British service by promises of similar indulgences in America, were now to be gratified, and were let loose upon the wretched inhabitants of Hampton without restraint." "The battle of Hampton," says another writer, "was marked by deeds of rapine and atrocity by the enemy, which would have disgraced a Vandal host, and reflected lasting infamy on the British name." It was in allusion to these outrages that Sir Sidney Beckwith, in a letter to General R. B. Taylor, who commanded the army in Norfolk and vicinity at the time, as before stated, made this forcible and striking remark: "Worthless is the laurel that is steeped in woman's tears."

Hampton is also much resorted to in summer for health and recreation. The inhabitants have long been noted for their hospitality and public spirit; and the moral character of the place compares favourably with that of others. The town has greatly improved in appearance within a few years, and continues to give evidence of prosperity and advancement. Old St. John's Church has undergone extensive repairs. There are several other churches in the place, all kept in good order, a court-house, and other public buildings, besides many neat and commodious private dwellings. There are several well-conducted public houses; among which we mention with pleasure, the Afton House, of which Mr. John Tabb is proprietor. The buildings are finely located; and the establishment presents very strong inducements to persons visiting this delightful little town in search of health and pleasure. The fare is exceedingly fine, and all the arrangements of the house are in good taste and excellent style; indeed, it is conducted by the worthy host and his refined and estimable lady, in a manner which, for polite attention, system, and good order, is scarcely excelled in any section of country. A substantial bridge connects the town with the road leading to Old Point.

Hampton is the birthplace of some notable men; among whom were the Barrons,—who distinguished themselves in the Revolution—one of whom was the father of the late veteran, Commodore James Barron, of the United States Navy. Captains Meredith and Cunningham, of the old State Navy, Major Finn, of the army, and other distinguished men, were also from this place.

Elizabeth City County was one of the divisions of the State made in 1634. It comprises a space of country eighteen miles square. The land is generally fertile, and in some places exceedingly rich and productive. Great attention is paid to the improvement of the soil, and agriculture has long been in a very flourishing condition in this excellent little county, which is considered by some the garden spot of the State. The inhabitants, for the most part, possess a sociable, obliging, and hospitable disposition. The population may be put down at four thousand.

Yorktown, in York County, ever memorable for the surrender of Cornwallis, is about thirty-five miles from this city. There are only a few buildings, many of which are in a decayed and dilapidated state. "The water scenery at York is fine. The river, full a mile wide, is seen stretching away until it merges in Chesapeake Bay—an object of surpassing beauty, when rolling in the morning light, its ripples sparkling in the sun; or when its broad bosom is tinged with the cloud-reflected hues of an autumnal sunset. On its banks stand the ruins of the old church. Silence reigns within its walls, and the ashes of the illustrious dead repose at its base."

"Long before the Revolution, the commerce of Yorktown had much declined, notwithstanding the wealth and power located in its immediate vicinity; and the Virginia trade was, in a great measure, diverted to our harbour, owing to its greater safety and facilities for business.

"The view from the ancient ramparts on the hill," says one who recently visited the place, "excited general admiration, while the locality of the venerable city, now suffering under the heavy yoke of time and legislative neglect, induced the hope that, under the new state of things, of which a faint beginning seems to have dawned upon our good old commonwealth, Yorktown might yet retrieve her former position among cities. The good people of the place are fully awake to her interests, and will leave no effort untried to advance her prospects. Captain Anderson, a wealthy and enterprising citizen, has built a strong and commodious wharf, and taken other steps towards that object.

"Leaving Yorktown, we pursued our course up the river, a distance of forty miles—its entire length—and a more majestic sheet of water we do not believe exists, nor one uniting so completely all the facilities of navigation. It preserves its breadth, say two miles, from its source to its mouth, and presents not the least obstruction to navigation by vessels of any size, in any weather. At West Point—the extreme end of King William County, and once advocated as the site for the capital of the

State,—a single vote decided in favour of Richmond—the Pamunky and Mattaponi form a junction with the York.

"The York River is, properly speaking, an arm of the bay, from its mouth to the point where the Pamunky and Mattaponi unite. In the early period of our colonial history, the attempt was made to build up at Yorktown a large commercial city; but long before the Revolution it proved abortive, notwithstanding its contiguity to Williamsburg, then the seat of royal authority in Virginia. Its magnificent water prospect is well calculated at first view to encourage the idea; and the ever-glorious reminiscences connected with its hallowed soil, even now, at times, engender such a hope."

"We were shown," says another writer, "the spot where Cornwallis delivered up his sword to Washington—the 'Moore House,' where the articles of capitulation were drawn up—the identical redoubts which were carried by Lafayette and Washington, sword in hand—the cave called 'Cornwallis's Cave,' and the old burial-ground, where some of the most ancient tombstones in Virginia can be found. One especially attracted our attention, which was inscribed to the memory of Hugh Nelson, buried 1745. The inscription is in Latin, with the family coat of arms cut upon the wall of the sides of the tomb. He was, doubtless, the ancestor of the Nelson family, and occupied a respectable position in the then colony. The ancient brick mansion of the Nelson family is also here; and in the eastern gable-end is a hole about eight inches in circumference, which was made by a cannon-ball from the American army, during the siege. The house must be at least one hundred years old, and is in tolerably good preservation."

Northampton and Accomac Counties, which embrace a small peninsula, with the wide Atlantic on the east, and the Chesapeake on the west, and reaching from the Maryland line south to Cape Charles, generally called the Eastern Shore, may certainly be regarded as comprising one of the most delightful and agreeable portions of our State. The land is level, the soil good, though light, and generally kept in an excellent state of cultivation. There is, in almost every direction, an appearance of thrift, industry, good husbandry, and good society. Some of the inhabitants are very wealthy, while a large proportion are in easy and prosperous circumstances. Taking them, generally, we may say, without adulation, we have rarely met with a more liberal, gentlemanly, and intelligent community. They appear contented, and, withal, greatly attached to their native place. The roads are excellent, living cheap, the climate salubrious, fine horses and vehicles are exceedingly numerous, and, with the deep and ever musical roar of the ocean always within hearing distance, it is truly delightful to make a visit to our Eastern Shore.

Northampton is a part of the territory originally called *Accawmacke*, which was the name of the tribe of Indians that held possession of the soil. In 1643, a division was made, and the southern portion was called Northampton. Eastville, a pleasant and flourishing village, is situated about the centre of the county. Capeville, Johnsontown, and other pleasant villages, are also located in Northampton.

This county has produced some eminent men, among whom we should mention Hon. Abel P. Upshur, formerly Secretary of State. He was a powerful orator, a brilliant writer, and an accomplished gentleman. His sudden death, while Secretary of State, occasioned by the explosion of a gun on one of the national vessels, is well recollected.

Accomac County, the northern division of the original *Accawmacke*, embraces a level space of country, forty-eight miles long and ten wide. This county is celebrated as the native place of Hon. Henry A. Wise, one of Virginia's greatest orators, whom we have already partially described. Drummondtown, a beautiful village, is the county seat. There are several other pleasant and handsome villages. Chincoteague is one of the beautiful islands on the coast, the view from which is sublimely interesting, and seldom surpassed in interest by ocean scenery.

A gentleman who recently visited Cape Charles, says: "We found the situation a delightful and commanding one; the broad Atlantic on the one side, rolling in all its grandeur, and the noble Chesapeake on the other. The point is susceptible of the most enlarged improvement, and far surpasses in advantages the celebrated watering-place at Cape May. It is in contemplation to purchase the place by a joint stock company, and we know of no enterprise that affords a better chance for a judicious investment. We trust the design will be speedily carried out, and suitable buildings established there before the next season. Every variety of fish can be taken in the water, and the adjacent country is fertile and abounds with game. The party met with a cordial reception from the citizens of the County of Northampton, deservedly famed for its generous hospitality."

Cape Charles is thirty-five miles from Norfolk, equal to an ordinary run of three hours. A steamboat would be profitably employed in making the run daily, touching at Old Point and Hampton; for the establishment at the Cape will rather add to than diminish the resort to these places, where the best table fare of our climate and waters is to be found, and the bathing is so generally approved. The distance from Old Point to Cape Charles is twenty-two miles.

CHAPTER LXIII.

Jamestown—First Settlement in British America—Situation—Old Graveyard and Ruins—John Smith—Settlement—Old Church—Battle with the Indians—Plan and Fortifications—Destructive Fire—Public Records Destroyed—Seat of Government Removed to Williamsburg—Yankee Monopoly—The Landing of the Pilgrims—Williamsburg—Situation—Capital—Population—Lunatic Asylum—William and Mary College—Trustees, President, and Chancellor—Endowment—Magazine—Dunmore—Statue—Old Buildings—Churches, College, Military Academy, &c.—Centre of Fashion and Learning—Society—Plan of the Town—Old Almanac.

The site of Jamestown, the first settlement in British America, and the first seat of colonial government, is on a small peninsula, or projecting piece of land, on the north side of James River, about eight miles south-southwest of Williamsburg. It is a sacred and melancholy spot. The old graveyard, and a portion of the steeple of the old church, are nearly all that remain to remind the traveller of those days long departed, when Captain John Smith and his company first landed on the banks of the noble James, and amid the dangers and privations to which they were subjected, commenced the foundation of the most powerful and flourishing of the colonies.

"Here stand the remnants of the first church built in America. Within its walls, nearly three hundred years ago, while the red man roamed the wild forest, a savage, in human form, was promulgated that gospel which assimilates man to his Maker. Here went up solemn hymns of praise, from those who braved the tempest, endured hardships, and planted the standard of liberty upon our native soil—those who, while they held the shield of Christianity in one hand, grasped the gun or sword in the other—those who suffered, that we, their offspring, might be happy, while they sleep mouldering in the silent sepulchre of death. Knowing these things, how deep a debt of gratitude do we owe our venerated sires.

"There are now but this old, lonely, dilapidated church, and the ruins of an old magazine, remaining to mark the spot where once stood the beautiful little village of Jamestown, so renowned in history. Like Jerusalem of old, one stone has not been left upon another, and the ploughshare and pruning-hook may be seen where was once heard the busy hum of a sprightly town."

According to the account of John Smith, "on the 13th of May, 1607, after a search of seventeen days, they (Smith, Gosnold, Newport, Ratcliff, Martin, and others), fixed upon a peninsula on the north side of the James River, about fifty miles from its mouth, and then in the possession of the Paspaheghs. This they pronounced a very fit place for a very great city; but there was some contention about it between Captain Gosnold and Wingfield, even after the provisions were landed. Here they commenced the settlement of Jamestown, which was, as it proved, the small beginning of our now great and prosperous confederacy."

Shortly after, the unprotected settlers were attacked by four hundred Indians: "a boy was slain, and most of the council, and thirteen others wounded. Had not a crossbar, fired from one of the ships, striking down a bough from a tree, frightened the savages, there would have been an end of that plantation."

The following is an old description of Jamestown, or rather of the *Fort*, which had attained to some dignity in 1609.

"A low and level lot of ground, of about half an acre, on the north side of the river, was palisaded in a triangular form; the south side, next the river, comprehended one hundred and forty yards; the west and east sides respectively, a hundred. At every angle or corner where the lines intersected, a bulwark or watch-tower was raised, and in each bulwark was mounted a piece of ordnance. On every side, at a proportionable distance from the palisade, was a settled street of houses, which was so laid out that each line of the angle had its street. In the centre stood the market-house, store-house, guard-house, and church.

"Thus was the town enclosed with a palisade of planks and strong posts four feet deep in the ground, composed of young oaks and walnuts. The principal gate from the town through the palisade opened on the river; at each bulwark there was also a gate, and at each gate, and in the market-place, a demi-culverin."

Shortly after this period the store-house took fire, and the houses of the town being thatched with reeds, burned with such violence that the fortifications, arms, apparel, bedding, and a great quantity of private goods and provisions, were consumed.

The public records were destroyed here in 1698, in a fire which consumed a large portion of the town; after which the seat of government was removed to Williamsburg.

"It is time now," says a New York writer, "that the merits of this Yankee monopoly of the first white settlements were examined into. The settlement of Jamestown, in Virginia, in 1607, was a little in advance of the landing of the northern Pilgrims of 1620."

Williamsburg, for many years the capital of Virginia, is situated on the division line between James City and York Counties, and on the east side of a small tributary of the James. It is distant sixty-five miles from Norfolk, and has a population of about 1500.

This place having been made the seat of government, in 1698, so continued until the Revolutionary war. The Eastern Lunatic Asylum, of Virginia, is located here, and is a large and lofty pile of buildings, properly enclosed, and very suitable for the purposes designed. This town is celebrated for its College of William and Mary, which was endowed during the joint reign of these monarchs, while Virginia was a colony of Great Britain. William and Mary College is, with one exception, the oldest in the Union. Francis Nicholson, Lieutenant-Governor of Virginia, and seventeen other persons, nominated and appointed by the Assembly, were confirmed as trustees, and were empowered to hold and enjoy lands, possessions, and incomes, to the yearly value of £2000, and all donations bestowed for their use. The Rev. James Blair was first President, and the Bishop of London first Chancellor. The King and Queen endowed the College with 20,000 acres of land, together with the revenue arising from the duty of one penny per pound on all tobacco transported from Virginia and Maryland to the other English plantations.

This ancient College is rapidly regaining its high reputation. It has now about eighty students. With so efficient and accomplished a faculty as William and Mary has now, it must succeed.

The old Magazine, erected one hundred and twenty years ago, from which Lord Dunmore removed the powder, in 1775, has been repaired, and is now used by the Baptists as a place of worship. There are, also, several old buildings formerly connected with Dunmore's palace. A statue of Lord Botetourt, one of the Colonial Governors, stands in the College square. The Methodist and Protestant Episcopal denominations have each a church. There are also here, a Female College, Military Academy, and other institutions of learning.

Before the seat of government was removed to Richmond, Williamsburg was "the centre of fashion, wealth, and learning in the Old Dominion," and the place is still noted for its good society, and for the refinement and polite hospitality of its citizens.

The streets of Williamsburg are regularly laid out, in the form of the letter W, in honour of William III. The site was originally called Middle Plantation. The writer has been handed, by a friend, a copy of "The Virginia Almanac, for the year of our Lord God, 1776, being bissextile or leap year, containing the lunations, conjunctions, eclipses, judgment of the weather, rising and setting of the planets, &c., also, a list of his Majesty's Honourable Council, and of the House of Burgesses, courts, roads, &c., and a variety of matter calculated for instruction and amusement, by David Rittenhouse, Philo., Williamsburg, printed by J. Dixon and A. Hunter." The typographical execution is very neat. This old literary curiosity is in a very good state of preservation. It is, indeed, an excellent work of the kind, although it contains some articles of doubtful propriety, and which we might publish, but for the fear that they might do more than merely amuse or interest some of our readers.

CHAPTER LXIV.

Smithfield — Situation — Beautiful Scenery—Stores and Residences—Shade-trees and Gardens—Appearance—Isle of Wight County—Enterprise—Soil—Bacon—Smithfield Hams—Brandy—Dried Fruit—Eggs—Poultry—Revenue —Suffolk—Situation—Railroad—Churches—Burnt by the British—Fire—Trade—Appearance—Hospitality—Branch of the Nansemond—Romantic Scenery—Matthews and Gloucester—Lands—Natural Advantages—Society —Perennial Charms—Local Attachment—Fair Daughters of the Sequestered Peninsula—New Church—Rev. G. S. Carraway.

THE beautiful and pleasant little town of Smithfield is situated in the northern part of Isle of Wight County, "on an elevated bank on the margin of Pagan Creek, a bold and navigable stream, commanding a splendid view of both land and water scenery—the country, for ten miles on the opposite bank of the James, being in full sight." There are about twenty stores, a number of handsome residences, and three or four churches;—population 1500. The place is tastefully ornamented with shade-trees, flower-gardens, &c., and has a social and very pleasant appearance. It has been said, with regard to Isle of Wight County, that "there is not a more thrifty and enterprising population in Virginia. Their soil is not remarkable for its fertility, but they make up in energy and industry that which has been refused them by the bounty of nature. An immense amount of bacon is annually shipped from this county, and the reputation of their hams is as world-renowned as those from Westphalia. They have ceased, in a measure, to make brandy from the apple, but engage in the more laudable and profitable business of cutting up and drying the fruit. This single article brings them an annual revenue of $20,000. The eggs sent to this market realize more than $5,000, and the poultry not less than $10,000."

Suffolk, the county-seat of Nansemond, is about sixteen miles southwest of Portsmouth, on the Nansemond River, and is on the line of the Seaboard and Roanoke Railroad. The situation is high, pleasant, and remarkably healthful. It contains four churches, a good court-house, and several other public buildings, besides a number of stores and neat family residences. Suffolk was burned by the British on May 13th, 1779, and not many years ago the buildings on the principal street were nearly all destroyed by fire. It has, for a long time, had quite a flourishing trade in lumber, corn, pitch, tar, &c. The place has a neat, rural appearance. There are two spirited party papers published in the town.

"The northern branch of the Nansemond abounds in scenery of the most picturesque and romantic description, and is well deserving the attention of Nature's admirers. The stream is of fresh water, winding some three or four miles in a northwesterly direction from Suffolk, and its average width is about fifty feet. In ascending its intricate windings, you are surprised at the different aspects presented to view. In some instances, the tall and majestic junipers are entirely submerged at the base, and, as you proceed, an elevation will suddenly appear, as if by magic, rising perpendicularly from the river at least twenty feet, rendering the contrast at once startling and delightful."

The hospitable inhabitants of the sterling county of Nansemond are also moving steadily onward in the march of improvement.

With regard to Matthews and Gloucester Counties, a gentleman, writing from the former (June, 1852), says:—

"This and the adjoining county of Gloucester are justly considered the garden-spot of the State. The lands are remarkable for their fertility, and generally are in a high state of cultivation and improvement. The country is salubrious at all seasons of the year; and the many navigable rivers, by which it is intersected, abound with fish of every variety, oysters, and, indeed, with every species of marine luxury. I know of no quarter, on this little terrestrial globe of ours, that presents so many physical advantages, and which, at the same time, is so picturesque and beautiful. The lands are finely adapted to the culture of wheat and corn.

"The society here is of a very superior order—refined, intelligent, social; and they have, perhaps, more of the 'amor soli' than any other people in the State. They cultivate this feeling as a principle, and consider it as almost essential to an enduring and discerning 'amor patriæ.'

* * * * * * *

"If I could feign or fancy, as in days of yore, nymphs or water-sprites under the waves of the majestic stream, from whose banks these lines are indited, I would faithfully and religiously pay my tribute to the Alma Dea of the waters. But the pleasant days of such poetic embellishments have passed away. Here, at least,. they have been superseded by the more real charms of the graceful, accomplished, and well-educated daughters, who reside on this sylvan and sequestered peninsula. Never did the sun of heaven shine on lovelier blossoms! but I must restrain my feelings, as I tread on holy ground. It seems like disturbing the perfume of the violet in its quiet retreat."

In an account of the dedication of a new church in Matthews, the same writer says:—

"There was a large assemblage present to witness the imposing ceremonies. The church is a neat and unostentatious building, located in a beautiful forest, where the pious and devout can offer up their adorations to the Throne of Grace, unmolested by the noise and pomp of the fashionable world. It was erected under the zealous and efficient ministration of the Rev. Mr. Carraway, formerly of Norfolk, who is doing much good here, and is beloved by all who are capable of appreciating true worth."

CHAPTER LXV.

Interesting Object—Lake Drummond—Hotel—Boundary Line—Connubial Parties—Location of the Lake—Dismal Swamp—William Wirt's Statement—Extent—Soil, Trees, &c.—Beasts—Undergrowth—Reeds, Vines, &c.—Dismal Swamp Canal—Seaboard and Roanoke Railroad—Jericho Canal—Lumber Trade—Draining the Swamp—Peat—The Lake—Interesting Scene—Graphic Description—The Poet Moore—Love Affair—Touching Lines—Deep Creek—Houses—Trade—Inhabitants—Washington Point—St. Helena—Lands—U. S. Government Buildings—Concluding Remarks.

THERE is in the vicinity of our city an object of considerable interest, of which little is known, even by many of the inhabitants. We allude to Lake Drummond, or, as the poet Moore called it, "The Lake of the Dismal Swamp." It lies about twenty-two miles from Norfolk, and four miles west of the canal, in which its waters are emptied through a lateral branch, two miles from the Hotel, which is situated on the east branch of the canal, with its centre on the boundary line of Virginia and North Carolina—a convenient stopping-place for connubial parties from the former State. The quiet and unruffled waters of the lake are to be found in the interior of the Dismal Swamp, through which, by the way, runs the dividing line of the two adjoining States, the larger portion of the swamp being in Virginia, and extending in a northerly and southerly direction about thirty miles, and averaging in breadth about ten miles. Mr. Wirt styled it the "Great Dismal Swamp," and in an account of the running of the boundary line, he stated that it was "more than forty miles in length, and twenty in breadth; its soil, a black, deep mire, covered with a stupendous forest of juniper and cypress trees, whose luxurious branches, interwoven throughout, intercept the beams of the sun, and teach the day to counterfeit the night." "This forest," continues that writer, "which, until that time, no human foot had ever violated, had become the secure retreat of ten thousand beasts of prey. Below is a thick, entangled undergrowth of reeds, woodbine, grape vines, mosses, and creepers, shooting and twisting spirally around, interlaced and complicated." The Dismal Swamp Canal, to which allusion has been made, runs through it from north to south, and "the Seaboard and Roanoke Railroad passes like a grand and densely shaded avenue for five miles across its northern part." Jericho Canal, a ditch about eighteen feet wide and ten miles long, also connects with Lake Drummond. Immense quantities of staves, shingles, &c., are transported through it on "flats," from whence they are conveyed in wagons or carts to the Nansemond River, distant about one and a half miles, and navigable for schooners of seventy or eighty tons.

This swamp, it is thought, might be drained, the fertile lands reclaimed, and, as the soil is vegetable, it is believed by some persons that it might be used as *peat*.

In this singular swamp, not very far from its western borders, strangely scooped out by the hand of Nature, is the concavity, averaging about twelve feet deep, that forms the bed of the Drummond Lake, which reposes peacefully in its romantic retirement. A solemn stillness pervades the shores—a silence broken only by the melancholy dirges of the breeze in the thick foliage above, the notes of the feathered songsters, the hiss of the venomous reptile, or, perchance, the splash of the leaping, fluttering perch. "It is delightful," adopting the language of the facetious editor of the Herald, "to drive along its banks, or skim its surface in the morning or evening of a summer's day, when the sun is just above the horizon; the mirror-like surface below reflects the trees, whose limbs embracing above, form umbrageous vistas, beyond which the eye now and then catches a view of an opening in the blue firmament; and the gilding of the sunbeams is relieved by the lengthened shadows of the objects upon which they rest. Then to inhale the delicious fragrance of the jessamine, the laurel, the eglantine, the wild rose, and various other aromatic shrubs and flowers with which the swamp abounds—not even the spicy gales of Arabia can surpass it, and no effort of the pictorial art can do it justice."

Thomas Moore, the Irish Poet, who, as already stated, visited this place in 1805, composed some touching lines on a legendary love affair connected with Lake Drummond. We shall give them a place, although they have been often published.

A BALLAD.

THE LAKE OF THE DISMAL SWAMP.

[WRITTEN AT NORFOLK, IN VIRGINIA.]

They tell of a young man who lost his mind upon the death of a girl he loved; and who, suddenly disappearing from his friends, was never afterwards heard of. As he frequently said in his ravings, that the girl was not dead, but gone to the Dismal Swamp, it is supposed that he had wandered into that dreary wilderness and died of hunger, or been lost in some of its dreadful morasses.

"They made her a grave, too cold and damp
For a soul so warm and true;
And she's gone to the lake of the Dismal Swamp,
Where all night long, by a fire-fly lamp,
She paddles her white canoe.

"And her fire-fly lamp I soon shall see,
And her paddle I soon shall hear;
Long and loving our life shall be,
And I'll hide the maid in a cypress tree,
When the footstep of death is near!"

Away to the Dismal Swamp he speeds;
His path was rugged and sore,
Through tangled juniper, beds of reeds,
Through many a fen, where the serpent feeds,
And man never trod before!

And when on the earth he sank to sleep,
If slumber his eyelids knew,
He lay where the deadly vine doth weep
Its venomous tear, and nightly steep
The flesh with blistering dew!

And near him the she-wolf stirred the brake,
And the copper-snake breathed in his ear,
Till he starting cried, from his dream awake,
"Oh! when shall I see the dusky lake,
And the white canoe of my dear?"

He saw the lake, and a meteor bright,
Quick over its surface played—
"Welcome!" he said; "my dear one's light!"
And the dim shore exchoed for many a night,
The name of the death-cold maid!

Till he hollowed a boat of the birchen bark,
 Which carried him off from shore;
Far he followed the meteor spark;
The wind was high and the clouds were dark,
 And the boat returned no more.

But oft from the Indian hunter's camp,
 This lover and maid so true,
Are seen at the hour of midnight damp,
To cross the lake by a firefly lamp,
 And paddle their white canoe!

Deep Creek, a pleasant village at the northern terminus of the Canal, is about eight miles from Norfolk. It contains about fifty houses, and carries on some trade in shingles, staves, fire-wood, &c. It is distinguished for the generous and social character of its inhabitants.

Washington, commonly called Washington Point, or Ferry Point, which occupies a portion of the angle formed by the confluence of the southern and eastern branches of our river, is a neat and pleasant little village. At St. Helena, situated on the south of Washington Point, and on the eastern shore of the Southern Branch, the lands have recently changed hands, and have been enclosed and much improved. The United States Government has purchased this property, which is immediately opposite the Navy Yard. Several large and substantial brick buildings, intended for store-houses, &c., have been erected, and the appearance of the grounds in this direction is rapidly improving.

We now bring these sketches to a close, and respectfully take our leave of the reader, whose clemency, we trust, has prompted him to make all due allowances. The sparsely scattered materials of historical and statistical information embraced in the work, were collected amid a variety of cares and duties, which tended greatly to interrupt the patient labour and attention so requisite, especially in preparing them for the press. An enlightened public will decide impartially, we believe, with regard to the performance of the task, and the character, interest, utility, and probable influence of the work. The consciousness that he has, at least, endeavoured to perform the duty as faithfully as attending circumstances would permit, will enable the writer patiently and cheerfully to abide by that decision, whether favourable or unfavourable.

With regard to his opinion of the present prospects of the City, as expressed on some of the preceding pages, and coinciding as it does, with that of many judicious and experienced individuals, both at home and abroad, he is constrained to express the sincere hope, that time may not prove it to be erroneous. May a full tide of prosperity, such as has never before been witnessed here, ere long roll in upon Norfolk, Portsmouth, and all the surrounding country! the merchants, tradesmen, and mechanics, all, increasingly busy and successful; the husbandman annually gathering in abundant harvests; and the members of all trades, professions, and classes, enjoying the reward of their labour and industry—receiving ample compensation for their toils, whether mental or physical.

May the borders of the City and all the neighbouring towns and villages be widened—new avenues opened, built upon, and occupied! May the principles of true religion and morality be spread abroad, and exert their genial influence upon the people, that no sad, calamitous visitation of Providence may ever be necessary to teach them their duty to the great I AM! May the number of spacious temples be increased—temples consecrated to Him who is the great and only source of all true happiness, of every blessing; so that the foundations of knowledge and virtue may be laid deep, wide, and strong, and many a noble, firm, and lofty mental and moral structure reared; so that the protecting care of Heaven may continue over all the inhabitants; for "except the Lord keep the city, the watchman waketh but in vain." May our beautiful town continue to increase in wealth, influence, and righteousness, until the mighty Heavenly messenger shall descend, and, with "his right foot upon the sea, and his left foot upon the earth," swear, in tones louder than sevenfold thunder, "that time shall be no longer!"

And when the affairs of this life shall all be wound up, its toils and cares over, the din of business for ever silenced, and the wonders and realities of the eternal world shall be revealed, may the names of the inhabitants, in thousands and tens of thousands, be found among those written in the register of Heaven, "the Lamb's book of life," entitling them to an everlasting habitation in "that great city,"

> "Where the rivers of pleasure flow o'er the bright plains,
> And the noontide of glory eternally reigns!"

INDEX.

* In the description of this building, page 178, for west, read *north*.

* Erroneously inserted Wellington, instead of Wilmington, p. 303.

* In the second name of the early settlers (page 40), the reader may substitute the letter *e* in place of the *a*, although it is probable it was originally written as printed.

THE END.

www.ingramcontent.com/pod-product-compliance
Lightning Source LLC
LaVergne TN
LVHW020918110826
845150LV00004B/706

* 9 7 8 1 4 2 5 5 5 5 4 4 3 *